# FROM HOLYHEAD TO BIR HAKKIM

## (and back)

the full story of

HMS *Tara*

Geraint S Griffith

*From Holyhead to Bir Hakim (and back), the full story of HMS* Tara
First published in Wales
on behalf of the author
in 2015
by
BRIDGE BOOKS
Pear Tree Cottage
Worthenbury
WREXHAM
LL13 0BF



ISBN 978-1-84494-103-2

A CIP entry for this book is available from the British Library

Printed and bound
by
printondemand-worldwide.com
Peterborough

# Contents

Preface 5

1. The *Cambria* Class 11
2. Preparations for War 26
3. Mobilisation 30
4. On Station 41
5. Irish Sea 55
6. To Egypt 75
7. Sollum Patrol 85
8. Attack 90
9. IGT H4 — SS *Moorina* 102
10. Search 110
11. Holyhead 116
12. In Captivity, November 1915 119
13. Egypt, November 1915 141
14. In Captivity, December 1915 144
15. Egypt, December 1915 159
16. In Captivity, January 1916 163
17. Egypt, January 1916 175
18. In Captivity, February 1916 (1) 181
19. Escape, February 1916 190
20. In Captivity, February 1916 (2) 208
21. War, February 1916 212
22. In Captivity, March 1916 221

23. Rescue 229
24. Alexandria 238
25. Homeward Bound 248
26. Epilogue 263

Appendix 1: Officers and ratings serving aboard HMS *Tara* at the time of her sinking 267
Appendix 2: *Moorina's* crew and passengers held captive with the *Tara's* crew 314
Appendix 3: Mercantile Marine officers and men appointed to HMS *Tara* who did proceed to the Mediterranean 316
Sources 319

Index 323

# Preface

If you ask any Holyhead resident with an interest in local maritime history to relate some tales from the past it is almost certain that HMS *Tara* will be mentioned. They will explain that she was the ex-London & North Western Railway Company's SS *Hibernia,* a steam packet which had been requisitioned by the Royal Navy on the outbreak of the First World War and converted to an armed boarding steamer at their Marine Yard Workshops and Dry Dock, at Holyhead in Anglesey. During the conversion she had been renamed, armed, her crew doubled and, with the addition of a sprinkling of Royal Navy personnel (including a captain), was sent to patrol the North Channel of the Irish Sea. In October 1915 she was transferred to the Mediterranean where she was torpedoed and sunk by *U-35*. The German submarine then towed the survivors in their lifeboats to the north African coast, where they were handed over to the Senussi and taken into the desert where, to all intents and purposes, they vanished until rescued by the Duke of Westminster's motorised column on 17th March 1916.

Although four books have been written specifically about HMS *Tara* and the ordeal of the survivors, none to my mind has provided the full details of the events of nearly one hundred years ago, particularly with regard to the story of the Irish Sea steam packets, their adoption by the Royal Navy as fleet auxiliary vessels and service prior to the events in the Mediterranean and north Africa during 1915. These four books were a valuable starting point for my research, but I have also consulted the diaries written by seven HMS *Tara* survivors; the diary of a member of the Emergency Squadron Royal Naval Air Service; the log books of various vessels (including *Tara*'s own) and reports from various Welsh, English, Scottish, Irish and Australian newspapers. From the National Archives, I have consulted the Royal Navy's files. I have also been in touch with families of crew members in Holyhead, Northern Ireland, Scotland, the United States of America and Australia. Hopefully, by using these and other sources many questions regarding the *Hibernia* / *Tara* have been answered.

For his assistance in researching this book, I would like to thank my very good friend, Aled L Jones, who helped enormously by finding relevant pieces of

*SS Hibernia leaving Holyhead for Kingstown on a summer's evening in 1906*

*[Courtesy National Railway Musem/Science and Society Picture Library]*

information from some very unlikely sources and for being always ready to carry out searches no matter how insignificant or pointless they seemed. I would also like to thank Peter John, researcher of the now defunct Naval Historical Collectors & Research Association, who would also find and search through various files and documents on my behalf at the National Archives, and William Davies, author of *The Sea and Sand*, to whom I am indebted for his encouragement and the loan of his photographs.

I would also like to thank the staff of the Anglesey Archives Service, the staff of the Holyhead Library, Campbeltown Library, the Belfast and Larne Libraries, the National Library of Ireland, Raymond Suddaby of the Imperial War Museum and the National Maritime Museum.

Individuals who greatly assisted me by supplying details from their family archives were: Mrs Ann Martin and Mrs Beryl Lloyd who gave me permission to use Quartermaster William Rowlands's diary and photograph; Miss Sharon Andrews and Mr Raymond Houston of Larne; Mr Donald R Gunn; Mr Thomas Ashmore; Mr Ann Denton of Milton Keyes; Mr Dewi Reily of Trearddur Bay; Mr Brian Jones of Holyhead; Captain Glynn Pritchard; Mrs Glenys Barton; Mr Gerald Burnell; Mr and Mrs Merfyn M Hughes; Mrs Dorothy Wise (daughter of Captain Albert Marsh); Mrs B Holmes; Mrs Gail Parillo; Mrs B Liepman; Wales Media Ltd.

Finally, I am indebted to the following organisations for their assistance: BRB (Residuary) Ltd; the Duke of Westminster's Estate; the *Campbeltown Courier*; the *Larne Times*, the National Archives. To any other institutions or persons that I may have overlooked I apologise.

I take full responsibility for any errors that may have crept into this book and to anyone whose copyright I may have unwittingly infringed, I offer my sincere apologies.

Geraint S Griffiths
Holyhead
2015

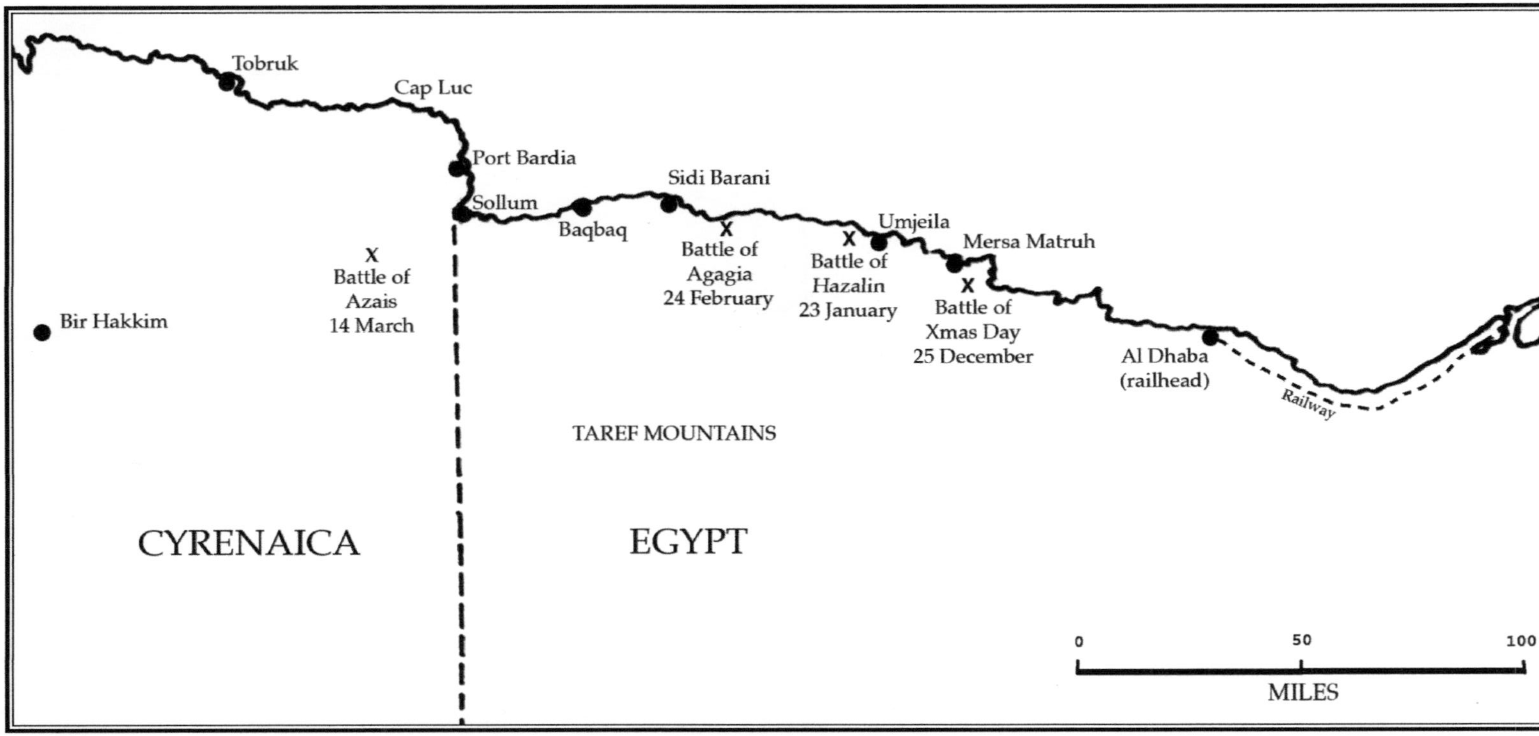


*North-east African coast, 1916*

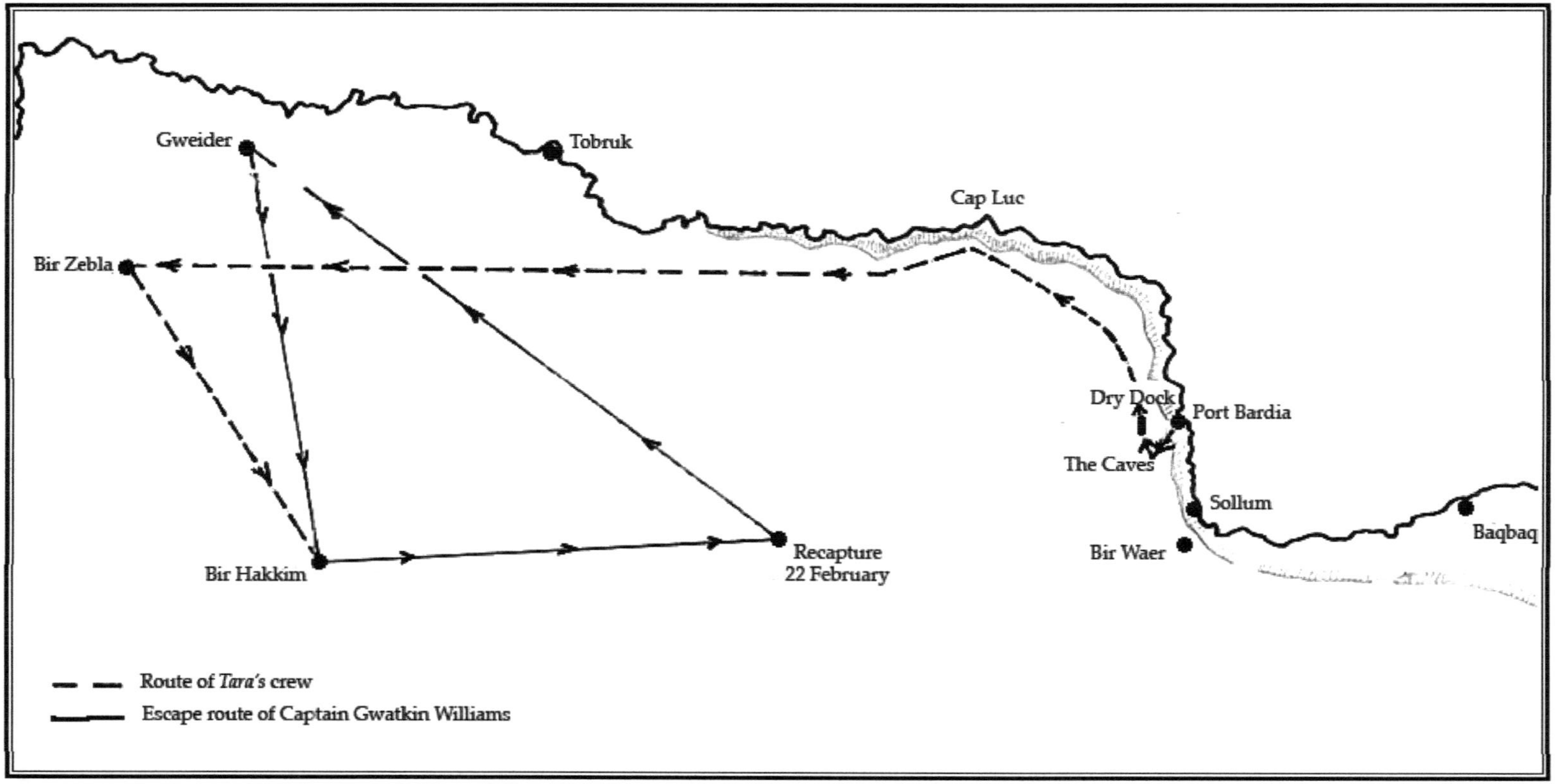


*Prisoners' routes 1915–16*

# 1. The *Cambria* Class

Although the London & North Western Railway (L&NWR) carried the Royal Mail from Euston to Holyhead, they did not hold the contract to carry it across the Irish Sea. Since 1850 this had been held by the City of Dublin Steam Packet Company (CoDSPC) whose side-paddle vessels – RMS *Connaught, Leinster, Munster* and *Ulster* sailed from the Admiralty Pier, Holyhead to Kingstown (now Dun Loaghaire) Ireland. In 1894, discussions for the renewal of the Royal Mail contract commenced but, as no interest had been expressed by either the L&NWR nor any other party, it was retained by the CoDSPC. The new contract commenced in 1897 but to accommodate its requirements, faster ships were needed and the CoDSPC ordered four new vessels from Cammell Laird's shipyard in Birkenhead to replace their four existing steam packets which were two-cylinder, steam-driven, side-paddle vessels built in 1859/60 and re-engined, re-boilered and re-constructed during the mid 1880s. The new vessels, although named after their predecessors, would be radically different in that they would have twin propellers, two four-cylinder triple-expansion engines, four double-ended boilers and would be capable of twenty-four knots. They were built to be driven as evidenced by a high turtle-back forecastle some seventy-feet long which would allow water to cascade off as they cut their way through heavy seas, thus enabling a high service speed to be maintained during the winter months. They were also to provide accommodation for both first-class and steerage/third-class passengers,[1] a new innovation for the mail and express steamers of both companies, as previous to this, steerage passengers were carried on the open decks but in inclement weather could pay to shelter within the accommodation (LNWR passengers had also the option of using the cargo/livestock spaces).

The L&NWR ran their vessels, both passenger and cargo, from Holyhead's inner harbour, past Kingstown and up the river Liffey to Dublin where they berthed at the North Wall and, although a longer route, it was direct to the heart of the Irish capital. Their passenger vessels the *Shamrock, Lily, Violet* and *Banshee*

1. Neither company operated a second class.

*The* Banshee *[Author]*

connected with the day and night express train service to and from Euston, and in consequence the vessels were known as the express steamers. These four vessels were also side paddlers, all built between 1876 and 1884, and had been re-engined and re-boilered but, with the advent of modern triple-expansion engines and more efficient boilers, were obsolete. Even though their passenger accommodation was limited and cramped, passenger numbers on the route had been steadily increasing and the L&NWR decided that they too would introduce four new vessels onto their Holyhead–Dublin route. The mainline service from Euston had recently been upgraded so that by the mid 1890s, it only took 5½ hours (with one stop at Crewe) to reach Holyhead. In addition they were to spend £20,000 on refurbishing the North Western Hotel in Dublin and to enlarge the refreshment rooms at the Station Hotel in Holyhead.

The L&NWR's four new vessels were to be built over a period of five years and would all be to the same design. Tenders had been sent to a number of yards, including Harland & Wolff, but it was William Denny & Brothers of Dumbarton in Scotland who were given the contract. In 1895–6 they had built two new passenger and livestock carriers for the company's Holyhead– Greenore service, the sister ships SS *Rosstrevor* and *Connemara*. The first built, the *Rosstrevor* had run at eighteen knots on her trials, but on service could only make seventeen. Denny's, after running model tests in their testing tank, discovered that cavitation caused the propellers to slip in the water so they took her back and replaced her specified two four-bladed propellers with two three-bladed propellers, which increased her service speed to 17½ knots. The modification resulted in Denny's losing £2,339 on her construction but earned them a very good reputation with the L&NWR.

The new vessels were designed to be fast and the L&NWR had specified that their registered tonnage was to be kept as low as possible and despite their restricted draft so as to navigate the river Liffey, they needed to be good sea boats and free from excessive vibration. Passenger capacity was to be of 623 saloon and 755 deck passengers. First-class passengers were to be accommodated on the awning and main decks amidships, and on the lower deck forward of the boiler rooms, whilst steerage would be accommodated on the main and lower decks aft.

The ships were not expected to carry cargo, but would be carrying passengers luggage and parcel post.[2] For this they would have one hold forward and a small hold aft on the lower deck.

For the new vessels it was decided to resurrect the names of the old Chester & Holyhead Railway's steamers of 1847 — *Anglia, Cambria, Hibernia* and *Scotia.*

The first of the new express steamers to be built was the *Cambria* and the class took its name from her. She was ordered on 20th November 1896 at an estimated cost of £84,250, launched on 4th August 1897 and handed over to the owners on 23rd November of that year. The *Cambria* made her maiden voyage from Holyhead to Dublin on Wednesday, 15th December under the command of the commodore of the fleet, sixty-eight-year-old Captain Thomas J Varian who had been master of the old *Cambria* when she completed her last trip some twenty-five years previously. The *Cambria* replaced the old *Shamrock* and was very well received by the press, her crew and, most importantly, her passengers. After a few months of satisfactory and reliable service a second vessel, the *Hibernia,* was ordered on 21st October 1898 as a replacement for the *Lily*, a paddle vessel which had entered service in 1880. The *Hibernia's* specifications and fitting-out details were:

*Hull and machinery*

Dimensions — 337.1 feet overall length, 329 feet perpendicular or waterline x 39.1 feet beam x 15.7 feet draught.

Propulsion — by two three-bladed propellers, driven by two four-crank triple-expansion engines, numbered 492 and 493; cylinder diameters 26 inches, 40 inches, 43 inches and 43 inches, stroke 33 inches the engines delivering 398

2. Although not holding a contract for the Royal Mail, the L&NWR's vessels did carry the GPO's parcel service.

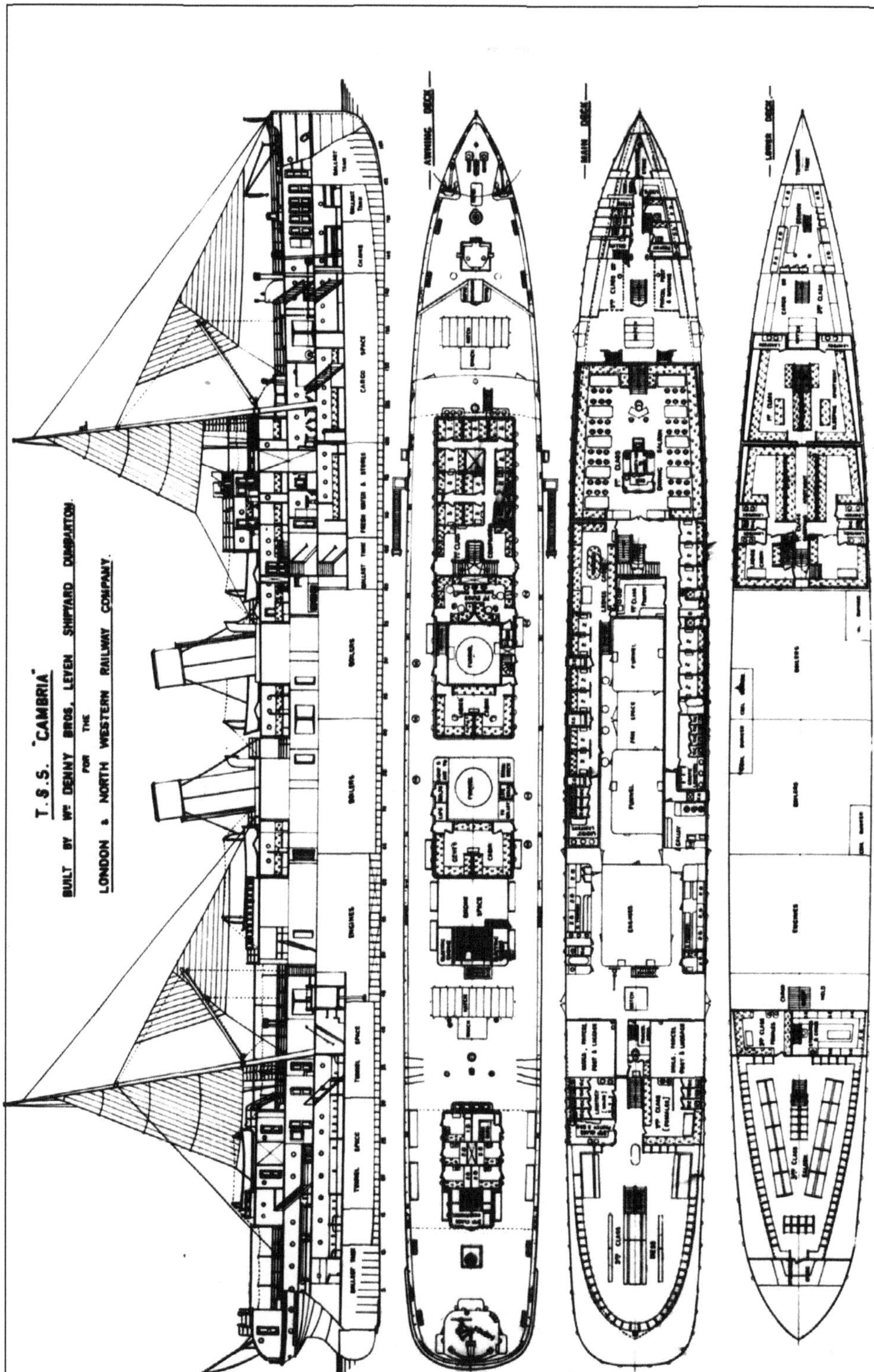
T.S.S. "CAMBRIA"
BUILT BY Wm DENNY BROS, LEVEN SHIPYARD DUMBARTON
FOR THE
LONDON & NORTH WESTERN RAILWAY COMPANY
AWNING DECK
MAIN DECK
LOWER DECK
BOILERS
ENGINES

nhp. Built by Denny's and designed by Walter Brock, the chief designer of Denny's. They were to be light and of the Yarrow-Schlick-Tweedie type, briefly this was an engine balancing system where the low pressure expansion stage was divided between two cylinders, one to each end of the engine. This resulted in the crankshaft being better balanced, giving a smoother and faster responding engine which ran with much less vibration

Boilers – eight single ended Yarrow tubular boilers with a working pressure of 160 psi, fitted within enclosed stokeholds. She had a bunker capacity of 101 tons of coal.

Electrical power — generated by two dynamos, each driven by a steam reciprocating engine, sited to port and starboard on a flat within the engine room at awning deck level. Also sited on this level was the main switchboard through which electrical power was distributed throughout the vessel. The installation of all lights, fittings, switchboard, etc was carried out by the electrical department of the L&NWR workshops in Crewe, where the dynamos, engines, fittings, etc were also produced.

Funnels — two, fitted with spark arresters so as to prevent sparks falling onto passengers. (This was to be a feature on all subsequent L&NWR/LMS coal fired forced draft steam vessels.)

Deck machinery; one capstan windlass fitted forward, two steam winches — one forward and one aft together with a warping winch sited aft, all built by Clark Chapman & Co.

Steering gear — steam, built by Brown Brothers.

A mild steel hull which could be sub-divided into ten watertight compartments.

Two decks; main and lower, plus an awning deck; fore and aft schooner rigged with two tapered and raked masts.

*Holds*

One cargo hold of 8,790 cubic feet forward and one small hold (capacity unknown) aft on the lower deck. The main deck aft cargo space contained two secure rooms, sited to port and starboard for parcel post and passenger's baggage and valuables. The main deck forward cargo space could be utilised to erect two room's/lockers, one to port and one to starboard for passengers

*Facing: The plans of the* Cambria *[National Maritime Museum]*

baggage and parcel post - these however were of a temporary nature so could be dismantled and the space used for third-class passengers, under this space on the lower deck there was another space designated cargo or third class.

Ventilation of all passenger and crew spaces was supplied by electric fans and all passenger and crew spaces were fitted with electric lighting. In case of failure/emergencies paraffin lamps fitted on gimbals were fitted in all passenger/crew spaces.

*Lifeboats*

Six twenty-four foot lifeboats (Nos 1, 2 ,3, 4, 7 and 8) and two twenty-two foot cutters (Nos 5 and 6), all clinker built with number plates and lettered with the ships name and port, arranged to port and starboard of the centre accommodation.

*First-class passenger accommodation*

Awning Deck. From the first-class companion an alleyway led forward into the first-class sleeping accommodation which contained four two berth and six three berth cabins, all panelled in sycamore and fitted with sprung mattresses and folding washing facilities.

The first-class companion was accessed from the awning deck by doors to the port and starboard sides. On the forward bulkhead, to port and starboard Moroccan leather upholstered benches were fitted. From the companion, stairs led down to a foyer on the main deck and to a first-class ladies cabin and a first-class sleeping apartment on the lower deck. Both companion and stairwell were floored with rubber tiles and panelled in ash, framed in walnut with sycamore mouldings and a reeded walnut dado.

Aft of the companion was the first-class gentlemen's smoking room; panelled in ash, framed in walnut, with sycamore mouldings and floored with encaustic tiles and the bar was situated to the after end, on the starboard side. The room was furnished with circular marble topped tables; chairs and benches were upholstered in buffalo hide; screens containing leaded stained glass panels were fitted in way of doors and air shafts so as to prevent drafts; on the ceiling the stained-glass, panelled skylight was equipped with an electric fan to extract smoke, fumes and stale air.

The first-class ladies cabin was sited aft of the forward funnel; panelled with polished sycamore, decorated on the frieze, dado and pilaster; to the ceiling a leaded stained glass panelled skylight was fitted; all furniture, benches and chairs were upholstered in blue frieze velvet.

The first-class gentlemen's non-smoking cabin was aft of the after funnel; decorated in the classical style with polished teak decorated frieze, pilasters and panels; the sofas within could be converted to sleeping berths and a leaded stained glass panelled skylight was fitted to the ceiling.

*First-class cabin Awning Deck [Author]*

*Main Deck*

Forward of the foyer was the first-class dining saloon which could seat eighty people on ten tables; the bulkheads were panelled in matt polished teak, framed with polished oak in the Grecian style with incised and gilt decoration, it had sideboards of polished oak with marble tops and was also equipped with carving tables and hot presses. Lighting was provided by both electric and natural light — the natural light being provided by large portholes and that light let in from a large

*Gentlemen's smoking cabin (SS* Scotia*) [Author]*

*First-class saloon, looking aft [Author]*

*First-class saloon, looking forward [Author]*

four stained glass panelled skylight on the awning deck, forward of the bridge, it came down trunking and into the saloon through stained glass panels on the centre casing within the saloon, on whose after end was situated the bar. Both bar and centre casing were panelled to match the saloon's bulkheads. The floor was carpeted with a heavy Brussels carpet, with runners of the same laid in the first-class alleyways.

The first-class ladies saloon was to port of the foyer but separated from it by a door and bulkhead both fitted with stained glass panel's, so as to allow light in whilst maintaining a degree of privacy for the occupants. Running aft within the Saloon were six two berth, first-class ladies cabins each fitted with sprung mattresses and folding washing facilities, aft of the cabins were toilets and a bathroom. Opposite on the vessels starboard side were six two-berth gentlemen's cabins (equipped as per ladies cabins), toilets and bathroom.

*Lower deck*

Stairs from main deck foyer led into the first-class sleeping apartment; fitted with benches which could be converted to berths; it also contained washing facilities and toilets – the apartment was to be used nominally by ladies but could be utilised for gentlemen. To the port side of the stair was a separate first-class ladies cabin fitted with toilet and washing facilities and whose benches converted to sleeping berths. The cabin sides were painted in white enamel.

Forward of this space was another first-class sleeping apartment, for gentlemen but was accessed from the dining saloon; it contained folding beds with sprung mattresses; washing facilities; the sides were painted in white enamel.

Ceilings of all cabins, apartments and companion were panelled and decorated to suit those spaces. An electric bell call system was fitted throughout the first-class accommodation and water was supplied to all washing facilities.

*Steerage passenger accommodation*

Main deck (aft) — third-class mess, accessed via double doors and stairs on the after end of the companion house on the awning deck. The mess had two large wooden dining tables with wooden benches situated in the centre of the space. Sparred wooden benches were fitted around ships side which were divided into two-foot spaces by solid arms so as to prevent passengers using the benches as berths. Forward on the starboard side was a female's saloon complete with benches and toilets. On the port side was a third class pantry and bar, male toilets and washing facilities.

Third-class saloon — accessed via a double stair from the third-class mess, sparred wooden benches fitted to ships side, it had no tables but did have two long wooden benches fitted either side of the stairway and a smaller one aft of the benches. Forward in the space on the port side was a female's cabin.

All washing facilities had water supplied.

Steerage accommodation/cargo spaces, forward of the first-class accommodation on the main and lower decks. These spaces could be utilised for passengers or cargo, the lower deck being fitted with wooden benches along the ships sides.

*Crew accommodation*

Funnel Deck — captain and chief officer's cabins, toilets and bathroom situated under the bridge.

Companion house, awning deck aft. Cabins, toilets, bathroom and mess for second and third officers. Chief, second, third and fourth engineers and mess.

Forecastle, main and lower decks; berths, toilets, bathroom and mess for fourteen seamen.

Main deck amidships, port and starboard; berths, toilets, bathroom and mess for fourteen firemen and trimmers.

Lower deck starboard, forward of third-class saloon; berths, toilets and bathroom for twenty stewards and cooks.

On 10th October 1899, Yard N° 618 was launched as the SS *Hibernia* at Denny's Leven Yard by Lady Houldsworth, wife of Sir William Henry Houldsworth, MP, who was a director of Denny's, and whilst the ship was being towed to the fitting-out berth, the launching party made their way to the Model Hall for lunch. Amongst the guests was Captain W H Binnie, superintendent of the port of Holyhead, who was standing by the *Hibernia*'s building to ensure company requirements were complied with and to be on hand to give authorization of any modifications that might be required.

As time went on and the fitting out progressed, more crew members were sent up from Holyhead to Dumbarton until finally, by December, she had a full complement. On 21st December, she ran her first trials on the Clyde and, with a displacement of 2,260 tons, attained a speed of 21.12 knots, her shafts turning at 172.5 rpm and her engines showing 6,943 ihp.[3] However, as with all trials, some minor defects were discovered and, after they had been attended to, she ran further trials on 10th January 1900 when, during the first run over 102 nautical miles, she averaged 21.3 knots. On the 12th, she ran a distance of 117 nautical

3. For the *Cambria's* trials the L&NWR had specified that their men would man the engine and boiler rooms – under Denny's supervision, and the coal she would burn would be from the north Wales coalfield – the same coalfield which supplied the companies Holyhead vessels. The L&NWR stated that they would undertake the cost of the additional expense. Whether the same arrangement was specified for the *Hibernia* is not known.

miles and achieved 21.5 knots – 0.5 knots in excess of contract speed. All being well she was duly signed over to L&NWR.

The *Hibernia* was of 1,862 tons (gross) and 313 tons (net). She was given the official number 111027 and the identification letters RLWT. Her total cost to the company was £93,153.

On 17th January 1899, *Hibernia* left Dumbarton for Holyhead where she arrived dressed overall and where, over the next few days, was no doubt visited by various superintendents, officers and crews of the other Holyhead vessels, office staff and workers of the Marine Yard and various other railway departments, as well as the wives and families of her own crew, all eager to have a look around the new vessel.

At 03.55 hours on 2nd February, she sailed on her maiden voyage from Holyhead to the North Wall, Dublin. On board, amongst the invited guests who had spent the previous evening and night at the Station Hotel at the company's expense, were P Denny (representing William Denny Brothers), W Brock (of Denny's engineering department), A T Orr (engineering superintendent for L&NWR in Holyhead) and the general managers of various Irish railway companies (Great Northern Railway, Great Southern & Western Railway, Waterford and Central Ireland Railway). Also aboard were journalists from various national and local newspapers.

On arrival at Dublin and after lunch, the guests and journalists were invited to inspect the ship and, although the weather had not been at its best, the press later wrote glowingly of her sea keeping qualities, of her appointment and equipment, and they were very much impressed by the new third-class accommodation.

Soon the *Cambria* and *Hibernia* were running a tandem service to Dublin. On 2nd May 1900, they were joined by the *Anglia* and eventually by the *Scotia* which made her maiden voyage on 23rd April 1902.

It was not long before the *Hibernia* saw some excitement. On 28th December 1900, whilst under the command of Captain Thomas G Clay, she was making her way back to Holyhead from Dublin in a terrific gale. Nearing the South Stack, she came across the steel barque *Primrose Hill*, bound from Liverpool to Vancouver, which was being driven onto the rocks in Abrahams Bosom, Penrhosfeilw. She tried to sail close to the barque to pass a line, but suffered a steering-gear failure and had to give up the attempt and was only just able to extricate herself and make Holyhead, by steering with her engines. The *Primrose Hill* was driven onto

*The steel barque* Primrose Hill *[Gwyn Pierce]*

the rocks and broke up, her crew of thirty-three, which included twelve apprentices, were drowned or dashed onto the rocks and only one man, a thirty-seven year old Swede – Johan Petterson survived having been rescued by a local farmer (twenty-three year old John Owen of Tai Hirion Farm, Penrhosfeilw) who had climbed down the cliff. As a wave swept the badly injured Petterson up the rocks some forty feet, Owen caught and clung to him and, even though the seas were constantly breaking over them both, he managed to hang on until help arrived. For his bravery Owen was later awarded a medal by the Royal Humane Society and paraded through the town on a horse and cart (which had been presented to his father by Lord Stanley of Penrhos) to the cheers of the town's people. Petterson, after spending some time in the local Stanley Sailors' Hospital on Salt Island, made a full recovery.

On 17th November 1903 Edward Jones, a boatman employed by the L&NWR was awarded the bronze medal of the Royal Humane Society for diving into Holyhead harbour on 1st September to rescue a Mr James Regan who had fallen off the quay whilst boarding the *Hibernia*.

On 4th March 1905, at 06.30 hours in thick fog, whilst in mid channel on passage to Holyhead, the *Hibernia,* under the command of Captain J F Pinchin, collided with the cargo vessel SS *Medway* which was on passage from Cardiff to Glasgow. Luckily both vessels were proceeding slowly and as their bows touched both had immediately put their engines astern. Momentum however caused the

*Medway* to scrape down the *Hibernia*'s side damaging the taff-rail and bulwark in way of the bow. An investigation revealed no underwater damage to either vessel and, after some thirty minutes, both continued to their destinations.

On 5th June 1906 an inquest was held in Dublin into the circumstances surrounding the death of James Williams of 10 Porthyfelin, Holyhead. His body had been pulled out of the sea earlier that morning by a boat lowered from the SS *Hibernia* whilst she was on passage to Dublin. The body was identified as that of Williams who was a twenty-year-old labourer who had been missing since 1st May when it was thought that he had gone to collect seabird eggs from the cliffs near Holyhead mountain. He was presumed to have missed his footing and fallen into the sea. The jury found a verdict of death by drowning and commended the captain of the *Hibernia* for stopping the vessel and bringing the body to Dublin.

In 1907 the L&NWR appointed a new marine superintendent to the port of Holyhead, Commander Gerald Edward Holland, CIE, DSO.[4] On 17th March 1908 news was released that as from 1st April the L&NWR would be transferring its passenger services to Kingstown, which had previously been used solely by the CoDSPC. The express steamers would continue to run a pattern where another would be the day boat, one the night boat, one vessel would be on stand-by should one of the running vessels suffer a breakdown, whilst the fourth would be laid up for maintenance and overhaul. The day boat would leave Kingston Pier at 13.45 hours, arriving Holyhead at 17.10 hours, whilst the night boat would leave Holyhead at 19.15 hours and arrive Kingstown Pier at 21.50 hours. Needless to say, the transfer of the L&NWR express steamers to Kingstown generated a lot of ill-feeling on the part of the officers and crews of the CoDSPC and no doubt amongst the Irish population.

4. Born in Dublin in 1860, educated at Radcliffe's College, Leicestershire he joined the Royal Indian Marine in 1880 and was promoted lieutenant 1882 and commander in 1893. He took part in the Burma expedition of 1887–9, the Chin Lushai expedition of 1889–90 for which he was awarded the Distinguished Service Order. He was in command of the RIM Warren Hastings when she was wrecked on Reunion Island whilst carrying troops of the Kings Royal Rifle Corps, 2nd Bn Yorks & Lancaster Regiment and the Middlesex Regiment to Mauritius. He was reprimanded by the court martial, but a Commendatory Order by the Viceroy of India for his efforts in saving life was printed with the findings of the court in appreciation the KRRC made him an honourary member of their officer's mess. During the Anglo-Boer War he served on the Natal Transport Staff at Durban as a marine transport officer (Indian Contingent) from 2nd October 1899 to 20th October 1900 and as the divisional transport officer in Durban from October 1900 to April 1901. For his services during there he was created a Companion of the Indian Empire – a unique award for the Boer War – and received three mentions in despatches. General Buller wrote that Commander Holland '... had served at Durban throughout. His genius for organization and knowledge for transport requirements is, I should say, unrivalled. He undertook the alteration of the transports which were fitted

*On 11th June 1911, Steward Lewis Owen of the* Hibernia *jumped overboard to rescue a passenger who had fallen into Holyhead harbour. He was later awarded the Royal Humane Society's Bronze Medal, given a reward by the Board of the L&NW and the Carnegie Hero Fund.*

In April 1912, the sinking of the RMS *Titanic* and the resultant large loss of life highlighted the inadequate number of life-boats passenger vessels had been legally required to carry – the number depending on the tonnage of the vessel rather than the number of passengers carried. Due to the ensuing public outcry, the Board of Trade moved swiftly to legislate to increase their number to ensure a seat for every passenger carried. However, a number of shipping companies foresaw this and to generate public confidence in their vessels, started to fit additional lifeboats before the legislation took effect. The L&NWR was one such company and in May, work started on the fitting of additional lifeboats and life rafts (or buoyant deck seats) to all their passenger vessels. They also ensured that there were more than enough life jackets for every person on board. For the four express steamers this resulted in the fitting of two additional 24-foot lifeboats atop the companion house on the awning deck and, taking advantage of modern technology to further enhance lifesaving, Helsby wireless telegraphy apparatus was fitted to the ships during June and July.[5]

On board the *Scotia* on 25th October 1912, Commander Holland presented prizes to the L&NWR winners of the annual four-oared with coxswains rowing races, held between the ships' lifeboats of the L&NWR and CoDSPC vessels during the annual summer regatta. After the presentation, he complimented the winners and stated that owing to the *Titanic* disaster it was inevitable that the Board of Trade would soon require all seamen to be qualified to man a lifeboat, both under sail and oars and to give the company's men some encouragement, added that from the following summer there would be money prizes for the men in the first two boats as well as the winners in a series of rowing races which he intended to arrange.

at Durban as hospital ships, and the result of his work has been universally admitted to have been a conspicuous success ...' From May 1901 to 1904 Holland had served as port officer in Rangoon and and retired from theRoyal Indian Marine in 1905. The following year he was appointed marine superintendent of the L&NWR port of Heysham.

5. Wireless Telegraphy Operators J D Cannon and D T Rockey were appointed on 9th and 10th July 1912, respectively. To which vessels they were appointed is not known.

On the 19.00 hours sailing to Kingstown on Friday, 4th July 1913, as the *Hibernia* was rounding the Holyhead breakwater, Thomas Chadwick, the galley boy went missing. He had last been seen by the cook, Walter Jackson, when he left the galley to throw the stove ashes overboard. At the subsequent inquest Jackson surmised that after Chadwick had dumped the ashes, via the ship's side door, which it seems was common practice, he had returned, replaced the bin in the galley and had then gone back to shut the door. Jackson speculated that a gust of wind, or wave may have caught the door as he was closing it pitching him into the sea. After a brief search of the galley area, the alarm was raised and Captain John Evans reversed course to the approximate position where it was thought that Chadwick had dumped the ashes. He brought the ship to a stop and a boat was speedily lowered and a thorough search of the area made but there was no sign of the missing man. The boat was eventually recalled and the *Hibernia* circled the area a few times before proceeding to Kingstown. Initially it was thought that Chadwick could have been dragged into the propellers and therefore there would be no trace of his body. However, on the afternoon of Wednesday, 30th July Harold Smith, an engineering student who lived in Cliff Bungalow, Valley was out in his boat in Beddmanarch Bay, near the Stanley Embankment, when he saw a body floating near some rocks. The police were informed and the body was recovered by PC R H Williams of Valley and later identified by his clothes as Thomas Chadwick of 24 Thomas Street, Holyhead. His body was later interred in the Catholic cemetery in Cleveland Avenue, Holyhead.

On Sunday, 5th February 1914 the *Hibernia's* chief engineer, Robert Paton, died and his position was taken by Harold O Roberts of the SS *Greenore*, a vessel on which he had served since she was built.

Over the winter of 1913–14 the *Hibernia* and her sister vessels would continue to plough their way, backwards and forwards across the Irish Sea, in storm and calm. Later, in the spring and summer, the stand-by or off-turn vessels would continue the tradition of taking excursions from Holyhead every now and then, out south towards Bardsey Island or east to Puffin Island or the Great Orme.[6]

6. The last vessel to make such an excursion before the war was the *Scotia*, under Captain Pinchin. She left Holyhead at 13.30 hours on 14th July 1914 for a supposed trip to Puffin Island, the 350 passengers aboard, who paid two shillings (10p) per head, had a bargain as he took them on to the Great Orme before returning to Holyhead, where she berthed at the Town Quay at 19.00 hours.

# 2. Preparations for War

As early as 1904 the Royal Navy had reached the conclusion that should war come it would most probably be against Germany whose expansionist policies and rapidly expanding navy was seen as a threat to Britain's trade routes with her empire. This caused some concern at the Admiralty, and they had to consider how best to contain the German threat in the event of a future conflict. As a result, the Navy's ship-building programme went ahead and in 1906 it stole a lead with the launching of the new HMS *Dreadnought* which overnight made all other battleships obsolete. She was the first of the 'all big gun' ships, carrying ten 12-inch guns, was coal and oil fired, driven by steam turbines. *Dreadnought* gave her name to a new class of warship, with between one and five vessels being launched every year until 1914, by which time the Royal Navy possessed twenty-six of the new battleships. Also leaving the slipways of the ship builders during these years were modern, turbine-driven battle-cruisers, heavy and light cruisers and destroyers.

Realising they would need vessels to fetch and carry spares, stores, and personnel for this modern fleet the Admiralty sought suitable vessels that could

*The captain, officers and crew of SS* Hibernia *c.1900*

work with the Fleet during a time of national emergency. As they had done over past centuries the Navy looked to the Mercantile Marine, which at the time was the largest merchant fleet in the world, composed mostly of cargo vessels and tramp steamers which plodded along at 7–10 knots. Although these vessels were adequate for their purpose, they were totally unsuited to the Royal Navy's needs; the latter wanted vessels that were capable of attaining and maintaining high speeds so as to keep station with the Fleet. The Director of Transports at the Admiralty had in mind vessels that could steam at and maintain a speed of at least 18 knots for 200 miles out and 200 miles home. They should also be able carry enough coal and water to stay at sea for four days whilst cruising at 10–18 knots. Having looked at various types of ships they came to the conclusion that, with some modification's, cross-channel steam packets would be ideal.

In the spring of 1909, the Admiralty approached the railway and shipping companies for details of suitable vessels which could be requisitioned in the event of war. As time went on and the size of the Imperial German Navy grew, so did the Admiralty's concerns and plans were drawn up detailing specific requirements for the number of vessels required and the modifications needed to bring them up to naval requirements. For these ships the Navy was to create a new class, that of Fleet Messengers, which eventually numbered more than eighty vessels. The majority of vessels within this class would be used for logistic support but it did contain vessels as diverse as an icebreaker, a salvage vessel, kite balloon ships and yachts.

The L&NWR raised some objections to the scheme, one of which was the taking up all of their express steamers would drive business into the hands of the CoDSPC which they might find it difficult to regain. The Admiralty replied

> ... that it [the question] was not of practical importance as the fastest boats of [your] competitor will have been similarly told off for Admiralty service ... and that ... it is thought highly likely that in the circumstances contemplated the companies owning cross channel steamers would find themselves unable to continue their ordinary business.

By 1912 it had been decided that sixteen vessels would fulfil the Admiralty's requirements, but that all would not be taken up at once. If war was declared, eight were to be immediately requisitioned, as 'First Requirement', but the second eight, the 'Second Requirement', would only be requisitioned when all movements of reservists between Ireland, England and the islands had been completed.

For the First Requirement, five of the vessels were to be steam packets from the port of Holyhead, the L&NWR's *Anglia, Cambria, Hibernia, Scotia* along with one of the passenger/cargo vessels, either the *Greenore* or *Rathmore,* whilst the London & South Western Railway Company would supply the SS *Normania* and *Hantonia* and the Midland Railway Company the SS *Duchess of Devonshire.*

By 6th November 1913 the requirements had been altered. The Admiralty now only required six fleet messengers — four to be taken up on First Requirement, stressing that the ships should only be those capable of 20 knots and fitted with wireless telegraphy equipment, and two on Second Requirement. As a consequence, for First Requirement the *Anglia, Cambria, Hibernia* and *Scotia* (already fitted with Helsby wireless telegraphy sets) were chosen, whilst for Second Requirement the *Duchess of Argyll* and *Duchess of Cumberland,* both from the Yorkshire & Lancashire Railway Company were to be taken up.

The vessels of the Cambria Class were coal fired and had a fuel consumption of 145 tons per day whilst steaming at 21 knots (their nominal full speed) and 34 tons per day whilst cruising at 12 knots. But, as built, each could only carry some 100 tons of coal in their permanent bunkers. Feed water for the boilers was also a problem as they were not fitted with evaporators or distillers and therefore could not make their own. Water therefore had to be carried in the vessels own 85-ton double-bottom tanks which were sited below the engine room, but this was only sufficient water for 3½–4 days steaming.

In order to meet the Admiralty's steaming requirements, space for additional feed water and coal had to be found. Whilst the additional feed water could be carried in the vessel's five ballast tanks, it was decided that coal could be stowed elsewhere — 190 tons on top of the propeller shaft tunnel in the third-class saloon, 106 tons in the forward cargo hold and 154 tons on the lower deck forward. Fully bunkered, each vessel would carry 550 tons of coal and, whilst the additional weight would increase their draft by four feet and reduce their speed from 21 to 17 knots, the Admiralty still thought their speed was adequate.

The stowage spaces for the coal had been chosen as they were accessible from the main deck via the forward and after main-deck hatches, through which the coal could be bunkered and from which the coal could be hoisted (in sacks) via the vessels own derricks to replenish the permanent bunkers. To transfer the coal from the stowage spaces to the bunkers, the Admiralty had specified that each vessel would require twelve additional deck hands, and to maintain speed they would also require one additional engineer and ten firemen. All told it was envisaged that each vessel, under Royal Navy manning requirements, would carry a total of 117 men, amongst which would be the commander (a retired Royal Navy lieutenant), signaller and nine Royal Fleet Reservists. There was more than enough space for these men as the ships had enough berths for their usual crew of fifty-six (although in the *Hibernia*'s case, in 1914 her normal complement was fifty-seven) as well as 214 first-class passengers. There were also passenger spaces — lounges, smoking rooms, etc which could be stripped out and converted to mess-decks and dining areas for the additional crew.

It had been envisaged that no alterations to the ship's structure needed to be carried out, although it had been mooted that they could be armed which would necessitate the stiffening and strengthening of the decks in the proposed gun positions. Magazines to hold the ammunition would have to be constructed under the main deck – somewhere in the vessel's bowels. In addition, signalling equipment, binoculars, a telescope, charts, chronometers (two), deck and engine-room stores for two months and victualling stores for two months, mess tables and utensils, bedding, blankets and coal would also be required. Some of these would be supplied by the Admiralty and the rest at the Admiralty's expense. The requirements also stipulated that the weather-work paint should remain roughly the same as their peacetime colours, but that their funnels should have any distinguishing colours or marks removed and then blacked. The ships' names and ports of registry should be dulled, so as not to be easily read by passing shipping. All lights should be screened, binnacle lights shielded, dead lights or scuttles fitted to port holes, portable wooden shutters fitted to all windows above the main deck (in the accommodation, wheelhouse, charthouse and deck houses) and painted canvas screens were to be fitted behind all the doors leading out onto the decks to prevent exposure of light when entering or leaving. Although designated naval vessels, the ships were to fly the Red Ensign, except when in company with other auxiliaries and naval vessels, when they would fly the Y.4 (the fleet messenger) pennant. These plans were finalised in February 1913.

# 3. Mobilisation

Despite the tensions which had been steadily rising in Europe, particularly in the Balkans, the government announced in March 1914 that, in addition to the annual naval manoeuvres, a test mobilization was to be held in July. This was not intended to be a real war mobilization and consequently the Royal Navy Reserves were invited to attend — they were not called out. On 10th July, operational orders were issued for the ships to assemble off Portland. All told some 460 vessels, including auxiliaries, attended comprising the whole of the Home Fleet (except for the 4th Destroyer Flotilla which was on policing duties off Ireland). The Reserves had also turned out and by 16th July, the whole Fleet was assembled in a state of mobilization.

Meanwhile in continental Europe, the situation had not outwardly altered since the assassination of Archduke Franz Ferdinand, the heir to the Austro-Hungarian Empire, and his wife Sophia on 28th June in Sarajevo, Bosnia. The German Kaiser was on his annual cruise in Norwegian waters and on 13th July the French President had left for the Baltic to meet the Russian Tsar. Off Portland, after the usual exercises at sea, the ships that had taken part in the Royal Navy's manoeuvres began to disperse on 23rd July and Admiral Callaghan ordered a Flag Officer's conference to be held at Portsmouth. On the same day, the

Hibernia, *leaving North Wall, Dublin [Author]*

Austrians handed the Serbs a very harsh ten point ultimatum which the Serbs eventually rejected and the Austrians declared war on 28th July.[1]

During the early hours of 24th July the text of the Austrian ultimatum was passed to the British Foreign Office which, realising the tensions between the European powers, found it contained a time limit of forty-eight hours. The wording was so provocative that the Portsmouth naval conference was immediately cancelled, but no orders were given to halt the dispersal of the fleet. Two days later, with the situation in Europe worsening, the fleet's dispersal was halted and on 27th July, orders were issued to those units which had already dispersed to return.

To avoid aggravating the situation, those crews who had been allowed to go on leave were allowed to remain on leave, whilst those that had been called to attend the test mobilization were told to remain with their vessels and the Royal Navy's Training Schools were not to reopen.

The Second Fleet,[2] along with 36 coastal destroyers and a few other vessels was ordered to ensure that all vessels had a full complement of crews and all officers temporarily appointed for the test mobilisation were to rejoin the ships on which they had been serving prior to the test mobilisation. On 28th July, the Grand Fleet was ordered to proceed the next day from Portsmouth, via the East Coast, to Scapa Flow. Both the Second and Third Fleets were ordered to take on board full coal bunkers, stores and ammunition but to do so as unobtrusively as possible. Four battleships of the Majestic Class – HMS *Mars, Hannibal, Magnificent* and *Victorious* were ordered to slip away quietly to protect the Humber. The

1. The Balkan War of 1912–13 had resulted in Serbia and Greece wrenching Macedonia from the Ottoman Empire and the defeat of Bulgaria, an ally of the Austro–Hungarian empire. The war had not only increased Serbia's territory but had also greatly increased her regional standing. Seeing this as a threat to their influence in their own back yard so to speak, the Austrian's used the assassination as a pretext to cut Serbia down to size. Germany, Austria's ally, was in complete agreement with this policy and saw Serbia as nothing more than a satellite or puppet of Russia, who, since the Russo-Turkish war of 1871, wanted to spread her influence throughout the Balkans and into the Mediterranean.
2. At this time the Royal Navy kept those vessels in home waters in three stages of readiness for war. The First Fleet (or Grand Fleet) was composed of her most modern vessels including the Dreadnought battleships and modern cruisers which were fully maintained, manned and ready. The Second Fleet was composed of her pre-Dreadnought battleships and those vessels built before 1906, mostly manned by specialist officers and 60% of their full complement, with the remainder of their crews housed in barracks, on courses, etc. These vessels could be ready for sea in a few hours. The Third Fleet was in effect a reserve with vessels bordering on the obsolescent, distributed in groups in various home ports, staffed by little more than care and maintenance crews and which would have to rely on the Naval/Fleet Reserves before they became fully manned, therefore they would not be ready for sea until sometime after mobilisation.

cruiser HMS *Forward,* on police duty in the Irish sea, was ordered to Lerwick where she was to form the Shetland patrol with four destroyers. A further eight destroyers of Nore command were ordered to proceed northwards on 31st July by which time the First and Second Fleets were at their war stations and those warships posted around the Empire were standing by ready to shadow enemy warships as unobtrusively as possible, on receiving notification of the imminence of war.

By 1st August events in Europe had escalated. Germany had declared war on Serbia's ally Russia, and the French and Belgians began a general mobilisation. In London, the Admiralty was watching the events in Europe unfolding and at 14.15 hours issued orders to start the requisitioning of colliers, oil tank vessels (tankers) and other ships from the Mercantile Marine and all recently appointed Third Fleet flag officers were to join and hoist their flags at once. Port admirals were ordered to report when the Third Fleet vessels were ready to receive their crews, and all that remained was to mobilize the Reserves. Later in the day, it was learnt that Russia, catching the Germans completely off guard, had invaded Prussia — the Germans had thought that it would take Russia at least six weeks to fully mobilise.

At 01.25 hours on 2nd August, Britain mobilised her naval Reserves thereby activating the Third Fleet. Consequently, when Britain did declare war, most of her cruiser squadrons were at their stations ready to enforce a blockade.[3] The First, or Grand, Fleet would be off the north of Scotland waiting to engage the German High Seas Fleet should it venture out to interfere with the transports taking the British Expeditionary Force (BEF) over to France. The date for the

3. Britain's war plans, first drawn up in 1904 and revised regularly, deemed that, on the outbreak of war with Germany, the Royal Navy would immediately enforce a mercantile blockade of Germany. They would have their cruiser squadrons off the Western Approaches of the English Channel, in the Dover Straits, on the Atlantic trade routes and elsewhere where, not only were they to seize German vessels making for their home ports but were also to stop and search all neutral vessels for contraband cargo which was directly or indirectly intended for Germany. At the outset of war, Britain had adopted, with some modifications, the terms of the 1909 Declaration of London – a treaty which she had never ratified. This declaration stated that during wartime, neutral nations were not to supply any belligerent nations with goods that could be used for warlike purposes; these goods were divided into three categories:

1. Absolute contraband – goods of a military nature, guns, explosives, etc;
2. Conditional contraband – goods capable of both military and civilian usage, e.g. fuel, clothing, and foodstuffs, these were subject to seizure only if destined for the armed forces of an enemy state;
3. A Free List of articles which could never be considered contraband such as raw cotton, oil, rubber and copper.

The goods included in the third category consisted of some of the most important materials of modern warfare, so the government decided to draw up its own list of contraband goods but, to avoid upsetting the USA, excluded cotton for a year, but thereafter bought it at ever increasing

BEF's crossing had originally been set for 7th August but, because the Territorials were at their summer camps and had to be recalled to their depots (they had not been recalled earlier so as not to inflame the situation), the crossings could not begin until 9th August.

On 3rd August, Germany had declared war on France and the following day her troops crossed the Belgian frontier. Britain immediately demanded that Belgian neutrality be respected or a state of war would exist between the two countries and issued a deadline of 23.00 hours GMT (midnight Central European Time) for a reply. That evening, locals in Holyhead saw another tangible sign of the worsening situation in Europe, with the early recall home of the local Territorials (H Company, 6th Battalion Royal Welsh Fusiliers), who arrived at the station from Aberystwyth where they had been at their summer camp since 25th July.

At 23.00 hours Britain, having received no reply to her ultimatum, declared war. At Holyhead, during the course of the night and the following day, the Marine Superintendent, Commander Holland, went aboard all the L&NWR's vessels lying alongside to explain the situation and to ask their crews to remain with their vessels as the company would be maintaining their cross-channel services. He later went aboard the company's other vessels when they docked. In the case of the *Hibernia*, the night boat which came alongside at 01.25 *a.m*, he boarded her and, after the last passenger had disembarked, asked the crew to assemble down aft, in the third-class saloon where he informed them of the outbreak of war, the intended requisitioning of the vessel, and requested them to remain with their vessel, at least for the time being, to maintain the cross-channel services.

During the afternoon and evening of 5th April soldiers, sailors, reservists and those recalled from leave or detachment arrived at Holyhead station, en route back to their ships, bases, battalions and depots in Ireland. The SS *Rosstrevor* sailed during the afternoon carrying some 370 soldiers whilst the *Hibernia*'s night sailing had to be delayed to await the arrival of a troop train; she eventually sailed long after her scheduled time with over 400 soldiers aboard. Many of these men were returning to their parent units that were stationed in Ireland as part of the 5th and 6th Divisions, the 3rd Cavalry Brigade, 3rd Brigade Royal Horse Artillery, 3rd Signal Troop Royal Engineers and the 4th Field Troop Royal Engineers.

The L&NWRs cross-channel passenger services were maintained, albeit rather erratically, until 8th August when Commander Holland received a telegram from

prices. The length of the prohibited goods list meant that most neutral vessels had to be stopped and searched.

the Admiralty's Director of Transports[4] announcing the immediate requisition of the four express steamers, which they had designated as fleet messenger N° 1 *Anglia,* fleet messenger N° 2 *Cambria,* fleet messenger N° 3 *Hibernia* and fleet messenger N° 4 *Scotia,* and work was to start immediately on fitting them out.[5] Those civilians wishing to cross to Ireland now had to use the vessels of the CoDSPC as from 4–6th August the L&NWR's passenger/ cargo and cargo vessels had come under War Office control and, with other requisitioned vessels, would be employed until the 22nd bringing across the Irish Sea the bulk of those Army units then stationed in Ireland.[6]

The 5th Division received its mobilization orders to be ready to move on 7th August although on the morning of the 6th its vanguard, comprising details of the 1st Battalion, the Cheshire Regiment, landed at Holyhead en route to Southampton (which had been designated a military port since the outbreak of war) and then to Le Havre, France. More troops landed during the afternoon and by 12th August, transportation across the Irish Sea was in full swing.

As the priority was to get the troops down to Southampton and over to France as soon as possible, the north Wales main-line regular train services had been put on a reduced service, and all excursion trains operating between Chester and Holyhead were cancelled. On the Bank Holiday weekend of 14–18th August, even this limited service was severely disrupted by units of the 6th Division and 3rd Cavalry Brigade which had started their move on the 13th. As the trains thundered towards Southampton on the down line, the up-line trains, full of coal from the north Wales coalfields, headed for Holyhead to feed the hungry boilers of the cargo ships and the additional bunkers – some 1,800 tons – required for the fleet messengers. These troop movements caused enormous disruption to the civilian railway services in north Wales.

These troop movements across the Irish Sea took until the middle of September and, although large numbers of troops did regularly cross both ways

4. The L&NWR had been warned of their likely requisition as early as 29th July.
5. For their fitting out (apart for the sighting and fitting of the guns) general guidelines had been issued by the Director of Transports, the interpretation of which was down to the individual shipyard, and whilst some yards would have carried out the bare requirements, others would have exceeded those requirements. Owing to the urgency for these vessels and to accommodate these requirements some calculations, drawings, etc would have to be done ... 'on the back of fag packets' and left to the expertise of the foremen and workmen of the yard. No doubt Commander Holland's earlier experiences of converting troopships during the Boer War would prove invaluable.
6. The SS *Heroic* (Belfast Steamship Co), SS *Londonderry* (Midland Railway Co) and SS *Kilkenny* (CoDSPC) had also been requisitioned. They began to transport the 6th Division over the Irish Sea on 15th August, sailing between Queenstown and Holyhead.

throughout the war, they never did so on this scale again until the formation of the Irish Free State in 1922. It was recorded that from 6–22nd August 1914, 323 officers, 29,391 men, 4,774 horses, 820 vehicles, 66 guns and 222 tons of baggage were transported across the Irish Sea. No doubt the whole being co-ordinated by Commander Holland and the Holyhead Station Superintendent, Andrew William Taylor, who, for this and subsequent work throughout the war, was awarded an OBE in 1919.

Whilst the 5th Division and other units had been preparing for their move over the Irish Sea, the Admiralty had also been busy taking measures to prevent German interference of these all important troop crossings. The 11th Cruiser Squadron, consisting of HMS *Juno, Isis, Minerva, Eclipse* and *Venus* (all Eclipse Class, 2nd Class cruisers built 1894–6), which had been patrolling the Western Approaches since 4th August, were ordered to patrol both the North and South Channels of the Irish Sea. HMS *Juno* was detailed to patrol the North Channel whilst the armed merchant cruiser *Caronia* (Cunard Line) and the rest of the squadron would patrol a line stretching from Queenstown to the Scilly Isles. Whilst HMS *Pelorus*, an old cruiser of 1896 vintage of the Bristol Channel patrol, and HMS *Challenger* (built in 1902), of the 9th Cruiser Squadron based at Portland, were to patrol the Bristol Channel and its approaches.

On 8th August all leave was immediately cancelled for the Marine Yard's workshop staff in Holyhead and work was begun on de-storing the *Cambria* and *Scotia*, the stand-by and off-turn vessels tied up on the Marine Yard berths, prior to their conversion. That evening and early the following morning, the day and

*Cross sectional view of* Hibernia's *sister ship ship* Cambria *showing where the additional coal was carried in this class of vessel, forward in the cargo space, above inthe lower deck cargo/3rd Class passenger space and aft of the 3rd Class Saloon. [Courtesy of the National Maritime Museum].*

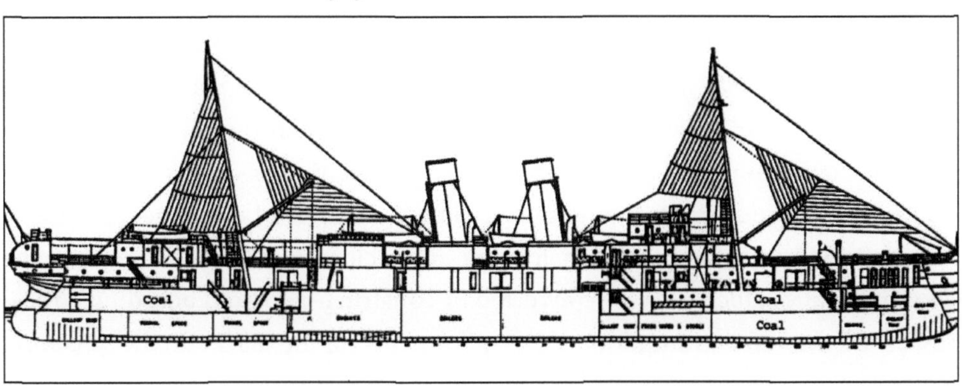

night boats, *Anglia* and *Hibernia* arrived at the station berths where, after the last passenger had disembarked, all crockery, linen and valuables such as company silver-ware, were removed and placed in the cellars of the Station Hotel. The vessels were then moved up closer to the Marine Yard. At 07.00 hours fitters, boilermakers and carpenters descended on each ship and the foremen of the various departments, already in receipt of instructions as to the work required, reported to the chief engineers and chief officers ready to carry out any repairs as well as additional or outstanding work which might be required down below or on deck. Fires in the boilers were drawn and, when cooled sufficiently, the furnaces were inspected and any repairs required to brickwork were made good, defective fire-bars replaced and the boilers themselves given a good and thorough clean. The main and auxiliary machinery was checked and repairs and adjustments made as necessary.

To accommodate the additional coal, the third-class saloon was stripped of all benches and all portholes were shut and their deadlights closed and secured. Although no workbooks from the Marine Yard have survived, it is thought that to accommodate the 154 tons of coal, the forward first-class sleeping apartment had to be stripped out, again the portholes and deadlights shut and secured, the stairway up to the first-class dining saloon removed and the opening plated over. The bulkhead between the first-class sleeping apartment and the third-class / cargo space forward was opened up and a bulkhead fitted so as to separate the seamen's accommodation from the new coal bunker. It is also thought probable that some of the other passenger spaces were stripped of carpets, furnishings and fittings to convert them to mess decks and store rooms for the additional crew.

Commander Holland received notification that all four vessels were to be painted dark grey and that three Hotchkiss 6-pounder guns were to be fitted to each, which were due to arrive from storage in Liverpool by train on 9th August. The guns to be fitted to the *Hibernia* came from HMS *Howe*, a battleship which had been built in 1881 and scrapped in 1912, whose rifling had been worn almost smooth from their years of service. Boilermakers and shipwrights were put to work strengthening and piercing the decks for the proposed gun positions. A magazine for the ammunition was also to be constructed below the main deck, as were ready-use ammunition lockers sited close to the guns. Within the accommodation, lockers were converted or constructed to hold boarding cutlasses, small arms and ammunition. All requirements for the blackout, the screening of lights, doorways, etc were taken in hand by carpenters, sailmakers, and coppersmiths. The Admiralty felt some concern regarding the Helsby wireless telegraphy equipment as its range was only some 150 miles, but it was deemed acceptable for the vessels' intended work, although it was noted that some additional equipment may be required for it to reach naval wavelengths.

Later that day, Commander Holland was asked by the Admiralty to supply the names of the captains, chief officers and chief engineers of the fleet messengers as they were to be given temporary commissions in the Royal Naval Reserve (RNR).[7] He replied that in addition to these ranks most, if not all, other deck officers and engineers also held certificates of competency (or 'tickets'), therefore should not these men also be eligible for temporary commissions? The Admiralty concurred and whilst the officers and engineers were given temporary commissions in the RNR, the crew, both petty officers and ratings, became members of the Mercantile Fleet Auxiliary (MFA), the forerunner of today's Royal Fleet Auxiliary. But, whether officer or rating, each civilian that sailed on these vessels was obliged to sign Form T124, an agreement where the signatory stated that he was willing to be attached to a named vessel and would serve under Royal Navy terms and conditions relating to discipline, victualling, insurance, rates of pay (which were 25% higher than L&NWR rates) and uniform.

On the same day, *Hibernia*'s new commanding officer, Captain Rupert Stanley Gwatkin-Williams, RN (Ret'd), arrived on board. After twenty-four years of sea service and three years of shore service with the HM Coastguard, he had retired from the Royal Navy in 1912. In the summer of 1914 he had been in Oporto, Portugal, learning the language, something of the culture and the country before trying to find employment in connection with the development of the Portuguese railways and harbours. On 2nd August he had received his notification of the call out of the reservists from the British vice consul in Oporto and immediately made arrangements to return to Britain. The following day, he found a berth on the SS *Hilary* and embarked, at his own expense, under an assumed name and heavily disguised, in case of capture by the enemy! The outbreak of war found the *Hilary* at sea travelling at full speed and blacked out at night. Passing through the cruiser squadron patrolling St George's Channel, she reached Liverpool on 6th August.

7. Captain Tanner was given the rank of lieutenant, RNR; Chief Officer C E Copland, Second Officer W Hughes and A Marsh the rank of sub lieutenants, RNR; Chief Engineer H O Roberts became engineer, RNR; Second Engineer H Jones, Third Engineers R E Jones and G H Roberts and Fifth Engineer H Hughes were all given the rank of assistant engineers, RNR; J G Thomas, being uncertificated, became third mate, MFA.

Captain Gwatkin-Williams caught the first train to London and reported to the Admiralty at Whitehall but, much to his disappointment, was told there was nothing for him yet and he made his way to his home in Portsmouth. The following day he received three telegrams all ordering him to report to Holyhead to take command of the SS *Hibernia*. Upon receipt of the first, he rushed to the nearest military tailor to be measured for his uniform, shirts, boots, etc then caught the first train to London and then onwards to Holyhead where, to show some authority whilst on board ship and waiting for his uniform to arrive, he took to wearing a civilian suit, a bowler hat and, strapped around his waist, a belt from which hung a naval boarding cutlass!

The placing of a Royal Navy captain on a Mercantile Marine vessel with the resultant demotion of her regular master may have been seen as a slight by the L&NWR officers and crew, but the Admiralty's instructions were quite specific; whilst Captain Tanner had sole control over the handling of the ship, Captain Gwatkin-Williams would act in an advisory capacity, interpreting Admiralty orders and acting as a link when working with other naval units. In the event of an emergency however, Tanner was bound to accept Gwatkin-Williams' orders subject to his receiving them in writing. As the latter was to recount later, this dual control arrangement was fraught with difficulties as a ship could only have one master. But, thanks to the two men's mutual respect and understanding for each other, the command structure did work.

On 10th August, three naval ratings arrived from Chatham: Yeoman Signaller H G J T Allan, RFR;[8] Leading Seaman W P Millward, RFR (who would be the gunner with responsibility for looking after her guns and training up the gun crews) and Able Seaman C Lacey, RFR.

On 11th August, William Thomas Davies, an electrical engineer, was appointed purser to the *Hibernia* and later the same day, Commander Holland notified the Admiralty that he had now appointed pursers to each fleet messenger as instructed, all of whom were well-educated young men, and he asked whether these men should also be given commissions? The Admiralty agreed believing it would be good for each ship's internal organization and accounts whilst off station. Consequently, each was given the temporary rank of assistant paymaster, RNR.

8. Allen's diary would later be used as the basis for a book called *A Black Hole in the Desert* which tells the story of HMS *Tara*.

As for her crew, *Hibernia*'s peacetime complement numbered fifty-seven, which included three stewardesses. These ladies were paid off, along with four stewards who were not required under the new Royal Navy manning arrangements, and also those who had no wish to serve under the Royal Navy (only two men from all four express steamers). Other crew members had left a few days earlier when members of the Royal Naval Reserve and Royal Fleet Reserve had been mobilized, and were now serving with the Fleet.[9] There was no disruption to the sailings however as the reservists had been replaced either from the Marine Yard's Shore Gang[10] or by a number of local volunteers, both ex-seamen and shore workers.

As the steam packets were to work with the Royal Navy, their crews were now expected to maintain a twenty-four hour rolling-watch system, working four hours on and eight hours off. Their off time would, however, be interspersed with additional duties: painting and chipping; drill; general quarters or action stations; look-out duties; coaling; gangway guard whilst in port, so additional crew members were required to maintain the watch system and it was thought that most of these men could be found locally. However, fulfilling the Admiralty's requirements of recruiting twelve additional seamen and ten additional firemen for each vessel was not so easy and Commander Holland had to inform the Director of Transports that this could well be beyond the capabilities of both the L&NWR's Marine Office and the local employment office. The Director of Transports had envisaged this situation and had, sometime previously, arranged for the Shipping Federation at Canning Place, Liverpool to supply the required number of men.[11] After a flurry of telegrams between the Federation and Holland,

9. So great was the urgency for the mobilisation of naval reservists, that it had been necessary to call out Holyhead's Post Office staff early on the Sunday morning to deliver the telegrams. This resulted in the L&NWR loosing some fifty-nine men whilst the CofDSP lost about twenty men. That night, as the Holyhead reservists assembled at the station prior to proceeding to Portsmouth, they were joined by sixty-four Irish naval reservists who had crossed from Dublin. Owing to the large number of passengers and reservists to be carried, additional coaches were fitted to the Irish Mail which pulled out at 00.25 a.m. amidst the cheers and tears of mothers, wives, daughters and girlfriends, and shouts of 'Good luck' from the huge crowd which had assembled to see them off.

10. The Shore Gang, consisting for the most part of ex seamen, firemen and stewards, were used in the Marine Yard and dry dock as labourers for chipping, scraping and painting ships' hulls and decks, cleaning holds, tanks and boilers, and supplying mate's (or helpers) to the various trades within the Yard. They were also used by the company as a local pool to replace those crew members of the company's vessels who had been taken ill or were on leave. This practice continued until the 1970s.

11. From 3rd to 21st August 1914, the Marine Office had managed to find and engage locally, sixty seamen, thirty-eight firemen and forty-nine coal trimmers. These figures suggest that they had not only found enough men to replace the naval reservists who had been called out on 2nd August, but

these men arrived in Holyhead between 11th and 13th August, some without kit and some who refused to sail. Things were eventually sorted out and the requisite number of men were attached to each ship, but it did not bode well for the future! Fortunately, unlike the L&NWR's men who were on six-monthly articles, the new men were only on three-monthly articles, in effect a three-month contract of work and, as their articles came to an end, the troublemakers were discharged. Consequently there was a turnover of men for the first six or nine months on all four ships.

During the second week of August, an artificer and an electrician were appointed to each vessel, the former were all boilermakers from the Marine Yard Workshops who had volunteered to serve at sea. George M Cox was appointed to the *Hibernia*, where a workshop or work area was undoubtedly made available to him, as were the tools of his trade necessary for the maintenance of the boilers as well as any modifications or structural repairs which might be required due to weather damage or an encounter with the enemy. The electrician appointed to the *Hibernia* was Ernest Lawton of the L&NWR's Crewe workshops, who would take over the electrical duties from the vessel's engineers, in particular the third engineer who in peacetime, in addition to his own duties, was the vessel's electrician. Whilst he or the other ships' engineers could deal with most faults such as shorts and breakages, any major fault which might occur whilst at sea would have to be isolated and dealt with by the Marine Yard's electricians once the vessel had returned to port. A quartermaster, leading stoker, two coal trimmers and a cook were also added to each ship's crew.

On 12th August, to conform to the Royal Navy's requirements, Howarth Hughes was appointed to the *Hibernia* as an additional engineer. Although nominally a fourth engineer within the company, he would serve as the ship's fifth engineer. On the same day, Frederick J Chambers was appointed as a second wireless operator, as Commander Holland had telegraphed the Admiralty to say that 'one man cannot be on continuous duty'. He clearly knew what the Admiralty expected of these ships and how they wanted them run. He also knew where to get hold of men and was not afraid to make suggestions — perhaps his experience as a Naval Transport Officer in Durban during the Boer War had come in useful.

also sufficient to meet the Admiralty's requirements for the new manning levels. However, after the arrival of the Federation's thirty-six seamen, twenty-four firemen and twenty-one trimmers, all locally engaged men were discharged. This does seem to indicate that the Federation men took precedence over the local men, and that the Marine Office was not aware of the manning arrangements between the Admiralty, Federation and the L&NWR.

# 4. On Station

It had been hoped that the *Anglia* and *Cambria* would be ready to put to sea by 10th August and the *Hibernia* and *Scotia* the following day, but the painting, coaling and arming of the vessels caused some delay.

Two guns had been fitted on the foredeck, one to port and one to starboard, so their fields of fire would extend from bow to beam. Their positioning and fitting had been fairly straightforward but the positioning of the after gun had raised some problems. In order to achieve a field of fire which would extended from the port beam through the stern to the starboard beam, it was necessary to fit the gun onto the after deck house which contained the vessel's steering gear. However, situated on the open deck, atop the deck house, was the emergency manoeuvring position, in effect an emergency bridge with two narrow decks extending out to the ship's sides, from where the vessel would be steered and manoeuvred should the bridge have to be abandoned. This emergency position was equipped with a binnacle, wheel and pedestal, and two telegraphs. This wheel, normally disengaged, could in an emergency be engaged to the steering gear in the deck house below. Aft of the platform, the roof of the deck house curved downwards to the awning deck and the ensign staff was fitted onto the curvature of this roof. Due to these factors, it was thought at first that it might not be possible for the vessel to accept a gun on the deck house. However, thanks to the gun's size it was found to be small enough to be fitted to the centre of the steering position, although the wheel and pedestal would have to be disconnected and removed. Emergency steering was still possible by way of a wheel fitted directly onto the steering gear within the deck house. The telegraphs, being close to the forward handrails were retained and a new ensign staff was made and fitted to the after end of the companion house.

At this time, the decision was taken that all four vessels were to fly the White Ensign, not the Red as originally intended, and they would all become His Majesty's Ships. On 13th August, HMS *Anglia* and *Cambria* were commissioned, whilst the *Scotia* and *Hibernia* were commissioned the next day. Prior to the *Hibernia*'s commissioning, she had to have her name changed as there was

*Pre 1908 stern view of the* Scotia, *HMS* Tara's *younger sister alongside Holyhead, clearly showing of the deck house roof, the ensign staff and emergency steering position [Courtesy of the National Library of Ireland]*

already one HMS *Hibernia* in the Navy, a pre-dreadnought battleship built in 1905 and having two vessels of the same name would only lead to confusion. Why, when, or by whom the name *Tara* was chosen is not known, but it is known that she was the first vessel in the Royal Navy to bear this name.

Whilst the ships were fitted out, the decision was taken that two of them, *Hibernia* and *Scotia,* would become examination vessels and work with the Royal Navy's patrol cruisers in the Irish Sea, in their search for suspected contraband carriers. The Admiralty had discovered that the Germans had used a disguised merchant ship, the *Königin Luise,* to lay a minefield to the north of the Thames on 5th August which had claimed the new cruiser HMS *Amphion* the following day. A few days later, minefields were discovered off the Humber and Tyne and the Admiralty now feared that the Germans were using disguised merchantmen and trawlers as minelayers and contraband carriers (although it would be thought that the contraband carriers would keep well out to sea to avoid the patrols), so they now wanted all foreign ships stopped and searched whilst all foreign trawlers were to be sent into British ports for inspection. Admiral Jellicoe, Commander-in-Chief of the Grand Fleet, also wanted all the east coast ports closed, but the Admiralty felt this was too drastic a measure. Admiral Beatty, Commander-in-Chief of the Battlecruiser Fleet, however stated that time did not permit the boarding of all foreign ships and that with growing U-boat activity, the threat to the patrolling cruisers in coastal waters would be extremely dangerous. This was reinforced on 22nd September when the *U-9* sank the armoured cruisers HMS *Hogue, Aboukir* and *Cressy* who were on patrol in the southern North Sea with the loss of some 60 officers and 1,400 men. After this disaster, the Royal Navy, to augment their patrols, opted for more examination vessels or armed boarding steamers as they became known. The vessels taken up were, like the *Tara*, mostly small passenger carrying vessels which the navy considered ideal as they could patrol coastal waters, had the accommodation and spaces for additional crew and, with some modifications, could stay at sea for some time. They were fast and should they be lost were a lot cheaper to replace than the Royal Navy's armoured cruisers. Ultimately there would be some thirty-eight such vessels taken up of which fourteen were eventually lost.

At 07.30 hours on 15th August, with all work completed, fully bunkered and in all respects ready for sea, HMS *Anglia* left her berth to anchor in the outer harbour to await the completion of the *Cambria*. At 19.30 hours, both vessels left Holyhead to join the Grand Fleet at Scapa Flow. During the days that were to elapse before *Scotia* and *Tara* left, further work was carried out to make them suitable for examination duties. It is not at all certain what this entailed, but for patrol work the most obvious would be the fitting of a crow's nest to the fore mast, searchlights to port and starboard and, in case of action with the enemy, the removal of as much as possible of all inflammable and unnecessary gear from within and without the vessels — panelling, carpets, unnecessary furniture, fixtures and fittings, deck benches, etc. Whilst this was going on, the crews were divided into their respective watches and lifeboat stations. Work was also handed out as were drills (gun, fire and lifeboat drill, action stations, etc).

Eventually at 10.44 hours on the morning of 18th August 1914, HMS *Tara* left Holyhead, all work completed and her hull and upper-works painted grey; although her funnels and mast were to be painted grey during the first few days on her patrol billet, which suggests that she had left with a degree of urgency. As she steamed out of Holyhead, the local superintendents of the L&NWR, the families, relatives and friends of the crew, workmen and other townspeople stood on the quayside to see her off.[1] She steamed out into the bay then slowed down.

1. HMS *Scotia* left the Refit Berth at the Marine Yard at 08.30 hours on 19th August, the last of the quartet to leave. She was to be based at Pembroke Dock and, in conjunction with HMS *Pelorus*, would patrol the southern channel of the Irish Sea.

Leading Seaman Millward and Able Seaman Lacey called the gun crews to drill, whilst Captain Gwatkin-Williams and Lieutenant Tanner left the bridge and went down to the captain's cabin to open the sealed orders. They were disappointed to discover that they were not to head for foreign and warmer climes but to the Mull of Kintyre in the North Channel of the Irish Sea where they were to report their arrival to the Coastguard station[2] at Torr Head in Antrim. The orders explained that they would be working in conjunction with HMS *Juno,* patrolling between the Mull of Kintyre and Rathlin Island and would come under the senior officer on the Coast of Ireland, Vice-Admiral Sir Charles Coke, based at Queenstown.

At 11.55 hours gun drill came to an end and *Tara* turned northwards, increased speed to Full Away, 17 knots, passing the Skerries, a group of rocks some six miles to the north of Holyhead. She arrived off the Mull of Kintyre at 21.35 hours after an uneventful passage, and was told to proceed with her patrol as outlined in her orders. After a quiet night, morning broke to find her lying to, with Rathlin Island to westwards. Spotting a fishing vessel she slowly got under way. At 05.00 hours all hands were called for General Quarters and at 05.32 hours, she hailed the trawler which turned out to be the *Dorothea* of Milford Haven, which was allowed to proceed.

After breakfast, at 07.00 hours, the crew were detailed to clean ship and four hours later the afternoon watch was called to rifle drill. After lunch the stewards were given cutlass drill, whilst the morning watch was given rifle drill. At 16.00 hours another vessel was sighted, General Quarters was again sounded, and the crew mustered at their action stations. The ship turned out to be the Admiralty collier, the SS *Highgate,* on her way south. Later, at 19.30 hours *Tara* challenged the *Calgarian* who was also heading south. At 21.45 hours she received a message from Torr Head Coastguard station informing Captain Gwatkin-Williams that, when he required coal, water or any stores, he was to proceed without being relieved, to Larne in Northern Ireland and then return to his designated patrol area without delay. Later that night two further vessels were challenged.

This would be the pattern of *Tara's* work, steaming backwards and forwards across the channel at various speed and courses, stopping and searching suspect vessels or chasing vessels that had slipped through the net, whilst the crew maintained the routine of watches and lookout duties and the endless work of

2. The Coastguard at this time was a part of the Royal Navy and remained so until after the war.

*HMS* Juno *[Author]*

maintenance, chipping and painting. On most days, for the off-duty watch, there would be a drill of some sort be it General Quarters, rifle or cutlass drill for the seamen, firemen or stewards; pistol drill for the officers or boat drill. At nightfall, night sights would be fitted to the three 6-pounder guns in case of a night action, and just before the break of dawn, the gun crews would be closed up should the enemy be in sight as it became light. At any time, day or night, and in any weather, if a suspicious vessel was spotted then the alarm would be sounded, the gun crews closed up and whilst the crew were assembling at their action stations the vessel would be requested to stop either by flags or wireless transmission and a lifeboat manned and lowered.[3] With Sub-Lieutenant Copland in charge the boat would go over to inspect the stranger's cargo manifest and crew list. Even on the blackest of nights, or in the dirtiest of weather, the first man up the ship's side, silhouetted by the searchlight, armed with a cutlass and a pair of pistols would invariably be Assistant Paymaster William Davies, RNR. If her papers were found to be in order the vessel would be allowed to proceed.

On 22nd August it was found necessary to have Bosun's Mate Richard Williams seen to by the doctor aboard HMS *Juno.* The cruiser was contacted and a rendezvous arranged. At 08.00 hours the following morning both ships came

3. The lifeboat's crew contained an armed party. Should contraband cargo be found, the ship would then be instructed to make for Larne under an armed guard, where the contraband cargo would be discharged before the vessel would be allowed to proceed. It was known that some German nationals living abroad, signed on as crew members of neutral vessels so as to try to get back to Europe in order to make their way to Germany to enlist. The passenger and crew manifests had also therefore to be checked.

together and stopped, and Williams was rowed over to *Juno*. The nature of his complaint/injury is unknown but he was off duty for four days (he was later paid off and died at home on 25th June 1915).

At noon each day the coal and water consumption was carefully logged and by 24th August it was decided that the *Tara* would call at Larne to top up her bunkers. Firstly, what coal was remaining in the new storage spaces had to be tidied up to make bunkering quicker and easier for the coaling contractors once she was alongside. Once this had been completed the ship was then washed down to get rid of the all-clinging coal dust and at 08.00 hours on the 26th she informed HMS *Juno* by wireless that she was heading to Larne for coal and water.

*Tara's* first visit to Larne may have been with some trepidation and a lot of curiosity as the town had been in the papers a few months earlier, due to the activities of Ulster Unionists who, on the night of 25th April, had landed the major part of a smuggled cargo of 216 tons of rifles and ammunition from the SS *Clyde Valley* at Larne (the remainder having been landed at Bangor and Donaghadee), destined for the Ulster Volunteer Force which was intending to resist the implementation of the Irish Home Rule Bill which the British government had been trying to push through Parliament. However, the crew need not have worried as they found themselves welcomed with open arms. At 11.40 hours HMS *Tara* picked up the Larne pilot and by 13.00 hours she was tied up alongside and bunkering had commenced. As the coaling was carried out by contractors, shore leave was granted to the off-duty watch.[4] By 01.30 hours the next morning coaling had been completed, 252 tons taken on board, and three hours later she departed for her patrol station where she arrived at 06.15 hours. At noon all hands were 'turned to' to wash down the coal dust, the bane of coaling a ship! The following morning the crew started topping up the permanent bunkers from the new storage spaces. Generally speaking coaling, watering and storing the ship at Larne would be repeated every eight to thirteen days. This continued until March 1915 by which time the base had become too congested with the ever-increasing numbers of drifters, trawlers and yachts of the Auxiliary Patrol force and the *Tara*, was ordered to use Campbeltown in Argyllshire.

4. On commissioning, warships split their crews into two watches, which were given various names e.g. the 'duty' and 'off-duty' watch or the 'Red' and 'Green' watch etc. On board HMS *Tara* they were called the 'Port' and 'Starboard' watches. This ensured that, when the vessel is in port and shore leave had been granted, enough men were left on board to sail the vessel in the event of an emergency.

During their first call at Larne it seems that there had been some trouble whilst the off-duty watch was ashore, whether some of the crew had returned late or drunk is not recorded — although the public houses in the locality had to be searched for missing crew members. Once at sea, Captain Gwatkin-Williams mustered the whole crew and read the Articles of War. Unfortunately, this did not seem to have worked and on 8th September (after she had bunkered and stored the previous day), Seaman J Mitchell was found to have failed to return to the ship and was logged as a deserter and Alfred Hughes, Gerald Byrne, James Gannon, Ernest Banks, Thomas Jones, Michael Ryder, William Black and Albert Milner, were ordered for extra duty and fined one day's pay for having broken leave whilst the ship was alongside, and Milner was also fined seven days' pay for being drunk. The Admiralty was notified of these incidents of insubordination and consequently, Charles Mintram, RN, a ship's corporal (in effect a ship's policeman) joined on 18th September, along with four RNR and two MMR ratings.[5]

On 24th September at 05.30 hours on a dark, overcast morning, the lookouts spotted a large steamer escorted by two smaller vessels having what appeared to have guns on their forecastles. The officer of the watch called the captain to the bridge, rang the alarms, altered course and increased speed. Once they had overtaken the strangers, the *Tara* signalled 'Stop your engines' and a boat was lowered and an armed party, under the command of Sub Lieutenant Copland, went over under the cover of her guns. Once aboard, the ships' papers were examined and found to be in order, Sub Lieutenant Copland and party then returned to the *Tara*. It appears that the stranger was the whale factory ship *Svend Foyn 1* of Sandefjord on her way south to the Antarctic via Cardiff, the armed escorts were her whale catchers and the 'guns' were their harpoon guns!

During October, the Admiralty received word that a German minelayer had

5. Leading Seaman James Marwick, Seamen James McKinven, William Ralph and Alexander Ross, and two Mercantile Marine ratings from Holyhead, Seamen John Jones (who was to replace Seaman Mitchell), and Fireman John Bagnall (who was to replace Fireman Richard Evans who had been taken ill on 2nd September whilst *Tara* was on patrol. On coming alongside at Larne, Dr Thomas Killen had been called who recommended that Evans be admitted to hospital. He was paid off, but his condition deteriorated and he died in the Moyle Hospital in Larne on 12th December. He is interred in St Seiriol's Churchyard, Holyhead). Seaman John Jones is believed to have been John Lewis Jones, one of the *Hiberia's* peacetime quartermasters. Although agreeing to go on active service on HMS *Tara*, Jones was not aboard when she sailed on 18th August and did not re-join until 18th September, but as a seaman, by which time Robert Abbit had been promoted in his place. Why Jones did not claim back his position is not known.

been sent to work in the Irish Sea. Consequently on the 16th, HMS *Tara* was ordered to leave her station and head south to search '... for a suspicious craft, presumably a minelayer'. She was to patrol within an area bordered by a line running from the Anglesey coast to the Isle of Man and from the Isle of Man to the Mull of Galloway. By 01.40 hours on the 17th, she was off the South Stack light and at 02.30 hours she came across and signalled the SS *Connaught* and SS *Slievemore,* both bound for Ireland, and later at 03.40 hrs the SS *Greenore* bound for Dublin. Receiving the correct replies, no doubt the wireless operators then exchanged news with their colleagues on the Holyhead vessels. Not finding any suspicious vessels, the *Tara* returned to her patrol area in the North Channel.

The minelayer in question was the *Berlin,* an ex Norddeutsher Lloyd liner now converted to a minelayer with 200 mines aboard. She had left Wilhelmshaven on 14th October with instructions to lay a minefield at the mouth of the Clyde, as the Germans knew that a large troop carrying convoy was to leave Canada in October and assumed it would make for the Clyde (it actually made for Plymouth). However, as she was making her way down the Scottish coast in atrocious weather, the *Berlin* began to pick up radio chatter, possibly emanating from those units of the Grand Fleet anchored in Lough Swilly.[6] So, at midnight, when just off the Mull of Kintyre, and between the Isle of Islay and Rathlin Island, with the chatter becoming louder and fearing discovery, she turned round and headed back out into the North Atlantic. Luck had been with her, HMS *Tara* into whose patrol area she had steamed, was not on station as she had left to coal at 0800 hours that morning and did not sail from Larne until 0900 hours on the 22nd. But, the Berlin still hoping to disrupt British trade, returned the next night to the coast of Northern Ireland and laid 200 mines in two parallel lines, some nineteen miles NNW of Tory Island, with the intention of fouling those vessels making for the Clyde, Liverpool and Belfast via the North Channel. These mines on the 27th claimed the SS *Manchester Commerce* and, the next morning, the new battleship HMS *Audacious* of the 2nd Battle Squadron of the Grand Fleet which was proceeding out into the Atlantic for gunnery practice. Her loss was initially thought to be by torpedo. But, on hearing of the sinking of the *Manchester Commerce,* the Admiralty suspected that mines had been sown. But who or what had laid them off Tory Island — a warship, a disguised merchantman or a submarine — was unknown and, most importantly, had another field been lain elsewhere?

6. The Grand Fleet had been dispersed to various anchorages as Scapa Flow, owing to submarine sightings and scares, was not yet considered secure.

The loss of the *Audacious* resulted in the blockading of part of the Grand Fleet in Loch Swilley. It could not put to sea until a passage had been cleared and four mine-sweeping trawlers were hurriedly sent from Milford Haven to sweep the area, but they were hampered as they knew neither the extent nor size of the field.[7]

The mine laying activities of the *Berlin* had revealed the inadequacies of the Auxiliary Patrol in the Irish Sea. More needed to be done and it had to have a more professional approach. As a result, Commander H G F Berekely, RN (Retired), was sent to Larne during the last week of October as the senior naval officer (SNO) of the North Channel Patrol Force. He was provided with the armed yacht *Oriana* and four drifters, the *Boy Scout, Dick Whittington, Ocean Harvest* and *Ocean Retriever*. These were to be based at Port Charlotte, Islay whilst searching the Scottish coastline from the Mull of Kintyre north as far as the Isle of Mull. This flotilla was known as the northern division. On 16th November these drifters were relieved by four armed trawlers from Lowestoft, the *Riano, Cerealia, Revello* and *Liberia*. A similar number of drifters were also sent to Milford Haven. In Liverpool, twelve tugs were commandeered which, once armed with rifles and pistols, were sent to assist; six to the *Tara* in the North Channel and six to the *Scotia* at Milford. Those attached to the *Tara* patrolled its southern end and were known as the Southern Division. The addition of these vessels was very much welcomed, although it soon became apparent that they did have their limitations, one of which was the *Oriana's* wireless transmitter, which soon proved itself inadequate due to its limited range of some nine miles. This necessitated SNO Larne having to send a tug up to fifty miles from her patrol station if he wanted to communicate with the *Oriana*.

Further limitations which soon became apparent were: the size and sea-keeping qualities of the tugs (because of the danger of their foundering in a rough sea, compelled them to seek shelter in heavy weather); the time each tug could spend on patrol (this between eight to eleven days, caused by their differing engines, boilers, coal consumption and bunker capacities) and the tugs' fenders (which were an obstacle to the hoisting inboard of boats after examination duties in a heavy sea which led to commanding officers limiting their examination of suspect vessels to steaming as close as possible around them). Finally, there were desertions amongst the tugs' crews and by the last week of November, the SNO

7. By the end of the month a channel had been swept clear thanks to the addition of the Royal Navy minesweepers *Circe, Leda, Jason, Speedwell* and *Skipjack*, thus freeing the Grand Fleet.

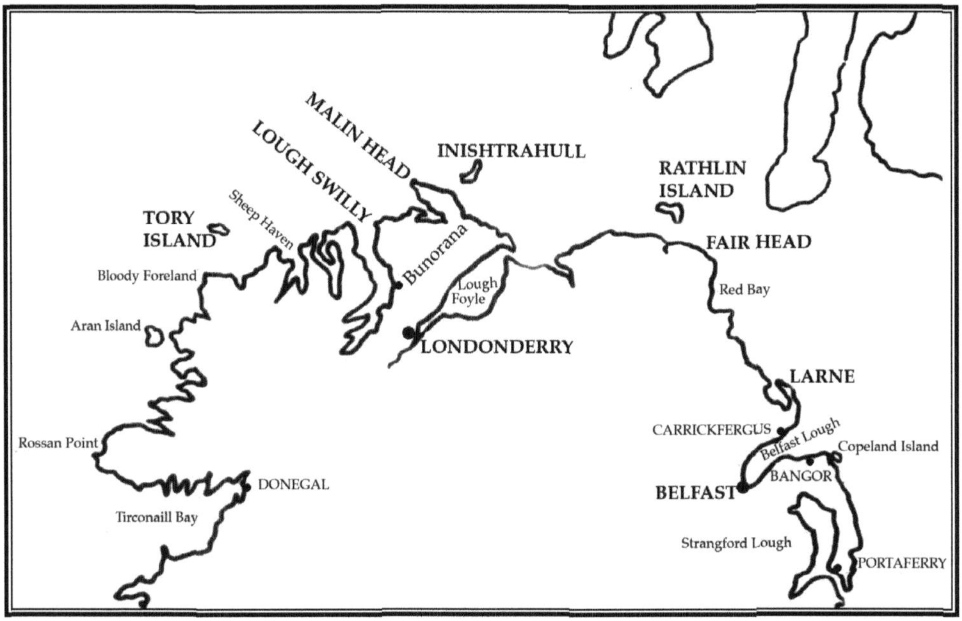


*Northern Ireland*

Larne was reporting that the departure on patrol of several tugs was being delayed by up to 36 hours due to the great difficulty of finding replacements. He went on to say that the principle cause was that crews quickly learnt of the high wages being paid to the crew of the *Tara* and the relative comfort offered in a large vessel as compared to the harsh conditions under which they had to serve.

By November, the Tara was undergoing changes to her routine. Due in part to the inadequacies of the *Oriana's* wireless telegraphy equipment, she (equipped with a more powerful equipment) would, in conjunction with her own patrol work, rove in both the northern and southern divisional areas acting as patrol leader, ordering the trawlers and drifters to their various tasks as instructed by the SNO Larne. Commander Gwatkin-Williams was given a degree of latitude in interpretating these orders and, owing to the lack of wireless transmitters on the trawlers and drifters, extensive use was made of signalling (by means of flags and semaphore) to pass messages between the vessels on patrol as well as the coastguard stations.

*Tara* called at Larne for coal twice during this month. Whilst alongside on the 10th, John Williams, the second cook, was relieved by John Pritchard. Around the same time, those men supplied by the Shipping Federation's Liverpool office were discharged as their three-month agreement had terminated, although it does seem that the more disciplined and conscientious were retained. Their replacements were supplied by the Federation's office at Belfast. On the 23rd, whilst making her way to her patrol area, it was discovered that Fireman Edward Jones of Holyhead had jumped ship, and one week later both Wireless Telegraphy Operators Robert Neill and Frederick J. Chambers were promoted to warrant rank as Wireless Telegraphist, Royal Navy Reserve. Finally, during the last week of November two of the patrolling tugs, the *Herculameum* and *Hornby* nearly foundered in atrocious weather, clearly a sign that things had to change and that vessels with better sea-keeping qualities were needed.

On 2nd December five trawlers arrived from Plymouth for the Larne patrol which, after storing and coaling, were ordered to anchor. However, owing to bad weather, the *Devara, Nellie Braddock* and *Angerton* dragged their anchors and grounded. Fortunately all were dragged off by the tug *Hornby* without damage. On the 6th, *Tara, Oriana, Revello* and the tugs *Blackcock* and *Herculaneum* were ordered to conduct a search of the Forth of Clyde for a reported submarine, but nothing was found. *Tara* then returned to her patrol billet, but the smaller vessels, owing to the rough weather, had to remain under the lee of the land and did not return to Larne until the 9th.

On the 10th, *Tara* noted that her sister ship, the Fleet Messenger *Anglia* passed north at 10.30 hours, en route back to Scapa Flow from dry dock Holyhead, no doubt the watch-keeping wireless-telegraphy operators on both vessels chatted to each other passing over the latest news and gossip of Holyhead.

The following day, after a very busy but uneventful four months, Captain Gwatkin-Williams received orders from Torr Head to proceed to dry dock in Birkenhead. Unfortunately for the Holyhead men, the *Tara* could not be accommodated at Holyhead as the *Cambria* was already in dry dock and would be followed immediately by the *Scotia*. But first *Tara* had to call at Larne to discharge most of her coal to reduce her draft to enable her to clear the sill of the dry dock. Two days later at 07.30 hours, she entered the Cammell Laird basin and moored alongside another armed boarding steamer, HMS *King Orry*.

At 07.30 hours on Sunday, 14th December the *Tara* was manoeuvred into the dry dock, the gate replaced and pumping commenced. As the dock was emptying, the yard's shipwrights were busy shoring her up whilst the shore gang scraped the weed and barnacles off her hull. A gangway was put in place to enable fitters, boilermakers and other dockyard workers to clamber aboard. The ship was in dock for seventeen days for what may have been a scheduled dry dock as the L&NWR's passenger-carrying vessels generally had their refits during the winter periods when passenger numbers were at their lowest. As well as the scheduled work, all deficiencies to the structure, accommodation and hull that had been exposed in the rough waters of the North Channel had to be made good; permanent shelters were erected on each bridge wing as well as a wheel / chart house on the after end of the bridge deck.

Although discipline was slowly but surely tightening up, there were still incidents of insubordination and irresponsible behaviour such as the desertion of Firemen Edward Jones (on 23rd November) and Walker (on 4th December) whilst she was alongside coaling at Larne. It had been decided that cells were needed, whether these were especially constructed or simply unused and stripped out cabins or converted storerooms is unknown.[8] During this refit it is likely that additional work was carried out to bring her up to the standard required of an auxiliary warship. A communications system between the bridge and the after (or emergency) steering position was installed; all the remaining wood panelling and inflammable and unnecessary materials were removed from within and without the vessel; wire-netting was fitted within the engine room – just below the skylights, over the tops of the engines and auxiliary machinery, and under the vents to prevent shell splinters and rubbish falling into the main and auxiliary machinery — the jamming of any moving part could prove disastrous should they be in action with the enemy.[9]

Whilst the ship was in dry dock, leave was granted and the off-duty watch left Birkenhead for Holyhead and a well-earned rest. Three days later, they returned and the duty watch went for their spell of leave. Taking advantage of this, Fireman Thomas Doughty married Miss Ellen Parry at Hermon Chapel, Llangadwaladr, Anglesey on 21st December.

On the 22nd, Chief Engineer Roberts, not a well man, was relieved by Thomas Jones and, due to the mess the ship's papers and accounts were in, Assistant Paymaster William Davies, RNR (who, in his defence, was not a clerk but an electrical engineer) was relieved by Alfred Dutton, a clerk from the L&NWR's

8. The first man placed in the cells was a Federation man, Seaman David Hayes, who had jumped ship on 13th January 1915, whilst *Tara* was coaling at Larne. The Belfast police had been notified and he was caught in Belfast and returned to the ship the following day and sentenced to seven days in the cells and fourteen days loss of pay for attempted desertion.

9. Skylights are somewhat akin to steel shutters, a series of which are fitted to port and starboard aft of the funnel(s) directly over the engine room. They are opened to allow additional ventilation of the space and can be closed during rain or heavy seas and were generally opened and shut using a chain pulley arrangement.

Marine Office in Holyhead. On the 31st, having dropped the Mersey pilot, HMS *Tara* left for Holyhead at 11.55 hours, berthing on the eastern side of the harbour at 16.00 hours.

The ship remained in Holyhead until 2nd January when she sailed at 19.50 hours for her patrol area, announcing her arrival to the Torr Head Coastguard station at 05.00 hours. She then crossed the channel and announced her arrival to the Mull of Kintyre Coastguard station some thirty minutes later and was told to proceed with her patrol.

On 4th January, *Tara* stopped the SS *Laupar of Tonsberg* bound from Stavangar to Liverpool, the boarding party from this time being led by Sub Lieutenant Marsh. Two days later, she took aboard two ratings from a patrol boat, Seaman Gunner Lacey (who had been noted as an absentee and would be discharged on the 11th) and Able Seaman Charles McNaughton, RNR, a new man.

On Saturday 11th January *Tara* called at Larne for coal, but had to anchor overnight. At 13.30 hours the next day she came alongside the pier and coaling began. At 18.00 hours all work was stopped when a sling of coal bags fell on one of the coaling contractor's labourers, John Williams, and fractured his left leg. First aid was rendered by Sub Lieutenant Marsh and Quartermaster R. Williams and the man sent off to hospital. Earlier Able Seaman Lacey was discharged to the naval barracks at Plymouth.

Whilst alongside Commander Gwatkin-Williams learnt that there had been some changes to the North Channel patrol. On 4th January the Northern Division based at Port Charlotte had been done away with resulting in the *Oriana* being ordered back to Liverpool and the drifters *Liberia, Riano, Revello* and *Cerelia* being ordered to Moville in Lough Swilly. The Southern Division had also been done away with and its tugs had been sent back to Liverpool. The patrol would now be using armed trawlers, some of which had arrived at Larne whilst *Tara* was refitting, and others would join over the next few weeks, eventually totalling eighteen vessels. Some of these had sailed from Plymouth and some from the east coast ports and in getting to Larne had sustained weather damage and not a few required some work on their engines or auxiliary machinery. These repairs were immediately taken in hand either at Larne or Belfast. Those trawlers without damage were allocated to one of three groups, numbered 68, 69 and 70, each with six trawlers. These groups, although not yet complete, were sent on patrol, and the trawlers awaiting repair were to join them as soon as the work had been completed. Eventually the groups comprised: Group 68 — trawlers *Nellie*

*Braddock* (leader), *Fishtoft, Davara, Alsatian Minor, Hungarian* and *Angerton;* Group 69 — trawlers *Goshawk, Walthem, Bittern II, Clonsit, Rose II* and *Cerasia;* Group 70 — trawlers *Margaret Duncan, Diver, Glenroy, Berkshire, Roxana* and *Dragoon.*

Patrol work within the North Channel continued, but during the latter part of January, owing to a collision in Scapa Flow, the battleship HMS *Conquer* was ordered to Cammell Lairds in Birkenhead for repairs and, because of the dangers of submarines and drifting mines from the Tory Island field, the vessels of the North Channel patrol were required to act as additional escorts through the North Channel.[10]

At the end of the month, a mine was reported to be off Port Rush and the trawler *Alsatian Minor* was despatched to the scene to tow it back to the *Tara* where it could be '... dealt with in accordance with instructions received by the Admiralty.'[11]

10. The Tory Island minefield had been found following the SS *Tritonia* running onto a mine on 22nd December, although its full extent was still unknown. Since he 27th November, trawlers under Lieutenant Sir James Domville Bart, of HMT *Kapherda,* working under SNO Larne, with eleven trawlers, had been searching for this field. By April it was thought to be cleared but in June a Norwegian vessel ran onto another mine and was sunk. A further mine was found in 1917.
11. *The Holyhead & Anglesey Mail* of 19th March 1976 carried an article headed 'Have you seen this before' making reference to a piece of a German mine that was inscribed 'This piece of guncotton taken from a German Mine at Portrush Ireland, January 25th 1915, HMS *Tara*'. It had been found in 1946, attached to a piece of wood, on a beach in Cemaes Bay, Anglesey by Ll. Williams of Cemaes Bay.

# 5. Irish Sea

Since the outbreak of war, German U-boats had been steadily increasing their area of operations and by early 1915 had started to make their presence felt in the Irish Sea, forcing the Admiralty to reorganise the Western Auxiliary Patrol areas.[1] On 15th February, they became flag officer commands and each was to have its own fleet of armed trawlers/drifters and yachts. The North Channel (Auxiliary Patrol Area XVII) was given to Admiral Charles Barlow, DSO (Retired), the Kingstown or Irish Channel area (Auxiliary Patrol Area XVI) was given to Rear Admiral Evelyn Le Marchant, and the Milford area, including the St George's and Bristol Channel areas (Auxiliary Patrol Area XV), to Rear Admiral Charles Holcombe Dare. Liverpool was separated from the whole as was the Clyde, whilst in Belfast a 'flying squadron', comprising six armed yachts, the *Valiant II, Jeanette, Marynthea, Medusa, Narcissus* and *Sapphire II,* was to be established.

During the autumn of 1914, the Admiralty began conducting experiments to net the Straits of Dover to prevent U-boats passing through – but peculiarly only during daylight hours. They did however eventually manage to close the Straits by using a combination of nets, minefields or barrages, and patrols – although a determined U-boat commander could still get through.

By 10th February 1915, sufficient nets were available for the Admiralty to decide to net the North Channel so as to give a degree of protection to shipping using the western ports of Liverpool, Belfast and Glasgow and thereby ensuring the safety of the all important troop movements between Holyhead and Dublin. They did, however, dispense with the need for a mine barrage as, owing to the rough Atlantic weather, a small number of mines were breaking away from the Tory Island field and becoming a nuisance to shipping, adding greatly to the

1. In January 1915 the *U-21* (*Kapitänleutnant* Otto Hersing) sailed from Wilhelmshaven to the Irish Sea via the Dover Straits and English Channel, she was spotted by HM Drifter *R R S* off Bardsey Island on the 28th, but went on to shell Barrow and was driven off by the Walney Battery. Off the River Mersey on the 30th she sank the SS *Ben Cruachen,* SS *Linda Blanche* and SS *Kilcoan,* The following day she was spotted twenty miles east of the Kish Light Vessel by the RMS *Leinster*. Off Fishguard on 1st February she fought off the armed yacht *Vanduara*. She returned home to a hero's welcome, each of her crew being awarded an Iron Cross. She was the first German U-boat to venture so far westwards.

work load of the vessels of the North Channel patrol and it was felt that another minefield would only add to these problems.

On assuming command of Patrol Area XVII on 20th February, Admiral Barlow was instructed to deny the North Channel to enemy submarines and minelayers. For this he was given the armed yacht *Clementina,* eighty drifters – forty of which would be armed – and the eighteen trawlers of groups 68, 69 and 70. He would also have under his command the armed yachts of the Belfast Flying Squadron which he could use at his discretion. His orders went on to say that the North Channel was to be forbidden to all vessels, irrespective of size or nationality, a prohibition which was to be brought to the notice of all ship owners and governments. All traffic wishing to pass through the North Channel would now have to use the three-mile wide channel which passed between Rathlin Island and the coast of Antrim, and no vessel would be permitted within four miles of Rathlin Island between sunset and sunrise.

Although the North Channel was only half the width of the Straits of Dover, due to rough weather, tides and currents, it required twice the length of net. The Straits contained a large number of wrecks and the shallowness of the water made it very difficult for U-boats to dive and clear the nets, so one or two lines were thought to be sufficient. The North Channel, however, was deeper (average depth some seventy fathoms) and diving underneath a line of nets was a

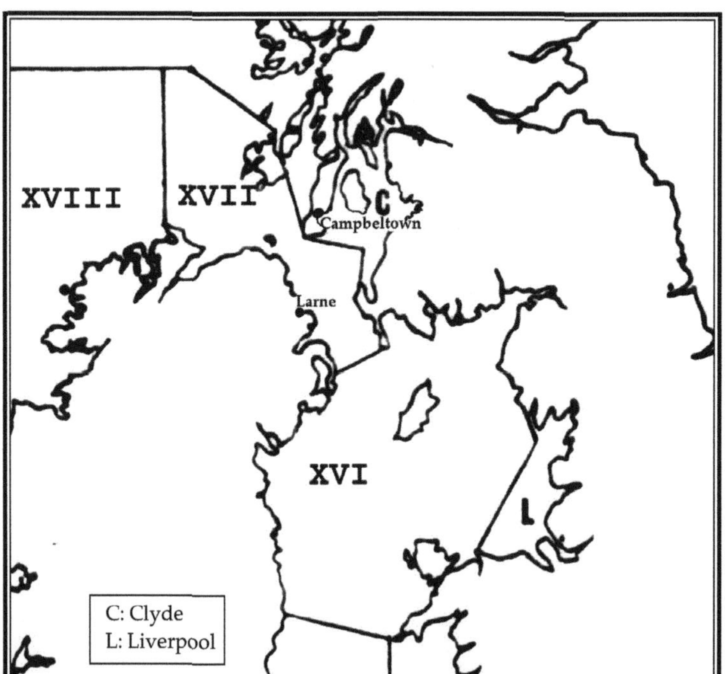


*Irish Sea and North Channel Auxiliary Patrol Areas, February 1915 [Author]*

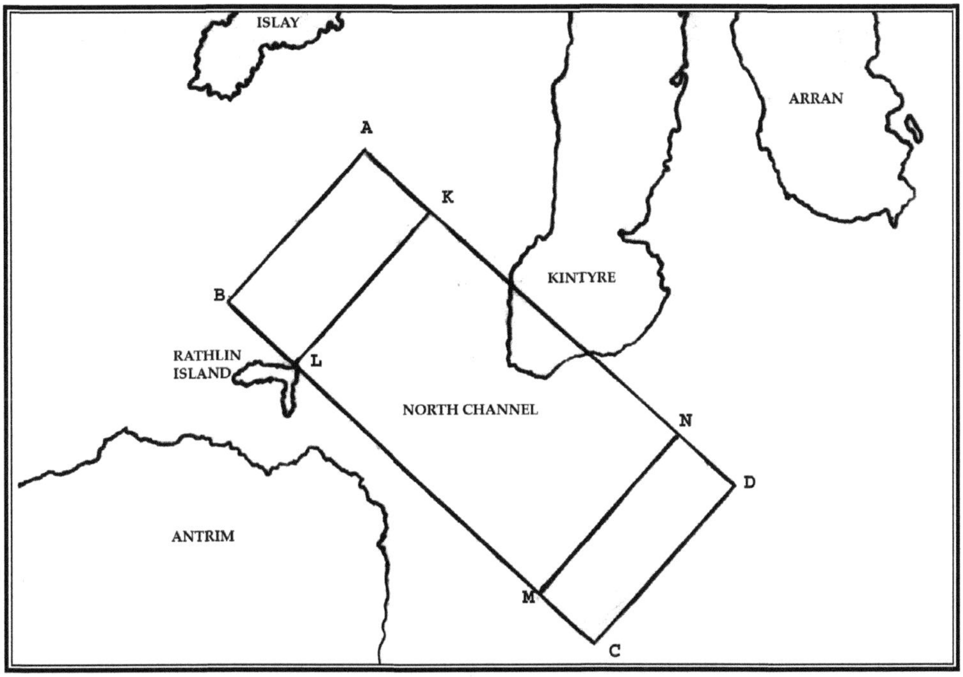


*Netted area within the North Channel and the five-mile extended patrol area and the safe channel between Rathin Island and the coast of Antrim [Author]*

relatively simple matter, therefore another system had to be devised. A designated patrol area, measuring approximately 20 miles x 11 miles (area K, L, M, N on map above), was to be established in the North Channel with its north-west point (L) at Rathlin Island. Within this area, a number of drifters, in four or five lines, would each tow steel nets (measuring up to half-a-mile in length) back and fore across the channel to keep the submarines down.[2]

While drifters towed the lines of nets, roving patrols of armed trawlers and other vessels would be within the netted area (K, L, M and N) making it almost impossible for any U-boat to surface for at least twenty miles. To extend this area, the armed patrols were pushed out a further five miles on either side (A, B, C and D), making a total distance of some thirty miles which U-boats had to travel underwater. It was believed that travelling this far underwater would either drain a submarine's batteries and/or foul the air within her hull, thereby forcing it to the surface where it could be dealt with by the guns of the vessels on patrol within or without the netted areas.

2. A single net was made of high tensile steel, measuring 100ft x 60ft or 30ft deep and supported by glass buoys, a number of nets could be connected together to form a line to the required length.

HMS *Tara* patrolled both inside and outside this netted area, but she was not confined to the North Channel but roved over a wider area as evidenced by the fact that on Thursday, 4th February, she was at anchor in Holyhead Bay having sent a boiler-feed water pipe to the Marine Yard workshops to be repaired. At 04.30 hours next morning, after the pipe had been refitted she hauled up her anchor and set out on patrol.

As time went on there were changes and additions to *Tara's* crew — on 5th February, Quartermaster William Thomas was granted leave following his wife's death in an accident in Holyhead and a week later Assistant Steward William James relieved Charles Gooding. On 23rd February, two RN signallers, Ordinary Telegraphist Raymond Fulcher and Boy Telegraphist George Tanner joined, as the ship was often the only vessel on patrol fitted with W/T apparatus and would be required to pass on orders and messages to the trawlers, drifters and yachts in her patrol area. On 26th February, an additional assistant paymaster, Walter Street, RNR, was appointed onto Captain Gwatkin-Williams' staff (but would not join until 3rd March).

A few days later, after returning to her patrol duties *Tara* was tasked to escort the SS *Redbreast* and *Vulture,* both carrying boiler spares from Ardrossan to Belfast. Having safely delivered her charges she resumed her normal patrolling duties. At about this time the SNO Larne reported to the Admiralty that

> The Auxiliary Patrol Vessels in the North Channel have now for some weeks been put under the direct orders of the Commanding officer of HMS *Tara,* who assigns stations and movements to them according to the varying requirements of patrol work, conditions of wind and weather and number of vessels available at the moment. This arrangement has proved satisfactory in that it has insured a more thorough cooperation between the *Tara* and these vessels, and it has yielded better results than those which were formerly attainable.

As for the other Larne vessels, they patrolled as far west as Sheephaven, north to Skerryvore and south to Holyhead; six trawlers had also been sweeping in Morecambe Bay, and predictably, owing to the damage sustained due to the rough winter weather, a number had been in dockyard hands but towards the end of the month the trawlers were disposed as follows:

*Group 68.* Patrolling the trade rotes between Oversay Island and Skerryvore, one trawler was detached to search the coastlines of Colonsay and Islay on its NW side.

*Group 69.* Two trawlers [were] patrolling the NW coast of Ireland from Fair Head to Malin Point, two others were on the trade route north of Inishtrahull and Rathlin Island – this group is still awaiting the arrival of the trawler *Clonsit* (in dock yard hands).

*Group 70.* On patrol in the North Channel under the orders of HMS *Tara.*

By the end of the month, of the eighty drifters ordered to Larne for the anti-submarine defences, sixty-five had arrived, of which thirty-three were now complete as to nets and bouys.

Although the Larne force had greatly expanded this was no guarantee of success and on 9th March, the SS *Princess Victoria* was torpedoed sixteen miles north-west of the Liverpool bar and the SS *Clan Macbrae* was chased by a U-boat. In the early morning of the 11th, the armed merchant cruiser HMS *Bayano* was sunk and that afternoon HMS *Ambrose* was attacked three times as she approached the channel. The SS *Helen* was attacked off Liverpool, the U-boat being driven off by the destroyer HMS *Dee,* one of two attached to the port, whilst further south in the Bristol Channel the SS *Florazan* was torpedoed. During the evening of the 12th, the SS *Atlantic City* was attacked off the South Rock, near Belfast and the following day the SS *Hartdale* was sunk south-east of the South Rock. The culprits of all these attacks were the *U-20* and *U-27*. This was a disappointing result for the Royal Navy considering the size of the force which Admiral Barlow had in his command but, as he later explained, the strength of the tides made it impossible to keep the nets positioned across the channel and none of his armed patrols were fast enough to deal with those submarines that were sighted. Admiral Jellicoe had become so alarmed by the submarine activity (as the Clyde was the coaling base of the 10th Cruiser Squadron which was enforcing the blockade in the North Atlantic) that he lent Barlow HMS *Faulknor* and six destroyers from the Grand Fleet until the 18th.

*Tara,* whilst on her anti-contraband patrol, came across evidence of *U-27*'s handiwork. On the morning of 11th March at about 09.30 hours when off the Rhinns of Galloway, some ten miles NNW of Corsewall Point, she spotted a coaster, the SS *Balmarino* lying to and blowing off steam. This in itself was sufficiently suspicious as many U-boat commanders were still stopping vessels to give the crew a chance to abandon ship before sinking their vessels. The officer

*SS* Bayano *in peacetime [Author]*

of the watch called the captain to the bridge, rang General Quarters and increased speed to 'Full Ahead'. With her gun crews closed up, *Tara* zig-zagged her way to the coaster and, as they neared the *Balmarino* it seems that their suspicions were justified as she had one of her boats out. Peering through their glasses however *Tara*'s officers could see the surface of the sea littered with rafts, spars, overturned and smashed boats, clothing and papers and within a matter of minutes their ship was surrounded by this wreckage amongst which were the bodies of the *Bayano's* crew, some floating spread-eagled but mostly floating upright in their life jackets. The *Tara's* engines were stopped and men rushed to the handrails and other vantage points to keep a lookout in case the U-boat was still lurking in the vicinity, and at 10.00 hours the order was given to lower a boat and the search for survivors commenced.

The *Balmarino* (under the command of Captain James Foster) had come upon the scene at about 08.30 hours that morning whilst on passage from Belfast to Ayr. Her lookouts had spotted a low-lying object in the water which, as they neared, they could make out to be men on rafts, some of whom were waving an oar with a piece of clothing tied to it. Captain Foster ordered a change of course and, as they closed they could see there were about twenty-four men on two rafts and an upturned lifeboat. Two of the men were clad only in their shirts whilst others were in their nightclothes. In addition, one man had a deep gash to his head and was covered in blood whilst most of the others were also bloodied and bruised.

As soon as she came to a stop, the *Balmarino's* lifeboat was launched under the command of the mate, Robert Murphy, accompanied by three men. After rowing over, they began the task of transferring the men off the rafts to the *Balmarino,* the operation taking some time as it was difficult to lift the almost helpless survivors off the upturned boat and raft into the lifeboat and then from the lifeboat onto the ship. However, having completed one trip Murphy was about to return to take the men off the second raft when the *Tara* came into view, lowered her lifeboat and took the rest of the men off. In all the *Balmarino* rescued eighteen survivors and the *Tara* eight. All of them had been in the water or on the rafts and boat for over four hours and were wet and suffering from the cold and possibly exposure, two of them were in a very bad way. Captain Foster thought that they would not last much longer. As soon as the survivors were brought aboard, their cuts and injuries were attended to, they were dried, given dry clothing, wrapped in blankets, placed into beds and fed hot soup and drinks. Captain Gwatkin-Williams suggested that all the survivors should be brought aboard the *Tara* so she could take them to Stranraer but this notion was rejected by the survivors on the *Balmarino*. Captain Foster said he would take them onto Ayr where the ship was bound and where they were eventually landed. Two of the worst cases were sent to Ayr Hospital, fourteen to the barracks of the Royal Scots Fusiliers and two were accommodated at the Ayr Station Hotel.

Aboard the *Tara,* similar care was being show to those survivors picked up by her lifeboat — Lt-Commander K A F Guy, RN; Surgeon K H Hole, RN; Surgeon Probationer R E Batson, RNVR; Midshipman H A Wright, RNR; CPO R A Wood, RN (115347); PO 1st Class G A Glover, RN (177130); carpenter's crew S V Brailford[?], RN and Able Seaman J Hayes, RFR (5517). Whilst her lifeboat was being hoisted aboard and stowed, *Tara* got underway and headed for Stranraer where she arrived at 11.35 hours and dropped anchor within the harbour. The survivors were then ferried ashore and taken to the King's Arms Hotel where they were given warm clothing and generally looked after by Captain Moreland, the agent of the Shipwrecked Mariners Society. At 18.30 hours, her duty done,

SS Balmarino
*[J Kelly & Co Ltd]*

Tara's *boat returning with survivors of the* Bayano *[BRB (Residuary) Ltd]*

*Tara* raised her anchor and steamed out of Stranraer to resume her patrol. No doubt the whole episode had been a sobering experience for the crew.

The men rescued by the *Tara* and *Balmarino* were the only survivors of the *Bayano's* 223-man crew. The ship had left the Clyde the previous night and not wishing to enter the netted area during the hours of darkness had slowed down. Unknown to her, the *U-27* (*Kapitänleutnant* Bernd Wegener) was lying ahead waiting. As the *Bayano* came towards the submarine, her captain put one torpedo into her; the time then being about 05.00 hours. Within a short time, there was a second and more violent explosion, resulting in much damage and causing her to sink rapidly. She went down so quickly — within three minutes according to one witness — that most of the crew who were in their hammocks or beds did not have time to get on deck, let alone get the lifeboats away. However she had been carrying three large rafts and there had been time enough to cut the lashings of two which had floated off as she sank, as did a lifeboat which the survivors had managed to climb into or onto. A short while after the *Bayano* had sunk the SS *Castlereagh* had come across the scene, steaming through masses of wreckage and dead bodies. Captain McGarrick had slowed the ship down and was starting to search the area for survivors when one of the lookouts spotted a surfaced submarine. McGarrick immediately rang for Full Speed and after some twenty minutes managed to outrun the submarine. There were so few survivors of the *Bayano* that the usual Court of Enquiry was not convened.

Owing to the ever increasing number of Auxiliary Patrol vessels now using the small port of Larne, *Tara* was slowly but surely being squeezed out. In addition, Larne was now geared for the handling, repair and maintenance of the armed trawlers and drifters, their minesweeping gear and stores. It was therefore decided that sooner rather than later, a new base would have to be found for *Tara* within the patrol area. After some searching, Campbeltown on the Mull of Kintyre was selected, and she was ordered to proceed to her new base on completion of her patrol. She arrived alongside at 08.00 hours on the 12th and shortly afterwards coaling commenced; by early the next morning all had been completed and the ship washed down and sailed at 04.00 hours to resume her patrol duties.

The Admiralty had been shaken by *U-27*'s attacks in the Irish Sea and the ease with which she had torpedoed the *Bayano*. This had revealed the general vulnerability of the Armed Merchant Cruisers of the 10th Cruiser Squadron to submarine attack as they sailed through the North Channel to and from Liverpool to coal. By coincidence in February the Admiralty had decided to permanently strengthen the North Channel patrol. On the 16th, four destroyers, HMS D*ee, Dove, Garry* and *Thorn,* left the Scapa Flow Local Flotilla to form this permanent force in the North Channel. They would come under the command of Commander Gwatkin-Williams of the *Tara*. Although all the destroyers had only been built at the turn of the century, by 1915 they were technically obsolete, but had to suffice. This new force become the Larne Patrol Flotilla and, although the destroyers were to be based at Stranraer,[3] *Tara* would continue to be based at Campbeltown. On 3rd March, she became their depot ship, accepting mail and messages to and from these vessels, and responsible for each destroyer's accounts, victualling, pay, leave, etc. In August, a doctor would be appointed to her, presumably to look after the personnel of the flotilla. As things turned out, however, *Dee* and *Dove* spent most of their time working out of Liverpool under the SNO of the port. Also, on 3rd March, *Tara* took aboard some twenty RN / RNR personnel, probably in lieu of a crew change. Also joining on that date from HMS *Thorn* was Assistant Paymaster Walter F Street, RNR who would assist Assistant Paymaster Alfred Dutton, RNR, with the additional paperwork which the formation of the flotilla had generated.

Of the new RN and RNR men who joined, their ranks ranged from Skipper[4] to Seaman and Engine Room Artificer to Stoker. It is almost certain they were sent to replace the men, supplied by the Shipping Federation, who had proved to be problematic. By now, both the Admiralty and *Tara's* officers had had enough of their insubordination and general unsuitability, and whilst most of the

3. There was some concern about the use of Stranraer as a coaling base at the time as due to the lack of manpower available to coal the destroyers, as most of the local labour was now employed in building a new military airship station nearby at Luce Bay, some 17 miles south of Stranaer. Luce Bay was one of a network of military airship stations now being being built so that airships / blimps could patrol both the North Channel and the Irish Sea.
4. Two Skippers and three ERA's were appointed, why is not yet understood. After the *Tara* left the Skippers served respectively on HMS *Garry* and *Thorn*.

inefficient and troublesome men had been weeded out and replaced by company men sent from the L&NWR's Marine Office in Holyhead or employed locally at Larne (or would be during her time at Campbeltown), it was felt that more had to be done. The only permanent cure was to replace these men with naval personnel. It would seem that problems with the Federation's men had affected all four of the express steamers, as early as the first crew change on 11th November 1914, the ex-L&NWR captain's of the *Anglia* and *Cambria*, L J Manning and W J Nash, (both by March 1915 serving as RNR lieutenants on their old commands) had asked for the Federation men on their ships to be replaced by RNR personnel, and they were.

In January 1915, just prior to her second crew change, Lieutenant Manning of the *Anglia* wrote to the Director of Transports regarding the re-signing on of the naval reservists '... the crew are [by now] practically all permanent men in the employ of the L&NWR with the exception of 21 RNR ratings, a corporal [ship's corporal] a yeoman of signals and two gunners.' By now this state of manning probably applied to most of the ex-Holyhead vessels.

During March 1915, there were also changes amongst *Tara's* junior officers, as despite the war company promotions continued. On the 9th, Sub Lieutenants Charles P Copland and William Hughes were recalled to Holyhead on being promoted to captain and chief mate respectively on the company's other vessels. Their places aboard the *Tara* being taken by Sub Lieutenants Leslie T Dudgeon and William T Griffiths. The exchange was carried out whilst the Tara was at anchor in Red Bay in Northern Ireland.[5]

On 2nd April 1915, Rear Admiral the Hon Robert Boyle succeeded Admiral Barlow in command of the Larne patrol area. At once he set about trying to obtain more drifters, and by the end of the month, he had managed to increase the size of the fleet from 80 to 130 vessels. At first they were organised into nine sections each with nine drifters then, as more drifters became available, the number in each section was increased to twelve. Whilst six sections were at sea, three would be in port for rest and maintenance; the drifters worked four days in port and four at sea. As each drifter could hold half-a-mile of net, it became possible for six sections i.e. 72 drifters, to keep some 36 miles of net in action within the patrol zone. Boyle also divided Patrol Area XVII into five sectors – V, W, X and Z – and,

5. This bay is just to the north of Larne, and it was where *Tara* had, since September 1914 regularly used to anchor to pick up mails, supplies or to shelter from storms and heavy weather. She also used this bay to station herself whilst waiting to intercept shipping.

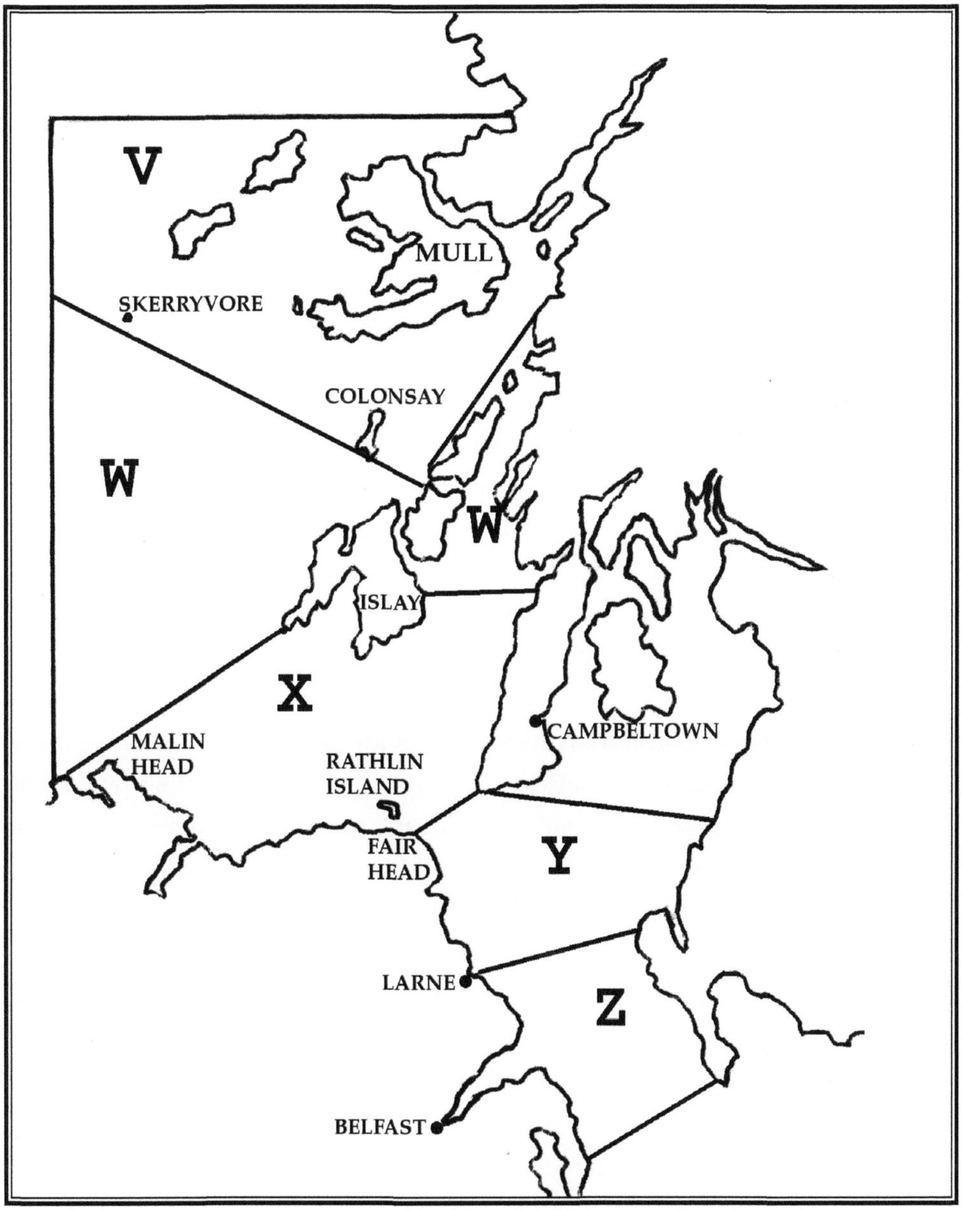


*Patrol Sector XVII, showing the five sectors V, W, X, Y and Z within [Author]*

much to the chagrin of the other SNOs of the Irish Sea patrol areas, he used the yachts of the Belfast yacht squadron, aided by some of the armed trawlers, to patrol the hundreds of coves and bays where a submarine might hide in the northern sectors. Other trawlers from the three groups were also used to patrol in the southern sectors, the eastern channel (the eastern side of the netted area) and within the netted area with the destroyers HMS *Garry* and *Thorn*, whilst *Tara* patrolled the western channel (the western side of the netted area). To assist with the roving patrols within the netted area, Boyle had also been given four destroyers of the 8th Flotilla (the Firth of Forth Defence Flotilla).

*Tara* certainly was not wary of using her guns in support of her patrol activities as was shown on the morning of 20th April when she fired three rounds across the bows of the SS *King's Lynn* which was steaming into the netted area. Ordered to stop, the *King's Lynn* was boarded by an armed party under Sub Lieutenant Marsh who ordered her captain to explain his actions in attempting to enter a prohibited area. Marsh explain to him that he was prohibited from entering the netted area and that Rathlin Sound was closed to shipping after sunset. That same evening the *King's Lynn* was again intercepted attempting to enter Rathlin Sound and Tara again fired across her bow. Commander Gwatkin-Williams later described the errant ship's captain as 'an apparently very stupid man'. How often Tara had opened fire during the previous months is unrecorded but Gwatkin-Williams, in his weekly report to the Admiralty, asked for an increase in his ship's allowance of ammunition from fifty rounds per gun to one hundred. He also asked for an additional armed trawler to be stationed in Red Bay to assist in the policing of the three-mile channel as Larne was unable to provide one.

Although attached to the netted area patrol, *Tara*'s work of stopping and searching merchantmen continued, with occasional forays down into the Irish Sea in search of non-existent submarines and suspicious vessels reported to the authorities by coast watchers, merchantmen and fishing vessels. Nothing was ever found, however numerous rocks and whales could testify to the accuracy of her gunnery. The miles she steamed within and without her patrol area slowly told on her and at 02.00 hours on 24th April she left the area for her four-monthly refit in Holyhead, where she berthed at 10.30 hours under the Shear Legs at the Marine Yard from where, after her coal had been discharged into railway wagons, she was manoeuvred and hauled into the dry dock and half the crew were sent on leave. During this period Gwatkin-Williams (who had been promoted to captain on the retired list on 6th April) had a false bow wave painted some two yards aft of the bow, on both port and starboard sides, which it was hoped would make her speed difficult to estimate by an attacking submarine. Finally, after all underwater work had been completed, she was hauled out of the dock to lie alongside the Marine Yard whilst work on her main and auxiliary machinery continued.

During her time in dry dock there had been some changes to her crew; it is known that six men joined, so it can be assumed that six men were discharged. Among those joining was Electrician Wallace C V Cooke (who relieved Ernest Lawton), Fireman John Williams of Holyhead, Fireman George A Wright (who had transferred from the paddle minesweeper HMS *Lynn*, the former GWR PV *Lynx*) and Seaman John Hodgson (from the recently decommissioned Fleet Messenger *Anglia*). Unfortunately the names of the other two men are unknown.

At 06.00 hours on 12th May, all work having being completed, she left Holyhead, passing the breakwater light at 06.26 hours heading for her patrol area, with orders to call at Campbeltown on the 17th to top up her bunkers.[6] Two days later, whilst on patrol, *Tara's* steering gear broke down. The engineers connected up the emergency steering and she made for Campbeltown, leaving HMS *Garry* and *Thorn* to patrol. Two days later, HMS *Garry* proceeded to Pembroke Dock for a refit, so the yacht *Clementina* (designated as the SNO patrol vessel in the absence of *Tara*) relieved her. However, owing to the commitments of his patrol vessels Admiral Boyle wrote to the Admiralty requesting more vessels, as the loss of both *Tara* and *Thorn* would be sorely felt. They replied that there were no other vessels available but more yachts would be sent as soon as possible. At 20.45 hours on the 22nd, her steering gear now repaired, *Tara* took over from the *Clementina* and resumed her usual patrol on the western side of the North Channel.

On 12th July 1915, Admiral Sir Lewis Bayly was appointed to replace Vice-Admiral Coke at Queenstown. With U-boats now sailing into both the Atlantic and the Irish Sea the size of the command had also grown and Admiral Bayly become C-in-C Western Approaches and the Irish Sea; his command including the bases at Queenstown, Larne, Kingstown and Milford and to which was later added the Isles of Scilly subsidiary base which was transferred from Falmouth command.[7] He now had at his disposal some 450 vessels and although many of the drifters had been absorbed into the North Channel net barrage, which had become so effective that it could be regarded as submarine proof. Although it is

6. On 12th June, whilst *Tara* was taking on coal, Seaman William Ralph, RNR, deserted and enlisted in the 1/7th Bn Royal Scots Fusiliers. The authorities eventually caught up with him in 1918 but, because he had enlisted, the charge of desertion from the Royal Navy was dismissed.
7. During July, Auxiliary Patrol Area XXII was formed, the limits of which were defined as a line running from the tip of the Llŷn Peninsula in Caernarfonshire to the Mull of Kintyre, and a line running from the Great Orme to Barrow-in-Furness. It encompassed in all some 3,000 square miles. Its base, HMS *Amethyst III* (yacht ex *Nellie II*) was at Holyhead under the command of Captain A R Raby, RN, whose headquarters ashore was firstly at Rose Mount, Boston Street (next door to the Holyhead Post Office) and later Bryn-y-Mor, Turkish Shore, Holyhead (the former home of the L&NWR's marine superintendent).

uncertain whether any U-boats had attempted to get into the Irish Sea through the North Channel, the Admiralty however was convinced that nothing was getting through.

As for the southern entrance to the Irish Sea, Admiral Bayly planned that once a submarine had been sighted then all available patrol vessels within the locality would be directed onto her, forcing her to submerge and to keep her down until her batteries became exhausted. Due to this loss of power and the foul air, the crew would have no choice but to surface and she could be dealt with by the guns of the patrol vessels. Therefore submarine activity became fairly quiet for a time in the Irish Sea, although the U-boats did remain active in other sea areas around Britain.

Even though submarine activity had considerably eased, it was work as usual for *Tara*, in fact she was busier than ever stopping and searching merchantmen by night and day, interspersed with roving patrols, sometimes on her own and sometimes in company with armed yachts or trawlers, looking for suspected submarines or German mines which had broken free of their moorings.

By now *Tara* was regularly using her guns to police and to shepherd errant merchant men in the North Channel. However, their regular use was revealing problems, some of which were fundamental. In late June it was noted that the guns on the forecastle were useless in a seaway. Due to her speed, straight bow and lack of flare of the hull forward, she had a very wet forecastle. The water thrown up onto this area, even in a moderate sea, greatly hampered the gun crews on the foredeck, so it was recommended that during her next dry docking they should be moved up to the boat deck forward, abreast the foremast. It had also been found that the sweep of the after gun was limited; the dockyard staff at Campbeltown were informed and in late July, whilst the ship was alongside coaling, they took the opportunity to extend the gun's platform from the steering position, horizontally aft over the deck house's curved roof. Its after end was attached to, and supported by, two stanchions fixed to the main deck, and the emergency steering position's handrails were extended to encompass the new gun deck. The gun was refitted to its centre and it was found that this had increased its arc of fire by 90°.

Despite the war, L&NWR promotions continued and, at the end of July 1915, Assistant Engineer Robert Jones was signed off in order to be promoted to second engineer on one of the company's vessels in Holyhead. His replacement was Richard Lewis Phillips, a third engineer from the cargo vessels. A few days later, a doctor, Surgeon Probationer (Temporary) George Findlay, RNVR joined the *Tara* in Campbeltown, complete with medical supplies and equipment.[8] One of the cabins on the awning deck was converted to a sick bay / hospital, making the ship the only one of the express steamers to have such a facility.

At the beginning of August *Tara* was relieved by her patrol mate, the armed yacht *Clementina,* and returned to Campbeltown for coal. On the 5th, the *Clementina* collided with the SS *Adam Smith* and was holed on the port side and had to be beached on Tor Cor Point where her guns and ammunition were salved and the crew sent to Larne. Attempts were then made to salvage her, (but were abandoned by 25th September). In his report on the collision, Admiral Boyle asked the Admiralty for a replacement as soon as possible as the patrol duties were at times having to be left to the trawlers alone.

On 24th the trawler *Ceresia* relieved *Tara,* which then proceeded to Campbeltown for coal, leaving the patrolling of the North Channel to the trawlers *Dragoon* (which had just taken over from *Angerton*) and *Ceresia,* which led Captain Gwatkin-Williams to write,

> ... the amount of shipping passing through the North Channel has been steadily increasing in volume for the last two months Danish, British and Russian vessels [all] bound for Archangel. With the small number of patrol vessels generally available it cannot be satisfactorily over looked.
>
> The armed trawlers which generally have to do the duties of the eastern patrol have no method of challenging war vessels which use that side at night. Hostile vessels could probably pass through as easily as British, and without being recognised as hostile. Even if fired upon, the probability is that the SNO in the North Channel could not be aware of what was taking place, since there is no method of communicating with [the] patrol trawlers at night at that distance. It is quite likely that rockets and flashes of guns would be unobserved, except in very clear weather.

Due to the shortage of vessels, Tara hurriedly returned to her patrol area and on 7th August held firing practice, after which Captain Gwatkin-Williams wrote that the after guns new position had improved its sweep and that all guns were

8. RNVR surgeon probationers were for the most part medical students in their third, fourth or fifth year of training, and had been appointed for the duration only. Many sat their final medical examinations whilst still in uniform.

working perfectly, but because of their worn barrels were hopelessly inaccurate. By the middle of August it was noted that the destroyers were regularly absent, most of their time being taken up on escort duties and, with the loss of the *Clementina*, the North Channel Patrol force was becoming stretched. On 22nd August the *Thorn* was refitting in Belfast, the *Garry* was escorting a Russian convoy, the trawler *Angerton* was on the eastern (channel) patrol and the *Tara* on the western (channel) patrol. This constant patrol work was telling on *Tara's* boilers and machinery, the crew were also feeling the strain, and Gwatkin-Williams noted that she was badly in need of her four-monthly refit which was due the following month.

For her final patrol before refit *Tara* left Campbeltown at 07.40 hours on Wednesday, 8th September, after spending two days alongside storing and coaling. She sailed and served variously on the eastern and western patrols but at 15.45 hrs on the 10th went on general patrol. That night, which was described as very dark, with a strong south-east wind and a heavy sea running, Chief Engineer Thomas Jones went missing. It was later discovered that before going to bed he had gone down below to the engine room to see how things were, and have a chat with the watchkeeper, the Fourth Engineer. He left the engine room at 23.30 hours but next morning, not having appeared at breakfast, the steward went to call him and found the cabin empty and the bed not slept in. The bridge was immediately notified and Lieutenant Tanner ordered a thorough search of the vessel, but with no luck, and it was concluded that he had fallen overboard. Tanner then ordered the *Tara* to reverse course, reaching the estimated position where she would have been at midnight, allowing for wind, tide and currents. A thorough search of the area was conducted, but there was no sign of Mr Jones. Campbeltown was informed and, as her Second Engineer Hugh Jones held a chief's ticket, he took over the post of Chief Engineer and she was ordered to continue with her patrol duties. The news was then telegraphed to the Marine Office in Holyhead. On confirmation that the chief was missing, the Marine Office then had the painful task of informing his family, a wife and four young daughters.[9]

At 03.00 hours Monday, 13th September, *Tara* was relieved by the armed trawler *Nellie Braddock* and headed for her refit at Holyhead, where she berthed

9. On 2nd October Thomas Jones's body was recovered from Sheephaven, Co. Donegal. After an inquest, it was brought back to Holyhead on 6th and interred in Maeshyfryd Cemetery, Holyhead.

at 13.00 hours. The urgency for this refit was nicely encapsulated by Gwatkin-Williams in his report where he stated that the

> Volume of shipping using North Channel [is] increasing daily.
>
> *Tara* has been 4 months at sea, with all boilers alight since last refitted. I do not consider it prudent for her to continue longer without boilers being examined and cleaned and machinery opened up and refitted. During that time she has steamed 25,867 miles and 59,671 miles since 18th August 1914 when she first put to sea at the beginning of the war. During all this period she has only had one small breakdown to [the] steering telemotor.
>
> ... some efficient sea keeping vessel should assist *Tara* in [the] North Channel patrol duties. The two destroyers are useful in fine weather, but are constantly absent on escort duties and making good defects. Trawlers are practically useless, owing to [the] lack of experience of many of their Skippers, their slow speed and their inability to signal or communicate rapidly. No confidence can at present be placed on North Channel detecting in all cases vessels slipping through during the dark hours or hazy weather, nor can the increasing volume of shipping be adequately overlooked.

On her arrival in Holyhead the usual routine of removing most of her coal prior to entering the dry dock was carried out before she was hauled into the dock and the dock gate manoeuvred and sunk into position. Pumping then commenced and, when she was secured on the blocks, a gangway was placed on board and the workers of the Marine Yard went aboard. Routine maintenance and overhauls were carried out on the boilers, main and auxiliary machinery and all defects repaired. Down in the dry dock, below the waterline, the shore gang scraped off the weed and barnacles, after which the hull was painted.

As noted earlier another important job that was to be carried out during this refit was the re-siting of her foward 6-pounder guns which were removed from the forecastle, and as suggested by Captain Gwatkin-Williams in June, refitted on the boat deck abreast the foremast (see photograph above).

Sometime in the middle of September it was learnt that, after this refit, *Tara* would be sent on foreign service to the Mediterranean. This must have come as a complete surprise to the crew as she had been extremely busy in the North Channel. But, leaving aside patrolling duties, with no confirmed submarine attacks in the channel during the previous few months (thanks to the net

*HMS* Tara's *starboard, forward 6-pounder gun in its new position [R Houston]*

defences), and the building of airship stations around the North Channel[10] and down into the Irish Sea, the Admiralty may have felt that they had now contained the submarine threat in the Irish Sea and concluded that the need for the *Tara* was greater in the mediterranean than in the North Channel. As she was moving to warmer climes, the Marine Yard's sailmakers were put to work making canvas awnings which, once *Tara* reached the Mediterranean, would be rigged up on the main deck over the crew's accommodation to keep them cool, and underneath which both officers and crew could escape the sun's rays during the heat of the day.

Once again, there were some changes to her crew. Owing to the rank structure of the L&NWR's Marine Department, a new chief engineer had to be appointed; the man chosen was Robert J. Seaborne Williams, at the time chief engineer of the SS *Greenore*. He was appointed Engineer, RNR, on 18th September and signed on, on 5th October (his place on the *Greenore* being taken by John Jones, chief engineer of the SS *Rathmore*). Surgeon Probationer Findlay was relieved on 1st October by Surgeon Probationer John D. Arthur. RNVR, and on the 5th an additional engineer was signed on, Assistant Engineer David J. Davies, RNR, who would *Tara's* Sixth Engineer (an additional engineer had also been appointed

10. The military airship station at Luce Bay had been in service since 15th July 1915 with three airships. Experiments were however ongoing as to communications between them and the base/ships. With the loss of the *Tara*, Admiral Barlow asked for the Ballycastle wireless telegraphy station – with its greater range – to be moved to Rathlin Island so as to be able to communicate with his charges.

*HMS* Tara *in dry dock, Holyhead, 13th September–6th October [R Houston]*

to the *Scotia* prior to her departure for the Mediterranean). Moving station also meant that *Tara* would have to relinquish her role as the depot ship to the four destroyers. She would also loose some of the RN and RNR personnel who had joined her in February and March. These men were discharged at Holyhead to the destroyer depot ship HMS *Hermione* (guard ship *Southampton*), and it is believed that their places were taken by some seventeen local men:[11] Seamen William J Rowlands, William T Jones, Owen Hughes, Griffith T Jones, Thomas Pritchard, and Firemen Richard Jones (of Bangor), Hugh Hughes, John Jones, Rhys Jones, William Griffith, brothers Hugh and Harold Jones, brothers Hugh Ellis and Thomas Richard Wright, Thomas H Owens, Hugh Williams and Thomas Jones. As already noted, it is believed that ex-Quartermaster John L Jones, now serving on board as a seaman, also rejoined at this time from sick leave. One other man who would not be going with *Tara* to the Mediterranean was her second engineer, Assistant Engineer Hugh Jones, RNR who had been taken ill whilst the ship was in dry dock and so could not rejoin.[12] As no other second engineer was available in the port the Marine Office promoted *Tara's* senior third Engineer, Richard L Phillips to be a temporary second engineer. The Royal Navy was informed and concurred, allowing the decision to stand whilst they searched for a relief.

11. This is believed to be correct as the dates when these men joined HMS *Tara* are unknown, but lack of contrary evidence makes it probable that most, if not all, were employed to replace the RN and RNR personnel paid off during this refit. This lack of evidence is mostly due to the Royal Navy which had, since August 1914, chartered (i.e. hired) the L&NWR vessels and hence had become employers of any new men they wished to employ on 'their' ships. Any new 'civilian' crew members who joined were therefore not required to sign the L&NWR crew agreements. Instead they would sign the Royal Navy's T.124 crew agreements. Unfortunately HMS *Tara's* T.124 agreements cannot now be found. It may be worth noting that the L&NWR did continue to use their crew agreements to sign on and off existing company men whilst all four of the express steamers were under Royal Navy control.
12. On recovery, Hugh Jones was appointed temporary chief engineer on one of the Holyhead cargo vessels, his rank being confirmed on 6th November 1915. Sadly he lost his life in the sinking of the SS *Connmara* in Carlingford Loch, Northern Ireland, on 3rd November 1916.

In spite of all the additional work which had been thrown onto the crew to prepare her for Mediterranean service, all were glad at the thought of not having to face another British winter in the North Channel and were eagerly looking forward to spending some time in warmer climes.

The crew by now had settled down, the troublemakers had been weeded out and, although the remaining men's ages ranged from their teens to their sixties, all could be relied upon at any time. As Captain Gwatkin-Williams later recounted '... perhaps not all could pass a rigorous medical examination but a night alarm could find things cleared away and all guns manned in less than three minutes. The men had learned to run and move quickly.' He also praised the vessel herself and in particular the engine room staff adding that, '... in that first year we steamed 60,000 miles in the narrow waters ... we never had a breakdown and we faced out every kind of weather'.

# 6. To Egypt

By the summer of 1915, the war in the Irish Sea had quietened down whereas in the North Sea and Western Approaches, the number of U-boat attacks and sinkings were increasing. On land, the British had repulsed a German assault on Ypres in April, fought a number of major engagements in France, all at a heavy cost in casualties, and repelled an attack on the Suez Canal by the Turks. In German East Africa (now Tanzania), Colonel Paul von Lettow-Vorbeck and his Askaris were leading the British and Commonwealth troops a merry dance and would continue to do so until the Armistice. Things looked grim in Mesopotamia where the Turks were proving to be tough and able fighters as they were on the Gallipoli peninsula where the British and ANZAC (Australia & New Zealand Army Corps) forces were suffering terrible casualties, not only from enemy action but also from tropical diseases and sickness.

In trying to maintain her worldwide commitments, Britain was very heavily stretched as Kitchener's 'New Armies' which were then under training were not yet ready to take to the field. The Turks and Germans were well aware of this and in North Africa had begun to cultivate the Senussi people in an effort to

*Looking forward on the SS* Hibernia's *promenade deck, c1905 [Author]*

persuade them to attack Egypt's weakly-defended western border. The Italian protectorates of Tripolitania and Cyrenaica had been wrested from the Turks during the war of 1911–12 (the latter lying along the western border of Egypt), inland, some 150 miles from the coast, was the oasis of Jaghbub, the spiritual home of the Senussi who were neither a tribe nor a clan, but Arabs drawn from various tribes (including the Bedouin and the Berbers). They adhered to a more fundamentalist form of Islam than was prevalent at this time in North Africa. The movement had been founded by Mohamed bin Ali al Senussi. He was succeeded by his son, Mohamed al Mahdi, in 1859 and the Senussi people gradually spread their influence from Benghazi to Lake Chad, and from western Egypt far into the Sahara desert. During this time they became more warlike and al Mahdi eventually commanded a formidable body of regular troops called the Muhafizia. They were friendly to Egypt when it was ruled by the Turks and later the British. They were not, however, friendly towards the French who were continually pushing further and further into Libya from Chad and the Congo and suffered accordingly at their hands. During the Italian–Turkish war of 1911–12, the Senussi (since 1902 headed by Ahmad al Sharif, known as the Grand Senussi, the nephew of Mohamed al Mahdi) had allied themselves with the Turks whom they regarded as not very religious and little better than Christians. After their defeat by the Italians, the Turks started to supply the Senussi with arms and ammunition as well as military advisers, so that they could continue the fight against the army of occupation. After August 1914, Turkish agents became more active in Libya and the Senussi became more daring, so that within six months the Italians had been pushed back as far as Tripoli, whilst in Cyrenaica they had fallen back to Benghazi and Derna. During one incident the Senussi had attacked and decisively defeated an Italian column of over 4,000 men, taking many prisoners and seizing their arms and ammu-nition and a considerable quantity of gold. The Germans

*General Jafar Pasha al-Askari (left) after capture in February 1916. He later served as the prime minister of Iraq [Author]*

and Turks hoped that when the latter launched their attack on the Suez Canal in January 1915, the Senussi would attack Egypt's western border, prompting a rising by Egyptian nationalists, but this failed to materialise.

Pressure was being applied on the Grand Senussi by the very pro German, Nuri Bey, the younger brother of Enver Pasha, the Turkish Minister of War, who in February 1915 had been sent to take charge of the Grand Senussi's military affairs and to persuade him to attack Egypt, but he was largely ignored. The Germans and Turks knew they had to win over the Senussi and during April had used the German mine-laying U-boat, the *UC-12*,[1] to land the Turkish General Jaafar Pasha al-Askari, another pro German, at Port Sulliman, and from this moment British Intelligence started to detect a change in the Grand Senussi's attitude.

For the British military this change of attitude was giving cause for concern, even more so when, on 7th May the High Commissioner of Egypt informed the Foreign Office that the Italian minister had admitted to him that the coast of Cyrenaica had not been patrolled by the Italian navy for a long time. But thanks to Lieutenant Colonel C L Snow[2] and Captain L V A Royal[3] of the Egyptian Coastguard Service, and their Arab agents in the Senussi camp, the British knew that arms, money and agents had been smuggled to the Senussi, and now it was confirmed that they were most probably being smuggled into Cyrenaica

1. On the outbreak of war Germany had commandeered five U-boats being built for the Austrian navy in Keil. But during the early spring of 1915, they compensated the Austrians by sending to the Adriatic five UB-class submarines (UB-1, 3, 7, 8, 14 and 15) which were small coastal types that could carry two torpedoes each, and four UC-class boats (the UC-12, 13, 14 and 15) which could carry a dozen mines each.
2. Cecil Longueville Snow, an administrative officer in the Egyptian Coastguard Service, had, on the outbreak of the Italian-Turkish war, been sent to Sollum as commandant by the Egyptian government. His instructions were to keep the frontier secure and to gather intelligence on the activities of the Grand Senussi who, although based in Cyrenaica, had many adherents in western Egypt and in the Nile valley. Tension increased when in September 1914 the Grand Senussi and his army moved up to the border and set up camp at Amas'id, some two miles from Sollum. It was increased further when the Turks entered the war on the side of the Central Powers on 29th October and Italy sided with the Allies on 23rd May 1915. The Grand Senussi bore no ill will against the British, who had allowed caravans of food to cross the border during the recent war, but hated the Italians and did not care much for the Turks.
3. Leopold Victor Arnold Royle, a nephew of Lieutenant-Colonel Snow, had joined the Egyptian Coastguard service in 1900. Before the war he had travelled throughout Egypt making friends with both Arab and Bedouin and was one of the few Englishmen to have met and got on well with the Grand Senussi. It may have been partly because of this friendship that the Grand Senussi hesitated to attack Egypt in 1915. When the Germans and Turks started to urge the Grand Senussi to attack Egypt's western border, Lord Kitchener had Royle transferred to the Western Desert Force as an intelligence officer owing to his specialised knowledge of the western Bedouins and the Senussi in particular.

somewhere along this porous coast. The Italian minister went on to ask the British if they would co-operate with the Italian navy in patrolling the Cyrenaican coast. The British government then asked Vice Admiral Sir R. H. Peirse, KCB, RN, C-in-C East Indies, whether any of his vessels could patrol the coast; if not, could the Egyptian Coast Guard based at Port Said carry out the task? In his reply, Admiral Peirse stated that the most the Egyptian coastguard could do was to arrange for a coastguard cruiser, in reality a gunboat, to call once a week at the small British coastal post of Sollum, on the border between Egypt and Cyrenaica. He went on to say that he had no ships available without drawing one from the Red Sea where they were desperately needed.[4]

On 21st May, the day he sent off his reply to the Admiralty's inquiry, Admiral Peirse was informed that two weeks earlier fifty German and Turkish officers, along with six field guns, six Maxim guns, ammunition and an amount of gold, had been landed just to the west of Sollum. However, the British were aware of these clandestine voyages and, knowing of the Senussi's hatred of the Italians, and Britain's tense relations with the Senussi, Admiral Peirse thought it best that no Italian warship should appear off Sollum. Instead, learning that the armoured cruiser HMS *Cornwall* was passing through the Mediterranean on her way to Zanzibar, where British warships were blockading the German cruiser SMS *Königsberg* in the Rifiji delta, he asked the Admiralty if he could retain her to patrol the Cyrenaican coast. This they rejected, but allowed the ship to search the coastline some fifty miles to the east and west of Sollum between the 24th and 27th, but without any luck. To add to the Royal Navy's burden, the Imperial German Navy, due to all the Allied maritime activity in the Mediterranean, had decided to send an ocean-going U-boat to operate there. On 25th April, under strict security, *U-21* (still under the command of *Kapitan Leutnant* Otto Hersing) had left Wilhelmshaven and arrived at the Austrian naval base at Cattaro (now Pola in Macedonia) on 13th May. The voyage had been quite an undertaking for an unescorted submarine. She had been refuelled off the coast of Spain but the fuel oil received was of the wrong grade so could not be used and she only just made it to Cattaro. On the 20th, after pumping out her fuel tanks and rebunkering with the correct fuel, and repairing the various defects that had been discovered during the passage, she left on her first patrol. It turned out to be a spectacular success as she sank the pre-Dreadnaught battleships HMS *Triumph* on the 25th

4. The Egyptians only had four Coast Guard cruisers available: *Reschid, Abdul Moneim, Nour el Bahr* and *Abbas,* each armed with a single 3-pounder gun.

*HMS* Scotia *at anchor in Alexandria [Author]*

and HMS *Majestic* two days later, both off Gallipoli, in full view of British, Australian and Turkish troops (and embarrassingly the battleships' naval escorts). Ashore, both sides had stopped fighting to watch as the *Majestic* turned turtle and sank beneath the waves, some men even jumped out of their trenches to watch the spectacle.

With the deteriorating situation in the Mediterranean and the western desert, Admiral Peirse decided that he must have regular naval patrols running along the Egyptian coast to stem the Senussi's supply of munitions and also to try and locate a suspected secret fuel dump for submarines thought by both the British and Italians to be located somewhere along the coast. To this end, on 27th May, he acquired the use of the Royal Indian Marine's troopship *Dufferin* to patrol the Gulf of Sollum. On 4th June, she was relieved by the old cruiser HMS *Philomel* which had been taken from the Red Sea patrol and returned to Alexandria for replenishment. These two vessels would now be employed patrolling to and from Sollum. On 29th June, seemingly disregarding Admiral Peirse wishes, the Italian armed yacht *Misurata*[5] reported that she had searched the coast from Tobruk to Sollum for the fuel dump but found nothing. On 9th July the *Philomel* was ordered to Aden, leaving *Dufferin* to patrol alone. On 23rd July, the old Eclipse second-class cruiser HMS *Diana* arrived at Port Said from Devonport en route to India. Admiral Peirse's request that she be attached for a time to the Sollum Patrol was granted, and the next day she was ordered to make for Alexandria where she

5. Ex British Armed Yacht *Arrow* commissioned into the Italian Navy, 5th September 1912.

and the *Dufferin* would form a continuous patrol from Alexandria to Sollum, i.e. one would be on patrol whilst the other would be in port taking aboard bunkers, water and stores. These ships were also charged with preventing the landing of arms and ammunition, and supporting the Sollum garrison in case of attack. In this they were to be assisted by two Egyptian coastguard cruisers, the *Reschid* and *Abbas,* which in reality were small gunboats. The following day, *Dufferin* broke down and had to make for Alexandria for repairs. HMS *Diana* hurriedly took on board bunkers, water and stores and set off on patrol where she was told to remain until relieved by the Armed Boarding Steamer *Scotia* on 14th August.[6]

On 3rd August, the Admiralty received a notification from the Italian Navy that an attempt would shortly be made to smuggle arms and ammunition in steamships from Syria to Cyrenaica, and requesting assistance from the British to find and stop them. Admiral Peirse had also learned of this, but his information was more specific and stated that two Greek ships were to sail from the Aegean to land Turkish officers and munitions for an attack on either Sollum, Barrani or Matruh – with the help of the Senussi. A disturbing feature of this report was that the ships would be escorted by submarines which could play havoc amongst the transports entering and leaving Alexandria and Port Said, and with the fighting that was then taking place in Gallipoli, transport traffic was extremely heavy on that route too. Peirse asked the Admiralty for destroyers to escort the transports but they declined, stating that there were no suitable vessels available, pointing out that British waters were being stripped down to a dangerous level to try and supply enough vessels for other theatres. But, they did however direct Admiral de Robeck, C-in-C Eastern Mediterranean, to detach two of his B Class submarines, with an armed boarding steamer to act as their parent ship, to Alexandria if he could spare them. The submarines, they suggested could be stationed off Sollum to surprise the Greek steamers should they arrive, whilst

6. On 18th June the *Scotia* arrived at Holyhead and next day commenced discharging coal. She was dry docked on the 20th, and by the morning of 2nd July all underwater work had been completed, the dock flooded and she was hauled out to lay alongside the refit berth at the Marine Yard workshops. Work continued on her for a few more days, during which time three men were paid off and three signed on. She took on stores, spares, coal and water before departing for Devonport where, after topping up her bunkers and taking on fresh water, she left on 19th July, escorting HMS *Aquarius* (an ex-water tanker converted to a submarine depot ship) to Port Said where they arrived on 5th August. Leaving her charge, she steamed for Alexandria where she joined her patrol mate, the MFA *Heroic* (see footnote on page 81) for service with the Coast of Egypt patrol (and where on the 11th she sent one RNR stoker to HMS *Diana* for detention in her cells). Each vessel was to spend one week at sea and one week in port. HMS *Scotia* began her first patrol on 14th August, and a week later was relieved by the *Heroic*. She then proceeded to Alexandria for coal, water and stores.

the ABS should be kept out of sight. Consequently, on 13th August the ABS HMS *Heroic,*[7] and the submarines B.6 and B.11, were despatched to Alexandria and next day sent on to Sollum. The *Scotia,* which had arrived in Alexandria two days previously, left for Sollum on the 14th. The cruiser HMS *Minerva,* which had arrived at Alexandria on the 10th from Tenedos, also left for Sollum on the 15th, and it was she and not *Scotia* that was to relieve *Diana* as Senior Naval Officer patrol. On the 16th, *Minerva* dropped anchor at Sollum and sent provisions and a Maxim machine gun and crew ashore to bolster the defences. She would maintain the patrol with the *Heroic* and *Scotia,* and would call at Sollum at least once, sometimes twice a day, to ascertain that all was well and to send more provisions ashore. On the 23rd August she was relieved by the *Dufferin.*

With the arrival of all these vessels the situation had much improved, but the Admiralty was not happy with Admiral Peirse for sending large vessels such as the *Diana, Dufferin* and *Minerva* to Sollum as, owing to the large exposed bay there, they could quite easily become targets for submarines. Shortly after this, the service of these three vessels was cancelled, HMS *Diana,* returning to Alexandria for replenishment prior to proceeding to India as per her original instructions.

This left the coast of Egypt patrol to *Scotia, Heroic* and her two submarines, and it was felt that their presence was enough to deter the landing of arms, ammunition, etc and, should the Senussi attack Sollum, they also had the capacity to evacuate the garrison.

However, it was not long before *Heroic's* submarines were deemed unsuitable, as they had low speed, no deck armament and a small radius of operation; they also had numerous defects and were in need of docking. At the end of August, Admiral Peirse recommended their removal, the Admiralty hearing of this then ordered the *Heroic* back to Admiral de Robeck in the eastern Mediterranean. Peirse then pointed out that, if the *Heroic* left, then the patrol would be down to one ship. The Admiralty then asked the military whether the Sollum garrison could be strengthened to resist an attack until a vessel could be sent from Alexandria to evacuate the post (as they were unwilling to have a vessel permanently anchored off Sollum should the garrison need evacuating). Peirse responded by pointing out that the strengthening of the post might be seen by the

7. SS *Heroic,* a steam packet of the Belfast Steam Ship Co Ltd, had met the *Hibernia/Tara* in August 1914 when she was one of the vessels engaged in carrying troops from Queenstown to Holyhead. After her requisitioning on 18th November 1914, she had been attached to the West Coast of Ireland patrol, which was the patrol area next to that of the *Tara.*

Senussi as a hostile act and precipitate an attack. He therefore asked for another Armed Boarding Steamer, so that the patrol would have two vessels, one on the Gulf of Sollum patrol which would call daily at Sollum to ascertain that all was well, while the other was being replenished in Alexandria. In the meantime, he informed the Admiralty that he was strengthening the patrol with one Egyptian coastguard vessel, the *Abdul Moniem,* and the armed yacht *Drama* – pointing out that neither had sea keeping qualities for working far from base, nor the carrying capacity should the Sollum garrison have to be evacuated. They would therefore only operate as far as Mersa Matruh.

This it seems convinced the Admiralty of the necessity of sending out another Armed Boarding Steamer and on 13th September they informed Peirse that '... *Tara* will be sent out. You should endeavour to make her and the *Scotia* suffice as *Tara* is the last one available!' However, just before *Tara* arrived, the *Heroic* broke down and had been replaced by HMS *Lunka* (British India Steam Navigation Co Ltd), an Armed Boarding Steamer from the heavily stretched Red Sea patrol.

On 7th May 1915, the RMS *Lusitania* was sunk by the *U-20* (*Kapitänleutnant* Walther Schwieger) off the Old Head of Kinsale, Ireland, with the loss of 1,198 lives, many of whom were women and children, and amongst whom were 124 American citizens. Whilst the number of casualties appalled the Allied and neutral nations, it also caused the German government to fear that the killing of so many Americans would draw her into the war on the side of the Allies. Whilst the diplomatic row raged on and the question of whether the German government should rein in the U boats now successfully operating around Britain and in the Western Approaches, the Imperial German Navy's HQ in Berlin was receiving reports from the Mediterranean of the successes of the *U-21* and pleas for larger submarines to be sent there so as to maintain pressure on the Allies by attacking shipping on the Gibraltar to Alexandria and Port Said (for Suez Canal transit) shipping lanes, and the transports to and from the Dardanelles. They would also be able to help transport munitions to the Senussi. It was decided to send two more submarines, under experienced commanders to join the *U-21*. The Imperial German Navy's high command also felt that, as most of the vessels these submarines would be encountering would be Allied, there would be less likelihood of them sinking ships carrying American civilians.

Consequently, on 4th August, the *U-34* (*Kapitänleutnant* Claus Rücker) and *U-35* (*Kapitänleutnant* Waldemar Kophamel) left the heavily-fortified naval base on the island of Heligoland and nosed out into the North Sea, on passage to the Austrian naval base at Cattaro in the Adriatic, travelling around the Orkneys and far to the west of Ireland. Due to the secrecy of their mission, they had also been instructed not to attack shipping south of the latitude of the English Channel. After an uneventful passage they reached Cattaro on 23rd August.

Following a few days' rest for the crews, and with all defects experienced and discovered during the voyage made good by the dockyard staff, both boats were refuelled and sent out on their first patrol in the Mediterranean. During the first three weeks of September, they sank five vessels off the coast of Crete.

On 5th October 1915, *Tara*, newly-painted and carrying victualling stores for three months, engine-room stores for two months, and boiler and machinery spares for herself and HMS *Scotia*, left Holyhead. The crowds of people that were there to see her off did not realise that they would never see her again and that it would be some six months before the lucky ones amongst the crew would see their families and friends again. Just before she sailed, one of the crew had sneaked a black cat aboard. He was given the name Tom and by all accounts was a large, gaunt-looking animal, but extremely well behaved. On her way to the Mediterranean, *Tara* called at Devonport where she topped up her coal and fresh water and took on board two new crew members, Warrant Engineer James Hutton, RNR (who held a First Engineer's Certificate of Competency), and Stoker John McNee, RNR. Hutton, a survivor of the old battleship *Majestic* which had been sunk off Gallipoli on 27th May, became *Tara*'s second engineer, taking over from Second Engineer Richard Phillips who reverted in rank to third engineer.

Some three days later, *Tara* arrived on the 7th she sailed, and four days later arrived at Gibraltar and from where, fully bunkered and watered and the crew having had some shore leave, she set sail for Valletta, Malta. After an uneventful passage through the western Mediterranean, she arrived in Grand Harbour where she bunkered. took on water and supplies. The crew were given shore leave, but just prior to departure, Tom the cat jumped overboard and made for shore – a bad omen for the superstitious. A boat was hurriedly lowered and he was caught and brought back. Once on board, he was confined in a hen coop until the ship was well out to sea.

On 21st October, the *Tara* steamed into Alexandria harbour and tied up to N°· 1 buoy close to the *Scotia* which had arrived from patrol at 07.45 hours that morning. As *Tara* entered the harbour the decks of both Holyhead vessels were lined with their crews shouting and waving to each other. But, being wartime, there was no time for joviality and boats were quickly lowered and the transfer of stores commenced. Some men did take a chance and went to see their friends and relatives. Most got away with it although Sub Lieutenant Ifor Jones of the *Scotia* was caught and severely reprimanded by the captain, Commander Dawson, and his name entered in the log 'for improperly leaving the *Scotia* and proceeding to the *Tara* at noon.' As soon as the stores had been transhipped and stowed, shore leave was granted for the off-duty watch of the *Scotia* – from 13.30 hours to 21.30 hours – and no doubt shore leave of a similar nature was granted to the off-duty watch of the *Tara*. The men of both ships went into the city for a bit of sightseeing, a few drinks and to catch up on the latest news of home.

For Captain Gwatkin-Williams, however, it was a different matter. After the *Tara* had tied up to the buoy and whilst the discharging of stores commenced and the coaling and watering barges came alongside, he took a boat ashore and reported to the Senior Naval Officer (SNO) Alexandria. He was informed that he was to be SNO North (West) Coast of Egypt Patrol and that he would be working in the British-controlled Patrol Area X, an area bounded by a horizontal line running eastwards from the southern coast of Crete to the Island of Rhodes, southwards to El Arish on the Palestinian coast, westwards along the Egyptian coast to Ras El Tyn on the Cyrenaican coast and northwards until it reached the coast of Crete. *Tara* was to patrol the area's southern boundary, the coastal inlets, bays and waters of the Egyptian and Cyrenaica coast. Gwatkin-Williams was further informed that the Italians, who had declared war on the Turks on 21st August, would be patrolling Area XI, the coastal region of Tripoli in the Gulf of Sidra and adjacent to *Tara*'s patrol area and that it was known that arms and ammunition for the Senussi were being landed in these inlets and coves.

# 7. Sollum Patrol

The Libyan–Egyptian border ran into the Gulf of Sollum where, on the eastern side, was located the small Egyptian border town of Sollum which was ringed by 600-feet-high cliffs upon which sat a Turkish-built fort. Although this fort was occupied by a small detachment of the Egyptian Army in 1915, the heights were occupied by the Senussi. Down below, between the cliffs and the sea, was an Egyptian Coastguard barracks which housed a small garrison consisting of Lieutenant-Colonel Snow, Captain Richard Bazley White, Captain Leopold Royle and a detachment of the Coastguard Camel Corps, most of whom were Sudanese. Accommodated in tents on the beach was a small number of convicts who were used as labourers. In all, there were some 100 men, whose situation was described as precarious as, although the British were at peace with the Senussi, some of the latter, perhaps reacting to the urging of the Turks, had recently started to act aggressively.

On 16th August, the Senussi sniped at the two British submarines and on the night of the 28th about 100 of them took up positions only a few yards from Sollum fort.[1] Whilst others lined the cliffs surrounding the town, some came through the British lines and then refused to go back, and a number of armed soldiers marched into Sollum where they remained until early the next morning. It seemed that an attack on Sollum was imminent. As the nearest railhead to Alexandria was some 180 miles away at al Dab'aa and the Khedival road (in reality more of a rough track running from the railhead past Sollum in the

1. On 16th August the British submarines *B11* and *B6* whilst lying off Ras Lik (Ras Lakk or Cap Luc, north of Port Bardia) noticed a white officer (Dr Otto Mannesmann, see footnote on page 91) ashore waving a white flag, Lieutenant Holbrook, VC, *B11's* commander, ordered the submarine's collapsible boat to be sent ashore. Half way there some Arabs appeared and opened fire, killing one engine room artificer (George Kirman) and wounding an able seaman. The submarines returned fire, killing or wounding an unknown number Arabs or Senussi. This incident could have precipitated matters on the western border, but Colonel Snow managed to calm the situation. However, the Grand Senussi did remark that 'You know that we have posts all along the coast since the beginning of the war with Italy, and that Italian battleships often cruise off the coast and fire on our troops, and it was for this reason that I gave strict orders to all officers commanding the west coast to fire on the ships before they could do our men harm. It was not possible for our men to know they were British.' Presumably the British were well aware of the Grand Senussi's instructions and perhaps this is why a Foreign Office official called the affair an act of naval stupidity.

*Sollum from seaward, the Coastguard barracks can be seen on the shore, whilst directly above, on the cliff top, Sollum fort can just be made out [Author]*

direction of Tobruk) was thought to be so rough that it was unsuited for transport vehicles, instructions were issued to the patrolling ships instructing them to call at Sollum at least once a day as the garrison might require a speedy evacuation in the event of a Senussi attack.

Further concerns were raised on the day of *Tara*'s arrival, which was the start of the Moslem festival of Kourban Bairam which would last until the 27th October. Snow thought that this might be the time when the Senussi would launch an attack upon the town and requested the SNO Alexandria to have one patrol vessel standing by off Sollum during the seven days.

On the 23rd *Tara,* fully stored, coaled and watered, had set out on her first patrol. She carried two additional crew members, an interpreter named Vasili Lambriadis (later to be nicknamed Basil by the crew) and Paddy, a mongrel dog about the size of a fox terrier. Lambriadis was a Syrian Greek who was fluent in English, Arabic, Turkish and a smattering of French, who had been employed to question the captains and crews of the vessels that the *Tara* would be stopping in her searches for gun-runners and smugglers who it was thought were trying to get supplies through to the Senussi. Paddy had been spotted by some of the crew swimming in Alexandria harbour and was rescued and became the ship's mascot. It was thought that his previous owner may have been an Arab who had treated

*The 'adopted' dog, Paddy.*

him cruelly and had thrown him into the harbour to drown as, whenever he was approached by an Arab, perhaps remembering his treatment by his first owner, he would snap and bark, thus making him very useful as a gangway watchman.

On the 24th, just to the west of Sidi Barani, *Tara* met her new patrol mate HMS *Lunka,* (Lieutenant R W White, RNR) whose services Vice-Admiral Peirse had managed to retain. As the two ships closed, additional lookouts were posted around both ships and, once it was decided that there were no U-boats in sight, both vessels stopped, a boat was quickly lowered and at 10.46 hours Lieutenant White stepped aboard the *Tara* to meet Captain Gwatkin-Williams. Both vessels then forged ahead until, after about half-an-hour's talk, they again closed and White returned to the *Lunka,* and both vessels resumed their patrols. *Tara* stopped and boarded a handful of dhows and caciques belonging to Greek sponge fishermen who were questioned by Basil. Finding no contraband, they were then allowed to proceed.

That night, at 22.46 hours, *Lunka* called at Sollum and, finding all was well, proceeded to patrol slowly up and down the bay. Next morning at first light, on being assured that all was still well ashore she proceeded out to sea. At 06.10 hours, she exchanged signals with the Italian armed yacht *Misurata.*[2] At 08.10 hours, she received a signal from HMS *Tara* which informed her that the *Scotia* would be relieving her later that day. At 1.40 hours *Lunka* called *Tara* to say that she had seen the *Scotia* steaming westward towards Sollum and therefore she was now heading for Alexandria for coal and water.

Reacting to Snow's request, the SNO Alexandria had ordered the *Scotia* to move on 23rd October to commence coaling. The following day, the ship was

*HMS* Lunka *at anchor in Alexandria [Imperial War Museum]*

washed down and at 16.00 hours set course for Sollum arriving there at 17.00 hours on the 25th. Commander Dawson immediately proceeded ashore to speak to Snow and, on returning to the ship at 18.45 hours, moved her out to sea and remained standing off Sollum at a distance of about two miles for the rest of the night. Dawson ordered lifeboats 1, 3, 4 and 8 to be lowered, instructed the bridge watch to keep a good eye on Sollum should they signal to be evacuated, and made ready to sail at a moment's notice.

At 05.50 hours after a quiet night, and after being assured that all was well ashore, *Scotia* got under way and proceeded out to patrol in Sollum Bay. At 10.05 hours *Tara* appeared and both vessels came together and the two captains met aboard the latter. Knowing that the *Scotia* was scheduled to leave for a refit at Port Said, Gwatkin-Williams asked if she could continue to patrol in Sollum Bay for the afternoon whilst *Tara* patrolled out to sea until the evening to which Dawson agreed. At 16.00 hours Dawson was rowed ashore to see Snow and, on his return to the *Scotia* at 18.00 hours, receiving a signal to say that *Tara* was on her way back to Sollum, he set sail for Port Said.[2] At 12.10 hours on 28th October *Lunka* left Alexandria harbour and relieved *Tara* in Sollum Bay at 07.00 hours the following morning. *Tara* then returned to Alexandria for stores, coal, water and a boiler clean.

At 06.00 hrs on 3rd November, *Tara* left Alexandria on her second patrol. Her lifeboats, fully watered and provisioned, were swung out in case of submarine attack as was standard practice. At 18.30 hours she received a message from the old light cruiser HMS *Proserpine* (guard ship, Port Said and flagship of Vice-Admiral Peirse) reporting submarine activity on the routes to the north and west of Sollum. This message had also been sent to the patrolling *Lunka* who had also been told to intercept four Admiralty trawlers which were escorting a collier, the SS *Rosalie,* from Malta to Alexandria and warn them of the danger. In the meantime, if she heard of any submarine attacks, she could commandeer some or all of the trawlers to search for the enemy vessel. A few hours later, she intercepted the convoy and warned the trawlers to keep a good look out before continuing with her patrol.

At 01.45 hours on 4th November, *Lunka's* look-outs reported the *Tara* coming up astern. White ordered a reduction of speed as both ships closed and Gwatkin-

2. Where she arrived on 28th October and, in addition to a refit, was also to have her three 6-lb guns replaced by a single 12-lb mounted aft. After the refit she was sent to join the Red Sea patrol where she arrived on 2nd December.

*Thought to be the last photograph taken of HMS* Tara, *on patrol in the Mediterranean [IWM/Sub Lt Marsh]*

Williams signalled that he was relieving the *Lunka* and that the latter was to return to Alexandria but, on her way back, she was to divert to a given position to the north-east to investigate a reported submarine attack on an unknown merchant vessel. At 02.15 hours the *Lunka,* wishing the *Tara* good luck, steamed off at full speed to investigate but, finding nothing in the reported position, altered course and made for Alexandria where she arrived without incident the following morning.

Meanwhile, the *Tara* had continued to her designated patrol area and then turned around and headed for Sollum where she arrived at 19.00 hours. Gwatkin-Williams made his way ashore where he was handed a telegram received at Sollum from Alexandria informing him of further submarine activity in the area. After a brief chat with Snow, who assured him that all was well, he returned aboard. The *Tara* then up anchored and left at 20.00 hours. Once at sea he radioed the *Lunka* to acknowledge receipt of the telegram. This was the last message received from HMS *Tara.*

# 8. Attack

On 12th October 1915, the *U-35* left Cattaro for a patrol in the Salonika[1] transport routes. On the 18th, she sank the Italian cargo vessel *Scilla,* and five days later the SS *Marquette* which had been carrying the 26th Divisional Ammunition Column and the New Zealand Stationary Hospital, the personnel of which numbered 36 nurses, 22 officers and 588 other ranks. She sank with the loss of 167 lives and 541 animals.

From then on chances of a sinking became fairly sparse as the British authorities, knowing that a U-boat was operating in the area, ordered all transports to sail at night. The nights, however, were moonlit which made the chances of a sinking even less for the prowling U-boat, so she was eventually diverted to the Gulf of Xeros where the Germans had a listening station. On the 25th, the U-boat's commander, the newly-promoted *Korvettenkapitän* Waldemar Kophamel, received instructions to proceed to Orak Island, near Bodrum on the Turkish coast where he was to embark military officers and munitions to Port Bardia in Cyrenaica.[2] This was nominally an Italian possession but, thanks to their successes since August 1914, had come under the control of the Senussi.

*U-35* arrived at Orak Island on 31st October and loading commenced almost immediately. By the time she left the following night, she was carrying some 300,000 cartridges, 80 belts of machine-gun ammunition, 120,000 Turkish Francs, ten Turkish officers. She was also towing two sailing vessels which were loaded with a further 300,000 cartridges and 120 Turkish soldiers.

Although the weather was fair, the tow line broke four times during the night

1. In September, German and Austro-Hungarian forces started to mass on Serbia's borders in an attempt to finally crush her and allow direct rail communications between Germany and Constantinople. As a result, Britain and France began to transfer troops from the Gallipoli peninsula in October to Salonika in support of Serbia. Their efforts were, however, too late as on the 7th November the Germans and Austrians launched their attacks on Serbia from the north, and four days later the Bulgarians attacked from the east and south east. As a consequence of these events, the Allied shipping routes to Salonika from Gallipoli, Alexandria and Marseilles were attracting the attention of German and Austrian U-boats.
2. Ex-Port Suliman. This was later renamed Port Bardia, which is the name used throughout this narrative. It has since been renamed Bardiyah.

*The* U-35 *at Cattaro*

and the convoy could only make some five knots. By noon the next day, the wind had picked up and the tows were slipped. Later, the wind dropped and the *U-35* returned and picked up the tow of one of the vessels. By nightfall, they had reached the shipping lanes and, as the wind again picked up, it was decided that the sailing vessels could proceed alone. On the morning of 3rd November, *U-35* came across the SS *Woolwich* which was carrying phosphates from Safaga Island, Egypt to Plymouth and stopped her, ordering the crew into their boats before Kophamel ordered her to be sunk by gunfire. Later during the same day, she attacked the SS *Japanese Prince* which was carrying troops to Salonika but, after a four-hour chase, the ship managed to escape and the *U-35*[3] then returned to her course and arrived at Port Bardia the next day. The crew were much relieved the cases and crates stacked aboard had made movement difficult, added to which most of the Turkish officers had been seasick and the stench intermingled with the smell of diesel and the heat had made the voyage most uncomfortable.

As the submarine neared the cove, the Turkish flag was fixed to the retracted periscope which was then raised and the crew was welcomed by a committee of Turkish officers and soldiers, some Muhafizia and Dr Otto Mannesmann.[4]

The Germans were surprised to learn that there were no unloading facilities, so the U-boat closed to the shore, dropped anchor and unshipped her collapsible boat. Rope pulleys were rigged between the U-boat and the shore and the boat

3. For their work in outrunning the *U-35* both Captain A H Jenkins and Chief Engineer C James of the *Japanese Prince* were mentioned in despatches.
4. Dr Otto Mannesmann, a German national, came from a family of wealthy industrialists with considerable business interests in the French colony of Morocco. Since 1906, he had been a considerable thorn in the French government's side. To the dismay of the French, the Mannesmanns had befriended

*Korvettenkapitän*
Waldemar Kophamel

connected to the rope. The crates were then manhandled into the boat which was then hauled ashore. The whole operation took five hours.

Whilst the German sailors had been rigging up the unloading gear, Turkish and Senussi sentries had been stationed on the rocks and high points around the cove. After the unloading had been completed, sometime during mid-afternoon, one of the sentries thought he saw something on the horizon and raised the alarm. The gear and collapsible boat were hastily stowed and the U-boat went astern out of the cove. Turning she went out to sea but discovered there was no ship in sight. Kophamel then conducted a trial dive and a few other tests to prove *U-35's* seaworthiness. Satisfied, he returned and dropped anchor just off the cove.

Whilst the unloading had been going on one of the Turkish officers (or possibly Otto Mannesmann) had mentioned that there were two Egyptian Coastguard cruisers, the *Abbas* (built in 1891, of 298 tons, 1 x 3lb gun) and the *Nurh el Bahr* (built in 1884, 450 tons, 1 x 3lb gun) at anchor off Sollum. Mulling this over, Kophamel decided to attack the town the next morning.

Shortly after dawn the *U-35* headed towards Sollum. Once out to sea she dived and, as she closed the bay, the periscope was raised. Both Coastguard cruisers could clearly be seen riding at anchor close to the shore, totally unaware

a Moroccan rebel leader who later became Sultan and, once in power, granted the family very lucrative mining contracts which caused uproar amongst the international community. On the outbreak of war, although a reserve officer in the Ulhans, Otto was referred to the Foreign Ministry as an expert in North African affairs and transferred to their Tripoli consulate with a brief to subvert French influence in their colonies in North Africa and to win over the Senussi. In September, he had written to the Grand Senussi urging him to attack Egypt. In December he had leaflets printed urging the Senussi and the tribes in Cyrenaica to attack the British in Egypt. Some of these fell into the hands of the Italians who demanded his recall to Germany and, although they had no wish to antagonise the Italians who were then neutral, the Germans refused. In March 1915, the Italians seized a shipment of arms, hidden aboard a ship in Venice, that was destined for the Senussi, organised by Mannesmann. The Italians were outraged and this time Mannesmann was recalled. After a few weeks in Germany he travelled to Libya, posing as a salesman, and was smuggled into Cyrenaica via Crete where he was received by the Grand Senussi. He made his camp on the coast, just to the north west of the Senussi's camp at Sollum, where he was less likely to be spotted by the agents of Colonel Snow and Captain Royle. Here he continued to urge the Grand Senussi to attack Egypt and organised supplies for them using German and Austrian U-boats instead of the small steamers and sailing vessels which the smugglers had been using to break the blockade.

of the U-boat's presence. Kophamel had thought of attacking using torpedoes, but the bay was too shallow and, not knowing the shore defences, he felt they could be in danger if he surfaced to shell the vessels. Considering what to do, he ordered the *U-35* to turn around and head out to sea. At 09.00 hours he ordered her to the surface. As soon as she broke the surface, the lookouts rushed up onto the conning tower and began to scan the horizon. There, to the north-east, they could just make out a two-funnelled steamer coming towards them. Kophamel hurriedly ordered all hands down below and the *U-35* submerged to periscope depth and waited. The steamer was HMS *Tara* returning to Sollum for her daily visit, approaching from the north-east, not zigzagging, but pushing her way through the water on a steady course at 7–7½ knots, her shafts turning at 60 rpm.

The sun was already high in the sky and beaming down upon a blue ocean. Those officers and engineers who were off watch were starting to gather at the tables and chairs under the awnings on the awning deck to read, smoke and chat. To southwards, some eight miles away, Observation Point on the north side of Sollum Bay could be seen rearing out of the water and already some of the men were making their way to the handrails trying to be the first to spot the sea bottom through forty fathoms of crystal-clear water.

Ordinary Telegraphist George Tanner was on watch in the W/T Room, whilst Yeoman Signaller Allen, making his way up to the bridge, stopped and had a chat with the lower bridge lookouts Seaman William Gunn and Signal Boy Raymond Fulcher . On reaching the bridge he picked up a telescope and had a good look around. To starboard the coastline did not look inviting, with brown cliffs rising up from the shore and a drab and featureless plain with the low hills of the desert in the far distance. To seaward there was nothing but blue sea. Putting the telescope down he went back over to the port side. Suddenly there was a shout from the masthead look-out, William H Parry, which made everyone look up. They could see him pointing over to starboard. Tables and chairs were thrown aside as everyone rushed to the starboard side where they saw the unmistakable white wake of a single torpedo, some 300 yards away, as it streaked towards their ship. Everyone scattered away from the starboard side and Captain Gwatkin-Williams, trying to give those men in their cabin's a chance to come up on deck, just had time to shout 'Away all boats' before the torpedo struck. He looked down at his watch — the time was 10.10 hours and the ship's position was 31° 30'N, 23° 29'E.

On hearing the lookout, Sub-Lieutenant Albert Marsh, who was on the bridge, immediately ordered Quartermaster Richard Williams to put the helm over to hard a port and rang down a double 'Full Ahead' (Emergency Full Speed) on the telegraphs. But it was too late. Due to the *Tara's* slow speed she was sluggish in answering the helm and the torpedo slammed into the starboard side at the after end of the engine room. The ship shuddered as it exploded deep inside her, the explosion throwing up a great black column of water, containing coal, dust, oil and all sorts of rubbish which burst through the starboard deck, smashing into the firemen's accommodation, killing three men. It brought down the main and auxiliary wireless aerials and left a hole in the deck and a larger hole in the ship's side. It had also collapsed the stairway down to the steerage accommodation and blown off all the engine and boiler-room vents and had probably smashed the starboard main engine as well as the starboard dynamo or the switchboard situated above it as electrical power was lost instantaneously. The *Tara,* however, despite being mortally wounded, still kept on going ahead.

After the explosion, Lieutenant Tanner had run up to the bridge to ring down 'Stop' on the telegraphs, but received no answer so went over to the engine-room voice pipe to order the engineers to stop the engines and come up on deck. Receiving no reply to his whistle, he placed his ear to the trumpet but all he could make out was the gurgling and sloshing sound of water and surmised that all in the space had been killed – Warrant Engineer J Hutton, Assistant Engineer G H Roberts, Acting Leading Stoker Thomas Jones and Greaser John Jones. Those in the stokeholds were luckier as, having separate stokeholds which were separate from the engine room, they had been shielded from the blast and resultant flooding and were now making their way up the stokehold ladders and out onto the deck. But they had not drawn the fires, nor shut the main stops as steam was still being fed to the port engine.

As the crew made for the port-side lifeboats, some men launched the N°. 5 boat, the third boat from forward on the starboard side. Containing eight men it hit the water but, unfortunately, the combination of the *Tara*'s speed and port list – having recovered from the force of the explosion and inrush of water, she was now coming back upright before settling – resulted in the boat being upended and slammed against the ship's side before it could be unhooked from the falls. Consequently all eight men were tipped into the water with one man suffering a broken arm and another a broken leg.

As the crew had been making their way to the lifeboats Leading Seaman Millward had ordered the gun crews to their posts on the awning deck. Whilst waiting patiently by their guns they suddenly saw a feather of water from the U-boat's periscope which was poking out of the sea some 500 yards off the starboard side. The starboard forward gun opened fire at the periscope which, after the eighth shot had landed fairly close to it, disappeared. It had not been an easy target considering the *Tara* was still moving ahead, sinking slowly by the stern, and listing to port.

Meanwhile, three of the port-side boats N[os] 2, 4 and 6 had been lowered. Sub Lieutenant Marsh, noticing that there was no officer in N[o.] 2 boat, climbed in and took command. Although the boat was packed, he ordered it lowered, expecting at any moment the falls to snap or the boat itself to break. However, it reached the water safely where the after falls were let go and, with a great deal of difficulty, the forward falls were unhooked. The N[o.] 6 boat was manned and lowered, but, as it was to have been cleaned that morning, was missing its oars and bung, and in consequence started to fill as soon as it landed in the water. A rag was found and jammed into the hole and a pair of oars was handed over from another boat.

As for the men of the 00.00–04.00 and 04.00–08.00 hours watches who at that time of day were mostly in their beds, Leading Stokers William Jones and Robert Phillips had been killed instantly. Their cabin, sited on the starboard side directly above the after end of the engine room, had taken the full force of the blast. Also killed instantly was the third engineer, Assistant Engineer Phillips who, due to the additional officers and engineers appointed, had elected to take a cabin on the main deck, aft of the stokers' accommodation on the starboard side. He was up and about and had popped into his cabin shortly before the torpedo struck and was there when it was totally destroyed by the explosion. Sub Lieutenant Griffiths had been woken, just before 10.00 hours by the steward bringing his breakfast tray. As he sat up in bed with the tray on his knees he heard a terrific thud and felt the ship shuddering from stem to stern. The impact threw the tray off his knees, upset the teapot and scalded his leg. Having a good idea that the ship had been struck by a torpedo, he leapt out of bed and made a grab for a pair of trousers, missed and ran out of the cabin, across the deck, and jumped into the sea naked! Assistant Engineer Davies, the sixth engineer, had also been in bed at the time of the explosion. He got out of bed and went out on to the starboard side of the boat-deck. Noticing that there was nobody about and at least one lifeboat missing he went round to the port side where there was a hive of activity, with men jumping overboard and others putting on life jackets.

Of the three port-side lifeboats which had been lowered, two were already standing off and pulling men out of the water. Davies climbed down into the third, the N$^{o.}$ 6 boat, which was still alongside but which shortly afterwards pulled clear and went off to rescue a fireman who had fallen into the water. Fireman John Jones had run up on deck from his cabin, clad in his pyjamas and clutching a coat. Fireman Owen Gray had been lying on his bunk, clad only in his shirt, but had also run up on deck, not even bothering to look for a pair of trousers. Fireman William Andrews, who had been on watch in the boiler room, ran up the ladders and simply jumped over the side clad in his shirt and dungarees. Quartermaster William Rowlands, who had been on the 04.00–08.00 hours watch had just finished shaving in the seamen's washroom and toilets when he heard a 'terrific explosion' and had hurried up on deck to discover the ship sinking fast. He rushed down to his cabin for his life jacket then went up to the bridge to join the gun crews but was not required, so helped lower one of the port boats. He then slid down one of the falls into the boat, somehow receiving a cut to his head as he did so. Fireman John Parry had leapt out of his bed and had also reached the deck but decided to return to his cabin to collect some clothes. He was last seen in the cabin by another fireman, Owen Pritchard, who was making for the deck and had tried to dissuade him but without success. The deck boy, William Jones, later recounted that he had jumped from the awning deck into a lifeboat and on landing had immediately been felled by a punch from a seaman who told him never to jump into a lifeboat wearing his heavy boots as he could well have gone through the hull or at least damaged the planking.

By now the engineers had managed to shut off steam to the *Tara*'s engines using the remote stops. Those left on board consisted of Captain Gwatkin-Williams, Lieutenants Tanner, Birkby and Neill, the W/T operators who (now that the W/T was useless) had joined the gun crews standing by their guns. Ordinary Telegraphist Tanner had placed all the confidential papers, signals and code books, into a weighted steel box and it being so heavy, was calmly rolling it with his foot across the deck to dump over the ship side. Assistant Paymaster Dutton came up on deck and reported to the captain that he had destroyed the contents of the ship's safe and that when he left his office the water was already up to his knees. Seeing as it was fairly quiet, Captain Gwatkin-Williams took the opportunity to go to his cabin to collect his money, knowing full well that the Royal Navy would compensate him for the loss of his clothes and equipment, but not his money! As he stepped back out on deck, a dull thud and rumble came from down below; probably the engine room bulkhead giving way. The *Tara*'s bow then rose alarmingly into the air and she started to slide backwards faster and faster under the waves, forcing a great wall of water to sweep up the awning deck from aft, bringing with it all sorts of debris. For those left on board it was now a case of every man for himself, and all were either washed or threw themselves over the ship's side. Gwatkin-Williams ran to the ladder leading down onto the foredeck but was hit from behind by the wall of water and debris. With the *Tara* sliding rapidly under the sea he tried to dive overboard but was dragged back aboard by the suction and found himself trapped under the forecastle awning, going down deeper and deeper. Fighting furiously he managed to escape and shot towards the surface, all the while being buffeted by pieces of wreckage that had broken loose from the wreck. Finally breaking surface amidst the heaving and churning water, coughing and spluttering, he swam to a nearby life-raft. Then he swam to, and clambered aboard the keel of an upturned lifeboat, from where he surveyed the scene. He had lost his cap, was bleeding from his nose and had suffered a nasty knock to his leg. He looked at his watch it was 10.18 hours. It had only taken eight minutes for the *Tara* to sink. Fireman John Parry had not been so lucky and never managed to regain the deck. Although he was spotted by a number of the crew waving from the porthole of his cabin as *Tara* slid under the waves, it was assumed that the sudden force of the water sweeping into the ship had trapped him in his cabin. It was a sight which Fireman Hugh Jones never forgot.

After she had disappeared, the surface of the sea was covered with a dirty, black brown film of oil containing coal dust, bits of wood, rags, life-rafts and wreckage of every description. Every now and then the surface would be disturbed as planks and other light bits of wreckage came hurtling up from the depths, their momentum causing them to be driven out of the water. Also on the surface floated hundreds of life jackets, a left over from her passenger carrying days, and ominously, surfacing some two miles astern was the U-boat. As the survivors looked they could see men appearing on her conning tower and the German flag being raised on a small mast. More men could be seen climbing down to man the 88 mm gun on the fore deck which they trained onto the lifeboats. The U-boat moved slowly directly towards the lifeboats, ignoring those men in the water, whom she left for the lifeboats to pick up.

Captain Gwatkin-Williams could see the men swimming and floating in the water, most in their life jackets, some clinging to wreckage, some supporting those that could not swim, whilst others who had been injured were calling out for help. Close by floated the body of the cook, Walter Jackson, still in his cork life jacket. It was later discovered that Cooke the electrician had come across Jackson on the awning deck and, finding that he had suffered a nasty wound to the shoulder, had helped him with his life jacket, but owing to the *Tara*'s sudden sinking the men had become separated. All three boats continued picking up as many survivors as they could, Sub Lieutenant Marsh's boat picked up seven men from the overturned N°. 5 boat but Seaman James McKinven was missing. He had last been seen in the boat by Ordinary Telegraphist Tanner and, as he was known to have been a non swimmer, it was assumed that he had drowned. Another man, Stoker John McNee, had a broken arm, but for some time had managed to support the clerk, William Manning, another non swimmer, until they were both picked up. Also pulled out of the water was Quartermaster William Thomas, who was found to have a broken tibia. Although the boat already contained some forty-five men, Quartermasterss Rowlands and Williams and Surgeon Probationer Arthur pulled Jackson's body into the boat and tried to revive him and dress his wound. It was, however, hopeless; he was dead and although the boat was overcrowded space was found for his body.

After all the survivor's had been pulled out of the water and transferred from various rafts into the lifeboats, Gwatkin-Williams found himself in the same lifeboat as Lieutenant Tanner who had also been dragged down by the sinking *Tara* before popping to the surface close to where Paddy, the ship's dog, was swimming. Tanner had lifted the dog out of the water and placed him onto a piece of wreckage and from where he was later rescued by one of the lifeboats. As the boats came together the captain ordered them all to make for Sollum, but the *U-35's* commander had other ideas. He decided to rescue the survivors himself and hand them over to the Turks or Senussi at Port Bardia.[5]

It seems that Kophamel was convinced that his attack on the *Tara* had either been spotted from Observation Point, or the torpedo's explosion had been heard in Sollum. He later wrote in the *U-35's* log that he was surprised that no attempt had been made to rescue the British crew from Sollum, 'Therefore they shall have

5. Why did all the survivors have to be taken to Bardia as prisoners of war? True it was normal procedure during the 1914-18 war for a U-boat having sunk an Allied ship to take her Captain and Chief Engineer prisoners but all the survivors, in this case 92 men? During this patrol Kophamel sank many ships but left their survivors to their fate, as he did to others of the vessels he sank throughout his wartime career. Had he acted rashly in torpedoing the Tara so close to Port Bardia, which was only some 16 miles north(by land) of Sollum? There is no doubt that on landing at Sollum the survivors would inform the authorities of the U-boats attack, and although the British

to be delivered to Bardia as prisoners of war.'

The U-boat closed onto the lifeboats and ordered them alongside. After ensuring that there were no other survivors in the water they did as they were bid. Seeing as the boats were low in the water, one of the U-boat's officers ordered some of the men out of each boat onto the after casing. In all forty-nine crewmen climbed onto the U-boat's casing under the watchful eyes of the Germans, most of whom were armed with pistols. One ordered Allen, the yeoman signaller, to hand over his hat band which bore the name HMS *Tara*. Allen later speculated that it was it to be used by the commander as evidence to confirm the sinking. Whilst they had been clambering onto the deck, some of the U-boat's crew were making the lifeboats fast astern, and it was only once the survivors got aboard the submarine that they discovered she was the *U-35*. Thinking that the U-boat was going to tow the lifeboats towards Sollum, and knowing there were two Egyptian Coastguard cruisers at anchor in the bay, the Captain thanked Kophamel but declined the offer explaining that they could easily row the eight miles to Sollum, knowing full well that if Kophamel did spot the cruisers he would more than likely sink them. Kophamel replied that he was not going to tow them to Sollum, but to Port Bardia and that they were to be made prisoners of war.

As the two commanders talked, all three lifeboats were secured astern. Sub Lieutenant Marsh remained in the No. 2 boat to steer her; with him in the boat were Quartermaster William Jones and the body of Jackson. Meanwhile the U-boat had turned and was now gathering speed and heading north-westwards, her crew keeping an eye on the prisoners as well as scanning the horizon in every direction with their binoculars. As she ploughed her way through the water the Germans chatted with the survivors and gave them water (which tasted of diesel), biscuits and cigarettes. For the injured, they gave bandages and disinfectant and for the naked Griffiths they found an old pair of trousers. A pair of trousers was also found for Birkby who had jumped over the side in his pyjamas and whilst in the water had lost his pyjama bottoms.

After half an hour or so the *U-35* slowed down and turned towards land. As they neared the shore they could make out a small, land-locked bay or cove

did know that munitions were being landed on the coast, did they realise they were being landed by submarine so close to Sollum, practically under their very noses? Realising that a U-boat was operating in the vicinity may have compelled the British to patrol the local coastline rigorously, both by sea and land and they could well have discovered Port Bardia and the munitions landed yesterday. Because of his precipitous attack it seems Kophamel had no choice but to take the survivors to Port Bardia and hand them over to the Turks?

surrounded by rocks and boulders. The German flag was lowered and a Turkish flag was fixed to the top of the periscope which was then extended to its full height. Kophamel then shouted down to the prisoners on the deck that they were now prisoners of His Majesty the Sultan of Turkey. He ordered his crew to let go the life boats and told his prisoners to remain where they were whilst he took the *U-35* into the cove. Suddenly, on the rocks close by the mouth of the bay, men appeared, Otto Mannesmann and some Turkish officers (one of whom turned out to be General Nuri Bey, C-in-C of the Senussi's Army and a half brother of Enver Pasha, Turkey's Minister of War), some Turkish soldiers and a number of Senussi Muhafizia. A total of some forty men.

Kophamel ordered the submarine's collapsible boat to be unshipped and was then rowed ashore to discuss the prisoner's fate with Nuri Bey and Otto Mannesmann. After some twenty minutes he returned and informed Gwatkin-Williams that the crew were now prisoners of the Turkish Army but that he was personally to be taken back to the *U-35's* base at Cattaro where he would be made a prisoner of the Austrians. The captain pleaded to be allowed to remain with his men and Kophamel relented. Whilst the two captains had been talking, *Tara*'s lifeboats had been ordered alongside and those men on her casing were ordered into them, but before leaving most were given a cigarette or two, a drink of water or a biscuit by the submarine's crew.

Once in the lifeboats they were told to row towards land, not onto the beach but alongside some rocks, where they were ordered out of the boats and clambered ashore under the watchful eyes of the Turks and the Senussi. Most of the survivors were half clothed and those without shoes or boots cut their feet on the barnacle encrusted rocks. They carried Quartermaster William Thomas on a makeshift stretcher, made from the lifeboat's sail, whilst the body of Walter Jackson was carried on a stretcher made of the lifeboat's oars. Once clear of the rocks, they carried on for about 400 yards into a bare ravine at the head of the bay. There they sat in a miserable huddle in the sand under the blazing sun, surrounded by Senussi guards, all well armed with modern rifles and who stood or squatted on the rocks and cliffs above the ravine. Any movement by the survivors brought a threat and a levelled rifle.

Whilst the crew were being marched up the ravine, some of the Turkish officers decided to take a look around the submarine. Marsh was asked to steer one of the lifeboats whilst the Turkish officers rowed it to the *U-35*. Amongst the officers were General Nuri Bey, Otto Mannesmann and Major Jemal Bey. Marsh later recounted that he had his work cut out as they had no idea of how to row and were continually 'catching crabs.' Meanwhile Gwatkin-Williams, who was still aboard the submarine, was in conversation with Kophamel and, after finishing off a hot meal in the lee of the conning tower, came ashore at about 15.00 hours. Once he had re-joined the men in the ravine a roll was called and it was discovered that there were 92 survivors, with one man dead and eleven missing. William Thomas had a broken right leg broken and severe lacerations around the break; Stoker McNee had a simple break of his left arm and a bad gash on his left hand; H O Hughes had a rupture; Richard Lewis had injured his stomach having collided with the gangway as he abandoned ship; Allen, the yeoman signaller, had gone deaf as a result of an old injury being aggravated by his recent immersion in the sea, and there were numerous men with minor cuts, bumps and bruises.

Shortly before 16.00 hours, as the survivors were coming to terms with their predicament, the Turkish officers (apart from Major Jemal Bey who was to be taken to Cattaro) came ashore, the submarine started her engines and, going astern, manoeuvred slowly out of the cove. On turning, she did not head for the open sea but headed south and dived. She was making for Sollum where, on arrival, she surfaced and stood off in the bay and at 17.15 hours opened fire with her deck gun. She fired about fifty rounds at the Coastguards barracks and the town, sank the Egyptian Coastguard cruiser *Abbas* at her moorings and severely damaged the *Nuhr-el-Bhar*. Surprisingly, there were no casualties ashore or on either of the two cruisers. At 18.00 hours, with darkness descending and satisfied with his work, Kophamel ordered the gun to cease fire and the *U-35* headed out to sea to resume her patrol.

The following day, the U-35 sank the *Caria* (3,032 tons), the *Clan MacAlister* (4,835 tons) and the *Umina* (6,218). In the early morning of the 7th, Kophamel spotted the Indian Transport *Moorina* and made preparations to attack.

# 9. IGT H4 – SS *Moorina*

The Indian Government Transport *Moorina* had been built in 1906 by Actien Gesellschaft Weser of Bremen, as the *Thuringen,* one of the Franks Class of six ships built between 1905–07 for Nord Deutscher Lloyd's Europe–Australia trade.

On 30th June 1914 she had left Hamburg for Bremen and Antwerp before heading out on another Australian trip, intending to call at Fremantle, Melbourne and Sydney. All proceeded smoothly until the early hours of 29th August when some ten miles south-west of Rottnest Island, near Fremantle, the cruiser HMS *Pioneer* appeared out of the night, fired two shots across her bow, and signalled her to stop. As she came to a stop an armed party rowed over, forced their way aboard and made for the bridge and engine room. The German captain and his crew were outraged as they had been unaware of the outbreak of war as the *Thuringen* was not equipped with wireless. Once she had been secured, she was escorted into Fremantle where her officers and crew were taken off and sent under an armed guard to an internment camp in Rottnest Island.[1] The *Thuringen* then lay alongside until the prize courts decided on her and her cargo's fate. As legal proceedings went ahead, a decision was taken to load the *Thuringen,* and her sister ship the *Griefswald,* which had been seized at Fremantle on 6th August 1914, with the cargoes from other captured enemy vessels now lying in Fremantle for shipping to their consignees in the eastern ports of Australia. Accordingly, a crew of forty (British and Australians) was ordered for 8th October, their captain was a forty-nine-year-old Londoner, Thomas Ernest Cutler. On 16th October 1914, fully crewed and loaded, she left Fremantle, calling at Adelaide, Melbourne and Sydney, before arriving at Brisbane on 18th November. By 12th December she had returned to Sydney and had commenced loading for Calcutta. A few weeks later, the legal niceties of the prize courts having been observed, she was placed on the British register with a new name, SS *Moorina* (a town some one hundred

1. This camp, which held over 1,000 inmates, was made up of crews of interned enemy vessels and foreign nationals. It was shut in late 1915 and the inmates transferred to the Garden Island Internment Camp, Western Australian and finally to Holesworthy Camp, near Liverpool on the outskirts of Sydney, New South Wales.

*The SS* Moorina *(formerly* Thuringen, *photographed in 1906) [Author]*

miles NNW of Brisbane), given the official number 139026 and her port of registry as London. Her managers were to be Burns, Philp & Co of 7 Bridge St, Sydney, New South Wales with the Commonwealth government acting as her agents.[2]

Whilst under the Indian marine, she would retain her British and Australian officers and engineers, but her crew would be replaced by Indians – Hindu or Muslim seamen and firemen, with Goanese cooks and stewards.[3] From this time on the *Moorina* was employed transporting horses and stores from India to the Red Sea, Persian Gulf and the southern ports of France. Although she did return to Fremantle on 2nd May 1915, possibly for a crew change (as it is known that Captain Cutler and some of his officers were relieved), she left Fremantle on the 4th heading for Marseilles.

For her last voyage she was under the command of another Londoner, Captain Harry Septimus Seale and sailed from Bombay on 26th October 1915, carrying 106 officers and crew, with Captain Blayney S Hickey of the Remounts Department, Indian Army, Lieutenant Thomas Seth Apcar of the 32nd Indian Lancers and a

2. In some publications the *Moorina* is shown as coming under the Commonwealth Government Line of Steamers, but this shipping company was not formed until 1916. On arrival in Calcutta she was handed over to the Indian Government and came under the Royal Indian Marine for use as a mercantile transport, and given the number H2. Her sister ship, the *Lotheringen,* was seized at Melbourne and also become an Indian Government transport (number H1).
3. From the Portugese colony of Goa, where a sizable proportion of the population was Catholic and therefore had no objection to handling beef or pork – cattle being sacred to the Hindus and the pig unclean to the Muslims. This manning arrangement was common practice amongst those shipping companies which carried European officers and Indian crew.

Captain Harry Seale

Subadar Major of the Jodhpur Lancers,[4] 54 sowar's (lancers) and eight followers, grooms, etc and 548 horses.

Leaving Suez on 5th November, she passed through the canal, stopping briefly at Port Said to drop the pilot, before increasing speed to 'Full Away' and heading out into the Mediterranean. At 11.30 hours on the 7th, when about 600 miles west of Alexandria and 100 miles off the coast of Tripoli, the lookout reported that a submarine was astern, chasing her. Word quickly spread throughout the ship and Captain Seale ordered the officer of the watch, the third officer, to call Chief Officer Coalstead. He then asked the engine room for more speed, the boats to be swung out and made ready for lowering. Some thirty minutes later the U-35, now well within range, fired three shells as a signal for her to stop. Captain Seale, deciding that discretion was the better part of valour, ordered 'Stop' to be rung on the telegraphs then 'Finished with Engines', the signal for everybody to come up on deck. He then ordered the boats to be manned and lowered. The U-boat came alongside and informed the captain that they had twenty minutes to evacuate the ship. This gave enough time for most to gather warm clothing and, in the case of Lieutenant Apcar and Second Engineer Richardson, to pack and bring a suitcase each.

All the boats were lowered, although the N° 1 lifeboat's forward fall was let go precipitously, causing the boat to land awkwardly in the water and be smashed against the ship's side. The five other boats landed safely and were either pulled or drifted clear of the *Moorina*. Once all the boats were clear, the U-boat then closed onto the ship and fired 6–10 shells into the hull, close to the waterline. No doubt a few exploded within the holds, amongst the horses, causing a terrible carnage.

The *Moorina* rolled over to starboard and, with steam escaping out of the engine room, sank stern first. As she slipped under the waves, the men in the lifeboats could clearly hear the screams of the wounded and terrified horses. Chief Officer Coalsted went on to say, 'We watched our fine ship disappear with 548 lovely horses. It made me sick to think of the dumb, faithful creatures'. She sank about twenty-five minutes after the first shell had struck and, surprisingly,

4. Another source has it that he was Subadar Major Lunt of the 18th King George's Own Lancers.

considering the accident that occurred when launching the N° 1 lifeboat, all of the crew and troops managed to get away safely in the five lifeboats. After she had disappeared, all that was left on the surface of the sea were a few pieces of wood, some rags and papers, and two hen coops. The lifeboats then closed onto each other and all agreed to keep together for as long as possible and to head for the nearest land, Tripoli, which they knew to be under Italian control and therefore friendly territory. There was also the chance of being picked up by a passing ship as they crossed the trade routes from Malta to Alexandria.

Whilst the boats were together the chance was taken to redistribute their passengers evenly; the Chief Officer's boat taking ten men from another but later, finding that it had become overloaded, a head count revealed that it was carrying forty men (Chief Officer Coalsted, Second Engineer Richardson, Lieutenant Apcar, the subadar major, twelve sowars, the eight syces and grooms, a mess room boy (possibly A F Rodrigues), eleven Indian firemen and trimmers and four Indian seamen).

Whilst the survivors were busy sorting themselves out, the U-boat motored over and *Korvettenkapitän* Waldemar Kophamel, leaning out of the conning tower, shouted down to the captain asking for the ship's papers. On being told that they had gone down with the ship, he then asked for the name of the ship and what she had been carrying. The information was given and the U-boat then motored off without further contact and, surprisingly, bearing in mind the fate of the *Tara*'s crew, without taking any prisoners. Chief Officer Coalsted later remarked that Kophamel spoke very good English but with an American accent.[5]

In all boats sail was hoisted and a southerly course for Tripoli was steered, a steady north-westerly breeze sprang up and the boats made good headway under canvas. But, due to it being over loaded, Coalsted's boat soon found that it was lagging behind, although all the boats were now slowly but surely becoming separated. At about 20.00 hours a steamer's masthead lights were sighted and as she neared they could make out she was a hospital ship bound west. Hopes were raised immediately, but although all the lifeboats were burning blue lights, showing distress signals and were only a few miles away from the hospital ship, she maintained her course and eventually disappeared over the horizon.

5. U-35 eventually arrived back at Cattaro on the 12th having sunk a total of twelve ships on this patrol, totalling approximately 48,813 tons.

Coalsted's boat made good progress throughout the night and by next morning the low lying hills of Tripoli could just be made out on the horizon. All day they pressed on and at 16.50 hours, as they were nearing land, the Chief Officer saw in the distance the N° 4 boat, under the command of Second Officer A J Creer,[6] and did think of trying to sail towards him or attract his attention. However, seeing that Lieutenant Apcar, who had been very ill before leaving the ship, and who after a day and night in the lifeboat had become much worse, was almost helpless, he decided to land before dark and continued towards land without attempting to contact the other boat.

As they neared the beach, Coalsted found that, with the heavy sea running, landing would prove to be very dangerous and decided to lay off for the night. A watch was posted, but there was no sign of life along the shore until about 21.00 hours when two lights were spotted, possibly Bedouin campfires. Not knowing if they were friendly, Coalsted thought it prudent to remain at sea. At 03.00 hours, as light was breaking they tacked and stood towards the shore, but the breeze had dropped and they did not land till noon. As the boat reached the shore they were immediately met by a party of five armed Arabs, dressed in various items of Italian uniform and accoutrements, and who covered the men in the lifeboat with rifles.

The leader, who was dressed in an Italian officer's uniform, stepped forward and took Lieutenant Apacar's revolver before informing them that they had landed in a little bay called Defni, some thirty miles to the west of Sollum. Glad to be ashore and being very thirsty, they asked the Arabs for water and were taken to a well about a mile off. But, before leaving, three or four sowars were ordered to stand guard over the boat and its contents, and told that what water was left in the boat they could drink. At the well the rest of the survivors drank their fill before being marched about two miles to an Arab camp of three tents where they were given some boiled rice. After their meal, the Arab in the Italian officer's uniform informed them that they would have to go on to another camp where they would meet the commandant. They marched a further four miles over some very rough country until, at about 18.30 hours, they met the commandant on a very rough track. He turned out to be a Turkish Army officer

6. Alfred Joseph Creer had been born in Sydney, New South Wales on 11th November 1894. Although an Australian, he had been brought up on the west coast of Canada and had sat and passed his 2nd Officers Certificate of Competency on the 24th February 1914. Returning to Australia he found employment with the Union Steam Ship Company of New Zealand. After the *Moorina* incident he sailed with various Australian and New Zealand shipping companies.

who informed them that they were now prisoners of war. This came as a complete shock as up until now they had assumed that they were with pro Italian Arabs.

The commandant led them to his camp which seemed to consist of one large mud brick hut, two smaller ones and some tents and the three Europeans were separated from the Indians who were herded into the large hut under an armed guard. The Europeans were shown to a small tent, close to another which held some wireless apparatus. But, before they could settle down, the commandant invited them to his tent where he made some tea. As they drank, he informed them that they were lucky that the officer had been there when they landed as they could easily have been shot by the Arabs for what little valuables they carried, be it money or clothes. A little while later, the sowars who had been left to guard the lifeboat, arrived at the camp. They had been unarmed and, as time went on, had become apprehensive of the armed Arabs wandering about and so had abandoned the boat. They brought with them the three officer's overcoats, but had left behind the two suitcases belonging to Apcar and Richardson, which contained some very much needed underclothing.

Over the next seven days the Europeans and Indians were allowed to wander around the camp unhindered, allowed to mix freely and were fed regularly with rice and water. On 15th November, Coalstead, Richardson and Apcar, along with Rodrigues the Goanese mess boy, were informed that they were to be sent to a camp for Europeans. During the late afternoon or early evening the four men spotted a long column of prisoners in the distance making their way westwards. A short while later a party of guards came over and their leader ordered the four men to hand over all their valuables, including their pocket knives. The four men said their goodbye's to the commandant and Indians, then set off with their guards through the canyons and dried waterways to meet the marching column, whom they assumed would be their ex-shipmates.[7]

Of the *Moorina's* other lifeboats, N° 4, which was under the command of

7. The Indians remained at the camp for about a month and were then taken to Sollum, which by now was full of well armed Senussi with modern rifles and bandoliers of cartridges strapped across their chests. After five days the troops were separated from the Lascars and instructed to lead camels laden with stores of biscuits, barley, rice, etc eastwards. They were now part of a Senussi army of some 2,000 Arabs with three machine guns and 800 camels. After marching in the desert for eight days they encountered the British on 25th December and during the confusion of the Battle of Wadi Majid the Subadar told his men to slip off to the British lines in three's and fours which they did, apart from seven Sowar's and five followers.

Second Officer A J Creer, contained Third Engineer Frank Gradwell, Fourth Engineer J Webster, Captain B S Hickey, three Indian soldiers and thirty-six lascars. Soon after hoisting the sail and steering southwards for Tripoli they rummaged around in the lockers and discovered that they had thirty-six biscuits and twelve gallons of water. Creer immediately imposed a strict regime of rationing and a one-inch mark was made in a tobacco tin which was then used as a measure for the water doled out each day to every man on board. After three days, owing to their suffering, the ration was increased to two inches per man per day.

For two days all the boats had managed to keep more or less together, but after a stormy night they had become separated. On the third day Creer discovered they were alone with three broken and three sound oars. However, at 10.00 hours, land was sighted and as they closed the shore they could make out someone on the beach waving to them, so they turned and headed towards the figure. As they neared the shore, several shots rang out but, thanks to a favourable wind, they managed to quickly turn the boat around and take her straight out to sea, but not before the hull had been holed in about three or four places and the sail peppered.

The next day, the boat was becalmed all that day and night and, as they lay off the shore, they could see many Bedouin camp fires burning all along the coast. They looked very inviting, but remembering their experiences of the previous day, they remained at sea, keeping well off shore whilst creeping steadily eastwards. That night they passed Sollum and on the morning of the 11th they were spotted and picked up by the Egyptian Coastguard cruiser *Reschid* which then made for Matruh with the lifeboat in tow. Gradwell stated afterwards that 'owing to the sun's rays by day and intense cold at night, whilst only half clad many of the men were in a terrible state.' But, once aboard the *Reschid*, and 'after a whiskey and soda, three eggs and some bread and butter, life took on a cheerful aspect.'

On arrival at Mersa Matruh, the survivors were landed and taken to the quarters of the Emergency Squadron of the RNACD[8] in the Coastguard Station where the RNAS men did all they could for them, including providing a meal of bully beef, and biscuits. The lascars and sowars, being Hindu, politely refused the bully and contented themselves with rice and flour (from which they made

8. At this time armoured cars came under the Royal Navy's Royal Naval Armoured Car Division, whose personnel was drawn from the Royal Naval Air Service/Royal Navy Volunteer Reserve.

unleavened bread). The officers, however, ate both bully and biscuits and after an enormous meal recounted their story to their hosts and disclosed that they had kept a log of the voyage in the second officer's discharge book and that on the fourth day they had all signed their names in the book for identification in case of death.

Later, the survivors were driven in motor cars across one hundred miles of desert to the El Dabaa railhead where they entrained for Port Said. There Creer, Webster and Gradwell embarked on the P&O steamer *Arabia*, arriving in Sydney, Australia on 24th December 1915 after a very uneventful voyage.

Of the other three lifeboats, two had landed on the coast near Baq Baq, where both boats and survivors were taken to Sollum. The Italian armed yacht *Miserata*, whilst on patrol, came across the third lifeboat and took the survivors on board before landing them at Sollum. On the 11th, Alexandria despatched the Coastguard cruiser *Abdul Monyam* to Sollum and Mersa Matruh to pick up all the survivors, but owing to breakdowns and bad weather she did not arrive at Sollum for two days by which time Creer, Gradwell and Webster had left Mersa Matruh for El Dabaa by car. The *Abdul Monyam* returned to Alexandria the following day.

# 10. Search

Meanwhile at Alexandria, throughout 5th November, Admiral Peirse had been receiving increasing reports of submarine activity but it was not until the mid-afternoon of the next day that news was received from Sollum of the U-boat's attack and the failure of the *Tara* to make her daily visit. The delay in receiving the messages had been due to the Senussi who had cut the telegraph line during the *U-35's* attack and was not discovered until Colonel Snow tried to inform Alexandria after the submarine had departed. He sent an Egyptian linesman to find and repair the break but in the evening gloom he had been waylaid by a party of Muhafizia and assaulted. On his return to Sollum, Snow was informed that the Senussi had deliberately cut the wire and, fearing that the conflict had already started, sent a letter to the Grand Senussi, who next morning replied with a conciliatory note, regretting the assault on the repair man and explaining that he would send armed men to guard the line. From the tone of the note, Snow could only hope that the Senussi were still neutral.

In Alexandria the news of the attack and the cutting of the telegraph line was received with some alarm and apprehension about the *Tara*'s safety. It was known that her W/T set did not have the necessary range to reach Alexandria without a linking ship or station and the SNO immediately ordered the *Lunka* to raise steam and proceed to Sollum. After taking on coal and water she cast off at 15.54 hours and made her way out to sea. Once clear of the harbour she went to 'Full Away.' At 23.45 hours she came across two lifeboats full of men and hauled them aboard. Fifteen minutes later she came across another lifeboat and took those men on board also. In all she had rescued thirty-two men, all survivors of the SS *Woolwich* (Watts, Watts and Co), which had been sunk by the *U-35* three days earlier.

At 13.30 hours on 7th November, as *Lunka* was approaching Sollum, the crew were ordered to their action stations. As she neared the harbour they could see the damaged *Nuhr-el-Bhar* and the masts and upper works of the sunken *Abbas*. Coming to a stop, she dropped anchor and lowered a boat. Lieutenant White, with an armed party, was rowed ashore where he met Colonel Snow who gave

*HMS* Prosperine

him of the latest information which he had received from his agents in the Senussi camp. Returning to the *Lunka,* White radioed his report to Port Said (HMS *Proserpine* having been sent to dry dock, Admiral Peirse had moved his flag to HMS *Minerva* in Port Said), stating that the *Tara* had been attacked and sunk on the 5th by two submarines, one large and one small. The survivors, some seventy in number had been landed at Morraisa by the *U-35* and that Colonel Snow had already been in touch with the Grand Senussi concerning the whereabouts of the survivors. The latter had denied all knowledge of them, although he did say he would make inquiries as to their whereabouts.

Port Said, knowing of the openness of the bay and the danger of lurking U-boats (and believing that there were at least six U-boats operating around Sollum) cancelled all sailings of unarmed or unescorted transports carrying troops from Egypt to Salonika and, fearing for the *Lunka's* safety, ordered her to return immediately. At 15.30 hours she up anchored and arrived at Alexandria at 12.05 hours on the 7th where White reported that the *Lunka's* speed had been seriously compromised in that they could not make more than twelve knots without a boiler clean. Seeing that the situation in Sollum was relatively quiet, and that submarine activity had now diminished, Admiral Peirse gave his permission for the *Lunka* to be attended to and, whilst she was laid up, ordered the sloop HMS *Jonquil* (Lieutenant the Hon G Fraser, RN), which based at Milo in Crete, working under the French, and eleven trawlers, to patrol the Alexandria–Salonika transport routes. He later contacted his army counterpart and after meeting they decided that from their meagre resources they could despatch to Sollum, two 9-cm Egyptian

Army Krupp field guns and their teams, so as to counter gunfire should another submarine attack from seaward. Also, the Emergency Squadron[1] of armoured cars was despatched to establish land communications with Sollum. Two W/T cars were to be despatched, one to Sollum and one to Sidi Barani, so that Alexandria could maintain W/T communications with the Sollum garrison should the telegraph line be cut again. The SNO ordered additional armament to be fitted to the two remaining Egyptian Customs cruisers, a 12-pounder was to be fitted to the *Abdul Moniem* (which was already armed with one 3-pounder), and another 12-pounder was to be fitted to the *Reschid* (which was already armed with two 6-pounders). Once these modifications had been carried out, the *Reschid* would proceed to Sollum and remain on stand by in the bay should the Senussi attack and the garrison require evacuation. These instructions were to be implemented immediately. Consequently, at midnight, the Emergency Squadron, comprising of six Rolls-Royce armoured cars, eight Ford Model T tenders, two Talbot staff cars and two Wolesley W/T cars, along with sixty-two men under Lieutenant Commander Lister, RNVR, left their camp at Sidi Gabes, Alexandria heading for Gabarry Station where in a siding the cars were loaded onto wagons and the men directed into a filthy truck. They had been informed that they were heading to El Dabaa and were to patrol in the western desert so as to prevent Arabs cutting the telegraph lines from Sollum. Peirse also asked the French destroyer *Jannissaire*, which had arrived at Alexandria on the 9th, escorting a transport, to call at Sollum on her way back to her patrol area. Her commander acquiesced and after coaling she duly arrived at Sollum on the 11th. On being assured that all was well, she remained for a few hours before steaming off.

During the early hours of 10th November HMS *Jonquil* closed onto the Cyrenaican coast to search for any sign of the missing *Tara*. At 07.55 hours she dropped anchor in Sollum harbour where a boat was sent ashore to try to obtain information from the garrison but it returned with no news. At 08.40 hours she weighed anchor and proceeded out to sea again and resumed the search, but again found nothing. Later that day, *Lunka*, her boiler clean completed, left Alexandria to resume her patrol duties, so *Jonquil*[2] was ordered to return to her patrol area off Crete. The same day, a report from the light cruiser *Minerva* at Port

1. The Emergency Squadron was the balance of Nos 3 and 4 Squadrons, Royal Naval Armoured Car Division, from which one section of each had been landed and were then serving in Gallipoli.
2. At 05.00 hrs on 11th November, *Jonquil* picked up thirty survivors, from two lifeboats, from the SS *Den of Crombie* (sunk by the *U-35* three days earlier). At 05.45 hours she stopped the SS *Caledonia* and transferred the survivors over to her, before making her way back to Crete.

Said to the Admiralty stated that 'Our agent's information is positive that they [*Tara*'s survivors] are somewhere on the coast, west of the [Egyptian] frontier. The Sheik el Senussi however states that he has no information about them, but whether the facts are being concealed from him by his followers, or whether he is deliberately deceiving us it is difficult to decide.'

By the 13th, the men and cars of the Emergency Squadron had been distributed between El Dabaa, Mersa Matruh, Sidi Barani and Sollum. Some cars had broken down, including one W/T car which had to be abandoned but not before its W/T equipment had been removed and set up in a wooden floored tent, on a small plateau close to the shore in Sollum. However, W/T communications were not perfect so a number of motorcycles had been issued to the squadron.

On the frontier, during the night of the 14/15th, two Egyptian Coastguard sentries were severely assaulted and their weapons stolen. Snow was informed by his agents that there were six U-boats operating in the vicinity which was backed up on the 15th by an Egyptian State Telegraph linesman who reported seeing a submarine off Sidi Barani, and three more were reported the following day. Shortly afterwards, a private in the Coastguard reported seeing another. These reports, however, were all untrue as since the 12th, when the *U-35* had returned to Cattaro, no U-boats had been operating off the Egyptian coast. On the 17th, a small party of Muhafizia fired into the camp at Sollum killing two friendly Bedouin and again cutting the coastal telegraph line. The following night the Zawieil (a religious school) at Sidi Barani some forty-eight miles east of Sollum was occupied by a force of 300 Muhafizia and on the 19th the Coastguard barracks at Sidi Barani was fired on, killing one coastguard and on the 20th an Egyptian post at Salil, some thirty miles to the south east of Sollum, was an attacked. After this last attack it was deemed that a state of war now existed between Britain and the Senussi.

Earlier that day, two 9-cms Krupp guns and six Egyptian gunners arrived via the *Reschid*. Chief Petty Officer C V Sharkey of the RNAS, one of the Emergency Squadron's detachment at Sollum, noting in his diary that it bore the date 1870 on its breech. Before nightfall, two Ford tenders and one motorcyclist arrived bringing a further six Egyptian gunners. That night, as the men of the Emergency Squadron lay in their overcoats on a hillside by their guns, they could hear singing and chanting coming from the Senussi camp. To some it reminded them of Gallipoli when the Turkish imams had called the faithful to prayer. The moon was bright and the men felt very exposed when, suddenly, a shot rang out, then another, and the Egyptian sentries fell back to their trenches and redoubts and all stood to. All then went quiet again and remained that way throughout the night, although they did receive news over the wireless that Sidi Barani was being heavily attacked and two armoured cars were at the gates firing into the Senussi.

At Sollum on the 21st November, Colonel Snow received a note on which was written the names of Captain Gwatkin-Williams and another man (the latter undecipherable). The Arab who had brought it stated that the prisoners were some two days march to the west of Sollum. This news was passed immediately to Alexandria and, during the early hours of the 22nd, Snow cabled Alexandria to state that, if he was not reinforced soon, Sollum would be lost. As Sollum was some 290 miles from Alexandria, Admiral Peirse decided that it was too far away to be used as a base for an expedition against the Senussi. The bay was open to submarine attack and there were no fast patrol craft to guard the transports which would have to be used. It was therefore decided to pull all outposts back to Mersa Matruh which, although some 120 miles east of Sollum, did have a natural harbour, was well supplied with fresh water and was within one night's journey, by sea from Alexandria. It was also some seventy-five miles from al'Dabaa, the railhead of the Khedival railway which ran from Alexandria and which could be used as a second line of communication. After discussion with the military, it was decided to start moving troops from Alexandria to Mersa Matruh on the night of the 24th using three trawlers which, after dropping off the troops, would continue on up to Sollum to evacuate the garrison there and bring them to Mersa Matruh. These instructions were cabled to Colonel Snow.

On the morning of 23rd November, the *Reschid* sailed into Sollum and Snow seized the opportunity to evacuate the garrison, fearing that to wait any longer would invite their capture or death. The garrison, consisting of Colonel's Snow and White, three British officers and twelve British other ranks of the Royal Naval Armoured Car Division, two Egyptian officers and ninety Egyptian other ranks, embarked on the *Reschid*, but prior to leaving they had to disable four Ford light cars, three Douglas motorcycles, as well as throwing the sights and breech blocks of the 9-cms Krupp guns into the sea. The wireless apparatus was dismantled and carried aboard, along with government papers, money, most of the ammunition from the arsenal and the machine guns, the latter being mounted at various points around the ship.

As the last man stepped aboard the *Reschid*, hundreds of Senussi swarmed down the hills brandishing their swords, shouting and firing their rifles into the air. They stopped a few refugees from getting to the Reschid, the governor's house was ransacked and the soldier's tents pulled down. Whilst all this mayhem was going on, Senussi horsemen galloped around and around whipping the civilians and striking the few remaining Egyptian soldiers who, Although cut off, were trying to reach the ship. Heavily laden and overcrowded the *Reschid* finally sailed at 14.30 hours towing behind her two of the *Moorina's* lifeboats as a precaution should she be torpedoed. As she steamed out of the bay, the men aboard could see that the hills around Sollum were covered with thousands of white figures.

Although the evacuation was successful there was one blemish on the whole operation, as they had left behind one Egyptian Coastguard officer and fourteen other ranks who had not received the order to get down to the beach and had been taken prisoners of war.[3]

The same day, the evacuation of Bagbag and Sidi Barani by land went off somewhat better. Both posts were stripped of anything that could be of value to the Senussi, Although four light cars had to be disabled before being abandoned at Barani. During the march to Mersa Matruh and after their arrival, there had been desertions to the Senussi from amongst the Egyptian Coastguard Camel Corps — a total of twelve officers, two cadets and 120 other ranks having made off with their arms, equipment and 176 camels.

For the *Reschid* the passage was uneventful. She hugged the coast for fear of a submarine attack and, as they sailed passed Sidi Barani at 22.00 hours, they could see the town was a mass of flames. At 07.00 hours they arrived and dropped anchor at Mersa Matruh.

3. Just after their capture, one of the Egyptian soldiers had tried to escape and was shot. A few hours later, the Grand Senussi freed the others and, two weeks later, one officer and thirteen men marched into the British camp at Mersah Matruh having walked across one hundred miles of desert.

# 11. Holyhead

Whilst the Royal Navy was desperately trying to discover the whereabouts of the survivors from the *Tara,* the news of the ship's failure to report at Sollum had been telegraphed to the Admiralty. But, after three days with no further news forthcoming, it seemed that the *Tara* and her crew had disappeared. A press release issued in London at 16.20 hours on Monday, 8th November stated that:

> On the 5th inst His Majesty's armed boarding steamer *Tara* ... was attacked by two enemy submarines in the Eastern Mediterranean, and sunk. Thirty four of the crew are reported missing.[1]

Rumours of the press release reached Holyhead during the evening and had spread throughout the town, and large numbers of people (one source had it that there were hundreds) flocked to the railway station to await the arrival of the last train so as to buy the late editions of the evening newspapers. Some of the papers speculated that the vessel that had been sunk had a tonnage of 6,322 tons, which led many to hope that it was not the *Tara*. Further uncertainty was generated next morning when the national newspapers recorded that there were two vessels named *Tara*; the first was HMS *Tara* (formerly the *Hibernia*) of 1,682 tons and the second, the SS *Tara* of 6,322 tons, built in 1902 for the British India Steam Navigation Co. and registered in Glasgow. A reporter for one of the local newspapers contacted the L&NWR's Marine Office at Holyhead and was told that. Although they had received no official news, they believed that it was indeed HMS *Tara* and not the SS *Tara* that had been sunk. Throughout Tuesday, the 9th, families and friends of the crew contacted the Marine Office and were all told the same thing, 'We have not heard anything officially though we are in communication with London.' What the relatives of the missing men were going

1. It is not at all certain from where the information about the two submarines had originated; perhaps it was pure conjecture on the Admiralty's part, believing that, after sinking the *Tara,* one submarine had discharged her cargo on the Cyrenican coast whilst the other shelled Sollum? The number of casualties is also a mystery; how did they know there were thirty-four — did the information come from Captain Royle's agents in the Senussi camp?

through can only be imagined Although for at least four Holyhead and one Scottish family, it must have been even worse as each had two family members missing. Later that evening, seemingly accepting that it was indeed HMS *Tara* which had been sunk, John Clay, vice chairman of the Holyhead Urban District Council, drew the council members' attention to the sinking and asked for a vote of sympathy for the families of those who had perished, even though a casualty list had not yet been produced. Over the next few days, the homes of the missing men were visited by representatives of the company, relatives, friends and the ministers of their local churches and chapels. Many of the local seamen and their families were regular church and chapel attendants and at least two crew members were deacons of local chapels. The following Sunday, the places of worship were packed with congregations in a sombre mood and many prayers were said for those who may have been killed and for the continuing safety of any survivors.

There was no relief when the *Holyhead Chronicle* was published on the Friday, reporting that, up until 18.30 hours of the 11th, there had been no further news of the thirty-four crewmen/casualties and that most of the people of Holyhead were reconciled to the fact that it was HMS *Tara* which had been sunk. The newspaper went on to say (inaccurately) that, as the *Tara* carried a crew of 109 (although the *Chronicle's* sister paper the *Holyhead Mail & Anglesey Herald* recorded the number as 111 – the *Tara,* for her last patrol, had carried 104 officers and crew), there were seventy-five survivors, all but one being from Holyhead and district, and that many of the crewmen's relatives had sent telegrams to the Admiralty asking for more information, but no further news had been forthcoming.

On Monday, the 15th, Holyhead suffered another body blow when news was received that the *Anglia,* the *Hibernia's* sister ship (which had been converted into a hospital ship), had struck a mine and sunk off Folkestone with the loss of 140 lives, 22 of whom were crew members from Holyhead. Due to her sinking in English waters and the almost immediate arrival home of the survivors, stories of her sinking and tales of the rescue would dominate the local newspapers for some time. The lack of news of the *Tara* and her crew ensured that only a paragraph here and there would appear in the papers for a while yet.

On 21st November, the Secretary of the Admiralty announced that, although they had no specific information any survivors from the *Tara,* it was believed that they had landed on the North African coast, somewhere beyond the Egyptian

*HMHS* Anglia
*[IWM]*

border and that '... every effort was being made to discover their whereabouts, and who the survivors were.' On the 26th, the Admiralty announced that some information had come to hand which indicated that Captain Gwatkin-Williams and Lieutenant Tanner and the other survivors had been seen at El Aziat, which was two days west of the Gulf of Sollum. Although they had no further specific news of any survivors, the local newspapers did try to put an optimistic slant onto what they knew, picking up on any rumours as was evident in 3rd December issue of the *Holyhead Mail & Anglesey Herald* in which the editorial stated that (thanks to the press release of 26th November), 'The safety of the survivors is not now in doubt' and a story in the same paper added that, 'as some persons were sailing along the N. African coast they met some members of the crew who stated that they belonged to Holyhead and that on reaching their destination these persons communicated the facts and afterwards went home'. To whom they reported the meeting, where the survivors were destined and where was home, the paper did not elaborate. It did, however, go on to say that 'the news had been bought in by native runners who were attached to a search party.' It added, perhaps to reassure its readers, that 'the survivors are able to survive in the desert by chiefly eating dates'.

# 12. In Captivity, November 1915

After the *Tara* survivors had clambered ashore after the ship's sinking, they sat around in little groups on the beach at Port Bardia, talking amongst themselves, all were unaware that the sinking of their ship, the refusal of the Senussi to hand them over to the British and the outbreak of violence over the next few weeks, would lead a state of war existing between the British Empire and the Senussi. Owing to the lack of trained troops in Egypt, the authorities had no alternative but to abandon their outposts on the Egyptian–Cyrenaica border and pull their forces back to Mersa Matruh, leaving the prisoners to their fate until sufficient troops became available to effect a rescue. The prisoners' lives then became a daily grind for existence which would last for four months.

*Friday, 5th November.* The ravine was found to be close and baking hot and those men who were almost naked soon found their skins starting to blister and burn so were given the odd garment from those that could spare them, and nearly all started to tear up their lifebelt's to make hats and sunshades. As the afternoon turned to early evening Captain Gwatkin-Williams, Lieutenant Tanner and Basil, the interpreter, began to talk to the Turkish officers whom they discovered could speak fluent French and had a smattering of English. They found that some had been prisoners during the Turko-Bulgarian war and were very sympathetic to the predicament of the survivors. Surgeon Lieutenant Arthur, attended to the wounded, the worst injuries being Quartermaster Thomas's broken leg, Stoker McNee's broken arm and Fireman Hugh Hughes's rupture. Unfortunately there had been no time for him to bring with him his medical equipment and supplies so there was little that he could do, although he did manage to fix splints onto Quartermaster Thomas's leg and Stoker McNee's broken arm. Later, some skins of water were handed around the men, but this was foul, yellow in colour and smelt awful — possibly because of the spices the Arabs had used to cure the goat skin's — and it 'oozed' out of the skins. Although most were desperately thirsty after their immersion in the sea, not many could bring themselves to drink the water. Each was also given one ship's biscuit which the Turks and Senussi had taken from the lifeboats prior to abandoning them on the beach. At about 20.00 hours, a goat was brought down for the survivors to eat but, not being butchers, they asked one of the Arabs to kill it, which he did by slowly sawing at it's neck with a blunt bayonet until it eventually drew blood and the animal bled to death. The goat was then butchered and some of the cuts placed on or near the fire, other pieces were put onto skewers, but after cooking all were found (by those who had the stomach to eat) to be either burnt or raw, and tough. Fortunately, most of the crew had also taken biscuits from the lifeboat's lockers which, added to the biscuits given to them by the Germans on the *U-boat,* lasted them until noon next day. They were also given two ragged tents which were quickly erected but were hopelessly inadequate to house the 92 men.

Before it became dark they returned to the beach and buried the body of the cook, Walter Jackson, Lieutenant Tanner reciting as much of the burial service as he could remember. After the service, a simple cross was made from a broken oar lashed together and placed at the grave's head and the whole covered with a cairn of rocks and stones so as to protect the body from wild animals. Surgeon Arthur, in conversation with Lieutenant Tanner, remarked that, although Jackson's wound would most probably have proved fatal, the cook had in fact drowned.

Afterwards Captain Gwatkin-Williams, Lieutenant Tanner and Basil, the interpreter, were invited to share General Nuri Bey's tent, where with the other two Turkish officers, Hunsi and Fevsi (one of whom had arrived on the *U-35*), they were given rice to eat and Tanner, having lost his shoes, was given a pair of Arab slippers. The captain later described the general as a dark-eyed, gentle-looking, slightly-built man, with a straggling black beard, an ardent antiquarian and naturalist who wanted to put the survivors to work excavating historical sites in the interior. He also recorded that the general was a noted revolver shot, which was possibly why he had survived so long amongst the Senussi.

Whilst the Gwatkin-Williams, Tanner and Basil slept comfortably in the general's tent, the officers and men had to make do with the two small ragged tents inside which the lucky few slept, whilst the others had to sleep outside and endure the cold, damp night air. But, being lightly clad, most were unable to sleep and what clothing they had left was shared; Sub Lieutenant Marsh gave his jacket and socks to the wireless operators Birkby and Neill, whilst he was left with his white shirt, trousers and shoes.

*Saturday, 6th November.* At first light the noise of the camels woke up those men that had managed to get some sleep; for the majority it had been a miserable night with fitful bouts of sleep. Those inside the tents, although warmer than those outside, soon discovered they were verminous and had spent the night itching and scratching. As the temperature dropped a fog had rolled in and those outside, having little or no clothing, had spent the night shivering in the cold and clammy night air.

Soon after dawn, warming fires were lit and the men gathered around them to warm themselves whilst water, a ship's biscuit and cooked rice were doled out. After breakfast they were ordered back down to the beach to haul the lifeboats out of sight to a pond or lagoon some fifty-yards inland. Two were successfully hauled to the lagoon but were damaged in the process, the bow planking having been pulled out of their prows. The third boat, the waterlogged N°. 6 boat, was left beached as it was now almost completely submerged. They then checked Jackson's grave which had been 'much disturbed' — by animals, or Arabs — and tided up and rebuilt the cairn before being ordered back to camp.

They later moved camp some two miles further up the ravine. Captain Gwatkin-Williams speculated that the removal of the boats and survivors from the cove had to be done as they might have been spotted by one of the patrolling Italian warships. He was informed that the Italians were not averse to firing a few shells at any caravans which they assumed would be more than likely carrying supplies for the Senussi. A few days previously thirty-five camels had been killed in this way.

Their new camp was close to what seemed to be a family farm where there were two water holes, a couple of pathetic fig trees and a strip of cultivated land, which led many to speculate how anybody could survive there. During the afternoon, as many men as wished were allowed to go back down to the beach for a swim under the watchful eyes of some armed guards.

Whilst the survivors had been busy with the lifeboats, swimming and changing camps, the Senussi had also been busy loading the camels with the munitions landed two days earlier. Once fully loaded the animals were then driven, snorting and protesting, along a precipitous track up side of the ravine, which was so steep in places, and their loads so heavy, that three fell over the edge and were killed. They were stripped of their loads, butchered and the cuts taken away for consumption by the Arabs. The *Tara's* survivors, although starving, could not stomach the thought of eating camel.

For their evening meal what little goat meat they had was roasted over an open fire but it kept falling off the skewers into the fire and when they tried to eat it they found it was tough and stringy and gave to the guards.

All the men's money and valuables were collected by the Turks — the total value was reckoned to be over £100. That night a Turkish doctor, Becki Faud, arrived in camp.

*Sunday, 7th November.* After another damp and uncomfortable night the survivors were warned that they were to be marched into the hinterland, some five miles north-westwards. After a breakfast of boiled rice they were given some sheets of paper and told to write letters to their families. They were promised these would be delivered to Sollum as soon as possible. Some of the seamen went down to the lifeboats and returned with a sail and a pair of oars which they used to make a stretcher for Quartermaster Thomas who was to be carried by those men who had been lucky enough to have kept their boots or shoes, there being sufficient to complete two carrying parties who would take it in turns.

The letters were then collected and the men told to form up in a column two deep, then ordered to march. After a time the column became stretched out over a considerable distance, with the guards leading, then came the men in ones and twos and finally the stretcher party bringing up the rear. They were never chivvied by the two Turkish soldiers who seem to appreciate their difficulties. During the day's march they had two stops at a couple of wells where, although the water was brackish and full of sediment, it did serve its purpose. Their route took them along the coast up and down the steep sides of two ravines that ran inland from the sea. Finally, after a last long climb of some 600 feet, they reached their new camp where they were met by Jaafar Pasha, whom they later learned was a general in the Turkish Army.

As they looked around they could see they were on a plateau which had, at its centre, a depression surrounded by a low, now ruined wall. To one side stood some more ruins whilst on the other, numerous depressions or holes had been gouged or eroded into the rocks, which led Gwatkin-Williams to speculate whether they were in fact sepulchers and the site a possible Roman graveyard, however three of these gouges turned out to be entrances to some small caves which they discovered were to be their new homes. The entrances to the caves were only large enough to allow one man to enter at a time and once inside it was discovered that the caves were interconnected and took on the qualities of a rabbit warren. They stank and were filthy from having housed animals for centuries. The caves could however only hold about forty men, so the rest would just have to try to sleep in the cold, damp night air. Gwatkin-Williams was later told the site had been an old Roman farm, which it may well have been, but the sailor's simply nicknamed it the Caves.

As Quartermaster Thomas was unable to get into the caves, a tent was rigged up for him, made of the sails and oars of his stretcher. Although this provided him with some shade, he was to suffer dreadfully during his stay at the camp, baking hot during the day and freezing cold at night.

The survivors were fed with rice, some cooked goat's meat and were also given some fetid water from the goat skins.

Whilst the men either slept in the caves or under the stars, the Gwatkin-Williams, Tanner and Basil slept comfortably in an army bell tent with the Turkish doctor, Becki Faud.

*Monday, 8th November.* Most men had only a fitful sleep; those in the caves had found the floor lumpy, hard and cold and there was no room to move. For those outside it was another cold, damp night. All hands were up at 05.30 hours and during the morning a caravan arrived carrying food and clothing and Arab shoes, linen shirts and trousers were issued to all. Some blankets, woollen bernouses (14ft long and 4ft wide) were also issued to all but fourteen men, and for every three men a rush mat was supplied for them to sleep on. On trying on the new clothes Sub Lieutenant Marsh remarked that they would have fitted an elephant! All were issued with metal spoons (on which most would engrave their names) and small glass tumblers, two cooking pans about the size of a small bath, five iron cooking pots and five enamelled basins for eating out of. For ease of cooking and feeding and so as to get the best out of these utensils, the officers and men were divided into messes — officers, petty officers, ratings, seaman (the Welsh seamen messing separately), firemen and stewards.

Each man was issued with 1½ lbs of rice, one ship's biscuit, 1 oz of goat meat and each mess was given a small quantity of tea, sugar, salt and limited amount of water (it had to be carried some 2½ miles from wells sited near the coast by the wives and daughters of their guards). This same caravan also brought for Dr Faud a case of Black & White whisky, a present from General Nuri Bey. During the afternoon they were visited by General Jaafar Pasha who immediately handed out sheets of paper and pencils and encouraged the men to write to their families — he also told them what to write. After they were done, he collected the letters and took photographs of the men sitting around the mouth of one of the caves. Yeoman Signaller Allen later remarked that '[We] must have made a sorry picture — a crowd of lean, hungry looking savages, with beards and in rags after only a week's captivity.'[1] On his leaving they held out some hope that the letters would be passed onto the British at Sollum.

Again their food for the day consisted of a biscuit for each man and some rice.

*Tuesday, 9th November.* For most it was another uncomfortable night. On waking they were not allowed to wash because of the difficulty of fetching water. Fires were lit to boil water for the breakfast rice, after which the men went out under an armed guard to collect firewood. This would become a daily ritual throughout their captivity. The wood and brush were brought back to camp and stacked, after which there was nothing for the prisoners to do, so most crawled back into the caves to get out of the sun and sleep until 16.00 hours, when they awoke to cook more rice for tea. As a supplement to their diet they were given some green tomatoes with their rice and biscuit, but no meat (the survivors kept the empty tomato tins which were used as cups or measures for doling out the rice). The rice ration could be exchanged for flour which some of the men mixed with a little water to make dough. This was then placed on heated stones near the fire to make bread. By 18.00 hours it was dark and the Turkish guards and Senussi got out their prayer mats, turned to face east (towards Mecca) and commenced their evening prayers, whilst the sailors went back to sleep.

During the day both Turkish officers, Lieutenants Fevzi and Husni, had left the camp and the survivors now came under the charge of Doctor Becki Faud, who according to Gwatkin-Williams, was considerate, spoke French and was somewhat given to liquor! During their evening talk he explained that the Senussi were very religious and strict adherents to the Koran and that many times he had been ordered by the Grand Senussi to amputate the hands of those Senussi who had been found guilty of smoking, under penalty of loosing his own hand if he refused.

*Wednesday, 10th November.* After breakfast Dr Faud informed the survivors that he had received news that the *U-35* had sunk an Italian ship, a British ship named

1. Quoted in *A Black Hole in the Desert*, anon, London, July 1916.

*Chatham* (no vessel of this name was sunk until 21st May 1918) and raided Sollum where she had sunk the two Egyptian Coastguard cruisers and laid the port to waste. He later dressed the wounds of the injured — the first time since they had landed — and it was noted that Quartermaster Williams's leg had become gangrenous. During the morning, one of the Turkish officers still in the camp came across the firewood collecting party and said he wanted four men with brass buttons on their uniforms to go with him, but there was only three such men in the group, so they returned to camp where he asked Surgeon Arthur, who still had his jacket, if he would join them. Arthur declined, but another man volunteered and, after an exchange of jackets, the party made for Port Bardia. As they walked they learned that a small boat had been seen making for shore but on spotting the Senussi it had stood off.[2] It seemed to the prisoners that the Turkish officer wanted the men to act as decoys to entice the boat to shore. By the time they had reached the port the boat had disappeared, but on climbing a nearby hill they could just make it out heading towards a steamer. They were then dismissed and told to return to camp. On their way, they stopped at an Arab camp and were given food and water by its owner.

For those in the camp, the rations were the same as the previous day but one goat was now being slaughtered on alternate days. Each man was given an 1½ ozs of tobacco, which must have seemed like heaven to the smokers. During the day, they received a visit from a big, powerful, bearded man with a Mauser rifle and an elephant hide whip whom they were told was the uncle of the Grand Senussi. On his arrival, the Turkish officers and Dr Faud hurriedly concealed the whisky and buried their cigarette butts in the sand, whilst the Senussi guards treated him with great reverence and respect. He spent the day sitting in the doorway of a tent firing his rifle at any target that took his fancy. Towards evening, and much to the relief of everyone, he left and soon the whisky and cigarettes reappeared.

2. Captain Gwatkin-Williams in his book *Prisoners of the Red Desert* has this boat as belonging to the sloop HMS *Jonquil*, but her log book does not record the launching of a boat whilst on patrol off the North African coast. One of *Tara's* quartemaster's, William Rowlands, speculated that they could have been survivors who were picked up by a steamer. However, Mr Frank Gradwell, third engineer of the *Moorina*, records that on the third day after the *Moorina's* sinking, at 10.00 hours, as his lifeboat – the No. 4 boat, neared the coast, they saw someone waving at them. As they neared the land they spotted armed Arabs and, suspecting a trap, turned the boat around. Seeing the boat turn away the Arabs started shooting but, thanks to a favourable wind, the boat managed to escape out to sea – but not before the hull was hit and holed in four places and the sail pierced in a dozen places.

In Sollum, Captain Royle took a small boat 'in the direction of Baq Baq to try to find physical evidence of the sinking of the *Tara*.' Off the coast he found masses of flotsam amongst which he counted some fifty deck rafts and one unidentified body (possibly Barber?) which was hauled aboard and the boat returned to Sollum, where presumably the body was buried as an unknown British seaman. The number of deck rafts amongst the flotsam certainly indicated that a passenger- or ex-passenger-carrying vessel had been sunk. The other two ships which had recently been sunk in the vicinity were the *Woolwich* (on the 3rd) and the *Moorina* (on the 7th), both cargo vessels which would not have carried deck rafts.

*Thursdays 11th November.* Dr Faud returned the men's money and valuables, and around the camp there were high hopes that there might be a prisoner exchange with the British. Food was as usual — rice, biscuit and dirty water.

*Friday, 12th November.* Fed up of having very little water, a deputation of the prisoners went to see Dr Faud to ask if they could fetch it themselves. He readily agreed, so a small party was organised and issued with new skins and sent to the wells under an armed guard. After some time they returned looking like a flock of canaries — the saffron and peppers used to cure the skins having mixed with the water seeping out of the skins produced a dye which ran and stained the carriers. The long walk and steep climb however, took its toll and it was not repeated, but thanks to the additional water, the survivors were given a few pieces of soap so that each man could have a wash.

Food for the day consisted of boiled mutton, rice and one ship's biscuit per man.

*Saturday, 13th November.* This morning there was great expectation amongst the prisoners that they were going to be released but those hopes were soon dashed as they were told they were going to be marched further inland. Why this prisoner release rumour persisted is not very clear, perhaps because Otto Mannesmann was shortly going to be leaving the camp and might take word of their predicament with him.

Of more concern was Quartermaster Thomas who, due to lack of medicines, had been gradually deteriorating and was now in great pain. His leg had been properly set but the gangrene had spread and the wound itself was crawling with maggots. Fearing the worst, Surgeon Arthur consulted with Dr Faud and both decided that their only course of action was to amputate the leg if there was to be any chance of saving his life. They informed both senior officers and his messmates of their intentions, pointing out that they had no anaesthetic or medical instruments, only a blunt pair of scissors which they asked some the crew to sharpen on a rock. Owing to the flies which infested the camp during the daylight hours it was decided that it would be best to operate after dark when they would have disappeared. During the day Thomas managed to eat a little rice, some small green tomatoes and was given a ship's biscuit that had been soaked in Dr Faud's whisky.

At 16.30 hours the operation commenced, with Dr Faud supervising and Arthur cutting. Two of Thomas's mess mates held his hands whilst the leg was cut off at the knee. Not once during the operation did he complain or shout. Whether the actual operation was judged a success is not known but at 23.30 hours Thomas passed away through loss of blood and shock. Just before he died, Dr Faud paid him a visit and promised to send him to Sollum, which seemed to have raised his spirits somewhat.

After seeing the miseries of Thomas, Otto Mannesmann, whom by now the sailors were openly calling 'The German', promised to have words with General Nuri Bey to try to initiate a prisoner exchange as it was becoming increasingly evident that the Senussi were unable to look after the prisoners.

*Sunday, 14th November.* At first light, before it became too hot, some of the men went a little way down the valley where they excavated a grave. Not having any tools they used their hands, cooking utensils and flat stones. Breakfast was at 08.00 hours and half-an-hour later Quartermaster Thomas was buried, with Lieutenant Tanner reciting those parts of the burial service that he could remember, breaking down every now and then as did most of the prisoners. After the internment they sang one verse of the English hymn *A day's march nearer home,* and no doubt some Welsh hymns. After the service they erected a simple wooden cross made from a broken oar and covered the grave with a cairn of rocks. All were feeling very lonely and anxious about the future.

This was the second burial since landing and the more vociferous of the survivors started to voice their complaints. To Captain Gwatkin-Williams and Lieutenant Tanner it seemed that things had come to a head as there had been instances of minor insubordination in the mercantile crew, amongst both officers and men. On more than one occasion since they had landed, when the captain, in the absence of Lieutenant Tanner, had given a man an order, he had been told by the recipient that he worked for the L&NWR not the RN! As he later explained, it was not that they were a bad crew but simply a cross section of British society amongst whom were the good, the indifferent, the selfish and of course the bad. Now that they were off the ship some were trying to use the younger members of the crew to cause trouble. Thankfully most of these had been made to see sense by their fellow crewmen, although a number did remain troublesome. The two senior officers did not have the means to enforce discipline, so the captain decided to explain the situation to the crew. He clambered up on a rock close to mouth of one of the caves and called the crew to assemble around him. He firstly addressed their not unfounded fears (and not for the first time) pointing out that, unlike Mercantile Marine crews who, once their ship had been sunk the crew's wages would be stopped, the Royal Navy would continue to pay them (and of course the allotments to their families) until the ship was officially paid off. Discipline had therefore to be maintained until that time. He added that, as the senior officer, the Senussi held him responsible for the crew's behaviour and in future any breaches of discipline would be reported to them, and it would be they who would punish the offenders according to their law — with punishments such as the loss of a hand for stealing or being lashed for minor offences. After the speech, much to his surprise, most of the listeners clapped their approval and there was to be very little trouble during the rest of their captivity.

That night, whilst the Turks and Senussi turned to Mecca to pray, the prisoners held an informal church service in and around the officers' mess. All denominations attended, and both Welsh and English hymns were sung. This Sunday service was to continue throughout their captivity.

During the night, Otto Mannesmann left camp, taking with him the men's letters (which included Lieutenant Tanner's report of the sinking) and a list of the casualties. He also took with him a written parole which he had extracted from Captain Gwatkin-Williams, in which the latter had promised he would not try to escape unless he had given seven days notice of the withdrawal of his parole. Before leaving, Mannessman had also promised that their new camp would have every comfort in the way of location, food and water, and further promised that they would not be moved until transport could be arranged for them. Also leaving the camp was Dr Faud, 'kind hearted Dr Faud' as described by Lieutenant Tanner, and the rest of the Turkish soldiers. Taking over was the English-speaking Achmed Mansoor, who had brought with him a Senussi colonel, Mohamet Effendi, and some Muhafiazi with their wives and families. Mansoor was a short, plump man with a short, black beard, alert and very sure of himself. He informed everyone that he had come from Constantinople by submarine, but it was later discovered that in reality he was an Egyptian Coastguard officer who had deserted to the Turks — the sailors called him Captain Achmed.[3]

*Monday, 15th November.* At 09.00 hours, after a breakfast of boiled rice, Achmed Mansoor gave orders to strike camp — so much for the previous day's promise! He explained that they were to make their way to an oasis which was only some two to three day's march away.

The men, mustered in their messes, formed up in a column of twos and marched into the desert. They were headed by eight camels carrying their tents, rice, water in goat skins and petrol cans, the camel's drivers acting as guides. Following them was Captain Achmed who was mounted on an ancient white nag. Then came each mess — officers, petty officers, seamen, firemen and, as no string or rope was available, each man had to carry both his own and his messes mats, pots and pans. The whole was surrounded by some thirty guards who were armed with a variety of weapons ranging from muskets to modern rifles.

Owing to the varied ages of the sailors the column soon became stretched out with the youngest in front. Marching under the baking-hot sun they raised a huge dust cloud as they made their way up and down the rough hilly tracks of the gullies and ravines which ran inland until they reached the shoreline. They then turned into one of the ravines and continued marching until 16.15 hours when they were herded into a small ravine one hundred feet wide, with steep sides some 30–40 feet high, which ended in a sheer wall. It was instantly nick-named

3. *Prisoners of the Red Desert* records that on 14th November '... HMS *Jonquil* arrived at daybreak off Port Bardia. Sweeping the shore with their glasses the lookouts could make out the waterlogged N°. 6 boat, but as they were about to drop anchor they came under heavy rifle fire. As the British were not at war with the Senussi, their standing orders forbade them to return fire, so the ship manoeuvred in the narrow channel and proceeded out to sea. She then returned to Sollum where on arrival she was informed that *Tara's* survivors had been taken into the interior. HMS *Jonquil's* log book, however, shows that she was at sea off the coast of Crete on 14th November. British forces would not land in Port Bardia until an armed party from HMS *Lily* landed there at 14.15 hours on 22nd March 1916. They searched the area, found and set fire to *Tara's* boats and, at 17.00 hours, returned to the *Lily*, which then up-anchored and proceeded to the Sollum anchorage.

the 'Dry Dock' by the prisoners who on being told that today's march was over, immediately flopped down to the floor. As they rested water was distributed. They had marched all day in a north-westerly direction towards Marressa and had covered some twelve miles.

Sometime later, four men under a Senussi guard and an officer, were seen marching towards the camp. As they neared, the prisoners could make out that three were white men and immediately a rousing cheer went up. The men turned out to be Second Lieutenant Thomas Seth Apcar of the 32nd Indian Lancers, Chief Officer Charles Sverin Coalsted, Second Engineer Thomas Reid Richardson and Sola (real name A F Rodrigues?) a Goanese mess boy, all of whom were survivors of the Indian Transport *Moorina*. Coalsted had with him a tin of Traveller tobacco which he handed around and which was very gratefully received by the smokers. The new men explained that their ship had been sunk by the *U-35* and how they come ashore near Marressa and been captured by arabs, who then handed them over to the Turks.

As the men were talking, two goats were killed by the guards, butchered and the cuts distributed between the messes, but as it was now too dark to cook, the meat was kept until the following day and the men went to sleep under cover of the overhangs of rocks, but found it very cold and draughty. Worryingly, dysentery had started to appear amongst the *Tara* survivors.

*Tuesday, 16th November.* Owing to a fog which had drifted inland during the night, the prisoners again awoke to find their clothing soaked and discovered that half their meat ration and some of their possessions to have been stolen by the guards. After protestations by the senior officers, two goats were killed and butchered, the cuts then handed out to the prisoners and cooked with a little rice. Assistant Engineer Davies later wrote in his diary, 'We have to be very quick at eating here as the rice and meat after boiling is placed in a fair sized enamel basin and sixteen of us eat out of it. We have the skin of tongue and roof of mouths peeling off through trying to get your fair share of food!'

Captain Achmed demanded that they hand over all their money, watches, rings and valuables. This was complied with but only after Gwatkin-Williams and Tanner had drawn up a detailed list of the items taken. During the afternoon, the prisoners were surprised at the arrival of some twenty Muhafizia under the command of a Senussi officer, Mohamed Zoue, who, clad in a dark-blue robe, was seated on a fine horse. When he dismounted he was seen to be six-feet tall and had a magnificent black moustache, the ends of which were twirled upwards, much like the Kaiser's. Much to the envy of the prisoners, he smoked almost incessantly. The Muhafizia now took over guarding the prisoners. At 16.00 hours and were then ordered to form up two deep with their belongings and marched off, again heading northwards. They stopped for an hour at dusk near a military post, a tent which contained a Turkish W/T station manned by two men. They continued over a flat yellowish, brown countryside in and out of dry watercourses which looked liked huge ravines. It was very hard going for the heavily-laden men, but they were in good heart and for most of the journey all joined in singing comic songs which, according to Sub Lieutenant Griffiths, sounded very well in the open desert. At 23.00 hours they reached a village which consisted of five or six, mud or stone buildings, the occupants of which came out to see them. Here they rested for the night having been herded into a filthy yard where there was hardly any room for anyone to stand let alone lie down.[4] After some strong protestations the Senussi relented and allowed them to sleep in a nearby field which, although cold and uncomfortable, was decidedly cleaner. They were given no food, but it was very doubtful if they could have cooked it as most were extremely tired and went to sleep almost immediately, despite many having blistered and bloodied feet.

*Wednesday, 17th November.* Most men endured a bitterly cold night, but Sub Lieutenant Marsh later wrote that he had spent the night with Chief Engineer Williams and Assistant Engineer Roberts [sic] who shared their blankets and rug with one of the *Moorina's* officers. It had been '... tight fitting to get sufficient cover and to keep warm, [but had] slept fairly well, though rock bed very hard!'

For breakfast they were given two butchered goats and enough water to drink and to wash with, their washing having to be done in the cooking dishes. Some of the villagers offered them red peppers and eggs to enhance their rations, but as they had no money they had to refuse.

At 12.00 hours the camels carrying their food and water arrived, and after a rest the march to the north west resumed at 15.00 hours, but the guides soon lost their way. At 22.00 hours they came across an Arab camp of dirty huts and tent's where a halt was called for the night. The prisoners were given a verminous tent which was only large enough to sleep some of the officers so the others had to

4. Sub Lieutenant Griffiths called this village/yard a broken up convent and graveyard.

sleep in the cold night air. Food was provided but again too late to be cooked and the men too tired to cook it. For the sailors, the march had taken its toll as those who were shod had developed blisters whilst the unshod had their feet cut and bleeding. Sub Lieutenant Marsh recalled that his feet were blistered and that due to the continuing march there had been no chance for them to heal and that most of the men were in a state of collapse. However, appalling as it was, it was preferable to marching during the midday heat.

*Thursday, 18th November.* When those officers that had been lucky enough to sleep in the tent awoke they felt much refreshed, whereas those outside found their burnouses, mats and clothing soaking wet — thanks to another bank of fog which had drifted in during the night. For breakfast at 07.30 hours they were given a little rice and a drink of water, after which they were ordered to form up in a column of twos and march. After 1½ hours they arrived at a little building which they called a blockhouse, a small house built of mud blocks in the vicinity of Ras el Leucca (Cap Luc) which apparently they should have reached the previous night.

They were now close to the sea and in the distance could make out a ship being chased by a submarine, but they were too far away to see the outcome. It being deemed too hot to march during the middle of the day the men took shelter wherever they could and rested until the sun had gone down a little.

At 16.00 hours, after a drink of water and more boiled rice, the march continued, now heading westwards across a flat, featureless desert. The men were tired and soon the column became stretched out to over a mile in length.

Lieutenant Apcar had been running a high temperature for two days and was now in a pretty bad way and had to be placed on one of the camels. After a time, he slipped off and many thought that he was dying. At 22.00 hours the order was given to halt and the men simply flopped to the ground. Again it was too late to cook supper and, after a drink of cold, green tea, they fell asleep on the hard ground. Already a fog was drifting in and moisture was beginning to settle on their clothes and blankets.

*Friday, 19th November.* Most of the prisoners had a very bad night's sleep, and again awoke with their blankets and clothing damp and wet. For breakfast they had a little boiled rice, some goat's meat and a drink of green tea.

The march resumed at 08.00 hours and at about noon they halted about a mile from an Arab camp of three to four tents perched on a hillside. The prisoners were ordered to wait whilst the guards took the camels to the camp for water and to bring back food and water for them. As the day wore on the men become increasingly hungry until, at about 16.30 hours, their patience was rewarded when the guards returned with water, rice and two thin-looking goats.

When slaughtering and butchering the goats the Senussi would never give the prisoners all the cuts of the carcass; they would always keep something for themselves, be it the lights, the entrails, a hind leg or the fat. Today was no exception and after keeping what they wanted, the remainder was distributed to the individual messes. After a supper of mutton and rice the men's hunger may not have been sated, but all felt much better and at 20.00 hours they unrolled their rush mats and burnouses to try to sleep as best they could in the cold, night air, with the warning that there was to be an early start tomorrow.

*Saturday, 20th November.* By 06.00 hours the prisoners were up and the day started off normally enough with each mess lighting its own fire for cooking breakfast rice and dry their clothes after the night's mist. A deputation of stokers and stewards arrived to see Lieutenant Tanner to report the disappearance of Thomas Owens, a coal trimmer, who had gone missing during the night, his manner being described as 'wild'. This left the senior officers in an unenviable position; if they reported him missing, he could be caught before he could make it to safety, but if they did not report it then he could well be robbed and killed by a wandering band of Bedouin or could simply die of thirst in the desert. After a discussion it was decided that Captain Gwatkin-Williams should report his absence. On being told Captain Achmed immediately flew into a terrible rage, mustered the prisoners, held a roll call and threatened to march them all day without food. He then ordered the sergeant to beat the guards who had been on duty during the night with his cane and ordered them to keep a closer eye on the prisoners.

At 10.00 hours the camels were brought into the camp and loaded. Whilst this was going on Achmed had been rummaging in one of the mess fires with a stick and had pulled out a lump of burnt rice which somebody had evidently thrown into the fire.[5] He demanded the culprit be handed over at once, but it was blamed on Owens who had thrown it into the fire before he absconded. In a rage, Achmed mounted his nag and ordered the men to march and they set off and marched for

5. One of Thomas Owens messmates had noticed his absence, and so had kept his ration in case of his return but had thrown it into the fire on the order to march.

ten hours during which time, at a very brief halt, they were given a small piece of biscuit and a drink of water, a wine glass full, according to Sub Lieutenant Griffiths.

After they had halted for the night, they were given no food and although the men were tired, sleep was difficult due to the hard ground and the nightly, heavy, clinging fog which came rolling in off the sea.

*Sunday, 21st November.* After a very uncomfortable and damp night, the men only had time for a drink of water before the march continued. By now, some of the weaker men were starting to fall by the wayside. Just before noon, Dutton, the assistant paymaster collapsed. He was given a drink of water and placed on a camel, as was the third mate, Mr Thomas, who had also collapsed. Mohamed Zoue could see that the boilermaker, Cox, was also in a bad way,[6] and dismounted from his horse which he gave to Cox to ride whilst he walked alongside. At noon, a halt was called and the men were given a little water and some three hours rest before the march was resumed.

During the afternoon, so to maintain progress, Captain Achmed ordered the guards to use their rifles to impel the stragglers onwards. They halted at 19.00 hours and fires were lit and rice boiled. Some of the prisoners were so tired that they dropped to the ground and fell asleep and had to be woken to get their ration. Coal trimmer, Owen Gray, later recorded that,

> This march was the most terrible thing that I have ever experienced, marching, marching, hunger, hunger and nothing to drink and the sun scorching my almost naked body, and I had time to extract small stones and tiny bits of shell from my feet ... Our guards kept telling us that a paradise was waiting for us at the end of this march, so we were doing our utmost to get to the end, at times we were almost too thirsty and hungry to move but our guards were forcing us forward by pushing their rifles into our backs.[7]

*Monday, 22nd November.* After waking at 07.00 hours the prisoners were given water and marched from 08.30 hours to noon. They stopped at the wells at Bir Zebla where they made fires and cooked some sweet, (sugared) boiled rice. About

6. Cox was suffering from a stricture of the urethra and had lost his catheter during the Tara's sinking and in consequence was suffering dreadfully. Suprisingly, it was known he was suffering of this complaint since the Tara was operating in the North Channel.
7. Note written by Fireman Owen Gray held in the Anglesey Record Office, Llangefni.

three to four hours later, as the sun started to go down, they resumed their march until 20.00 hours. Flour was distributed for their supper which, after they had made a fire, the officers mixed with water and sugar to make some thin flap cakes or flap jacks. They then rolled themselves into their burnouses and went to sleep on the open desert.

Whilst on the march some of the crew had seen snails hibernating on the desert shrubs which they collected and, after supper, placed on some stones in or near the fires, on which they were roasted before being eaten.

*Tuesday, 23rd November.* Most of the men spent a miserable night and again awoke with their clothing and blankets soaking wet. They breakfasted at 07.30 hours, after which, as all were infested with lice, the Senussi ordered them to march to a well about a mile away where they were to wash themselves and their clothes — only their third wash since coming ashore! Afterwards, a party of men went out for the daily ritual of collecting firewood, walking some two to three miles under the watchful eyes of an armed guard.

During the morning Captain Achmed left the camp, the men hoping that when he returned it would be with more goats as they had no meat since the 19th. Unfortunately, when he did return it was without any goats, so for supper more rice and flour was issued and more flap jacks made. These had to be eaten when hot as when cold they were, according to Lieutenant Tanner 'awfully solid.'

After supper, Gwatkin-Williams noted that during the previous couple of days the march had become easier as the land was flatter, with stony outcrops here and there. It was waterless but covered with aromatic shrubs and there was plenty of wildlife about, snakes, hares, tortoises, larks, wagtails, a few vultures, ravens, hawks and robins, and quite a few butterflies, some of which were common in Britain. Whilst he had been writing lyrically about the land, Assistant Engineer Davies and some of the other smokers were experimenting, making cigarettes out of used tea leaves.

They turned in at 19.00 hours and about half-an-hour later a searchlight was spotted to seaward.

*Wednesday, 24th November.* Due to the fog many had again had an uncomfortable night and as dawn broke at about 06.30 hours they lit their fires for the usual routine of cooking their breakfast rice, drying their clothes and burnouses. It was at this time that Surgeon Arthur reported to the senior officers that Cooke, the electrician, was now running a high fever, whilst Cox, was having difficulty passing water and in great pain. Having neither medicines or equipment, he suggested that a hot bath in one of the large cooking pans might help ease the pain. It was tried but to no avail.

Captain Achmed informed the prisoners that for the next stage of their journey they would have to turn inland into the desert and that the camels would now only be carrying drinking water, there would be no spare water for cooking. All the ship's biscuits had been eaten and two day's rations of flour were issued with instructions to cook enough bread to last two days.

At 16.00 hours, when the hottest part of the day was over, the order to march was given. From Bir Zebla they turned south into the desert. It was an appalling journey. As darkness descended, the men blundered into rocks and stones over which they stumbled and fell. For the weak, the old or infirm it was particularly frightening. As the column lengthened they became terrified of being left behind in the desert to die of thirst when the sun rose and many pleaded with their shipmates to help them. Although their comrades did try to assist, they had enough trouble carrying their own and their mess's possessions and trying to look after themselves. Achmed, himself scared of being lost, urged the guards to use their rifles butts and muzzles to push the men on, whilst he threatened to have every straggler flogged. At 23.00 hours the moon rose which made things a little easier and a halt was called a short time later. The men dropped thankfully to the ground and waited for the stragglers to catch up. They were then given a little water and tried to sleep where they had dropped. For most, however, sleep was impossible and they spent the night shuffling about half clad in the cold. During the day they had covered some twelve miles.

*Thursday, 25th November.* After a bitterly cold night when most had only a fitful sleep at best, they were up and packed before daybreak. But because Captain Achmed had taken his time in getting ready it was not until 08.00 hours that the march commenced. By now, most of the prisoners had eaten their two day's rations of bread and had to go without all day. Mid morning they crossed the Enveiral road (which led from Sollum to Tobruk) running from east to west. At the noon halt the men were given rice and water. At 15.30 hours the march resumed which lasted until about an hour before sunset when, much to the men's surprise, they were given a further ration of rice and water in which to cook it.

*Friday, 26th November.* At 03.40 hours the prisoners were roused, although for most sleep had been impossible as due to the bitterly cold night they again had spent the night walking about and lighting fires to try to keep warm. Breakfast consisted of the usual boiled rice which they had with a little water. At 04.30 hours the journey continued and as they marched they noticed that the desert had become flatter and more barren, strewn with pebbles, coral and pieces of shell, and had taken on a red tinge. By mid morning they could make out a large white mound in the distance which they later discovered was the tell-tale sign of a well or wells. As they neared, they could make out another mound, a small stone blockhouse and a fine large tent out of which emerged an old Arab. He was a mullah named Osman who was in charge of the well. The sailors would later nickname him 'Holy Joe'. With him, was his plump wife and numerous children, and two older women. At 11.55 hours the men halted by the wells and wondered where they were and how anyone could possibly live in such barren and cheerless place.

Meanwhile Basil, who had been talking to Captain Achmed, returned to the prisoners to tell them that they had reached Bir Hakkim Abbyat, the Wells of the White Doctor, their new home. On hearing they were shocked, some of the men simply flopped to the ground or just stood where they were dumbfounded, so much for paradise! They looked around, nearby was a small date palm growing out of an ancient lime kiln, what few shrubs that grew were stunted and there were a few ancient graves nearby. Some two miles to the north were two other wells, the Wells of the Red Doctor.

The wells were said to be Roman and all of a similar design having being hewn out of the limestone rock. Each was bottle shaped, some fifteen feet deep and twenty-five feet in diameter at the bottom. At the top was an opening, about one yard square. The wells were usually found in pairs and sited in large, flat areas of rock at the lower levels of a slope, so that when the rains fell the water would run downwards into the wells' openings by a series of low walls. Once inside, the water would remain in the well for years, being kept cool by the surrounding rock; evaporation was kept to a minimum due to the small opening.

One of the Wells of the White Doctor contained about nine feet of water whilst the second was dry and partly filled with sand and rubbish. Next to each well was a mound made of the sand and stone which had been excavated from the wells. These two mounds were on the lower side of the slope below the wells and each stood some twenty feet high, resembling an orange, sliced in half and

Mullah Osman

upended. About thirty feet away stood a blockhouse, built of stone and mud blocks, slightly larger than an old fashioned pig-sty, where the stores and rations were to be kept. Adjoining was a sheep pen, near which Captain Achmed and Mohamed Zoue's pitched their tents. Achmed told the prisoners to make themselves at home.

The sailors found their tents were in a deplorable condition, there were no poles, ropes or pegs so they could not be erected, however they were assured that a caravan would be bringing these soon. They were once again given paper and encouraged to write to their families. Later in the day they were given water and rice. The wind which had been blowing hard all day had been steadily increasing and towards evening was a gale, carrying with it sand, small stones and twigs. To get out of the wind the men collected large stones and rocks and built a low wall to shelter behind, covering themselves with the tents which they used as sheets to huddle under. Their guards, now numbering about twenty men, all Muhafizia, slept in five tents near the mounds which they used as lookout posts. During the next few days they were joined by their wives and families.

*Saturday, 27th November.* The cold wind was still blowing and the men were still out in the open, but there was no sign of the caravan bringing the promised poles and ropes for the tents.

All messes maintained the routine of collecting firewood, after which some of the men wandered round the camp. They discovered that it was littered with shards of broken, red pottery thought by some to be of Roman origin. To the south east were half-a-dozen graves, whilst the countryside around the camp was littered with animal bones and here and there the mummified carcasses of donkeys and camels.

*Sunday, 28th November.* Osman, who was in charge of the wells of the White Doctor, had been in conversation with Achmed about using the prisoners to clear out the Wells of the Red Doctor before the rains fell. No objections were raised by either Captain Gwatkin-Williams or Lieutenant Tanner and so, after breakfast, a working party made up of petty officers and men was organised. Put under the command of Assistant Engineer Hughes, they duly marched off escorted by Osman and half-a-dozen armed guards.

On the working party's return at 16.00 hours, all prisoners were ordered to move camp to higher ground so as to bring it closer to the wells and blockhouse. The Senussi provided a tent for the officers to sleep in, an eighteen-foot square Arab tent through which, according to Chief Officer Coalsted, on any night, the stars could be counted! It was erected by the crew in the middle of the compound, after which they were forced by the Senussi, at the point of a gun, down into the dry well for the night. The tent held as many as thirty occupants, petty officers included, but during the night, finding the tent too draughty and cold, Sub Lieutenant Marsh and a few of the other officers and engineers joined the men down in the well where, although crowded (with some seventy-eight men), it was warm.

The flour ration had run out, so the men had four meals of rice and a little green tea at night.

During the day the Gwatkin-Williams had been informed that Owens had been re-captured and that they would be shortly joined by 150 crewmen from a sunken British warship.

*Monday 29th November.* The rations again comprised of rice and water and the working party departed for the Wells of the Red Doctor after breakfast. Owing to the lack of tents, all the other available men were then organised into working parties to start collecting stones and rocks to build blockhouses to house them. Somehow, the officers had managed to get hold of some tent cloth or a strip of canvas, which they used as a blanket when they turned in after their nightly cup of green tea.

The crew were again secured down into the well for the night.

*Tuesday, 30th November.* Thanks to the strip of material, the officers had a much warmer night inside the tent, but the crew were starting to become vociferous about being forced to sleep in the dry well. After breakfast, the working parties departed to their respective tasks. Later, the daily firewood collecting party returned to camp with the news that they had come across tyre tracks about a mile to the south of the camp. This was good news as it proved that motor vehicles could travel this far into the desert.

Gwatkin-Williams noted that the men were allowed a great deal of freedom around the camp and for a distance of about a mile from it, but no further, as there was a danger that they could be killed by marauding Arabs.

Although they had been given rice four times today and a small drink of green tea before going to bed, it was noted that the portions were becoming smaller.

# 13. Egypt, November 1915

The military in Egypt were well aware that the Senussi attacks on the border, although pinpricks, were causing unrest amongst the native population, especially amongst the Behera, a tribe who occupied the lands of western Egypt, and in consequence felt a deep bond with the people of Cyrenaica – indeed many were influenced by the Senussi's teachings. The British realised that they needed to act quickly and decisively, as any defeat of British arms might precipitate an uprising in Egypt. Therefore it was decided to assemble a force strong enough to defeat the Turko-Senussi forces, and to reoccupy Sollum as soon as possible. As already mentioned, it was decided to pull back all outposts on the border to Mersa Matruh, which would now become heavily fortified and be used as a base for the new force, the Western Frontier Force, for its forthcoming offensive into the western desert and reoccupation of Sollum.

The only troops available in Egypt who were not on the Suez Canal defences, were base details and un-brigaded units. From among these Lieutenant-General Sir John Maxwell, C-in-C Egypt, on the 20th November, ordered the formation of a force at Alexandria, the Western Frontier Force under the command of Major General Alexander Wallace. It was made up of:

A composite mounted brigade of three composite yeomanry regiments which had been raised from the 2nd Mounted Division under the command of Brigadier-General Julian Tyndale Biscoe. The brigade included elements of over twenty different yeomanry regiments.

A composite regiment of the Australian Light Horse, raised from details of Australian Light Horse brigades.

The Nottinghamshire Battery (TF) Royal Horse Artillery, ammunition column and auxiliary services.

A composite infantry brigade, under Brigadier-General the Earl of Lucan, comprising,

1/6th (TF) Bn, Royal Scots

2/7th (TF) Bn, Middlesex Regiment

2/8th (TF) Bn, Middlesex Regiment
15th Sikhs and auxiliary services
The divisional train of the 1st Australian Division
A detachment of the Egyptian Army Military Works Department (there were no Royal Engineer units available)

To make good and secure the single standard-gauge railway line from Alexandria to al' Dabaa, and to patrol to the Moghara oasis, General Wallace on 21st November detached the 2nd Bn, New Zealand Rifle Brigade, one company of 15th Sikhs, a detachment of 150 of the Bikaner Camel Corps (with an attached Egyptian Army machine-gun section) and one armoured train with the 1/10th Ghurka Rifles and two 12½-pounder guns of the Egyptian Army Artillery.

By the 23rd, the Western Frontier Force was considered complete and ready to move up to Mersa Matruh. However, owing to the number of U-boats now thought to be operating in the Mediterranean, it was decided that the safest way to move them west was for the Mounted Brigade to be moved from Alexandria to al'Dabaa by rail, then march the seventy-five miles to Mersa Matruh, whilst all the other units were sent from Alexandria by sea at night. However, due to a sand bar across the harbour entrance, only shallow draft vessels could be used. In consequence, two Egyptian Coastguard cruisers, the *Abdul Moniem,* and the now repaired *Nuhr-el-Bhar,* with HM Trawlers *Remagio, Rodosto, Comrade, Abergeldie, Falmouth III* and the *Rononia*[1] (which had been serving as outer guard to Alexandria's harbour) and four small local steamers were requisitioned. A third coastguard cruiser, the *Reschid,* was to be converted to a hospital ship.

On the night of the 23rd/24th November the first of the troops, 300 men of the 15th Sikhs under Lieutenant-Colonel Gordon, sailed in three trawlers from Alexandria and landed at Mersa Matruh the following morning. These sailings would become a nightly occurrence whilst during the days mounted troops and transports were carried by rail to al'Dabaa. Once the railhead became secure, detachments were then sent out to secure the wells at Abu Gerab, Bagggush and

1. The transportation of troops was proving to be very slow so the Admiralty asked Admiral de Roebock in command at the Dardanelles if he could help or, if not, ask the French to detach from Milo on Crete some British vessels working under their command. He had however, already despatched the sloop *Clematis* and six trawlers — *Abronia, Ocean Princess, St Clair, Scooper, Scuter II, Slasher* to bring a floating dry dock from Port Said to Mudros. On 26th November these were handed over to Admiral Peirse, the *Clematis* was placed on coastal patrol and initially two of the trawlers (and later all of them) were utilised to transport troops to Mersa Matruh.

Jerawla, the only sizeable wells in the eighty-five miles between al'Dabaa and Mersa Matruh. Unfortunately, the water level of the wells only allowed two squadrons to be watered at one time which impeded the movement of the cavalry to Mersa Matruh.

Meanwhile, civil unrest was starting to break out in Egypt and on the 29th, the 1st/1st North Midland Mounted Brigade, with the Berkshire Battery Royal Horse Artillery were sent to Fayoum, some fifty miles south of Cairo. On the same date, a squadron of Egyptian Army cavalry and fifty men of the Bikaner Camel Corps occupied the Wadi Natrun some forty-five miles south of Alexandria.

By 7th December, the Western Frontier Force (less five cavalry squadrons which remained at the railhead due to the shortage of water) had assembled at Mersa Matruh and General Wallace had moved his headquarters to the town.

Some twenty miles west of Mersa Matruh, near Ras Umm el Rakham, there was a Senussi camp estimated to be about 12,000 in number. Although the Grand Senussi had not yet declared his intentions, the Turkish General Nuri Bey and his followers had by now completely broken away from him. This camp was to be General Wallace's first objective.

# 14. In Captivity, December 1915

*Wednesday, 1st December.* By now, the meals and work were becoming routine. Over the previous few days Osman, who was in charge of the guards, had like them been armed with a rifle, but now changed it for a whip which he used with gusto if he thought there was any slacking. This treatment, which was also directed at the Senussi guards, was much resented by the crew who were quite willing to work as it gave them something to do. They did not, however, like to see some of the older or weaker men being whipped and it was pointed out to their captors that any failings on their part was due to lack of food and poor diet, and some of the younger and more able threatened to hit back at the Mullah. They complained to Gwatkin-Williams who advised them not to take any action and he had a quiet word with Achmed which seemed to work.

*Thursday, 2nd December.* The working parties again departed to their various tasks and during the morning a caravan of sixty camels arrived from Sollum which had to be watered. Whilst the animals were drinking, Basil took the opportunity to speak to their drivers from whom he learned that Sollum was some four to five days march away and there was fighting going on between the Senussi and the British and that the latter had fallen back to Mersa Matruh. This was news which cast a gloom over the camp. The caravan had brought more tents, poles and ropes and, after their day's work, the prisoners managed to erect two tents before nightfall, one for the petty officers and one for the ratings.

The men's Arab footwear had been gradually falling apart and many were now going around barefooted which, due to the broken shells, coral and stones which littered the ground, was proving very painful.

During the day, James Marwick was taken ill with a high fever.

*Friday, 3rd December.* The last of the tents was erected which meant that night all prisoners would sleep under shelter. Such a development may have been providential as many of the men had become quite vocal about having to sleep down the well and, although they had been boiling the water before drinking as

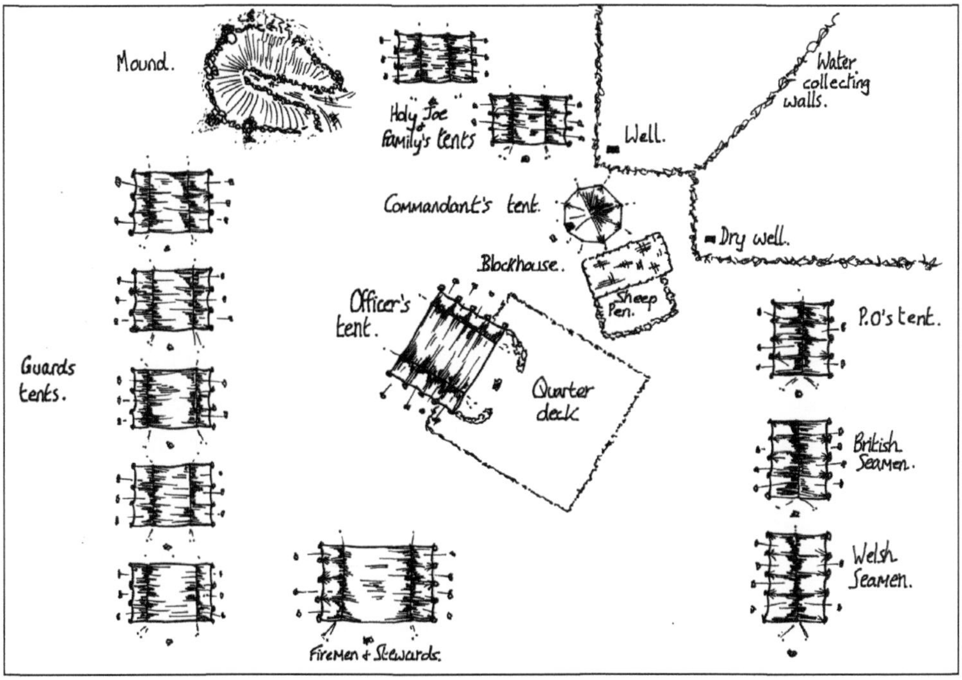


*Camp at Bir Hakkim [Author]*

recommended by the surgeon, dysentery and diarrhoea was becoming quite prevalent, causing the air in the well to became foul during the night. It became so bad that some of the men were having to be hauled out with ropes in the mornings! It was not only in the well where the air had become foul, Chief Officer Coalsted remarked '… that with dysentery and diarrhoea prevalent the stench in the [officers] tent where men were packed like sardines made sleep impossible ... and vermin had now made an appearance and [we] had no means of checking them.' Over the next few weeks, as the lice multiplied and, due to the lack of soap and washing facilities, most, if not all, of the survivors would become covered in sores caused by the men scratching, trying to relieve themselves of the lice bites.

Whilst scrabbling around the camp, Sub Lieutenant Dudgeon found a piece of glass which all used as a mirror. This was the first time they could see how much their appearance had altered, everyone appearing gaunt with long hair and beards. A row broke out as some of the men suspected that the officers were keeping food for themselves. It was quickly pointed out that, since the Senussi had started doling out the rations from the blockhouse, the food had been taken to the officers' tent where it was divided between the various messes in front of representatives from each. To ensure fair distribution they used an old 1lb jam tin to measure out the rice or barley flour for each mess and an ancient, blunt, sword bayonet and sharp stones, possibly flints, to butcher the carcasses. The officers divided their meat ration into as many pieces as there were men in their mess. The meat would then be cooked and, when ready, one man would leave the tent and sit outside, out of view. The cook would then pick up a piece of meat and shout 'Who will have this piece?', the man outside would shout someone's name. This procedure would be repeated until all the rations had been apportioned.

At about 16.00 hours, what was described by the Senussi as a wolf had killed a sheep belonging to Osman's flock. After much haggling late into the night, Achmed managed to purchase the carcass and, much to the prisoners' surprise, gave it to them. It was the first meat they had seen in fifteen days, and although it had been mauled about three-quarters of the carcass was still edible and all looked forward to having it the following day.

*Saturday, 4th December.* Now that all the prisoners were under canvas, the stone collecting parties for the blockhouses were done away with. Breakfast still consisted of boiled rice, but for the evening meal there was now mutton and boiled rice. The Senussi had shown all the messes how to cook the rice so that it was dry and not slushy. After the evening meal everyone felt much better and the various messes sat around their own campfires outside their tents until about 20.00 hours singing, talking and sipping green tea. For the officers, the main topic of the conversation was food, each man describing what he would love to eat and his favourite meal. It was, according to Tanner, one of the best nights they had had so far. During the day they had received the good news that some twenty or thirty goats were expected in the camp which, if true, meant that they could now look forward to having meat every alternate day.

*Sunday, 5th December*. During the early hours there was the usual heavy fog which soaked the tents, but it had been a warm night. It being a Sunday there was no work and awoke feeling better after the previous night's meal. For those suffering from dysentery and diarrhoea, however, the meal had passed straight through them and the stench in the tents was unbearable. The sufferers had no change of clothes and, after their messmates had washed their bodies, they had then to remain naked whilst their clothes were washed and draped over the surrounding shrubs to dry. This had become a daily routine if the weather was warm. If the weather was not warm enough to dry the clothes, the sick had to lie in their own filth and, to add to their miseries, everyone, whether sick or healthy, was swarming with lice.

Breakfast consisted of one ship's biscuit and they later had three meals of boiled rice. At dusk, in the officers' tent, the usual Sunday service was held, which a few petty officers attended. This evening the service had ended with the singing of *God Save the King* which caused Captain Achmed to fly into a rage. He rushed over to the officers' mess and made Lieutenant Tanner promise that the prisoners would never sing it again. In his defence, Tanner retorted that he thought he had received permission but apparently was mistaken. All hands turned in at about 20.15 hours.

At about 23.00 hours two shots were fired by the guards, who were no more than young boys, and there was great excitement in the camp. It transpired that Osman's dog had killed the wolf. One of the prisoners remarked that the wolf looked more like a large fox!

These same young soldiers would regularly fall asleep whilst on guard duty and the sergeant would give them a good whack with his cane whilst doing his rounds and their howls would wake up the prisoners. If their guards did not fall asleep, they would inevitably sing which would also wake up the prisoners!

*Monday, 6th December*. Work continued at the Well of the Red Doctor. Breakfast and dinner was of salted, boiled rice, whilst for supper there was sweetened, boiled rice, after which the officers sat around their campfire and had four glasses of green tea.

*Tuesday, 7th December*. The rations had again been reduced and each man was to receive about 1½ lbs of rice but in reality received much less and what there was had to be picked over carefully as it was full of dust, dirt, mouse droppings and other foreign matter.

During the afternoon the Senussi found a dead four-month old baby camel floating in the well which was thought to have belonged to a passing caravan and had fallen into the well during the night and drowned. Gwatkin-Williams volunteered to go down with a rope to recover it and the camel was hoisted out. The Senussi showed no interest in the carcass so it was given to the prisoners whereupon Quartermaster Rowlands who, in his youth had been a butcher's boy, volunteered to skin and cut it up. As a result, the officers dined on boiled rice and boiled camel's head and for supper, a soup made of its liver, kidneys and heart. Lieutenant Tanner later wrote that he 'Went to bed feeling well fed and content after a fashion, but we had been rather hungry or would not have eaten drowned camel.' Sub Lieutenant Marsh recorded that a lot of the men were now praying for more camels to fall down the well but unfortunately for them, the Senussi took greater precautions with all future caravans.

During the day a few more cases of dysentery were reported amongst both officers and crew and Cox, suffering of a stricture of the urethra, was now in great pain.

*Wednesday, 8th December.* Not much sleep was had during the night as the weather turned colder, the sentries noisier and Osman's two donkeys had brayed continuously and, having no grass to eat, grazed on the nearby bushes and nigh on demolished the prisoners' tents in their efforts to get at the bushes and scrub which the men had collected as firewood and stacked outside their messes. For some days, the prisoners had found each morning that their firewood stacks had shrunk. At first the officers suspected that the guards were stealing it as Paddy the terrier had actually bitten one as he attempted to steal some. The officers made a bed for the dog within the wood pile but the stack still shrank. Then it was discovered that, whilst Paddy may not have liked the Senussi stealing the wood, he did not mind the donkeys helping themselves.

During the morning, Tanner went out as usual with the firewood collecting party, believing that he was setting an example to both officers and crew regarding the importance of daily exercise. More importantly, he wanted to ensure that everyone in the party pulled his own weight. This morning, firewood party found a large snake amongst the shrubbery which was instantly killed.

On the menu was boiled rice for breakfast, camel meat soup and rice for lunch and cold camel meat and hard-boiled rice for tea and supper. During the evening, the officers had a sing song around the campfire till about 20.00 hours then turned in.

*Thursday, 9th December.* The weather had turned slightly warmer and most of the prisoners had slept well. In the officers' tent they had a breakfast of salted rice, followed by sweet rice for lunch and salted rice again for tea.

As a reward for removing the drowned camel from the well, Captain Achmed gave Gwatkin-Williams a ship's biscuit which the latter described as a 'Very great luxury.'

During the evening, the officers gathered around the fire to drink green tea until about 20.00 hours.

*Friday, 10th December*. Sleep had become easier for everyone during the past two nights. Dutton speculated that this was because they were becoming accustomed to the hard desert floor.

They were up at 06.00 hours for work at the Wells of the Red Doctor. Again there was boiled rice three times today and some green tea in the evening. Hopes of additional rations had been raised when some of the crew spotted the guards slaughtering a sheep, but it was not for them.

Very unusually, Captain Achmed was in a very amiable mood and, speaking fairly good English, was chatty with everyone. This was perhaps the result of the arrival during the morning of additional guards, their families and more camels. These same animals stampeded later during the day, injuring a woman and child.

Some eight to ten men were now suffering with dysentery each day.

*Saturday, 11th December.* Another very misty, damp and cold night resulted in the tents again being soaked through in the morning and few of the prisoners managed to get a decent sleep as Osman's large black dog had spent most of the night barking.

A goat was slaughtered and butchered but as usual some of the offal and fat was retained by the guards. The cuts were divided between the ninety-six men, which worked out at only 2 ozs each. In the officers' mess it was decided rather than roast the meat which wasted too much of its goodness, they would first use it to make soup for lunch and then have the meat for tea or supper. Consequently, breakfast was boiled rice, lunch was goat soup and rice and tea boiled goat and rice washed down with green tea.

The prisoners were still busy clearing out the Wells of the Red Doctor, where Osman urged them on as rain was expected any day. So far no great amount had fallen, which both officers and crew were thankful for as the tents were so full of holes they would leak like sieves.

It was a very hot day during which Gwatkin-Williams, with Achmed's approval, had drafted a letter to Nuri Bey asking if it were possible for the *Tara*'s and *Moorina's* crews to be exchanged for Turkish or Senussi prisoners.

All hands were turned in by 19.00 hours.

*Sunday, 12th December*. The fog lingered until 10.00 hours and the tents were again soaked through. As usual the men were up at 06.00 hours to stoke the fires on which to cook their breakfasts of boiled, salted rice. Later the working party departed for the Wells of the Red Doctor. During the afternoon the sun broke through which lifted the mood of the camp.

Rations were issued and one goat was slaughtered, again the Senussi retained what they wanted and handed the remainder to the prisoners, which worked out at about an egg-cup full of meat per man. For lunch the officers had boiled, sugared rice and for their evening meal, boiled goat and rice followed by a glass of tea.

During the evening there was hymn singing, and Sub Lieutenant Marsh remarked that it was nice to hear the Welsh crew singing in the tent alongside them.

*Monday, 13th December*.[1] A goat was slaughtered and handed over to the prisoners who were allowed to butcher it themselves. A bag of flour and a bag of rice were also issued with orders that they were to last for four days.

Hearing that Captain Achmed might soon be going to Sollum, Tanner compiled a list of survivors which he hoped could be forwarded to Commander Holland, the L&NWR's Marine Superintendent at Holyhead. This was the third such list he had compiled since their capture.

It was noted many of the men were now suffering with dysentery.

*Tuesday, 14th December*. The weather had warmed and the day broke with no mist or fog. Meals again consisted of the interminable rice, flour and goat. The Senussi guards kept one of the goat's back legs for themselves. Although they had been issued with flour in lieu of rice it did not last long and the collecting, cooking and eating of snails (now nicknamed 'Lily Whites') had become more popular. The downside of this was that some of the crew were always arguing and quarrelling over the snails, and the food ration in general, so much so that every now and then a fight would break out. Although the senior officers did at first try to restore order, they eventually decided to let the fights continue as by now the men were so weak that any fight did not last long and they were at best half-hearted affairs.

1. *Prisoners of the Red Desert* records that on 13th December HMS *Jonquil* paid a visit to Port Bardia and was fired upon so had to beat a hasty retreat. Her log has been consulted and it shows that on this date she was on patrol off the coast of Crete.

Dysentery was raging amongst the prisoners and Surgeon Arthur could do nothing as he had no medicines.

*Wednesday, 15th December*. At 11.00 hours Captain Achmed left camp for Sollum, taking with him the prisoners' mail, some of which had been hurriedly written. The letters included one from Gwatkin-Williams to Nuri Bey and Admiral Peirse and one from Tanner to Commander Holland. Achmed also took with him some forty camels which the Senussi guards had commandeered over the last couple of weeks from the Arab camps in the locality. He promised to bring them back laden with food and luxuries in time for Christmas Day. In his absence, Mahomed Zoue took over as commandant of the camp.

The usual working party departed for the Well of the Red Doctor, whilst in the camp the cooks of the various messes prepared the day's meals. In the officer's mess the cook of the day made 125 flapjacks, cutting them out of the dough with the lid from a tin of Traveller's tobacco. All the others left in camp, both officers and crew, spent their time either tending to the sick, gathering firewood, having vermin hunts (searching out lice in their clothes) washing and mending clothes — most of the men had by now made sewing needles out of slivers of bone which littered the camp and had unpicked one of the canvas sails from the lifeboat for thread. Most of the men had made or would make trousers and shirts out of the empty flour and rice sacks which were distributed evenly amongst the survivors, although the most deserving were always given preference. The garments they made, however, soon wore out at either the elbow, the knees or the backside.

Now that Achmed had left, everyone seemed hopeful that they would soon be free and the mood in the camp lightened somewhat as every now and then someone would break out with a laugh and even the smokers had got over their craving for tobacco. The petty officers were given a tent by the Senussi which they erected behind that of the British seamen.

Sub Lieutenant Griffiths came down with dysentery. He was already suffering from an old injury which affected his right-hand side, the result of a fall down a hatch when his vessel was working cargo at San Fransisco some years previously.

*Thursday, 16th December*. At about 07.00 hours the camp awoke to a cold grey morning with the threat of rain in the air. The desert was beginning to show signs of spring as the shrubs started to sprout leaves, but there had been insufficient rain, although there had been plenty of heavy dews and mists.

After a breakfast of boiled rice, a flour ration was issued from the blockhouse. Later, in the officers' mess, Dutton, the cook of the day, made a duff by mixing flour with boiled rice, kneading it and placing the dough into one leg of a pair of Arab trousers knotted at the bottom. Placed in a bucket of water it was boiled over a fire, and when thought to be ready, pulled out. It looked nice and plump and was divided into nine pieces and thoroughly enjoyed by all and washed down with a cup of green tea. For their evening meal, Chief Officer Coalsted cooked a fine soup of goat and rice.

Gwatkin-Williams spent some time talking to Mohamed Zoue and was told that the Turks were willing to exchange the prisoners but the British were holding things up. Mohamet Zoue went on to explain that if the Senussi had wanted to keep the prisoners they would have taken them further into the desert a long time ago. He added that rumours that the Senussi had either killed or mistreated their Italian prisoners were untrue as in reality they had been better looked after than the *Tara*'s survivors. This news was passed on to the other messes which put everyone in a good sense of humour, as they waited to hear news of the prisoner exchange. Earlier, there had been some excitement in the camp when one of the prisoners had captured a chameleon which fascinated everyone as it changed colour.

Quartermaster Robert Abbit was now suffering from dysentery.

*Friday, 17th December.* A dull, cold day. In the officer's mess all sat around after breakfast trying to remember what bread tasted like, then what bacon and eggs tasted like — but they soon gave it up as a futile exercise. Later in the morning Coal Trimmer Owens, who had escaped about a month before, arrived in camp under an armed guard of two Muhafizia. Everyone expected that he would be severely punished, but Mohamed Zoue merely contented himself by slapping his face two or three times and ordered him to be placed into the dry well for a few hours. During the afternoon he was given a biscuit and some water by the Senussi. Sometime later Captain Gwatkin-Williams managed to get him freed and asked him for an account of his adventure. Owens related that he had been found by some Senussi a couple of days after escaping wandering in the desert and been taken to Sollum where he was well treated and well fed. In his pockets he had a bar of soap and some priceless matches. Owens also mentioned that the journey from Sollum had taken five days.

Gwatkin-Williams learned from Mohamed Zoue that Captain Achmed was not returning and that the prisoners were now under Senussi control. He wrote that Mohamed Zoue '... was a humane and kindly man, much saddened by the war with Italy [and] who had at one time been a head man at Ben Ghazi, where his wife and family still remain.'

*Saturday, 18th December*. The weather had warmed a little but the prisoners rations had not improved. Boiled rice for breakfast, dinner and tea and many men were down with dysentery. Dutton complained of feeling very feverish and spent all day lying in the tent.

*Sunday, 19th December.* Dutton was feeling much better and rose at 06.00 hours to help cook the breakfast of boiled rice. The rice ration had been increased slightly so that each man had about 1lb and some 2 ozs of goat's meat. For lunch, the officers made this into mutton soup which they thickened with flour and had boiled rice for tea. Most of the officers and men were now regularly supplementing their diet by eating snails.

During the evening the officers sang hymns around the fire.

The last of the sugar was issued, the tea having run out sometime ago.

*Monday, 20th December.* Everybody was up at 06.30 hours and after breakfast, in addition to the working party at the Well of the Red Doctor, another working party was organised to clear out a small well. This was about three miles away, sited between the Wells of the Red and the White Doctor. It was full of sand and stone and Mohamed Zoue was keen to see it brought it back into use as it was to be named after him.

Dysentery and lice were affecting many, a situation which caused great concern to both the surgeon and the senior officers. Most had large sores on their bodies caused by the itching and scratching and most days lice hunts were a regular feature of camp life, the men picking the lice and their eggs from the seams of their clothes. To try and eradicate the infestations, on warm days the prisoners would boil their clothes and then drape them over nearby shrubs to dry. But it was hopeless and within a few hours the lice would return.

The weather had turned for the better as it was a glorious, warm day.

*Tuesday, 21st December.* Mid-winter day. The men felt that the weather could only get better.

By now the prisoners guards numbered only four Senussi who, knowing that they could not escape, left them to wander as they wished.

It was noted that Seaman John Hodgson was suffering badly from dysentery.

*Wednesday, 22nd December*. Owing to the increasing numbers of men going down with dysentery, Mohamed Zoue issued the prisoners with olive oil in which they were to boil their breakfast rice. During the day a caravan of eight camels arrived bringing eight bags of rice and six of flour.

During the evening, the working party, half starved and half clad, arrived back at camp from the well and asked Mohamed Zoue for an increase in their rations as the work was now becoming too much for them in their weakened state. Their request was refused as quite simply there was no food to spare. A small goat was killed for the guards, but not for the prisoners.

Captain Gwatkin-Williams had picked up a rumour that they could soon be sent to the Siwa oasis, which he believed was malarial and nearer to Egypt.

*Thursday, 23rd December*. At about 10.00 hours it started to rain, which soon turned into a downpour which lasted until 15.00 hours. The water ran in torrents through the tents and the tents themselves leaked like sieves, forcing the men inside to stand under any decent sized stretch of goatskin for protection from the rain whilst the water flowed around and over their feet. What it must have been like for the sick and infirm can only be imagined; everyone was very cold, wet and miserable. Dutton later remarked that this was the most miserable day so far. To try to lift the men's spirits fires were lit inside the tents, something which the Senussi would not do as it ruined the hides out of which the tents were made.

After the rain had stopped the daily firewood collecting party went out.

*Friday, 24th December*. A fine, sunny day and after breakfast the officers began to construct a low stone wall, some three foot high, around their tent, much as the petty officers and men had done. Not only would this make the tent feel snugger but it and would hopefully divert rain water around the tent during the next downpour.

During the day a Turkish officer, Lieutenant Mustapha, who on his way to Sollum, rested at the camp. Captain Gwatkin-Williams and Basil took him around the tents, pointing out the sixteen men with dysentery who were in a pitiable condition and asked if he would speak with General Nuri Bey on their behalf. He promised he would and left the camp at 17.00 hours taking with him the officers' letters, yet another list of the prisoners, a list of the valuables taken by Captain Achmed. He also promised to send Sub Lieutenant Griffiths a belt to support his injured side.

There were a total of twenty men on the sick list, some suffering from dysentery and others who were described as 'ruptured' — caused by uprooting shrubs for firewood? Lieutenant Tanner later wrote 'Not much of a Christmas Eve!'

*Saturday, 25th December*. Christmas Day, fine and sunny but cold. There was no working party at the well, but the men would have to work the following day instead. At 07.15 hours after breakfast, Captain Gwatkin-Williams, along with Lieutenants Tanner and Apcar, and accompanied by Basil, called at the blockhouse to wish Mohamed Zoue a Merry Christmas. To their surprise, he invited them in and gave them some unleavened bread and sugar. They spoke for a while and before leaving he gave each a handful of white beans to put in their soup.

At mid-day Gwatkin-Williams and Tanner paid each mess a visit finding that most of the men had already eaten their day's ration. Most of the messes had been saving a portion of their daily ration over the last week so as to have a good blow out on Christmas Day; now they had nothing to look forward to.

After their visits to the messes the three officers returned to their own tent for Christmas lunch, which had been cooked by Second Engineer Richardson. He had awoken at 03.00 hours to prepare the dinner which consisted of soup (made of 1lb of goat's bones, rice and the white beans, boiled rice and dough boys) and was served at 11.45 hours. Afternoon tea consisted of weak green tea (they had saved the used tea leaves from the last seven days) and 'Petty Officer's Pudding' which was made of flour kneaded with boiled rice and some sugar (saved for over a fortnight). The pudding, which weighed some 20 lbs, had been boiled for five hours in Lieutenant Tanner's trousers! After the meal most of the officers had to go for a walk to digest the pudding as it sat in their stomachs like a rock. There had been enough pudding to give each man some ½ lbs. For supper, they had another portion of boiled rice with 'ash cooked' bread. To end the night, all messes gathered and sang carols and hymns around their respective camp fires and retired at 19.30 hours.

At about 20.30 hours the stillness of the night was shattered by a woman's screams. Later, it was learned later that a messenger had arrived at camp with the news that Osman's brother-in-law had been killed in battle with the British near Mersa Matruh. During the day artillery fire could be heard intermittently to the north east.

*Sunday, 26th December*. At the Wells of the Red Doctor the working party had now been put to repairing and rebuilding the low walls which collected and diverted the water into the wells. Mohamed Zoue informed Captain Gwatkin-Williams that there had been heavy fighting near Mersa Matruh where the Senussi and Turks had killed over 3,000 British troops and had taken 900 prisoners, losing some 1,000 men themselves. Gwatkin-Williams doubted the veracity of this very much!

After yesterday's 'festive' meals most men were feeling well fed. The rations issued on this day were shorter than they had been for sometime and although a goat was killed, the officers decided to save their own meat ration so as to add it to the duff the following day. Rations for the ninety-four prisoners were now to be issued once a week — three sacks of rice and one of flour. The senior officers were concerned that some messes would go through their allotment within five days as they did not seem able to ration their food.

Fourteen Senussi arrived from the east during the day and camped nearby. More heavy gunfire to the north east was heard.

*Monday, 27th December.* A very quiet day, the plight of the sick and the lack of medicines was making the men feel very hopeless and depressed.

The officer's had a meat duff, made of finely chopped goat's meat, flour, rice and water all mixed and kneaded, then boiled in a cloth.

Gunfire was heard from dawn until about 09.00 hours and some men reported that during the night they had seen a searchlight to the north, in the direction where they thought Sollum lay.[1] The fourteen Senussi left heading westwards.

*Tuesday, 28th December*. Owing to all the sickness Mohamed Zoue ordered that the prisoner's rice must be cooked with olive oil, of which he only had a limited

1. On 27th December, the French Ministry of Marine issued the following communiqué – 'In the course of an exploration of the Bay of Sollum one of our cruisers bombarded and destroyed a Turkish battery. The trawler *Parisii* opened fire off the Ottoman coast on two large enemy submarines a great distance off [which] took to flight after being fired at for 2 hours.'

amount. A small ration of oil was issued to the officers from the blockhouse which was divided equally in front of representatives of each mess. The commandant also ordered that the sick, now numbering twenty-five, were to be placed into one tent. This caused terrible upset as some of the men who were turned out of their tents refused to sleep in other tents and the dysentery cases, without their mess-mates to look after, them just lay in their own filth. After protestations the order was soon rescinded.

*Wednesday, 29th December*. A caravan of four camels arrived in the camp from the east, carrying sacks of rice and herding twenty-four goats. The supplies were very welcome as the meat had run out some days previously and the rice ration had shrunk dramatically.

Gwatkin-Williams was informed that Captain Achmed was to return to Bir Hakkim within a few days with 130 British cavalry prisoners.

*Thursday, 30th December*. Sub Lieutenant Marsh wrote, 'Rice again for meals. It is strange that one does not grow tired of same – hunger I suppose!' Since mid December most of the messes had been cooking large numbers of snails, either roasted or boiled. Some men had refused to eat them. One of these was Yeoman Signaller Allen who a few days before had relented and begun to eat them, but on this day he went down with dysentery. This led some men to think that the snails might be the cause of the infection.

One of the firewood-collecting party found some wild garlic which was put into the pot along with the snails. It was found to be quite tasty and everyone started to look for garlic.

It had been quite a warm day, which was quite a change from the cold weather of the previous few days.

*Friday, 31st December*. Remarking on the goats which had arrived on the 29th, Quartermaster Rowlands speculated that one goat killed every other day and shared between ninety-four prisoners and about forty guards was not going to satisfy anybody's hunger. As if to prove the point, a small sheep was slaughtered and given to the prisoners — it worked out to about 1oz of meat per man.

Captain Gwatkin-Williams reflected that it was now eight weeks since the *Tara* had been sunk and, in spite of the difficulties and hardships, the time had flown. The men were becoming accustomed to hunger, squalor, dirt and discomfort, and while hope ebbed and waned, life was anything but dull. He thought that cheerfulness and religion were deeply felt by most. Politeness, at one time almost lost, was now sometimes seen and discipline, though of a peculiar sort, had been maintained in spite of the officers and men being herded together.

# 15. Egypt, December 1915

Now that all the preparations had been made, General Wallace was ready to make his move. At 07.00 hours on 11th December, 350 men of the 15th Sikhs, the 2nd Composite Yeomanry Regiment (three squadrons with three machine guns), a section of the Nottinghamshire Battery, Royal Horse Artillery, six armoured cars, three Fords and a wireless car of the Royal Naval Armoured Car Division, together with one section of the South Midland Field Ambulance, RAMC, moved out of Mersa Matruh to engage and disperse the enemy.

Marching along the coast road the column reached Wadi Senaab where the Senussi were entrenched in some strength. The cavalry pushed forward ahead of the column and engaged with the Senussi who were holding the southern side of the *wadi* in some strength. Due to the nature of the ground, however, the infantry had been unable to keep up with the mounted men and were unable to assist and things looked precarious until the arrival of a squadron of the Australian Light Horse during the afternoon. The enemy were finally driven from their positions, with a loss of some one hundred men killed or wounded. The British lost one officer and thirteen other ranks killed, and two officers and sixteen other ranks wounded. Unfortunately, one of those killed was Lieutenant-Colonel Snow who was shot by a Senussi whom he was attempting to persuade to surrender.

After dark, the column rested at Um Rakhum and the next day, owing to the tiredness of the yeomanry's horses, concentrated on clearing out the Wadi Shaifa, capturing some twenty-five Senussi and a number of abandoned camels and cattle. During the day, aerial reconnaissance revealed that the enemy had gathered in some strength at Ras Manas, thirteen miles west of Um Rakhum, so the column was strengthened by two company's of 1/6th Royal Scots and orders were issued for an advance on Ras Manaa the following day.

At 08.00 hours on the morning of 13th December the column moved out but, whilst crossing the Wadi Shaifa, was attacked by an estimated 1,200 Senussi supported by two artillery pieces and machine guns. The situation become rather critical until the arrival of two guns of the Nottinghamshire RHA and a squadron of the Australian Light Horse which managed to drive the enemy back about a mile before darkness put an end to the pursuit. The column retired for the night to Um Rakhum and the next day returned to Mersa Matruh. British casualties amounted to nine other ranks killed, six officers and fifty men wounded. The Senussi lost about 250 killed and wounded. On the night of the 15th, owing to their isolation, the British outposts at the wells of Abu Gerab, Baggush and Gerawla were withdrawn and from this date until 23rd December the time was spent organising and reinforcing the force at Mersa Matruh.

Meanwhile, the enemy had not wasted any time and concentrated their forces near Gebel Mewda, some eight miles south-west of Mersa Matruh. Aerial reconnaissance showed that by the 24th there were in the area an estimated 5,000 Senussi (about half of whom were Muafiazia), with four artillery pieces and a number of machine guns under the command of Gaafar.

Major-General Wallace decided to split his force in two. Command of the right column was given to Lieutenant-Colonel Gordon of the 15th Sikhs and the column was made up of the Royal Buckinghamshire Hussars Yeomanry, one section of the Nottinghamshire Battery, RHA, the recently arrived 1st New Zealand Rifle Brigade, the 15th Sikhs, 2/8th Middlesex Regiment, Notts & Derby Field Ambulance and the water section of the Australian divisional train. The left column (under Brigadier-General Tyndale Biscoe) was made up of the Brigade Staff and Signalling Troop (2nd Composite Yeomanry Brigade), Nottinghamshire RHA (less one section), two troops of the Duke of Lancaster's Yeomanry, one troop of the Derbyshire Yeomanry, two troops of the City of London Yeomanry, one squadron of the Hertfordshire Yeomanry, the Composite Regiment Australian Light Horse (three squadrons), the Yeomanry Machine Gun Section and the Yeomanry Field Ambulance.

At 05.00 hours on the 25th, the force marched out of Mersa Matruh, the right hand column going along the Khedival Road towards Gebel Medwa, whilst the left hand column took a wide detour southward around the flank of the enemy in an attempt to block his retreat. HMS *Clematis*, positioned off shore was to assist the right hand column by giving supporting fire.

At first every thing went well, but at 06.00 hours as dawn was breaking, the Senussi sentries gave warning of the approaching column by lighting huge bonfires and there was soon fierce fighting. It was obvious that the surprise that General Wallace had been hoping for had not come off, however by 10.00 hours the Senussi had broken and the British had broken their line. Skirmishing continued in the caves and ravines during which many Senussi were shot or bayoneted and many others captured. But it was not until 15.00 hours that the left column reached its required position between the Wadi Senab and Wadi Majid, but which time it was too late. Although decisively beaten, the majority of the Senussi force was able to escape westwards along the rocky seashore, where the cavalry were unable to follow. At 17.00 hours the pursuit was broken off and the cavalry returned to Mersa Matruh whilst the rest of the force camped at Gebel Medwa. The British had lost fourteen other ranks killed with three officers and forty-seven other ranks wounded. The Senussi had lost over 370 dead (a number of the dead were identified as deserters from the Egyptian Coastguard as they were still wearing their uniforms), eighty-two prisoners, eighty camels and much live stock and over 30,000 rounds of small arms ammunition and three boxes of artillery ammunition. The British also captured the personal effects of Gaafar which he had to leave behind in his flight. A subadar and eleven sepoys who had been captured by the enemy from the transport *Moorina* and used as camel drivers, took the chance to escape to the British lines during the confusion of battle.

Major-General Wallace now took the opportunity to clear the area between Mersa Matruh and al'Dabaa of Senussi, who were mostly Bedouin and a battalion of Muafizia. To effect this, a small force under the Earl of Lucan, consisting of six squadrons of cavalry, two sections of artillery, the 15th Sikhs and the 2/7th Middlesex Regiment (less two companies) was despatched on the 28th from Mersa Matruh to Bir Gerawla, twelve miles to the south east. Although several Senussi camps were visited, no resistance was offered, the Bedouin fleeing from their camps as the column approached. The column returned to Mersa Matruh on the 30th having destroyed some eighty tents, large quantities of grain and seizing over 100 camels and 500 sheep.

During December the Royal Navy continued with the anti gun-running patrols off the North African coast and provided additional firepower for the advance to Gebel Medwa. On the 17th December Admiral Peirse had some welcome news from the Admiralty in that the Flower Class Fleet minesweepers HMS *Magnolia, Mallow, Mimosa, Lily* and *Veronica* had been despatched to his command. On the 20th he was notified that the German *UC-12* was sheltering in Sollum Bay, damaged and short of fuel. Not wanting to miss the opportunity of destroying a U-boat, Peirse, only having HMS *Clematis* available, sent her towards Sollum with orders to contact the *Magnolia* and *Mallow*, who were escorting a convoy of transports from Marseilles, and take them to Sollum to sink the submarine. However, by the time the *Clematis* reached the convoy, the *Magnolia* was running short of fuel and had already left for Alexandria. Accompanied by the *Mallow,* the *Clemetis* arrived at Sollum on the morning of the 22nd where they discovered that the U-boat had left. The Germans had sent the *U-34* from Cattaro on the 21st to assist the *UC-12* and the latter, after undergoing repairs, had then sailed. Disappointed, the two warships opened fire and destroyed the pier and sank or damaged several small steamers and boats which, according to one source, had arrived full of arms and ammunition for the Senussi as soon as the town had fallen. Both ships came under fire from the two 9-cms Krupp guns — the Senussi had evidently found both the breech blocks and sights that the Egyptian Coastguards had thrown into the sea before departing. Both Royal Navy ships escaped without damage.

# 16. In Captivity, January 1916

*Saturday, 1st January 1916*. The day broke with a fine sunny morning and the men had again saved some of their rations over the previous week for another blow out. There was boiled rice for breakfast and lunch and a meat duff for tea at 18.00 hours which the men enjoyed very much and after which they turned in.

Captain Gwatkin-Williams reflected that New Year's Day had been celebrated much the same as Christmas Day, albeit less spectacularly. The prisoners are living in five tattered and filthy tents, their rations per man being 14 ozs of rice and a quarter-pound of flour, with 1 oz of mutton or goat flesh, or a salt-spoon full of olive oil every other day. The men washed regularly but had been without soap for weeks and all had unkempt, long hair and beards. Many were suffering with various ailments and up to twelve men were suffering daily with dysentery, six had ruptures, but there were no trusses, and Firemen Owen Roberts was dying of tuberculosis and the boilermaker, G M Cox, of uric acid poisoning. Perhaps surprisingly, no one was suffering with a cold. Neither medicines, medical supplies nor bandages were available nor were new or warm clothes. The sick were either fed the same meagre diet as the healthy or simply went without and all slept together on the ground in the vermin infested tents, their bodies covered with tattered clothes or sacking and where a fire burned all day and night.

There was plenty of good, clean water and thankfully it had not rained hard. The men were kept busy clearing out and repairing the old wells and low walls or collected firewood, cooked and tended the sick. It seems that everyone was coping, up to a point, with the constant, gnawing hunger but, the thinner they became the harder and colder the ground became when they lay down to sleep at night.

Some of the men tried to find different ways of cooking their rations whilst others tried out different combinations of the rations, their efforts being much appreciated as were those individuals who could remember songs, hymns, or poetry. They had received no news of the outside world since they landed and had no knowledge of whether their families knew if they were alive or dead. There was no reading material in the camp, other than an old French magazine dated 1870!

Lieutenant Tanner hoped that peace may be found during the coming year so that next New Year's Day would be spent at home. Whilst Sub Lieutenant Marsh was more pessimistic, writing that he expected to be in Bir Hakkim for sometime as the government would not bother with their rescue as the men required for the attempt would be needed elsewhere.

Assistant Engineer Davies was also very down, writing that they could not hold out much longer, and that the Chief Engineer, Abbit, Cox and Hodgson were suffering terribly with dysentery.

As if to dampen the men's spirits, the rain poured down all day.

*Sunday, 2nd January.* Rain again during the morning with a cold north westerly wind and more rain at dusk. Again the tents had leaked and all were soaked and cold. Sub Lieutenant Griffiths noted that all eighteen in the officers' mess huddled together miserably. From Osman they learned that this was a rather mild winter with not much rainfall, for which the prisoners were very thankful! Everyone hope that there would not be many caravans passing through as the camels need quite a bit of water and could easily empty the wells.

The prisoners had boiled rice for all meals and during the evening there was hymn singing in the officers' tent.

*Monday, 3rd January.* Although it was a fairly hot day, more rain fell during the afternoon and evening. Again the water had poured in through both the holes in the tents and the recently-built wall around the officers' tent. All the prisoners were soaked through, cold and sickness was rife. The health of the chief engineer, Cox, and Hodgson (all suffering badly from dysentery) was causing concern and the combination of bad weather and the sickness raging in camp made everyone feel gloomy, markedly so during this evening when there was a very sombre mood in the officers' tent as they sat around the fire, nobody felt very much like the usual light hearted banter.

Only boiled rice for the prisoners' meals again. Basil completed building a hive-shaped oven which was fired up and pronounced a success.

*Tuesday, 4th January.* A bright, sunny day but cold, with a strong breeze blowing which thankfully dried out the tents. A goat was slaughtered and for the officers it was rice for breakfast and tea whilst for lunch there was mutton soup thickened with a little rice, 1 oz of meat and a dough boy for each man.

One of the petty officers found and killed a leveret which was cooked in their mess and given to the sick, one of whom was Cox — now recorded as gravely ill.

*Wednesday, 5th January.* This day began much as another day, albeit with rotten weather of hailstones and rain. Camp routine was as normal, the working parties going out to the wells and to collect firewood. Those remaining in the camp looked after the weak and the sick, had a lice hunt and prepared the evening meal.

Sub Lieutenant Griffiths recorded that they had not seen soap for eight weeks '... and when we do have a dirty wash we use the shirt we wear to dry our burnt skin.'

At about 20.00 hours, just as the officers were settling down for the night, a petty officer called at their mess to inform Lieutenant Tanner that Cox, the boilermaker, had passed away at 19.15 hours. The officers went over to the petty officers' mess with Surgeon Arthur who confirmed that Cox was dead, his death being attributed to uric acid poisoning and malnutrition. The doctor speculated that if they had been prisoners in Europe, then Cox would have survived. News of his death was quickly passed from mess to mess and cast a dark shadow over the whole camp and all prisoners felt very sad and very, very far from home.

*Thursday, 6th January.* After breakfast, Cox's body was prepared for burial, being carefully sewn up in rice and flour sacks. His grave was dug some 2–300 yards south of the camp by the prisoners using their bare hands, lids of cooking utensils and flat stones.

Once dug to the required depth, or as deep as they could go, the body was carried gently from the petty officers' tents and at 10.00 hours was lowered into the grave. All those able to attend gathered, standing bareheaded around the grave whilst Lieutenant Tanner conducted the burial service and recited as much of the burial service as he could remember. All hands then recited the Lord's Prayer and sang *One day's march nearer home,* followed by Welsh hymns (one of which was *Bydd myrdd o rhyfeddodau)* after which there were prayers. During the service nearly all the men had broken down, crying freely, none feeling ashamed. After the service, the men covered his grave with stones.

Afterwards, Lieutenant Tanner noted that 'Cox had suffered a great deal of pain, but in the end passed away peacefully and without suffering' and Sub

Lieutenant Griffiths noted that 'Abbit and Hodgson [were] very bad [and] not such a thing as a luxury of another kind to give them.'

*Friday, 7th January.* A wild night after a cold and windy day, the men were still very gloomy over the death of Cox but life had to go on and the daily routine gradually picked up. There was boiled rice for breakfast and tea whilst for lunch a meat duff. Due to their meagre rations more and more men were eating snails, but so far Sub Lieutenant Marsh had resisted the temptation, but for how long he could last he was not sure.

*Saturday, 8th January.* Last night the wind blew from the north west and during the early morning, rain arrived, and once again the prisoners were soaked through. Needless to say most had a sleepless night.

In lieu of the meat or olive oil ration, some sugar was issued to each mess. The officers used theirs to add to a duff, made of flour, sugar, wild garlic and water. The dough was then boiled in the leg of a pair of Arab trousers. Owing to the success of Christmas and New Year's Day dinners, they decided to save a little of their daily rations for one good blow out each week.

*Sunday, 9th January.* There was no work today and the weather was warm and pleasant. Again there was boiled rice for breakfast, lunch and supper with which each officer had two flap jacks (made of flour, sugar and water). During the evening, there was the usual Sunday night hymn singing around the camp fire. Sub Lieutenant Marsh, in the officers' tent, remarked that the singing in the Welshmen's tent was beautiful.

Whilst Captain Gwatkin-Williams recorded that some of the Senussi were now starting to suffer from dysentery, so was hopeful that they would now make an effort to obtain medicines.

*Monday, 10th January.* The morning broke with a beautiful sunrise and the day gradually got warmer, but there was a slight cold wind. Breakfast was of boiled rice after which the working parties departed for the well. A goat was slaughtered, so for lunch they had one ounce of mutton, a flap jack and some soup to which had been added a few grains of rice. But before tea, at 15.45 hours, Seaman Hodgson died, having been suffering with dysentery, piles, lack of adequate food and the absence of medical treatment. Lieutenant Tanner later wrote that he had not suffered, but had just grown weaker and weaker until he eventually slipped away. His death, the second at Bir Hakkim, again cast a gloom over camp, in which there was now some twenty-five cases of dysentery, of which Chief Engineer Williams, Quartermaster Abbit and Fireman Owen Roberts were the worst, and their condition was causing a great deal of concern. However, they were well looked after — as well as their circumstances permitted — as each mess tended its own sick, where the healthy cleaned, washed and fed, and generally looked after the infirm. The prisoners had been given another cooking pan so were now busy, boiling the soiled clothes of the sick, trying to wash off the filth and lice — but owing to the lack of spare clothing the washing still had to be done on a sunny day so the clothes could dry and be returned to the sick on the same day.

Three camels carrying six bags of rice left camp, heading west.

*Tuesday, 11th January.* After breakfast, the body of Hodgson was sewn up in sacking, the grave dug as deep as possible alongside Cox's. The funeral took place at 08.30 hours and was attended by all that were able. The prisoners made a pathetic picture as nearly all were half clad in ragged tatters of uniform or flour or rice sacks, bareheaded, barefooted, lousy, long haired and bearded. Lieutenant Tanner read most of the burial service but was overcome with emotion and was barely able to carry on. They then sang *Nearer my God to thee* and *Abide with me,* after which the Welshmen sang the hymn, *Yn y dyfroedd mawr ar tonnau,* and Fireman Hugh O Hughes, a deacon of one of the chapels in Holyhead, recited the Lord's prayer in Welsh. It was a very sad and moving service, leaving most in tears. The men again piled stones and formed a cross over the grave to keep the wild dogs from the body. Afterwards, all retired to their respective messes and during the evening the officers had a sweet duff for supper which helped to fill them up and then turned in.

Another camel left camp today, heading westwards carrying two bags of rice.

*Wednesday, 12th January.* During the night nearly all could make out the noise of heavy gunfire in the distance and many speculated on what was happening.

They awoke to a cold and dreary day with a meagre breakfast of boiled rice. Concerned that the flour and rice in the blockhouse was running low, Mohamed Zoue ordered Mohamed the Senussi's cook to go to Sollum to procure more and before he left Captain Gwatkin-Williams asked him to bring back medicines.

During the day the Senussi asked if the prisoners wanted to move their tents as it was the Arab custom to shift camp every month or so if only by a few yards, the prisoners having built stone walls around their tents declined, the Senussi acquiesced.

The Captain noted that there were now very few guards in the camp and that Mohamed Zoue was hopeful that the prisoners could be released before summer.

*Thursday, 13th January.* The weather was again very dull and cold with a full gale blowing, so most spent the day in their tents in which they lit fires to try to keep warm. For breakfast and lunch they had boiled salted rice and for supper sweet boiled rice.

*Friday, 14th January.* The working party at the Mohamed Zoue well had by now emptied it of rubble and sand but were still repairing the low walls that collected and diverted the rain water into the well.

The weather was chilly and breakfast was still boiled rice, lunch was dough boys and mutton soup. Mohamed Zoue informed the officers that Greece had entered the war on the side of the Allies which led many to speculate that the war could soon be over.

*Saturday, 15th January.* Another day of boiled rice and duff for their meals, but all went to bed still feeling hungry.

*Sunday, 16th January.* A day of rest. Over the last few days the rations had been slowly cut down and the prisoners could only afford to put a small amount of rice into their soup. For supper they had boiled sweet rice, after which the officers had hymn singing around the fire. Sub Lieutenant Marsh remarked that the second steward, William Barton, was of great help as he knew a number of hymns.

*Monday, 17th January.* More gunfire was heard during the night and on awaking they discovered that Mohamed the Senussi cook had returned from Sollum with a caravan and each prisoner was issued with a piece of Grecian made soap only the second piece to be issued to each man since they had landed in November. The caravan had also brought two prisoners, Indian troops[1] from the *Moorina,* who

1. Although described as 'troops', it is believed that at least one man was a fireman from the *Moorina.*

stated that they had been taken as far a Mersa Matruh, where there was a battle in which the Senussi had been defeated. During the confusion of retreat, thirty-one of the thirty-six Indian prisoners had managed to escape, but they (the two Indian 'troops') had been recaptured. They also reported that the Senussi had by now been driven back to Sollum. The two Indians were put into the petty officers' mess.

Lieutenant Apcar had managed to concoct two new dishes, pillaf [sic — pilau rice?] and kebabs.

*Tuesday, 18th January.* At 10.00 hours Mohamed Zoue left the camp with three camels and some Muafiazia. He explained that he was to attend a conference with the British at Sollum, but before leaving, Captain Gwatkin-Williams asked him to give Nuri Bey a letter which explained that he was giving the him seven days notice of the withdrawal of his parole as the general had not kept any of his promises. Through Basil he tried to explain what was in the letter and his reasons for the withdrawal of the parole, but Mohamed Zoue paid no heed and rode off. The new camp commandant was Salim Effendi, a kind-hearted man but he did not have the strength of character of Mohamed Zoue and was more of a diplomat than a soldier. He spoke Italian and at one time had been secretary to the Grand Senussi. He explained to the captain that the Senussi had made a mistake in attacking the British who were a different proposition to the Italians and that he believed that the prisoners would be free within a month or so. This bit of news was passed on to the sailors and raised the hopes of everyone.

More soap was issued which added the prisoner's sense of well being and the whole atmosphere of the camp changed. Everyone was in a much lighter frame of mind, there was laughter and jokes, men and clothes were being washed and the contrast was remarkable! To celebrate, the officers had a good sized sweet duff for tea, and it was noted that the Chief Engineer and Quartermaster Abbit were feeling better.

*Wednesday, 19th January.* The mood in the camp continued to be very optimistic. It was a fine day, although too cold for a lice hunt. There was rice for breakfast and lunch, and sweet rice for supper, with 1 oz of mutton for lunch.

Some concern was expressed about the amount of rice and flour in the blockhouse.

*Thursday, 20th January.* The Chief Engineer's health had again deteriorated and was causing a great deal of concern. He did not want, or could not eat, rice and had only been able to eat a few dirty scraps of biscuit which had been given for him and the other serious cases by Salim Effendi. The Surgeon Arthur and Basil had to beg and plead for these crumbs of biscuits or any other comforts for the sick. Every now and then the Chief, suffering from dysentery, would wish himself dead, whilst the other officers did their best to cheer him up, especially the two engineers Howarth and Davies who looked after him day and night, washing and feeding him.

There were rain showers on and off all day, but by the night the clouds had disappeared leaving a beautiful, clear, moonlit night. The officers had three meals of boiled rice with a portion of mutton at lunch time.

*Friday, 21st January.* The Chief was growing weaker and everyone was concerned as he had eaten hardly a thing for the last three weeks. Quartermaster Abbit and Fireman Roberts were also in a very bad way. There had been boiled rice and mutton for the meals again today and, as the weather had warmed, all hands had a good lice hunt in the hope that they could have an itch free, peaceful night's sleep.

*Saturday, 22nd January.* A cold day with some rain in the afternoon. The officers ate rather well, having for breakfast dry boiled rice; lunch consisted of mutton and rice; for tea they had a sweet duff, which had been boiled for 4½ hours, and for supper dry boiled rice again. Afterwards, most men turned in feeling bloated and, although it was raining hard, went off to sleep straight away.

*Sunday, 23rd January.* A very wet and stormy night, the rain lasted until three in the afternoon, after which the usual firewood collecting parties went out. Every day they went out but were having to go further and further afield to find the brushwood. Most of the men had neither shoes nor boots and so came back with their feet cut, bleeding and bruised.

For breakfast there was boiled rice; lunch was boiled rice, mutton and mutton soup in which was a sprinkling of rice. During the morning, the last two sacks of rice were issued to the prisoners and they were told that these rations were to last until Thursday.

In the afternoon, a long awaited caravan of 12–15 camels arrived. Amongst the supplies it brought were twelve sacks of rice for the prisoners but unfortunately no medicines.

*Monday, 24th January.* The caravan had brought some news. Basil was informed by Salim Effendi that a two months armistice between the British and had been agreed in Sollum and that the last of fighting had been some eleven days ago. This news was passed on and Sub Lieutenant Marsh later wrote that he was excited and could not wait to be released. Captain Gwatkin-Williams recorded that everyone was extremely thrilled at the prospect and very optimistic but he was not so sure about the armistice and in consequence had started to contemplate escape. He reckoned that as one sack of rice had to last ninety-five men some four days, this equalled just under 1lb per person per day, so it would be difficult for him to save rice for his breakout and journey to the coast, and he had heard that the Sollum road was now mostly under water. He also noted that, thanks to the recent wet weather, wild garlic was sprouting around the camp and was eagerly collected to be added to the soup or the snails.

*Tuesday, 25th January.* Weather was cold but dry. There was rice again for all meals with a small amount of mutton and garlic.

Sub Lieutenant Marsh, whilst collecting water at the well, was disturbed to find he was being stared at by Mullah Osman's wife; apparently she was fascinated by his gold teeth.

*Wednesday, 26th January.* This morning Surgeon Arthur reported to the senior officers that the Chief Engineer was very ill. His dysentery was very bad and he had been moved for his convenience nearer to the door of the tent. He was fading fast, so much so that all that was left of him now was skin and bone. He must have known that he did not have long as he asked Fireman H O Hughes to 'Put a good word, up above for me' and to tell the men 'to dig my grave deeper than the other chaps, so that the wild dogs wouldn't get at me!'
The usual firewood collecting party went out after breakfast.

*Thursday, 27th January.* A much better day, dry and warm with a light wind, ideal to allow the men to strip off and have a lice hunt. The food was the same – boiled rice for all meals and a small portion of meat for lunch.[1]

*Friday, 28th January.* Again it was a lovely day but the wind had turned colder. Camp routine continued much as it had done for the last few weeks. Most days a few Arabs arrived at the wells from the direction of Sollum, there were mostly hungry and unarmed and had stopped for a drink before proceeding westwards. As the prisoners had not heard the sound of gunfire over the last few days they began to hope that they could soon be released and so today most had spent their time writing letters to their families, which they hoped would get through.[2]

At about 22.20 hours those in the officers' tent were awoken by the watchman with the news that Chief Engineer Williams had died. Most remained in their beds whilst the watchman put more wood on the fire and blew the embers into life and there by its light they could make out the still body of the Chief, supported by Davies and Hughes and with Surgeon Arthur in attendance. The smoke, which drifted this way and that, lifted every now and then allowing a better view of the group. The Chief looked little better than a skeleton, thin, pale and haggard but by the firelight he looked at peace. Captain Gwatkin-Williams recalled that when they first landed the Chief had been the most cheerful, even without his tobacco and his spectacles which had gone down with the ship. He continuously joked and even admitted that his eyesight was improving. However, as time progressed he was slowly but surely loosing heart until he was struck by dysentery, and for the last six weeks had just lain on his back in the corner of the tent, silent and too feeble to move. Since being struck by dysentery he had been attended faithfully by Hughes and Davies, the fourth and fifth engineers, who even though he would not eat cajoled him into trying little morsels and generally tended on him, washing his body and clothes. On warm days, they would carry him out into the sunshine — two days previously one

2. Quite understandably, the people of Holyhead (and in particular the families of the missing crew members) were becoming annoyed with the government's seemingly complacent attitude over the fate of their missing menfolk. Telegrams and letters had been sent and representations made to the government, to the local MP, Ellis Griffith (who had asked questions in the House of Commons), the Admiralty and to the board of the L&NWR but no news had been forthcoming. Finally, in an effort to get some response Mrs Elizabeth Hughes of 17, Queens Park, Holyhead, the wife of Fireman Hugh O Hughes, had organised a petition in Holyhead which resulted in her obtaining 2,896 signatures which she sent off to Mr Arthur Balfour, the First Lord of the Admiralty, with a letter praying for particulars regarding the survivors of the Tara. The response was a letter from Balfour's secretary, dated 27th January 1916, which read 'Mr Balfour has asked me to say that he has received your letter of 25th January, enclosing the petition of the relatives and friends of the crew of HMS *Tara*. The First Lord is glad to be able to tell you that some news has come to hand from Egypt, and is contained in the enclosed announcement, which will appear in the press of the 28th January. As you will see from this announcement, it is hoped that some further information may soon be forthcoming.' This 'announcement' read: 'A report today has been received from Egypt stating that there are 95 survivors of HMS Tara at present in the hands of the Senussi and that they are being well treated. An attempt is being made to send clothing, etc, to them. Hopes are entertained that the names of these survivors will soon be known, when they will be immediately published.'

had helped him write a farewell letter home so all in the camp knew that the end was not long in coming. The Captain went on to say about the fourth and fifth engineers 'No mother could have done more for an ailing child, nor with less hope of any earthly reward.'

Quartermaster Abbit, however, who had been too weak to move for the last three months, had suddenly taken a turn for the better, which led all to hope that he was getting better, especially Milward the seaman/gunner who had been conspicuous in his devotion to the quartermaster.[3]

*Saturday, 29th January.* After breakfast, Chief Engineer Williams's grave was dug in accordance with his requirements. Sub Lieutenant Marsh sewed his body in sacking which was then carried from the tent to the small cemetery by six officers – Lieutenant Tanner with Sub Lieutenants Dudgeon, Griffiths, Marsh and Assistant Engineers Hughes and Davies. The service began at 09.00 hours. Nearly all those attending, broke down again at some stage as most had known and sailed with the Chief for many years, and for a few of the crew probably since the Chief had first joined the company. By all accounts he was a very popular and a very well-liked man. The Lord's prayer was recited and the hymns *Abide with me* and the first verse of *Forever with the Lord* sung, after which a Welsh hymn *Bydd mwydd o rhyfeddodiau* was sung and Fireman H O Hughes recited an English and a Welsh prayer. Then the grave was filled and well covered with stones and a stone cross formed on top. Everyone then returned to camp in a very solemn mood. Sub Lieutenant Griffiths later recorded that everybody was touched by loosing a good friend and shipmate.

*Sunday, 30th January.* The weather continued to be dry but it was cold with a high wind which forced all cooking to be done inside the tents. Although the atmosphere was uncomfortable and thick with smoke, it was preferable to cooking outside where the high winds would quickly waste the meagre stock of firewood which the prisoners had to travel further and further afield to collect. It was also too cold for a lice hunt.

3. On this day the L&NWR's Marine Office in Holyhead received news from the Admiralty of the casualties sustained during the sinking of the *Tara*. The news was immediately transmitted to the families, and no doubt the whole of Holyhead soon knew who had been killed and who was still alive. But in a cruel twist of fate the families of those who had died since landing would learn of the deaths of their loved ones only after the survivors had been rescued. This was also the day when Mrs Jeanie McKinven in Campbeltown was informed by the Registrar General of Shipping and Seamen of the loss of her husband James.

During the morning, Captain Gwatkin-Williams and Basil were invited to share some sour camel milk in Salim Effendi's tent. The commandant seemed very confident about their release and the arrival of the long awaited (since November) caravan. He also explained that the Grand  was in direct negotiations with the British and that there were only some twelve Turkish officers in Cyrenaica who were no threat to the negotiations and could be ignored.

Later in the day, there was some excitement when the prisoners spotted a large caravan to the south-west which they thought was the long-awaited caravan. They were disappointed to see it disappearing into the distance.

By now, most of the prisoners were eating snails including Sub Lieutenant Marsh who had overcome his revulsion. He pointed out that to him they looked horrible, but some men were eating them by the dozen. After a supper of boiled rice and some mutton the usual hymn singing went on in the officers' tent.

*Monday, 31st January.* Owing to their steadily shrinking rations, a deputation of prisoners went to see Salim Effendi. During the previous eight days they had been given four sacks of rice, which worked out as a half sack of rice per day for ninety-four men. The commandant refused to increase the rations but changed the subject to say that there were forty people at the peace conference at Sollum trying to arrange a truce between the  and the British. This news was passed to the other prisoners which raised their spirits.

During the day, Captain Gwatkin-Williams learned that two men with three camels had arrived in camp. They had brought no stores but did deliver a letter from Sollum to Salim Effendi. When later asked about the men and the letter Salim Effendi denied that they had come from Sollum or that they had brought any letters or news.

The high wind continued, the men were still cooking inside the tents, and their meals were the same, boiled rice and mutton soup.

# 17. Egypt - January 1916

On 1st January, aerial reconnaissance discovered a village of eighty tents in the area of Gebel Howimil, thirty-five miles southeast of Matruh and fifteen miles south of the coast at Baggush. General Wallace ordered a column to be speedily formed to eliminate this potential threat. It consisted of A Battery of the Honourable Artillery Company (HAC), six squadrons of cavalry, machine-gun and signal sections, the 2/7th Middlesex Regiment (less two companies), 1st South Midland Field Ambulance, 137th Field Ambulance and the Water Section of the 1st Australian Divisional Train. However, before it could move, the weather confounded his plans as the following morning the skies opened and torrential rain fell for over a week turning the countryside into a sea of mud. By the evening of the 9th, the rain had stopped and three days later it was deemed that the roads could be used and the column set off. By 13th January it had reached Baggush and the next day Gebel Howimil, in the vicinity of which they destroyed several small camps and stores, seizing camels and herds of livestock. There was no opposition from the Senussi. Whilst this operation was in progress, the RN Armoured Cars took the opportunity to re-establish the telegraph line between Mersa Matruh and Dabaa which had been destroyed some time previously. On the 15th, A Battery HAC (which had arrived as reinforcements in late December, along with the 1st New Zealand Rifle Brigade and two naval 4-inch guns) and two squadrons of the Australian Light Horse left the force for the railhead at Dabaa to return to Egypt. The remainder returned to Bir Gerawla and the following day moved to Mersa Matruh, bringing with it thirteen prisoners, 140 camels and 50 cattle. It had been a difficult operation thanks to the recent wet weather.

Whilst these land operations had been progressing, Vice-Admiral Peirse had received word that supplies for the Senussi were being landed at Sollum and Bardia. On 14th January, HMS *Latona,* a converted second-class cruiser laid forty-five mines off the ports, each secured some twelve feet below the surface, in an effort to catch any U-boat that might try to land arms or supplies. It had not been an easy job as it had to be executed at night and the coast was poorly charted. But

*Latona* had laid her cargo as close to the shore as possible, so close that the crew later recounted that they had been able to smell the Senussi's cooking fires.

On 19th January, Captain Royle (the Western Desert Force's intelligence officer) acting as an observer in a reconnaissance aircraft, spotted the main Senussi camp twenty-five miles south west of Mersa Matruh at Halazin. It contained at least 100 European and 250 Bedouin tents, including one that held the Grand Senussi. The size of the enemy force made General Wallace pause and wait for the 2nd Regiment of the South African Infantry Brigade which had arrived in Alexandria from England. This was moved by sea to Mersa Matruh over the 20th and 21st.

Reinforced, Wallace's force moved at 04.00 hours on the 22nd and marched some sixteen miles to Bir Shola where it camped for the night. At 06.00 hours the next morning it marched off, having been split into two columns. The right column, commanded once again by Colonel Gordon with one squadron of the Duke of Lancaster's Own Yeomanry, the Nottinghamshire Battery, RHA,[1] 15th Sikhs, 2nd South African Infantry Regiment and 1st New Zealand Rifle Brigade.

The left-hand column, under Brigadier-General Tyndale Biscoe, with one squadron Australian Light Horse, three squadrons Royal Buckinghamshire Hussars Yeomanry, one squadron Dorset Yeomanry, one squadron Hertfordshire Yeomanry, the Mounted Brigade's machine-gun section and A Battery, HAC.[1] In reserve were two troops of Yeomanry, 1/6th Royal Scots (less half a battalion) and the South African Ambulance who all moved half-a-mile in the rear of the right-hand column. The armoured train, with half a battalion of the 2/8th Middlesex Regiment, remained at Bir Shola.

At 08.30 hours on 24th January, when the right-hand column was about seven miles from Bir Shola, the left-hand column reported they could see the enemy about two miles ahead of their scouts. Shortly afterwards, the Australian Light Horse engaged the enemy and the Buckinghamshire Hussars and the HAC were sent forward to support them. At the same time, the right-hand column, with the 15th Sikhs leading, opened the attack. The cavalry, now relieved by the infantry,

1. With the evacuation of the Gallipoli more units were available in Egypt, so a start could be made to reorganise the Western Frontier Force. At the beginning of the month the 1/2nd South Midland Mounted Brigade consisting of the Buckinghamshire, Berkshire and Dorset Yeomanry and the Nottinghamshire Battery, RHA (TF) was ordered to join General Wallace. The Composite Yeomanry Brigade was also reorganised and now consisted of only the Hertfordshire Yeomanry and the 2nd County of London Regiment (Westminster Dragoons), with one squadron each of the Duke of Lancaster's Own and the Surrey Yeomanry.

pressed on trying to outflank the Senussi on their right and at the same time tried to cover the left flank of Gordon's column, who were spread over a front of a mile-and-a-half and had to work their way towards the enemy over ground that was devoid of any cover. A mirage made the locating of the enemy's position almost impossible and, as a result, the infantry suffered from the enemy's fire. However, the Senussi were eventually pushed back some three miles to their main positions, their retirement conducted with great skill as they did not allow the attackers to get to close quarters. By 12.45, the South Africans, some of New Zealanders and the Sikhs, had reached the Senussi's main line of defence, but due to the mud their flanks had not kept up. Consequently, small parties of Senussi managed to work their way around both north and south, and were slowly forming an arc around the attackers. So great was the danger that the 1/6th Royal Scots had to be called up from reserve to restore the situation.

By 14.30 hours the danger was past. One hour later, on the extreme left, the cavalry of the left-hand column were being pushed back. Two companies of New Zealanders were put in and the Senussi were driven off. By 15.00 hours the enemy had been driven out of their positions and their camp was occupied and burned. The work was completed by 16.30 hours.

As darkness was approaching and the troops and cavalry horses were exhausted, it was decided not to pursue the fleeing Senussi. Orders were issued for the force to make camp some two miles to the east of the Senussi's camp where the Field Ambulance was now quartered and from where it, and the ammunition column, could not be moved owing to the deep mud.

The mud had hindered operations throughout the day, so much so that the RN armoured cars could not be used, and the men had to spend a wet and cold night under the stars as the train could not be brought up and neither could any other transport. They also had to do without supplies and blankets.

At daybreak, there was no sign of the Senussi and at 08.30 hours the force started their march back to Bir Shola. It was a tiring march and all transports had to be hauled by hand. The wounded suffered, those that were unable to ride had to be stretchered, which threw a great strain on the troops who were already tired and thirsty after a cold and mostly sleepless night. They eventually met the train some three miles west of Bir Shola and the wounded were placed aboard. The force then marched to camp, arriving at Bir Shola at 17.00 hours.

On 25th January, the weather cleared and the whole force marched to Mersa Matruh, arriving there at 16.30 hours. The British casualties during the action of the 23rd (later to be called the Battle of Halazin) amounted to one officer killed and ten wounded; eleven other ranks killed and 164 wounded. For the Indians, three officers wounded, nineteen other ranks killed and 114 wounded. It was not known what the enemy's losses were, but it was thought to be in the region of 200 killed and 500 wounded and, although the Senussi had suffered a severe blow, once again they had escaped to fight another day. Wallace, believing he had done what had been asked of him and no doubt feeling his age, asked to be relieved. General Maxwell reluctantly accepted his resignation and having decided it was now time to reoccupy Sollum, appointed Major-General W E Payton, CB, CVO, DSO in his place, who would assume command on 9th February.

Meanwhile, the RN armoured cars had been withdrawn and replaced by the 1st, 2nd and 3rd Light Armoured Car Batteries (LACBs), under the command of Major Hugh Richard Arthur Grosvenor, the second duke of Westminster. The 1st, 2nd and 3rd LACBs had originally been formed during the autumn of 1914 as one of the armoured-car squadrons of the Royal Naval Air Service. The Duke of Westminster, had served during the Anglo-Boer War as a second lieutenant in the Royal Horse Guards. Resigning in 1906, he then joined the Cheshire Yeomanry and by 1914 had risen to the rank of major. On the outbreak of war, although second-in-command, he was not mobilised with the regiment but spent the best part of three months working with Rolls-Royce engineers developing the armoured car at his own expense. On 7 November 1914, he was granted a commission as a temporary lieutenant-commander RNVR, and appointed to HMS *Pembroke III* at Chatham for service with armoured cars. Later, the cars moved to Wormwood Scrubs in London and came on the books of HMS *President* at Crystal Palace, their official title becoming the Royal Naval Armoured Car Division. The Duke was then given command of No. 2 Squadron.

In March 1915, after training at Sheerness and Wormwood Scrubs, the squadron moved to France and was detailed to work with the cavalry during the battle of Neuve Chapelle. The lack of movement in the war on the Western Front and the establishment of trenches which ran from the Swiss border to the North Sea, limited the use of the armoured cars and No. 2 Squadron was based at the White Chateau on the Poperinghe road, acting as armoured taxis for staff officers travelling to and from the front lines.

On 31 August 1915, control of the armoured cars passed to the Army which necessitated their reorganisation and further training and the squadron returned to England. The Duke, by now a RNVR commander, reverted to the rank of major in the Cheshire Yeomanry and was attached to the Machine Gun Corps (Motors), urging his men to remain with the squadron. Those drivers that elected to stay were transferred from the RNAS to the Army Service Corps (ASC) from where replacements (where possible with Rolls-Royce experience) were also found. For the machine gunners who remained it meant joining the Motor Machine Gun Corps (Motors) and those that departed were replaced by cavalrymen who, owing to their small build, were thought to be best suited to the cramped turrets of the armoured cars.

On 15th October 1915, N^os^ 1, 2 and 3 LACBs crossed over to France but, were not destined to remain there for long. The duke, fed up of inaction and having friends in high places, badgered the authorities for an active command. This was granted and on 24th December 1915 the cars entrained at St Omer bound for Marseilles. On 8th January they embarked for Alexandria aboard the SS *Anchises,* arriving in Egypt five days later. The cars and their crews then embarked onto HMT *Borulas* which sailed for Mersa Matruh on the 24th. The passage was scheduled to only take some fourteen hours but, due to a storm, took two days and three nights. When the storm first struck orders were issued to lash the cars down so as to prevent them crashing about in the hold, but it was hopeless and the ropes snapped like string and it was with some relief that, when the third day dawned, the sea was flat calm and Mersa Matruh appeared on the horizon. On arrival, the *Borulas* anchored in the bay and the twelve armoured cars, the duke's Rolls-Royce tourer and a few Model 'T' Ford tenders were unloaded using the *Borulas's* own derricks and two lighters. Once landed, all were driven and/or

*The vehicles of N^os^ 1, 2 and 3 Light Armoured Car Batteries just after their arrival at Mersa Matruh* [Trove – *National Library of Australia newspaper website]*

pushed to a camp which had been established about a mile inland. The crews spent the next few days recovering from the voyage, repairing the damage caused by the storm and preparing the cars for the desert conditions before starting to patrol aggressively.

# 18. In Captivity, February 1916 (1)

*Tuesday, 1st February.* The weather was still windy and cold, but dry and the messes continued to cook inside their tents — boiled rice for all meals with a very watery mutton soup.

During the morning, Salim Effendi asked Captain Gwatkin-Williams to write letters to the Grand Senussi, Captain Achmed, Mohamed Zoue, Tarrick Bey (the commandant of Sollum) and the commanding officer of the British forces at Sollum, to speed up the supplies of medicines, food and clothing. He also explained that for weeks they had eaten nothing but rice, salt and a small quantity of mutton. The letters left camp during the early evening.

During the afternoon, six Senussi officers who were travelling westwards from Sollum, visited the camp. On seeing them Salim Effendi rushed over and hugged each one, kissing both their cheeks and hands. To celebrate their arrival he gave orders a goat to be killed and a meal prepared for them, but there was to be no meat for the prisoners. Gwatkin-Williams and Basil later spoke to the officers and explained to them that the fighting between the Senussi and the British was now over and that soon the prisoners would be taken to Sollum and set free.

*Wednesday, 2nd February.* The weather was unchanged and the prisoners continued to cook their rations inside their tents. Concern was growing regarding the health of Fireman Harold Jones.

*Thursday, 3rd February.* The wind had risen to gale force, blowing from the east, and the temperature had dropped. It was too cold to go for a walk, so nearly all spent the day indoors making themselves as snug as possible. Breakfast was the usual boiled rice and dinner soup and rice. During the day, a goat was killed for the prisoners but the guards retained the liver, kidneys, entrails, head, fat, neck and feet. Sub Lieutenant Marsh was noted to have remarked, 'Oh! I could do with a good feed.'

*Friday, 4th February.* Fed up with the negligible rations the men were getting,

Gwatkin-Williams went to inquire of Salim Effendi what food, and how much of it, was left in the blockhouse as the sacks of rice they had been receiving were now only a quarter full. He was told that there were nine bags left but that a caravan was expected any day and when it arrived there would be plenty of food for everyone. Salim Effendi went on to say that should the caravan not arrive then he would commandeer food from the Arabs encamped in the locality.

*Saturday, 5th February.* The wind died down somewhat but it was still cold and the prisoners continued to cook inside the tents. More goats were killed for the Senussi while the prisoners looked on hungrily.

Quartermaster Abbit and Fireman Roberts were recorded as being 'gravely ill.'

*Sunday, 6th February.* At last the wind had died down and it was a glorious sunny day and the temperature had risen, being described by Dutton, the assistant paymaster, as extremely hot. The prisoners got the cooking pans on the fires and, as soon as the water was heated, all had a good wash using the small scraps of soap that they had managed to retain. Afterwards all basked in the sunshine. For their meals they had a small quantity of rice. During the evening there was hymn singing in the officers' mess.

*Monday, 7th February.* The weather was a bit colder but there was good news as a sheep had come down with sickness and had been killed by one of the guards. The Senussi refused to eat sick or diseased animals so the complete carcass was given to the prisoners to butcher and eat. Marsh, by now thoroughly at home eating snails, recorded that he was eating snails galore and enjoying them! As for the rice, he conceded that it was the same old fare — 'enough to make you cry!' Lieutenant Tanner did not seem to mind eating rice as Surgeon Arthur had explained to him that by eating it for so long all uric acid should have been purged out of his system.

*Tuesday, 8th February.* At noon, two messengers arrived in the camp from Sollum. One brought a small amount of medicine for dysentery which, if doled out carefully, might last the day. The other brought a letter from Nuri Bey and Salim Effendi immediately ordered Gwatkin-Williams to draft a reply in French, not English, as the Turks to whom he had previously written could not understand

English! Salim Effendi told him to write down how many pairs of boots, shirts and trousers were required, and what food and medicines were needed. He was also to state how many men had died and how many were sick. This had come as a shock to the captain, as he had been under the impression that the Turks could be disregarded. However, he hurriedly drafted a reply whilst the surgeon wrote out a list of the medicines he required. These were then handed to the messenger who immediately set off for Sollum. Sub Lieutenant Griffiths was amazed that the captain thought that these supplies would be forthcoming but recalled that he believed the Senussi story that a German submarine had towed boats full of munitions from Constantinople to Tripoli. Griffiths, recalled how the old Chief Engineer regularly pulled the captain's leg about what he thought was plainly a ludicrous idea.[1]

*Wednesday, 9th February.* The weather was cold but dry with a strong wind which forced the men to again cook their meals inside the tents. Breakfast and supper consisted of boiled rice, whilst dinner was a very weak mutton soup which left everyone feeling hungry. Some rice had been given to the prisoners from the mullah's own store, which, according to Quartermaster Rowlands, 'wasn't much and must have been lying there for some years as it was all mouldy.'

Due to the recent rain, the grass and vegetation had started to grow and the desert had taken on a green tinge. Wildlife also started to make an appearance and hares and ravens had been spotted. The snails which the men had been eating, usually found stuck to the underside of rocks, were now beginning to stir after their hibernation and starting to feed on the vegetation. Whenever a northerly wind blew small butterflies appeared.

*Thursday, 10th February.* The weather was still cold and the meals were the same as yesterday. Lieutenant Tanner, by now fed up of the cooking of Portuguese Joe (their nickname for Sola the Goanese steward), ordered him to move to the seamen's mess. The officers had allowed him to sleep in their tent as long as he cooked for them, their reasoning being that having been a mess room steward on the *Moorina* he should be an expert on cooking rice. The officers had discovered that they could cook rice better than him. Tanner noted that the steward would feel better living amongst the men.

1. In reading Captain Gwatkin-Williams' and Sub Lieutenant Griffiths' diaries it is obvious that there was a degree of animosity between them.

The officers had their ration of Osman's rice, which led Tanner to note that the rations were now very small and of poor quality. The rice was more like flour and was musty having been kept in the blockhouse for over three years. During the previous few days they had received about ½ oz of goat bones from the Senussi with which they have been trying to make soup, but it was very weak and had the consistency of dish water.

Sub Lieutenant Marsh recorded that the Senussi were continually telling them all sorts of lies: Captain Achmed and Mohamed Zoue's caravans were to arrive any day; boots had been sent for; the British and Senussi were great friends — but these were all lies and Marsh suspected that, as it was part of their life, they could not help but lie!

*Friday, 11th February.* A south-easterly gale blew all day then, at nightfall, it veered to the west. There had been no working parties at the wells since the previous Wednesday. The rice ration was awful, turning to glue almost as soon as it touched water, making cooking it without burning almost impossible. In the officers tent, Lieutenant Tanner was amongst the few that had managed to get his share down without being sick.

Sub Lieutenant Marsh had his twenty-ninth birthday, but there no cake for him, only rice.

*Saturday, 12th February.* The prisoners were eating great quantities of snails to supplement their meagre rations.

Captain Gwatkin-Williams received a reply from Tarik Bey, the Turkish commandant of Sollum, dated 10th February 1916

> I have received the letter you have sent to His Excellency General Nouri Pasha [sic], I will send it at once to the general. I have read it and understood it. I hope you will be repatriated in some months at least 2–3 months. Because of the general war this fatality to the civilised world will be finished in the next summer. As soon as the General has accepted your demand, I will send you all — whatever it is to your destination. The general is at Matruh. I am going to see him and after my return I will do the necessary [this part is almost undecipherable]

Having read the letter, Gwatkin-Williams was unsure which letter Tarik Bey referred to, the letter of 18th January (in which he withdrew his parole) or the last, dated 1st February. He was also suspicious that not all of his letters had got through as, when Captain Achmed had been in command, some of the *Tara's* officers had seen torn up bits of papers on the floor of his tent in the Lieutenant Tanner's handwriting. The news was, however, very disappointing to everyone — so much for their early release!

During the previous few days the guards had been acting suspiciously, some had been seen busy packing bags and boxes and sorting out the camels, and lately the firewood collecting party had not been allowed to go to the high ground to the north of the camp. The officers thinking possibly that from this high ground they may spot the Senussi army in retreat. In the evening some of the guards were seen leaving the camp carrying their belongings, heading north westwards.

During the night, Mahomet the cook arrived back at camp and told the Gwatkin-Williams that Mohamed Zoue would be returning in a couple of days. But, having been lied to time and time again, the captain discounted this bit of news.

*Sunday, 13th February.* The meagre rations of the last few weeks were beginning to take their toll, the men were becoming thinner, weaker and some were beginning to loose heart, although there were some who were still hopeful of rescue. Lieutenant Tanner tried to be optimistic about the situation by telling those in despair that, as they could be used for ransom or bargaining, they were of more value to the Senussi alive than dead.

*Monday, 14th February.* A quiet day; the meals were of the usual rice and for some reason the sick seem to have taken a turn for the worse.

Some of the prisoners who had refrained from eating snails had decided, owing to their starvation diet, they that they should now do so and a larger than usual snail collecting party went out. Due to the activities of earlier snail collecting parties the area around the camp had been denuded of snails and they had to venture further afield to find sufficient quantities.

The favourite way of cooking the snails appears to have been to roast them. The snails were placed on a stone in the fire and, when the steam escaped out of their shells, it whistled and once this stopped they were ready to be eaten. Alternatively, the snails could be boiled with a few wild herbs. To pick the snails out of their shells most of the men had made a needle or skewer out of the many camel or donkey bones which littered the camp. Outside each tent or mess door there were great heaps of white snail shells. One man, known only as the Snail King, was recorded as having eaten as many as 1,000 in one day! Captain Gwatkin-Williams could not face eating snails and later wrote that 'even extreme hunger cannot make me eat the sandy morsel, which hangs limply from its shell with its horns out as though alive.' Quartermaster Rowlands on the other hand was quite upbeat and noted that it was 'St Valentine's Day good quantity of snails gathered for our tea.' Chief Officer Coalsted remarked that 'In spite of their looks, and the sand and grit inside them, we were glad to have the snails ... the following day two small meals of mouldy rice and snails were being eaten by all.'

*Tuesday, 15th February.* Rain fell all day, forcing the prisoners to remain in their tents. Thanks to the recent deaths and the bad news of the last few days there was a mood of depression hanging over the camp. Quartermaster Abbit, already suffering badly from dysentery and dropsy, had now developed a cataract on his left eye and had been sick since 16th December.

Osman the Mullah and Mohamed the cook left the camp to go to Grass, one day's march away, where there was purported to be a military dump or store, to try to obtain shoes or boots for the prisoners.

*Wednesday, 16th February.* Another depressing, wet day. Captain Gwatkin-Williams spotted some of the guards taking five sacks of rice out of the block-house and place them on camels which then set off to the north. Half-an-hour later a small caravan arrived from the north-east carrying ten sacks of dates and unhooked barley. Later he was given a handful of dates by Salim Effendi which, after all the goat and rice, tasted delicious.

*Thursdays 17th February.* No rain. Lieutenant Tanner decided that owing to their starvation diet those officers and men who had not yet eaten snails must now do so. A snailing party was organised which managed to collect about 1,000, which were then boiled for five minutes, shelled and boiled again for a further twenty minutes. A little of the musty rice was added to thicken the gravy. Tanner remarked that they were not bad at all, whilst Sub Lieutenant Marsh found them to have a rather fishy taste when cooked that way. He preferred his boiled, in salted water for ten minutes, picked out of their shells; then he closed his eyes, popped them in his mouth and ate them.

*Friday, 18th February.* The bad rice was still being doled out and the men were still complaining to their officers. Lieutenant Tanner and a handful of officers went to see Salim Effendi to demand an increase in the ration, which had some effect but there was not much food to spare. Salim Effendi explained that it had to be smuggled over the Egyptian border as the caravans had to evade the Egyptian coastguards.

In their free time, the prisoners had now begun making souvenirs out of the camel bones which litter the area.

*Saturday, 19th February.* At 09.00 hours Fireman Owen Roberts died, Surgeon Arthur recording that death was due to tuberculosis, dysentery and lack of medical care. Roberts had been in failing health since landing and had simply wasted away, getting thinner and weaker day by day. He was only twenty-eight years of age. Again a deep grave was dug and the body sown in sacking before being carried from the tent to the little cemetery at 15.00 hours. Lieutenant Tanner read the burial service, the hymns *Abide with Me* and *Forever with the Lord* were sung. Fireman Hughes recited the Lord's Prayer in Welsh and led the singing of a Welsh hymn. During the service many of the men broke down and cried quite openly, the singing being very subdued. After the service the grave was filled in and covered with stones. Captain Gwatkin-Williams later wrote of Fireman Roberts: 'Poor fellow, his limbs were but pipe stems when we buried him; there seemed not an ounce of flesh left on his body, in spite of the tenderest care from his companions. I had often been touched on visiting his tent to see how those starving men had set aside for him practically the whole of their combined day's meat ration.'

*Sunday, 20th February.* The weather had been gradually improving and for the previous four days Salim Effendi had been supplementing their rations with a handful of dates. Although half of these appeared to be rotten they were still

*The four graves at Bir Hakkim [BRB (Residuary) Ltd]*

eaten. For their meals the officers had dates for breakfast, the stones of which were carefully saved and ground to make 'coffee'; a little meat and soup for lunch and boiled rice for supper. But they still went to bed feeling hungry, some believing that they were being subjected to slow starvation.

A messenger took the prisoners mails to Sollum at 09.00 hours and at night there was the usual hymn singing in the officers' tent.

Captain Gwatkin-Williams had determined to try and escape and head for Sollum. He had noticed that for some time the guards had not bothered to keep a careful eye on the prisoners and did not mustered them for a head count. Perhaps more importantly, Osman, the most observant of the Senussi, had been at Grass for five days. Gwatkin-Williams recalled that the route they had followed when travelling to Bir Hakkim was around three sides of a square, which had been carefully observed by using the stars in the night sky by himself and the ship's officers. He estimated that all he had to do was head to the north east, diagonally across the square, marching at night and using the stars to navigate, until he reached the coast where he could turn south and head for Sollum.

In preparation for the escape attempt Gwatkin-Williams had saved two days of his rice ration and as more rations were issued on Sundays he was able to draw an advance of a further two days rations. After a word with Morris, the chief steward who did the issuing, he managed to get another ration from the general issue. Seeing that he was determined to escape, the other officers all contributed to give him enough for a further ration. When this rice was boiled it would become very heavy and he calculated that it would weigh up to 14 lbs.

Knowing that the Senussi did not like sickness, the officers had over the last few days let it be known that the captain was seriously ill and Gwatkin-Williams had kept out of sight in the tent. The ruse had worked and the Senussi did not bother to investigate but did provide him with about a pound of barley flour as a medical comfort. This was made into biscuits for him by Basil. Altogether he reckoned he had six or seven days supply of food which comprised of rice, about ½ lb of mutton from the officers, some broken biscuits, a pound of dates and a little sugar which Basil had stolen from the blockhouse.

Gwatkin-Williams divided the food into six separate portions which he packed into his spare pair of Arab's trousers which had the appearance of a string of sausages which he could hang over his shoulders. The dates and sugar would be in a bag around his waist. For water he would have to use a water skin but, try as they might, none of the officers could find a watertight skin, all the new ones seemed to have disappeared. They selected the best they could find, into which they put about a gallon of water which he would have to carry on his back like a ruck-sack and for which Basil had made the shoulder straps. He would also take with him: an iron horse shoe (not only for luck but on which to use to roast snails); a diary and pencil; a list of officers and men; half-a-dozen precious matches; a stump of candle for night signalling should the opportunity arise; a pipe and tobacco pouch in which he carried his bone sewing needles and some thread; his tomato-tin drinking cup; his old pair of worn out shoes; a few letters and a map of Bir Hakkim, which he and the officers had prepared. He would also take with him Tarrick Bey's letter to prove he had withdrawn his parole to escape in case of capture. All told he thought that he was well prepared and could manage a ten-day journey. He had so far escaped the ravages of dysentery and other sickness and for some weeks had surreptitiously been exercising barefoot around the camp so now felt fit enough to attempt an escape. There was also the added urgency that the days were now lengthening and becoming hotter. During the day he went through the whole plan with Lieutenant Apcar in whom he had great faith, describing him as a realist who would not allow his mind to be clouded by optimism. Apcar agreed that the chances were about 50/50 and that he should give it a shot.

At 18.45 hours, before the moon rose, he made his bid for freedom.

# 19. Escape, February 1916

Captain Gwatkin-Williams made a record of his escape attempt, commencing on 20th February.

*Sunday, 20th February.* Our mails left for Sollum at 9 p.m. We went through the usual farce of writing home, through we have never yet had any assurance that our letters have gone through or that our countryman have any knowledge of our existence. But it eases our minds.

This was the day on which I had for some time determined to escape, and which if I succeeded would end an intolerable situation. The Senussi were obviously of opinion it was quite impossible and had almost ceased to guard us, and we were rarely mustered. They had brought us by an 11 days march round three sides of a square, and geometry was to them unknown. We had never traversed the direct track, or anywhere near it, to Sollum.

The country was almost waterless, and the rare wells guarded by soldiers. The natives were hungry and hostile, and the chances were that any European met with would at once be killed for the sake of his clothes or anything he had. Their marvellous eyesight at once detects any moving thing while miles away, and our fairer skins and ignorance of Arabic were an additional difficulty, not to mention our lack of money to bribe, and weakness and lack of shoes for walking.

My plans were as follows, and though my messmates at first believed the whole affair madness on my part, and did their level best to dissuade me, yet later they came round to my views, and gave their whole hearted assistance, and believed as firmly in it's practicability as I did. Ever since landing I had kept a diary of distances covered, and I knew the distance to Port Sulliman from Sollum within ten miles or so, and had a general idea of the configuration of the coast. Plotting these out, I made a rough map, showing Sollum to bear ENE some 80 miles only. Secondly we had heard gunfire on several occasions and seen a search-light, which we believed came from the direction of Sollum. These bore exactly ENE thirdly by carefully questioning through others camel-men and the two Indian prisoners who had been sent back here from there, the average time taken by camels (not going it a straight line but from well to well) was five days, or about 100 miles, and probably 80 as the crow flies. Fourthly the general direction of caravans known to be going there was ENE.

From all these I felt perfectly confident of the general direction and distance to Sollum, and my ability at least to strike the coast in its vicinity. The two Indians also gave descriptions of the country which tallied exactly with each other, and stated they had met no one on the whole journey. This removed much of the danger of discovery, and I intended to lessen it still more by travelling only at night and hiding during the day. If I saw anyone I could slightly alter my direction and trust to my Arab clothes and sunburnt face hiding my identity. If, however, I were really caught, I had several sentences written out in Arabic, by which I would state that, although I had no money on me then, if they would guide me safely to Sollum, they would receive much gold. I had no doubt of Sollum being in British hands, as the Indians had themselves witnessed it, and the repeated assurances of Selim that there was a two months truce with England made murder at sight less probable.

I determined to strike a course which would take me a little eastward of Sollum into Egyptian territory, and when I believed I had passed it strike north for the coast. If, however I had underestimated the distance, and struck north too soon , I knew that sooner or later I must strike the road running west from Sollum in Senussi territory, and by keeping to the southward of it and moving east, readjust my position and obviate the danger of getting into the area on the west side of Sollum Gulf . The moon was nearly full, and there would be tonight be just an hour's darkness between sunset and moonrise, giving me just the chance I wanted to slip away. I would then have a full moon to walk by for several nights, and however cloudy, its position could generally be seen sufficiently to give me an indication of the course too be steered, though on clear night the stars would, of course, be a much better guide. By observing carefully, I knew exactly the positions occupied nightly by the 'Bear' or 'Huntsman's Clock' and so could tell the time, and from that judge the distance covered, as I had been a great pedestrian all my life.

For, shoes I borrowed Lt Apcar's (Arab shoe's). He had been sick ever since he landed and they were the only pair in the camp not worn out, and fitted me to a nicety. For food, I had been saving a little rice from each meal all the week, although a bitter pinch it was. Rice rations for to days were issued that morning, so I was able to draw two more days in advance, and I drew another from the general supply (with the connivance of the Chief Steward). By shamming dysentery, I was able to cajole a little flour out of Selim and make a pound of bread, and as he never went near sick people the chances of my absence being discovered at once were very much decreased. Indeed, I had every hope of three or four days start and the chance that they would think I had escaped towards the Italian town of Tabrouk [sic], which was closer. Thus I had four rations of rice, weighing boiled, over 12 lbs (rice requires exactly twice its own volume to cook it) and two days smaller rations of bread. These I tied carefully as separate one-day rations, three in each leg of my cotton Arab drawers, with the rice to come first, as I was afraid it might be sour before the first four days were up. The mess contributed to me generously a large piece of meat, which I cut up, and put one piece with each ration, and I had also dates I had saved in a bag at my girdle, also added to generously by my messmates from their scanty store. For water, I carried a half filled kid skin on my back containing I suppose, one and a half gallons. The trouble was, all our skins were leaking badly. But I got the best, and hoped that, with economy it would last me at least eight days. Thus I had six days full provisions (but of a terribly heavy type and weighing at least 30 lbs) and I knew I could go for many days without food if necessary, living on snails and roots. I calculated I could walk at least 20 miles a day (in spite of weakness and impossibility of training), so that if Sollum were only 80 miles away, as I believed I had a very ample margin. I did not attempt to escape sooner in the year, because there was then every prospect of our release or exchange, and besides, there was the matter of my parole. But I felt that if I put it off longer I would be loosing strength all the time. The nights would be shorter, giving less time to walk, and the heat greater, making exertion greater and water more necessary.

I was the only one in the camp who had never known a moment's sickness or had a sore foot, and I had unlimited faith in my own endurance. Going alone was far safer, and two people would only hamper each other as much as leashed greyhounds. Besides, I fancied a change of scenery, and the whole prospect was delightful. It was a case of then or never. So off I started about 6.30 that evening, well up to programme time, with a very light heart and many a hearty hand grip from those I had not known were my friends.

I slipped away without the sentry having a ghost of an inkling. The fires were made to blaze extra high so as to help dazzle him, and in some twenty minutes I lost sight of them behind a rise and was stumbling over the stones in the darkness.

Besides my provisions I carried a few letters for home a list of the crew, my diary, a small tomato tin for a drinking cup, my lucky horseshoe, my bone needle and thread for mending shoes. Tarrick Bay's letter (in case I were accused of breaking parole) , stout staff and a few other odds and ends. Also half my 'bernous' which originally was some 14ft long. My tattered naval uniform I wore under Arab clothes, for showing in an emergency, and I think the safety of my life was greatly increased by it.

At first my pack felt very heavy, the ropes feeling hard on shoulders which were little but skin and bones, and the water leaking steadily away soon soaked me through behind, I soon had little thought of anything else and gradually became more accustomed to it.

As the moon rose walking became better, but the night a full of alarms, and every now and then I had to lay flat under my sand coloured bernous to see if an object moved or not – the only way of deciding whether it were a bush or a human being

I could steer an accurate course by rising stars east at first and east by north later, and took short rests at, as far as I could judge 9 p.m. and midnight, when I ate a few dates and licked the outside of my wet water skin.

*Monday, 21st February.* I began to get a bit done with my heavy weight and the awful stone towards morning, but managed to keep going pretty steadily. My shoes were a little small, and both my big toe nails worked loose and had to be tied on with a piece of rag and I got somewhat of a blister on my left heel, not having worn shoe for two months.

I stumbled right into a caravan of eighty or ninety camels about 4 a.m. and lay flat in the dust, while the drivers went chanting past me at a distance of 4 yards, quite unsuspicious. Then the moon became totally obscured by clouds that I had to wait an hour before I could again determine my course. But on the whole I calculated I had done well and made good twenty-five miles, east by north when day broke.

Here I found myself in an area of very stunted bushes, only a few inches high, so after a short rest and a good look to see if the coast was clear, I moved on a mile or so to where they were higher. Here, however, I seemed to be in a very populous neighbourhood. Several large caravans passed with much noise, and isolated persons as close as 30 or 40 yards. It was anxious work, as I crawled from side to side to get the bush between me and them, but late I became more confident and dozed for a little. My chief anxiety was about the water, as the skin still leaked terribly, and I seemed to have already lost nearly half its contents, though there was no apparent hole.

An hour and a half before sunset, there being apparently no one about, and feeling much refreshed I ventured out and found myself at once in the immediate vicinity of an Arab camp of some eight tents, right in my course. But trusting to my disguise, and making as big a detour as I dared to avoid it, I passed it without mishap.

Many fire's were visible after dark, so this was evidently not the uninhabited desert I had imagined from the Indian's descriptions – but they probably went on entirely different route. It is very disquieting though. Tramped on until midnight, averaging, with steps, some 2½ miles per hour.

*Tuesday, 22nd February.* Plodded on at something under 2½ miles an hour with short rests until dawn, when I fairly dropped from exhaustion into the nearest bush, being quite unable to lift my feet further.

A leopard was making [the] night hideous by his caterwauls in the near vicinity, but I was too done to notice him, and after a few brief calculations, dozed off happily in the knowledge that I had covered in all some 51 miles in the 36 hours since leaving El Hakkim. More than half way to Sollum. But my water-skin was now nearly empty and dripped continuously as I watched it. I hung it from the bush and left my tin cup under it to try and catch some of the precious drops, and then fell fast asleep.

It must have been an hour later when I awoke with a start and found the whole country around me alive with men and camels moving in all directions. I lay as flat as possible, and trusted that providence would help me again as she had done so often, so that I had begun to get careless or I would never have been trapped like this. But the water skin was my undoing. Evidently its unfamiliar appearance in the bush attracted their attention, and I saw three men making my way with guns and loud ejaculation.

I covered my face with my bernous and pretended to be asleep, hoping they would not like to awaken me. But it was no good and soon felt myself roughly seized and shaken. I opened my eyes lazily, and then attempted to go to sleep again. But the game was up, and I was pulled to my feet, while the tree villainous looking rascals stared and shouted at me loudly.

My captors, who were of a low type of Bedouin, soon went through my belongings and stripped me, and I should have been in a bad way had not more powerful thieves appeared on the scene, who assuring me that the first would cut my throat, took me away from them and went over my person even more carefully. I was soon the centre of some 20 or 30 cut throats, the leaders of whom eventually took charge of me, as being their special prey.

All this time I was working in my carefully prepared Arabic sentences, about my having nothing of value on me, but that if I could be conducted to Sollum, there would be much gold. This was readily understood, and when they discovered I really had nothing of value, beyond my clothes, it began to have it effect, though I was in danger at one time by laughing and displaying my gold teeth. They appeared to think removing my head was the easiest way of getting it.

I was then marched off to the nearest encampment, [of] some 30 large tents, on the journey to which they displayed the usual Arab and Turkish ideas of humour by firing their guns over my shoulder or in my direction. But this not appearing to answer expectations, they later contented themselves by exhibiting me for the rest of the day, much as dancing bears used to be in England. They displayed great curiosity in my diary, and treated it with great respect.

I kept on quoting the name of the Grand Senussi and Nouri Bey, etc, about any article for which they showed a special acquisitiveness and in the end I had nothing taken from me, except my much prized steel needle. This I resisted by force, and then later gave it to its would be purloiner as a present. This made him very ashamed and I hereby gained a friend, who saved me much annoyance, and whom at one time I had great hopes would conduct me to Sollum (until we were rescued by the Armoured Cars we all believed Sollum to have remained in the hands of the British since Xmas and that there was peace between them and the Senussi. Both these surmises were contrary to fact).

Late in the afternoon I was turned over to two Turkish soldiers (Cretans) who appeared to be billeted in the camp, Ali Hassan, thick set, vulgar and of Negroid type; Mahmoud, well set up and good looking, more refined and able to read and write. They always reminded me of the two comic villains of a pantomime, and their talents being complimentary, they had become quite indispensable and inseparable, the one from the other. As I spent a whole week in their society, I had some opportunity of studying them. When any robbing or threat was necessary, Ali Hassan, the old campaigner, was much to the fore. But when it was a matter of finesse and diplomacy, he kept his ungainly person out of sight and Mahmoud came to the fore to cajole a night's lodging, a bowl of milk or a feed of dates.

Between them they appeared to get on very well, but having no idea of direction they came to rely almost entirely on me to pilot them to unknown places, of which I never knew so much as even knew the name. In fact I was quite a 'Star' turn where-ever I went. I was always asked to tell the inhabitants the directions in which different places lay, and which, after a glance at the stars and the rough map I had made, I was easily able to do to their undisguised astonishment.

The two soldiers having gone over my person with a dexterity evidently acquired from log practice (and realizing that what the Senussi had left couldn't be worth much), then listened to my story and were sympathetic on the subject of gold at Sollum. My hopes of successful bribery again rose, and I displayed my uniform (worn under my Arab shirt) and medal ribbons, to emphasize my importance. But I soon discovered they were only 'kidding' me, which was indicated by whistling loudly, to show I was a 'bird' or someone who had flown. Their incredulity they expressed by pulling down the corner of one bloodshot eye.

Facial expression appears to be very limited among the Arabs, and I soon fell into the spirit of the game by doing my 'tricks' which generally got us a more liberal supply of food. The 'tricks' being no more than assuming an expression of *hauteur*, superciliousness, contempt or vanity. These caused unfailing yells of laughter and had to be many times repeated, and after displaying, and after displaying my gold tooth, tattoos, medal ribbons and diary, the show was considered finished and we were generally well repaid with dates and milk.

Civilized dental treatment always aroused great interest in this land of perfect teeth, and I well remember an occasion when Lt Tanner put the whole of our guards to flight by opening his mouth and letting his upper plate of false teeth suddenly fall.

The night I spent in this camp, between my two soldier friends, each with his Martini [rifle] at his side, a hand on my shoulder and a big camel rug over us.

We had the usual supper of dates and milk, and soon I learned the etiquette. The large wooden bowl of milk goes from hand to hand and you may only drink it with loud indrawing of the breath. An exhausting process, but equalizing the amount you all get.

Dates you eat as fast as you can, stoning them with one hand all the time, and it is *de rigueur* to throw back the debris in the bowl. I broke my best tooth trying to eat fast enough for my share, but never had a chance, though among my fellow-prisoners I had at one time been very unpopular on account of the rate at which I bolted my food.

Shoes you always took off, and hats you always kept on. This annoyed me much in bed, where my feet were cold and my head hot, but there was no appeal.

The evenings were always spent round the bright fire at the entrance to the tent, well screened from the cold winds, and where I was to display my 'tricks'. The women, who are never veiled, and generally very well dressed in red and other bright colours, squat round as interested spectators in the background. They always appeared to me to be treated with the greatest kindness and consideration, but to have a definite place in the order of things, which they never tried to exceed. They a generally very small compared with the men, but well proportioned and comely, and invariably disfigured by tattoos or slit nostrils.

I was much truck by the luxury and richness of most of the tents, which by fire light appeared like vaulted Gothic buildings inside. They were all quite new and very large and covered with magnificent carpets and rugs of wonderful colours and thickness.

But food beyond kids, dates and milk, appeared to have disappeared from the country, and in most camps the whole population appeared to subsist entirely on roots, herbs and snails. To see a whole family gorging on the latter, cracking the shells on stones and with smeared faces from the brown juice is a disgusting sight. The bowls we ate from were inevitably filthy beyond measure, water being too rare a commodity for any form of washing to be ever indulged in, and its lack of course never noticed.

The village doctor was generally one of our guests. (Whoever happened to be present always joined in the feed). He is generally a powerful, saturnine looking man and was invariably introduced by drawing a finger across the throat. This I gathered was intended to inform me that he combined the gentle art of medicine with the more trying duties of Lord High Executioner. And such I believe to be the case, since my friend, Dr Bechi Faud, had told me he was compelled by Achmed Shereef to amputate the hands of for culprits guilty of smoking.

Catching 'lodgers' and throwing them in the fire was an invariable evening entertainment evening amusement, in which all joined, so that the lack of bridge and other games was not felt.

*Wednesday, 23rd February.* Had a very disturbed night, thanks to the two rifles in my ribs, cold feet and the noise of camels and dogs, and the fact that my two friends 'lodgers' evidently considered me 'fresh fields and pastures new' and moved accordingly. When one is already weak, the loss of this blood and sleep nightly is a serious consideration.

We turned out at earliest sunrise and then spent the morning moving from on tent to tent getting dates at one and milk at another, and showing my 'tricks'. This continued until about 2 p.m. The country as far as I could see in every direction, was covered with lines of tents and the great frames for weaving carpets, etc countless camels, sheep and goats. There appeared to be no water supply, and the few pints I saw were bright yellow from the clayey soil, and I fancy had been gathered from shallow holes dug in the ground to catch the rain.. Taking a hawk with us (these beautiful birds can be purchased for a shilling or so), we moved along and soon loosened it at a hare, with the only result I have ever seen in this country – the loss of both bird and quarry!

Soon we came to a deserted part, where to my surprise I found a camel, two men and a girl, evidently waiting for us. The soldiers mounted and the procession started and once more I was happy in the belief that my bribes had prevailed, and that they were thus secretly taking me to Sollum. We passed a man mercilessly beating his wife on the ground, but I was prevented from interfering, which perhaps was wisest.

And then to my surprise the soldiers got down and moved off, leaving me in the charge of the strange camel man. I felt rather disquieted again in this lonely spot, as it somehow looked like a prelude to murder and the division of the spoils. But then I felt reassured by the fact of a woman being present. They would hardly have brought her to witness it.

We moved on, on a devious course, saw someone, and coming closer., I discovered to my surprise that it was my two soldiers friends again, with a very fat lamb just killed, and a bright fire which they had recently lit.

In an incredibly short time the animal was skinned, hewn in pieces and cast on the fire, and as each part was cooked it was taken out, portioned and devoured. The first part cooked was the feet, then the liver, light and kidneys, then the entrails and stomach and head, and lastly the carcass. The whole animal disappeared in less than half an hour from the time of my arrival, and I have enjoyed many a good dinner at home far less, though we had neither salt nor bread.

The Arabs tore the flesh like wolves, and cracked the bones with their teeth to extract the marrow, and I followed their example as well as I was able. So cooked, the entrails (quite uncleaned) were by far the best part of the animal, and filled with its mother's milk, as deliciously crisp and tender. The liver and light have a seductive taste no frying pan can give them, the feet (hoofs, hair and all) not at all bad, and the stomach decidedly palatable. In fat it was all very good, and I felt very much better after such a quantity of nourishing food, and after this never had any doubts as to the good intentions of Ali and Mahmoud with regard to myself.

After eating, we at once departed, but I was able to gather this was the solution of the provisioning problem that had been troubling my soldier hosts. They had again and again asked me for money to buy food for the journey, and failing this, had commandeered the animal.

The camel men were then sent ahead to fill my water-skin at a well, whose yellow mound, was plainly visible, while the soldiers and I went off in another direction. Their intentions soon became evident. Another large flock of sheep and goats was passing.

A very simple process of acquisition was then gone through. Guns were levelled at the shepherd by Ali, until he ran for his life, while Mahmoud carried on and tried to pacify the irate shepherd's wife. Ali suddenly sprang on the fattest lamb and bore it off bleating on his shoulders. We then joined the camel-men again and proceeding a mile or so a fire was lit, the lamb killed and another orgy commenced. This time we only did half a job, and the remainder of the flesh was put on the camel.

Soon after dark we arrived at an Arab camp, and after being accommodated with the usual dates and milk, the lamb's carcass was put into a large iron pot and boiled. The resulting broth (only about two quarters were made from three quarters of a sheep), was very good, but being evidently despised by my hosts, was given to the women. We six persons had then eaten two complete sheep within four hours. That night I felt no hunger, but very decided pains! My Arab fiends, however, were in no way inconvenienced and were quite surprised and annoyed when I wished to curtail the usual evening pantomime. Though I had been kept walking since sunrise, our apparent progress this day was only some 16 miles to the NE and I had no idea yet where they were taking me.

*Thursday, 24th February.* Dragged out at sunrise, feeling very piano, the result of excessive mutton. We visited tents for some hours, whereby Mahmoud was able to get us invited to partake of several bowls of milk, but no dates.

We then proceeded to do the usual robbery of a fat kid, it taking a little longer this time, as its owner was not to be intimidated by Ali Hassan, or his wife to be cajoled by Mahmoud with a signed paper. It was only when the animal had been completely cooked and eaten as before, that they ceased their protests. While we ate, the camel strayed and it took us a weary three hours march in the hot sun before we came up with it.

We were sill in the vicinity of the yellow well mound seen the previous afternoon, and happening on another flock, again seized the fattest lamb without either explanation or apology. The appetite seemed to grow with the eating. This was the fourth, but last, however for as we bore it off on the camel, at a great pace to the NW we saw eight sturdy shepherds with guns, following us in skirmishing order.

We increased our pace, which I found pretty hard going, in my footsore and weary condition. Firing soon commenced on both sides, and the bullets were soon merrily knocking up spurts of sands all around us, but without anyone being the worse. The girl was put on the camel, and with a kick I was told off a camel-driver, which I readily did. The whole situation was so humorous, with the girl holding the struggling, bleating lamb on the camel (the latter tacking in every direction), and myself sweating, beating and limping behind, that I fairly yelled with laughter, in which the girl merrily joined.

Eventually the shepherds came up and I was told to disgorge the prey. The man who received it, evidently well satisfied, saluted me courteously, but was followed later by a hail of bullets from my robber friends as soon as he had retreated some 300 or 400 yards. This again, fortunately, without any accidents.

We then marched off NW once more in a hot sun, passing the Sollum road and telegraph posts abut 3 p.m. until we got to another Arab camp, where we spent the night and got an excellent date and milk supper. Apparent progress about 16 miles NW though we must have actually covered close on 30 miles in various directions. The country here was not so thickly populated as the place where I was recaptured, and where the lines of tents stretched for miles in every direction. But even here there were immense flocks of sheep and goats, mostly moving to the west. The soil is firm clayey sand, with large numbers of dried up Roman wells or cisterns.

*Friday, 25th February.* Had a cold night of it, my *bernous* having been on the camel the previous day, which did not arrive before dark, being very slow. Out at sunrise, and Mahmoud having cajoled three lots of dates and milk, we started off at 5 miles an hour to the NW as though determined to make up for the time wasted on previous days. I found the pace very killing in my weak and footsore condition. Fortunately the day was cloudy. We continued all day, at never less than 4 miles an hour, with hardly any rest of any kind, pulling herbs and roots as we went along on a very zig-zag courses between west and NNW happening suddenly on an Arab camp we sought, one and a half hours after dark, and when I was utterly done. The lights suddenly shone out in a hollow, as we topped the rise. Apparent distance made good only some 20 miles WNW but we must have covered well over 30 miles; the soldiers had no idea of direction. The country here is the same firm sand and clay soil, covered with scrub. There are several low ridges of hills and a higher one, running east and west, and which gradually receded, lay to the southward of us. There are many small valleys running towards the coast, green and full of grass and large bushes, with signs of many recent camps in them. But the country was then nearly bare of inhabitants, except some very small flocks, who's impoverished owners were busy eating snails and roots and could give us no other food, but indicated the direction we should go in. At the camp where we slept we were given rice, the first I had seen since my escape. All this land must be very fertile and well watered in the winter months, and edible roots and plants were especially abundant.

Went to bed very hungry, not having then learned the rules as to eat rice. The latter is brought in, smeared round the sides of a large wooden bowl. Each diner at once scoops all he can with his hands and rams it down his throat, and it is all gone in ten seconds. I was not quick enough and got hardly any. Our hosts was a very kind, white bearded old gentleman, of a refined type, who spent the evening nursing his family, and with whom I made great friends. We spent the night warm, under luxurious rugs.

*Saturday, 26th February.* Out at sunrise and at once started again on our wild zig-zag at a very fast pace. We had nether breakfast nor water, but I had had a refreshing nights sleep, and we gathered what roots we could as we went along.

The country was much the same as on the previous days, but the valleys flatter and broader and the hills to the south gradually were lost to sight. To the NW the land appeared more uneven, and I noted what resembled very large well mounds. The whole gave me the impression that the coast was not far away.

I had a bad day of it, with no food or water, and covering at least 35 miles; the lack of water I did not feel, only the hunger. Towards 3 p.m. it became obvious that my guides were utterly lost, as they were then heading due north, so I took the matter in my own hands and made them follow me to the WSW where I saw what I thought were tents. On nearer approach they proved to be a very large number of well mounds, with a kind of pharos and what had evidently been a Roman town. The soldiers evidently recognised it and were overjoyed, and we found an Arab tent near by, whose owner was able to put us on the right track. Going a couple of miles about SE across a couple of valleys filled with large lilies in flower, we came on numbers of telegraph posts and, if my memory serves me right, saw a road.

A little further on, we came upon the huts and tents of the Turkish camp. Judging by the debris this had apparently at one time been of a considerable size, but at this period did not contain more than I think, some twenty soldiers, clad in their tattered khaki uniforms. The officer's quarters was a rough board building of two stories, like a very small railway signal box, from whose upper story ran the telephone wires, and through whose chinks whistled the bitter wind. The upper storey was reached by a rough outside stairway, under which was the sentry box.

At the entrance I was met by Capt Achmed, clad in an English khaki uniform, of which, he being somewhat short and stout, the knees were buttoned round his ankles, and Mahomet Effendi, late our Senussi Commandante. They regarded me with stern faces, and Achmed said to me 'This is very bad' while Mahomet repeated in broken English 'Captain no good.' I told Achmed it was nothing of the kind, and that if had been a prisoner in Egypt he would have been only to glad to escape himself.

He said 'But why try to escape? You are mad I believe. What shall we tell the English Government if you had been killed by Arabs?'

I replied that he could tell them the truth for once, that I quite realised he had the right to kill me now if he wished, that I was no more mad than he was, and that the reason I tried to escape was that we had no news of home since we landed, and I wished to get to Sollum to inform the British of the real state of affairs and how we were treated. He said 'You believe then that Sollum was in the hands of the English?' I said that I knew it was, and at this he smiled. His relief at my safe recapture was obviously great an the atmosphere had become less thundery. I was conducted upstairs to the telephone room, where there was a bed and a dozen or so of Russian magazine rifles. The joyful news of my safe recapture was then telephoned through to all parts of the country, my ears catching the names of Matruh, Bomba and Sollum, which I thought to be only a 'bounce' on his part. Towards dark I sank in a comatose condition on the floor, worn out. To my surprise I was soon afterwards woken up a brought a delicious bowl of peppered and saffroned rice, followed by the sweet, syrupy Arab tea which I had not tasted since Christmas. In my pocket I had what I called my 'liberty pipe' (a pipe which I had in my pocket since I swam for it when the *Tara* sank). This I had sworn not to smoke until I had liberty. Some kind Senussi officer giving me cigarettes (very strong and vile Italian tobacco) I now indulged in this luxury to commemorate the two days freedom I had had. Later in the evening I was allowed downstairs with the other officers (some five or six Senussi, mostly elderly men, and Achmed), and was indulged with more tea, while they listened to as much of my adventures as I thought it wise to give them. They were much amused at the story of the soldiers and the sheep and this way of raising food especially pleased Achmed. I told him how good they had been to me, and specially commended their loyalty in refusing all my bribes. At night I slept with all the officers on the ground floor, my head on what I could feel to be a sack of macaroni.

*Sunday, 28th February.* Everyone extremely civil to me in the morning, especially a young and good looking Senussi officer, absurdly like Lewis Waller in appearance. He gave me dates and innumerable cigarettes, and then he and the cook, Mohammed, shaved and generally preened and decorated themselves. Even Achmed unbent so far as to give me a cigarette and converse in a friendly way, and gave me the latest Turkish war news, some of the items being that the canal had been crossed in two places near the centre some 10 days previously; that the Germans were within 15 kilometres of Paris and that the French Government had been moved to Bordeaux. I assumed successfully an air of respectful belief, which evidently pleased Achmed, and he further informed me that the British had been driven back beyond Matruh, and now only held Baba [El Dabaa?], at the end of the Egyptian railway.

Late in the morning, my two soldier friends were brought forward, and each being rewarded with a silver dollar, departed, after a hearty handshake with myself. Achmed informed me that the name of the camp where we were, was Arkoma (its real name was Gweider, it was in the vicinity of Tabrouk), and that our last day's march had been 30 miles. As far as I could understand, my soldier guides had called it Tabrouk – which I understood to mean the Turkish camp covering the Italia town of that name. I had never had any opportunity of judging how far we really were from the sea, but I was told we were close to Zebla. Achmed, however, never erred on the side of truthfulness.

Achmed also told me that the Italians would not fight, that they only had one hundred black soldiers at Tabrouk (the rest having been withdrawn for the European War), and that Sollum being closed, the Italians were letting through provisions for the Turks. I however, saw practically noting to confirm this, except very small quantities, Mahomet Effendi departed during the morning, and Ached told me he was going west, but would later return to the wells of El Hakkim.

I spent this day resting, washing and trying to get some of the vermin off my person, having no desire for these momentos of my soldier guardians. There is a very good well here, full up to the top with water. A prisoner was brought in during the day by two soldiers; an Arab found with modern weapons in his possession! These, by Turkish orders, should all have been given up, the natives being only allowed firearms of obsolete pattern. Of the later there seems to be a fine collection in the country – flintlocks, dating from the Napoleonic wars, fitted with a fixed bayonet, Minie rifles of 1875, percussion rifles and double barrelled sporting guns of all varieties. The prisoner having had his face well smacked, was put in the sentry box under the stairway, and left there for the night – I do not know what his subsequent fate was. The soldiers who had brought him in were each rewarded with a small silver coin. The rifle, a Russian magazine, very popular with the Turks, was added to the store in the telephone room.

This telephone station is evidently of importance as there is always an officer on duty there and sleeps beside it at night. Messages are continually coming and going all day long. Achmed is commandant here, being busy and important, and evidently enjoying life; he seems to have the handling of a good bit of money.

I was allowed to wander within 50 yards of the telephone station during the day, and was amused to see the stampeding of an Arab horse. Those that I had seen hitherto had always been to old and infirm for such frolics. But they are wonderfully adapted for the country in which they live, and seem to be able to endure thirst for periods approaching those of a camel. Five days without water is quite a common thing and one I had often observed in Mahomet Effendi's ancient steed.

Salim Effendi arrived during the afternoon with four soldiers from El Hakkim and sat in the dust looking much depressed. But seeing me smoking amiably with Achmed soon tumbled to the alternate state of affairs, and all spent a merry evening together quaffing tea, to which I was not invited. Macaroni and oil for breakfast and peppered rice in the evening, joyful luxuries, but in very small quantities, owing to the, from my point of view, unfortunate advent of guests, whose share I might otherwise have had.

I was locked in the lower room for the night by myself, the whole place having been cleared of officers and the sacks of provisions it originally contained. I lay down in the dirt , and as soon as the last flickering flames from the box of embers I had been given as a light expired, the fleas literally descended on me in showers and shovelfuls. I never knew anything like it, and there was no sleep for me. But my kind friend Lewis Waller visited me at some late hour, and filled my pockets with dates and my heart with gratitude. There are kind hearts everywhere, but there is none more generous that the Arab, or chivalrous than the true Turk. The trouble is that their memories are so short.

*Monday, 28th February.* I left at sunrise, escorted by Selim, the four soldiers and an old woman driver, after an early bowl of milk, Selim who was kindness itself and ever thoughtful, made me feel somewhat shamefaced, for I could not but be aware that had I not been recaptured, he himself would have been punished by disrating from officer to private, an apparently fixed rule.

We trudged steadily south at a good 4 miles an hour, over a very nearly level country, until at 11 a.m. we came on a small Arab camp, where we stopped for dates and milk. Once again due south, good going over the firm oil and bushes, but weary work for me with my raw and aching feet, and the fatigue of eight days marching and uncertain food. On, up to the east and west Sollum road, here 20 feet wide, and on up the incline which miles away had looked like mountains but was merely a slight plateau like elevation of the ground. On this rise we heard a great sound of firing, and saw a small party (four or five) of Turkish soldiers, but I did not ascertain the cause. Stopping we were soon joined by them, and I found them to be commanded by a fine specimen of Albanian, fierce looking and clad in flowered silks , a magnificent great silver ring on his finger, with a large mysterious looking stone in it. On his breast he wore a very large decoration which he informed me was Turkish. We soon made friends and I was proffered the inevitable cigarette, though I found it a very poor substitute for food. On parting, we turned back to the north, recrossed the Sollum road, and found an Arab camp close by, where we spent a very comfortable night, boiled mutton being forthcoming as well as milk and dates. Distance covered 28 miles south.

*Tuesday, 29th February.* A very refreshing night's sleep, with soft lying and warm rugs to cover me; spared also the prolixity of rifles and strong odoured soldiers as bed-mates, to which my former captors had made me almost resigned. Out with the sun, we crossed the Sollum road about 7 a.m. heading ESE at 4 miles an hour. It soon became very bad going over the red and black soapy flints and limestone rocks so familiar around El Hakkim, and I was very glad when at 11 a.m. we pulled up near an Arab camp. The soldiers were sent in as usual, but returned soon after to my great disappointment, with no food. Apparently there was none to be had there.

There were an enormous number of old Roman wells in this neighbourhood, one of which had apparently been recently repaired. After half an hour we moved on, this time to the SWW looking at first for some other camp but without success. We continued thus at 4 miles an hour, over stony ground, for the rest of the afternoon. I was utterly done and had been foodless and waterless all day except for part of a small tortoise the soldiers gave me, and three hard set Lark's eggs which I found and ate, warm and raw, I shall not forget in a hurry their unpleasant wriggles as I swallowed them! There were enormous numbers of hares about in this bare country and the soldiers in vain tried to stalk them with their rifles. A hawk was also loosed and lost. I was soon too utterly done to go a step further, and Selim again showed his kindness by getting off his camel, which I rode for nearly two hours. This was all the more remarkable, as I found afterwards his feet were blistered from end to end, caused by his forced march to Gweider for me. The soldiers also loudly protested against a culprit like myself being so honoured.

About 4.30 p.m. when I had quite given up hope of reaching our destination (as we had apparently made no landmarks), we saw the stone beacon and water walls of El Hakkim. Selim and his soldiers fired a fusillade of shots in the air, and very soon the whole garrison, now reinforced to sixteen, came running to meet us, headed by the black priest Osman and followed by the women and children.

Osman greeted me by a blow on the shoulders with his rhinoceros-hide whip, and followed it up by some seven or eight more on the head and back. Someone else smacked my face, and the women threw ill-aimed stones and spat. But I seemed to hardly feel it. I was driven forward to the blockhouse and then confine in the sheep pen at the back. My coat, shoes, possessions and precious diary were taken from me, the four sentries put on guard making a parade of loading their rifles, and no one was allowed to approach.

I didn't believe Selim intended actual violence should be done to me, but he was ever weak if kind-hearted, and they all seemed to hold their priest (who had no real temporal authority) in great awe.

Here in the sheep pen I remained the night, apparently half naked and hungry. But as soon as it was dark, and other British prisoners could no longer see, my clothes and bernous were brought back, two mats were given me (one of which I made a roof of), and I was given water and a liberal supply of dates. With a thankful heart I was asleep in a few minutes, to woken a little later by Mahmoud, the bright eyed nine year old body servant of Selim. In his hand he had brought a huge bowl of rice and watched delightedly while I ate it. It was in fact Selim's own supper, and so liberal that I could not finish it (the first and last time while I was a prisoner). I often thought regretfully in still hungrier days later on, of the part I had left uneaten and failed to put in my pocket. The sentry himself also gave me a cigarette to smoke and a large fire burned all night to keep me warm.

Such is the Arab character!

*Wednesday, 1st March.* I enjoyed a rest cure all day Wednesday in the sheep pen, being rather glad of it than otherwise, as was given an unusual amount of food and did not feel very strenuous after my nine days of roving and the weather was mild. Towards dark however, at Lt Tanner's urgent solicitations, I was allowed to return to the officer's tent where I got a very warm and hearty greeting.

# 20. In Captivity, February 1916(2)

*Monday, 21st February.* As the men awoke, the camp routine began as normal, the guards not having noticed the captain's disappearance. The meals throughout the day were the usual rice, dates and meat for the healthy and a little flour for the sick — all in hopelessly insufficient amounts.

Later during the day Lieutenant Tanner reflected that at first he had been against the escape attempt as the chances of success were not too good, but seeing the captain was determined and one of the strongest of the prisoners and had explained that he reckoned the distance to Sollum was some eighty to one hundred miles to the east-north-east and that he would march during the night, avoid all wells and tracks and rest during the day, Tanner thought there was a chance of success.

*Tuesday, 22nd February.* During the morning Osman called at the officers' tent looking for Basil who had developed a painful abscess at the bottom of his spine. On entering the tent he immediately noticed that the captain was absent. The officers quickly explained that he had been hungry and had left the tent during the night/early morning, but they had no idea of where he had gone nor the direction he had taken. The alarm was raised and guards sent out into the desert in all directions. Salim Effendi was greatly disturbed no doubt wondering what Nuri Bey and the Grand Senussi would say and do to him if the captain escaped. He explained to the officers that the captain was very foolish as he could come across some Arabs who could murder him. All hands were then called out of their tents and mustered for a head count, the first for a very long time. Expecting some harsh treatment they were surprised to be then given an extra date ration!

Seeing that Basil being in great pain, Surgeon Arthur later lanced the abscess with a razor to relieve the pressure.

Dutton noted that a lark had flown into the officers' tent whilst a cat slept on the tent and wondered if these were good or bad omens?

*Wednesday, 23rd February.* As punishment for the captain's escape attempt, the Mullah informed the survivors that their boundary area would now be shortened to thirty yards outside the camp during the day and ten yards during the night. Anyone found outside this area would be shot. This meant they could only use the water from the new well, which was dirty, for their drinking, cooking and washing. The water collected from the well was full of sand and grit as it had not had time to settle after the recent rains. The clean water in the old well was now to be used by passing caravans only.

Nearly all were now supplementing their meals with snails. In the officers' mess they had heard that two men in another mess had eaten over a 1,000 snails during the day, Tanner remarking that the most he had eaten in one sitting was eighty!

*Thursday, 24th February.* A quiet day but the rations were getting even smaller and the men becoming weaker. The snails, which were now coming out of hibernation, were found to be full of sand and very gritty.

*Friday, 25th February.* A cold day. Chief Steward Morris reported that the stores in the blockhouse were running very low and if a caravan did not come soon would be exhausted. Lieutenant Tanner was worried as all were weak and anxious.

Sub Lieutenant Marsh, speculated that the captain may have reached Sollum and could be sitting down to ham and eggs for breakfast after which he would be lambasting the lieutenant-colonel about the prisoners' plight, urging him to organise a rescue attempt. He also recorded that he and Sub Lieutenant Griffiths, together with Assistant Engineers Hughes and Davies, had often discussed the idea of an escape attempt whilst they still had the strength.

*Saturday, 26th February.* Salim Effendi left camp first thing this morning accompanied by six guards. It was later discovered they had gone to bring back the captain who has been captured in the desert by some Arabs. It was also thought that he had been wounded. During their absence, the Senussi sergeant was put in charge of the camp.

The prisoners' rations were reduced by half which led Lieutenant Tanner to go to the blockhouse to see the sergeant and ask for an increase and to make it clear that if any more men died then it would be the sergeant who would be held responsible. As they were arguing some of the prisoners made their way to the blockhouse to see what the fuss was all about. Thinking that the prisoners were going to rush the blockhouse the four guards left in the camp fired six shots over their heads, whilst their women rushed out of their tents and attacked the prisoners with sticks and long poles. The prisoners scattered and the sergeant ran amongst the guards and their wives pelting them with stones until they quietened down and the prisoners returned to their tents.

Once order had been restored the sergeant promised to provide the prisoners with one goat or sheep per day, but although sympathetic with their plight he would still have to reduce their rice and date ration by half as there was simply not enough to last.

Later, in the officers' mess, Sub Lieutenant Griffiths made some date coffee which Lieutenant Tanner thought tasted excellent. The coffee had been made by roasting the date stones, then grinding them down and wrapping the grounds in a cloth which were then boiled.

*Sunday, 27th February.* A day of rest for the prisoners was disturbed during the morning by shouts and arguments coming from the guards' tents. This was soon settled by the sergeant who waded into the throng and lashed about with his cane. The prisoners later learnt that the argument had been over who should have the head of a goat which had been slaughtered for the prisoners. Dutton later remarked that it had been quite exciting for a Sunday morning.

Extra guards and camels arrived with two bags of dates. The daily ration was now ¼ lb of crushed barley, ¾ lb of dates and 2 ozs of goat meat. At 11.00 hours the firewood collecting party went out and during the afternoon a snailing party went out under an armed guard. Returning to the camp the latter party reported that the snails were becoming scare.

During the evening hymns were sung in the officers' tent.

*Monday, 28th February.* Not having saved any of the previous day's rice for breakfast, the day's first meal consisted of only snails. Later, two days rations of rice and dates were issued, about 1lb of rice and 1½ lb of dates for each man and a slaughtered goat was to be issued each day. Owing to the shortages they were now reduced to one main meal per day.

*Tuesday, 29th February.* The firewood party went out in the morning and the snailing party with Lieutenant Tanner and Sub Lieutenant Dudgeon went out during the afternoon. At about 17.00 hours the latter group heard some gunshots to the north of the camp and they immediately made their way back to camp. The Senussi women had rushed to the top of the mounds by the wells where they had started to cry. In the camp, the guards (numbering about twenty, including Osman the Mullah) formed up and marched out in the direction of the gunshots. After some time had elapsed the prisoners could make out a small party making their way towards the camp and, on their getting closer, they could make out Salim Efendi on camel back and Captain Gwatkin-Williams on foot, accompanied by six Muafizia.

When the group reached the camp the Mullah Osman strode up to the captain and struck him across the face with his whip whilst his wife threw stones at the captain's back. The Osman then ordered Gwatkin-Williams's coat removed and had him placed in the sheep pen near the blockhouse. As he was led away Salim Effendi returned his coat. The men, although disappointed that he had been captured, were glad to see that he had not been wounded and Lieutenant Tanner later received permission to send him a mat and sack to sleep on. Sub Lieutenant Marsh thought that they would now be in for a rough time.

# 21. War, February 1916

With the reorganisation of the Western Frontier Force almost complete, thanks in part to the evacuation of the Gallipoli peninsula and fresh units arriving from England, the Composite Brigade of Yeomanry was replaced by the 2nd Mounted Division and the remainder of the South African Brigade (the 1st and 3rd South African Infantry Regiments had replaced both the 15th Sikhs and the New Zealand Rifle Brigade). The Hong Kong & Singapore Mountain Battery was attached to strengthen the artillery and further transport units and services were added which did away with the necessity of the force having to return to Matruh for replenishment after every engagement. Preparatory to beginning the advancing along the coast, the armoured cars were sent to reconnoitre the route to Unjeila. As they approached the town they came across some Senussi outposts with whom they exchanged fire before returning to Mersa Matruh to report their findings. On 13th February, a force of cavalry, the Australian Camel Corps and two armoured cars were sent to attack and occupy the town. This accomplished, Unjeila became the advance depot for stores which would be required for the advance on Sollum.

Even though it was known that the Senussi were present in some strength in the vicinity of Sidi Barrani, on 20th February General Payton sent a force under Brigadier-General Lukin to occupy the town.[1] The next day, aerial reconnaissance discovered the Senussi main force encamped at Agagia, fourteen miles south-east of Barrani. This information was confirmed by some Senussi deserters who also added that in the camp were Nuri Bey and Jaafar Pasha. Sayed Ahmed, the Grand Senussi, had also been there but had recently left for the Siwa oasis. The news was relayed to General Peyton who considered the force large enough to handle the Senussi and ordered Lukin to continue with his march and to attack as soon as he was in sight of the enemy.

On 24th February, Lukin ordered camp to be made at Wadi Maktil and

1. It consisted of a squadron of Royal Buckinghamshire Yeomanry; Queens Own Dorset Yeomanry; Notts. RHA, 1st & 3rd S.A. Infantry Regiments a detachment of the 1/6th Royal Scots and two Field Ambulances.

declared that the next day would be one of rest prior to a night approach with an attack on the Senussi camp the following dawn. The plan was disrupted at 17.30 hours on the 25th by Jaafar Pasha who attacked the British force with two field guns and at least one machine gun. Although the attack was quickly repulsed with the loss of only one man killed and one wounded, it made Lukin alter his plans so that the British attack would take place in daylight.

On the morning of the 26th, a yeomanry scouting party discovered that the positions occupied by the attackers the previous evening were deserted. Aerial reconnaissance, however, showed that they had only retired to their old positions in Agagia. At 09.30 hours the assault force left camp, accompanied by six armoured cars under the command of the Duke of Westminster.

By 10.15 hours the Yeomanry had seized a hillock 4,000 yards north of the enemy's position and some forty-five minutes later the main attack began. In the centre, the 3rd South African Regiment advanced on a front of 1,700 yards; the Yeomanry, less one squadron and with two armoured cars, operated on the right flank with orders to pursue the moment the enemy broke. On the left were the remaining squadrons with two armoured cars whilst the 1st South African Regiment and another two armoured cars were kept in reserve.

The British advance was met by heavy machine-gun and rifle fire, supported by two or three field guns. As the 3rd South African Regiment advanced, the Senussi moved swiftly to try to outflank them on their left. They were met by a squadron of Yeomanry brought up from reserve and the counter-attack faded away. General Lukin then withdrew this squadron from the left flank and sent it to strengthen his main pursuing force on the right and there is no doubt that this move did much to ensure the success of the subsequent operations. By now the Senussi positions were only some 500 yards ahead, so Lukin threw in most of his reserves, which included the remainder of the armoured cars. At the same time he warned Colonel Souter of the Dorset Yeomanry, to be ready to attack.

Souter later recorded that at about 13.00 hours he received a message from General Lukin asking him to pursue the Senussi with a view to cutting off their retreat. Thinking that there might be barbed wire and trenches in the sand hills, Souter decided to allow the enemy to get clear of the hills before attacking him in the open. He gave the order to chase the Senussi on a parallel line westwards and to keep some 1,000 yards between them and the retreating enemy. This the Dorset's did, dismounting every now and then so as to rest the horses and to fire into the retreating enemy. At about 14.00 hours, by which time his men were on the open plain, Souter saw the whole of the retreating Senussi force for the first time. It extended for about a mile and had a depth of 300–400 yards. In the front were the camels and baggage train, escorted by irregulars, with Muhafizia and Maxim guns forming the rear and flank guards. He then decided on a mounted attack.

Souter dismounted at about 15.00 hours to give his horse a rest and to check the nature of the ground over which they were about to move. The Dorset Yeomanry then regrouped on him but the squadron of Buckinghamshire Yeomanry (with whom they had set out) had gone on ahead and were nowhere to be seen. Souter then decided to attack alone and the Dorset Yeomanry formed up in two lines and started to advance steadily towards the enemy. The Senussi, seeing the attacking Yeomanry, brought their Maxims into action. When they reached about fifty yards from the enemy's position the colonel gave the order to charge and, with much yelling and shouting, the Dorsets smashed into the Senussi who immediately broke and started to flee. In the middle of the line, Souter's horse was shot but staggered on for a few strides before collapsing and throwing the colonel to the ground within a few feet of General Jaafar Pasha, the Senussi's commander! Souter was not alone as with him were Lieutenant J H Blaksley and Trooper Brown (possibly W Brown) whose horses had also been shot from under them. Surrounding them were some fifty Muhafizia and the situation was decidedly dangerous until the arrival of a machine-gun section who despatched the Senussi. Jaafar Pasha and his staff were then captured and speedily escorted from the field. There can be no doubt that the cavalry was extremely effective against the Senussi but that success came at came at a price; the Dorsets lost five officers and twenty-seven men killed, two officers and twenty-four men wounded, and some eighty-five horses killed or missing.

This action, known as the battle of Agagia, brought the first part of General Peyton's advance on Sollum to a successful conclusion. Two days later on 28th February the port of Barrani was occupied unopposed enabling the remainder of the force and the supplies to be brought up by sea. The 1st Australian Divisional Train upon which the force had relied upon for its supplies was now required elsewhere and, although 2,000 camels had been provided in lieu, the army was very much dependant upon the Royal Navy. Fortunately, plenty of warning had been given and supplies were brought to Barrani about a week earlier than expected. By 8th March the remainder of the South African Infantry Brigade, the 2nd Mounted Brigade and two sections of the Hong Kong & Singapore Mountain Battery had arrived from Mersa Matruh.

The Senussi had retired westwards towards Sollum and the Egyptian Bedouin were now starting to desert them in large numbers. A number of their sheiks arrived at General Peyton's camp but, due to the necessity of having to push forward as quickly as possible, negotiations could not be entered into and they were dismissed. Aerial reconnaissance showed that the Senussi had occupied their old camps at Bir Warr and Msead, some two miles to the west of Sollum which had been the Grand Senussi's headquarters before the outbreak of war. It was thought that they might be intending to meet there with reinforcements coming up from Cyrenaica.

From Barrani there were two possible routes along which the British could continue the advance on Sollum — along the old Khedival road which followed the coast, or by climbing up onto the inland plateau using one of the available passes such as the Nagb Medean, and then travelling along the plateau towards Msaed.[2] This second route was preferable as it would save having to climb the cliffs at Sollum which rose steeply some 600 feet up from the shore and, if defended, would mean a heavy loss of life for the attackers. There was a good supply of water along the latter route at the wells at Augerin and in large cisterns at the Nagb Medean and Siwiat. It was thought that the use of these wells coupled with the imposition of water rationing would mean the attacking force could use the plateau road if it moved in two columns.

The first column, consisting of infantry and other slow moving bodies, left Barrani on 9th March under the command of Brigadier-General Lukin, with orders to secure a foothold on the plateau using the Nagb Medean, a pass south of Bakbak. The second column, comprising of the cavalry, horses and camels, was to leave two days later and reach Augerin a day later, after the Nagb Medean had been secured. In effect the whole force would be concentrated at Augerin with outposts on the high ground and ready to make its attack on Birr Warr and Msaed.

On the 12th it was discovered that the water at Augerin could not possibly sustain such a large force and that the cisterns at Medean and Siwiat were dry. This news necessitated a rethink on the part of the planners. It was known that the armoured cars had reached the plateau using the Alim er Rabia pass, telephone intercepts showed that the Turks did not know whether to fight or flee,

2. The route was along the top of the Taref mountains which rise up in the desert some thirty miles inland of Mersa Matruh and run westwards, converging onto the coast near Sollum where the cliffs rise steeply some 600 feet and surround the town.

and a cistern had been discovered at Alim Tejidid which held enough water for two battalions for one night. General Peyton, who was not keen on abandoning the plateau route, was averse to risking heavy losses attacking the Sollum heights. He decided to send Lukin, in command of two battalions of South African infantry, the armoured cars, a camel corps company and the mountain guns, along the plateau. The remainder of the force would travel along the Khedival road. The armoured cars were under instructions to make for the most westerly pass near Alim er Rabia. On reaching the top, they were to turn north west and proceed until they met the infantry who would be coming from Augrin and the passes of Nagb Medean and Aragib.

Things did not go according to plan however. On 11th March, following a sandstorm, the armoured cars had to be dug out before they could move. Despite the rough going they managed to reach the pass which was to be a steep climb. After a brief survey, it was thought possible so officers, drivers and gunners immediately set about clearing away all the loose scree, boulders and rocks so as to clear a route and, with engines revving, drivers changing gears furiously, much pushing, shoving and shouts of encouragement, the cars were bumped, staggered and lurched their way to the top of the plateau. They were then driven a short way into the desert where a camp was made for the night. The following morning they proceeded to the north west, met the infantry and continued the march towards Sollum.

By midnight on the 13th/14th, General Lukin was at Siwiat, and a few hours later the cars were ordered to move forward with the infantry. One crew, in a car named *Blast*, was detailed to go on ahead to reconnoitre the route but, after driving only a short distance, suddenly arrived at Halfaya Pass, only some three miles east of Sollum, where it halted to await both columns. General Lukin's column was first to arrive and was joined a few hours later by General Peyton's column and both then advanced on Sollum which they discovered to be abandoned.

At 09.00 hours on 14th March, reconnaissance aircraft reported that the Senussi were abandoning their camps at Bir Waer and Msaed. Peyton immediately called for the armoured cars and ordered the Duke of Westminster to pursue the fleeing Senussi 'with reasonable boldness'. The cars roared off and on arrival at the camps discovered the fires to be still burning but the sites deserted. The cars then gave chase. The Senussi were no doubt thinking that if they could put a day's march between them and the British they would be safe. These had been

*Men of the N^{os} 1, 2 and 3 LACB MGC (Motors) inspecting captured Senussi machine guns*

their tactics in the past but they had not considered the armoured cars, for which the conditions were ideal. The cars roared along, reaching speeds as high as forty mph, and soon came across hundreds of armed Bedouin, all fleeing westwards. These were ignored and they then came across the main body of the Senussi, the Muhafizia, about a mile off the track, some twenty-five miles west of Sollum, near the wells of Bir Aziz.

As soon as they spotted the cars the Senussi turned into the desert, whilst the Turks stopped and set up their artillery and machine guns and opened fire. The gun crews were quickly shot down as they bravely attended their weapons. As the flaps and turrets of the armoured cars had been closed down prior to their going into action, the interiors of the vehicles soon became a living hell. Heated by both the racing engine and the blazing sun, each car was now being filled with the smell of cordite and oil fumes emitted by the guns. The noise was also deafening, thanks to the screaming engine, the clattering machine guns, the Senussi's bullets that were striking the armour and the officers shouting their instructions. On top of all this, the drivers had to contend with hot cartridge cases spilling down on them from the machine gun, burning their bare arms.

As soon as the Turkish guns had been silenced the Senussi broke and started to flee westwards. The cars pursued them for some ten miles doing great execution before a halt was called and they returned to the battlefield. Three artillery pieces, nine machine guns and 250,000 rounds of ammunition were captured, along with thirty prisoners, including two officers. On the British side, one officer had been slightly wounded. It was said by the armoured car crews that during the chase, the camels of the Senussi's supply train, which were loaded with ammunition, blew up when hit. Those cars that had suffered punctures or damage were repaired and a camp was made for the night a short distance away from the battlefield. The following day, the 15th March, the cars returned with their prisoners to Sollum.

With the threat of a Senussi invasion now diminished and their forces scattered into the western desert where they could be dealt with by the Italian forces,[3] the unrest in Egypt immediately started to subside. There now remained the question of the whereabouts of the survivors of the *Tara* and *Moorina*.

There are at least three versions of how the military discovered the whereabouts of the sailors. Firstly, a letter written, by Captain Gwatkin-Williams, had reputedly been discovered in a house in Sollum. Alternatively, a letter written by Gwatkin-Williams had been found blowing in the wind in the desert. Thirdly, and most credibly, Captain Amphlett of the MGC (Motors), whilst his car was having a wheel changed, had come across a Wolesley car that had been abandoned by the Turks on the Khedival road. In this he found a variety of papers which he quickly stuffed into his pocket and later handed over to an intelligence officer in Sollum. One of the papers was found to be a letter, written in French at Bir Hakkim, by Captain Gwatkin-William, dated 1st February. Whatever was the true source of the letter, Captain Royle did not know the location of Bir Hakkim and started questioning the prisoners and found one man who knew of it and had watered sheep there with his father some forty years previously. Another prisoner declared that he knew that particular stretch of desert. Both felt sure they could lead a rescue party there.

Speed was of the essence as it was thought that the broken Senussi may now want revenge for their defeat and the casualties they had suffered, and might take revenge on the *Tara* and *Moorina* survivors. The Duke of Westminster at once made his way to General Peyton to volunteer to lead a column to affect their rescue. The general had to carefully consider this request as information was scant to say the least and the distance which they might have to travel was

3. Unfortunately the Italians were either reluctant or simply refused to tackle the Senussi and it would be up to the British later on in the year to invade Italian Cyrenaica, defeat the Senussi and capture Sayyd Ahmed.

*Hugh Grosvenor, second duke of Westminster, leaning against one of the armoured cars which he commanded in the Western Desert, 1916 (note the naval epaulettes on his uniform) [Rolls-Royce plc]*

unknown for certain, although Bir Hakkim was thought to be some seventy-five miles to the west of Sollum. The terrain through which they would have to travel was an added unknown factor as were the obstacles they might come across. Not the least of their problems was the threat of Senussi reinforcements coming from the west. Peyton,

> ... encouraged by the Duke's quiet confidence and having still fresh in [his] mind his brilliant leadership of March the 14th, and greatly influenced by the misery to which our fellow countrymen are being exposed to and to the still greater misery to which they would be indefinitely condemned unless a rescue was effected, ... decided to accept the offer.

The general then offered Westminster the use of his own staff car.

The Duke gave orders for the armoured cars to be readied for the journey; petrol, food, blankets and clothing were collected and loaded onto Ford Model 'T' tenders whilst he went to see Lieutenant-Colonel R R Lewis, OC the 16th General Hospital (now at Sollum) to request ambulances, orderlies and medical supplies for the rescue.

It was decided that the party would use the nine armoured cars which had been at Bir Aziz and which were still on the plateau, three Ford motor cars with machine guns, twenty-three other cars and ten motor ambulances; amongst the other cars were Ford tenders (carrying petrol, food, water etc), a Wolseley and five road cars used by General Peyton and his staff, as well as the Duke's Rolls-Royce tourer.[4] Thirty-two men of the MGC (Motors) would man the armoured cars and ASC drivers and RAMC orderlies would man the tenders, ambulances and road cars.

The column was supplied with enough petrol for a journey of 300 miles as well as food and water for three days. A staging camp was to be erected by the Berkshire Yeomanry and the Australian Camel Corps some way out in the desert at Bir Aziz.

All of the vehicles had to assemble, albeit with some difficulty, at the top of the plateau by the evening of the 16th, fuelled up, air filters and plugs cleaned, and stocked with spare tyres, inner tubes, water, petrol and oil. Most of the vehicles then had a tarpaulin draped over their engine to try to keep it warm and to prevent the dew getting at the electrics so as to ensure a quick start in the morning. Sentries were posted around the camp whilst the men of the rescue column turned in. They were to set off before first light the following morning.

4. Reports as to the number of vehicles used in the rescue varies greatly – dependent on whose report is read, I have used the figure given in the official announcement of the rescue dated 23rd March 1916.

# 22. In Captivity, March 1916

*Wednesday, 1st March.* Again there were snails for breakfast, after which, some flour and rice was issued which had arrived on a caravan the previous day. The issue worked out at about ½ lb flour and ¾ lb dates per man per day, plus what was left of a goat/sheep's carcass after the guards had taken what they wanted. A small tin full of rice was issued to the officers, some of the rice was added to the goat soup which they had for lunch with a little boiled rice, a biscuit (made of flour), date coffee and two or three dates for tea. Dutton noted 'How a man is supposed to live on these rations is a Chinese puzzle! We are getting weaker every day, officers complaining it takes them all their time to pull up the firewood.'

During the evening the Captain Gwatkin-Williams was released from the sheep pen and was returned to the officers' mess. Lieutenant Tanner gave his parole to Salim Effendi that he would not try to escape again. After Selim Effendi had left, the captain related his story and noted that escape was practically impossible as the Senussi were in control of Sollum. He went on to say that he had been caught on the morning of the second day after leaving the camp. To the other officers he looked awfully tired and worn out. He reckoned that he had walked some 200 miles since escaping and, although he maintained that he had been well treated by his captors, the rest of the mess were disinclined to believe him. Sub Lieutenant Griffiths noted that

> Tanner got him released and his officers had to go short at tea and thanked him in a most disagreeable way as he had most to eat when tied up, the camp was then spoilt, liberty stopped and [the] well quarantined at night!

Later, using the doctor's scissors, Sub Lieutenant Marsh cut Sub Lieutenant Griffiths and Assistant Engineer Davies's hair and trimmed their beards [torpedo] fashion. Afterwards, Griffiths obliged Marsh, who afterwards remarked 'What a treat, feel a new man.'

*Thursday, 2nd March.* Another quiet day.

*Friday, 3rd March.* During the day four Arab shepherds stopped at the camp to water their flock and the Senussi guards stole four of their sheep.

*Saturday, 4th March.* The men were becoming weaker and some were speculating that if no food arrived soon it would be too late as they would be too weak to march anywhere. Their shoes and boots had long gone and most were now barefooted whilst some had made moccasins out of old Arab goatskin tents.

*Sunday, 5th March.* After the usual hymn singing in the officers' mess in the evening there was a philosophical discussion on whether the end justified the means — was it permissible to do evil in order that good might come of it? Lieutenant Tanner noted that the following Sunday's discussion was to be on the biblical quotation 'Greater love hath no man than this, that a man lay down his life for his friend,' an action such as that of Captain Oates on Scott's Antarctic expedition.

Quartermaster Abbit and Seaman Thomas Pritchard were both ill, the latter causing the surgeon great concern.

*Monday, 6th March.* The men's weakness was being especially felt when gathering firewood, a chore which had to be done everyday.

*Tuesday, 7th March.* The last of the rice was handed out today and Lieutenant Tanner hoped that they might be given more meat or some barley meal in lieu of it.

Sub Lieutenant Griffiths noted that it was his brother George's birthday, and that he wished he was at home with him.

*Wednesday, 8th March.* About 7 lbs of barley meal was issued to each mess in the morning. The officers decide to make flap jacks with theirs which worked out as three flap jacks per man.

*Thursday, 9th March.* Selim Effendi left the camp by camel to try to procure more rations. The camp was again left in the charge of the sergeant and about seventeen guards.

A goat was slaughtered and some of messes added the blood of the slaughtered animal to their goat soup.

*Friday, 10th March.* For breakfast the officers had a few dates. During the day a sheep was slaughtered and the officers added its blood and some herbs to the goat soup, all agreeing that it greatly improved the flavour, giving it the taste of liver. Supper consisted of a few dates and a small flap jack.

During the morning a great row erupted in the guard's camp where some of the guards, whose wives and children were also starving, had stolen and hidden a sheep in a tent, then killed it and were now squabbling over its carcass. Lieutenant Tanner thought that the guards could probably live on less food than the prisoners and that for the latter only one or two day's rations, excluding meat, were left. Things were very grim and all were waiting anxiously for the return of Salem Effendi with food supplies.

*Saturday, 11th March.* The prisoners awoke in the morning to discover that there was neither rice nor flour to eat. Two sheep were killed and the officers were given the liver and lights [offal]. These were cut into sixteen portions, skewered and roasted over an open fire and eaten for breakfast. A meal which was very much enjoyed. Later, the officers received more meat and about 7 lbs of barley meal and the sergeant promised that if a caravan had not turned up before sunrise tomorrow he would march the prisoners to Achib Mabiad Wells where there were stores. Lieutenant Tanner doubted that the men could march more than about four miles a day and questioned whether the sergeant would take responsibility for moving the prisoners. To protect their feet for the possibility of such a march the officers began to make slippers out of the old goat skin tent they had been using as a blanket in their tent.

*Sunday, 12th March.* The men awoke at first light but there was no sign of the promised caravan and the blockhouse was empty. There was no more rice, flour or dates and there were only eleven goats and sheep in the pen. The sergeant explained that a messenger had arrived during the night stating that Salem Effendi would be arriving with the stores the following day. Osman, the old Mullah, who listened to the conversation disagreed, saying that the man that had arrived was not a messenger. During the afternoon, a shepherd called Howcutt, and his wife arrived in camp bringing with them a flock of twenty-two sheep and goats, and news that Salem Effendi would arrive the next day. The officers hoped that he would bring with him rice and flour as they could not see themselves lasting long on a meat only diet. Dutton remarked that 'We are living solely on three sheep [shared] between ninety-three prisoners and about forty to fifty soldiers and families.'

During the evening there was hymn singing in the officers' mess, after which there was a discussion, the topic of which had been changed to 'Love took up the glass of time' and 'Is love the greatest force of all?' Lieutenant Tanner noted that following week's discussion was to be on 'Answer to prayer.' Whilst some debated, some of the prisoners went for a walk to visit the graves of their comrades remarking, as they often did, 'Poor chaps, murdered.'

*Monday, 13th March.* The prisoners were now on a meat only diet and most were too weak to walk far or to do much work. Nearly all were feeling very light headed. The snail and herb collecting parties had stopped as the snails had now become too gritty and scarce and the herbs were just not worth the bother, but the firewood collecting parties still had to go out.

*Tuesday, 14th March.* Still no sign of the caravan, so three goats were killed, butchered and distributed amongst the prisoners and guards. When the firewood gathering parties returned to camp they reported that some of the men had been fainting.

During the afternoon a messenger arrived with news that a caravan was on its way and would arrive the following day, but he was not believed.

*Wednesday, 15th March.* Again there was no sign of any caravan and Lieutenant Tanner complained to the other officers about the constant lying by the Senussi since their landing at Port Bardia. Two sheep and one goat were slaughtered and their cuts distributed amongst the guards and prisoners. As usual, the guards took the liver and lights and kept the heads of two. The prisoners noted that there were only nineteen sheep and goats left in the pen. All were now very hungry all the time, very weak and lethargic, so much so that the men of the firewood collecting parties had to kneel to pull up the shrubs instead of bending over as they used to do. The loads they were returning with were becoming smaller. By now all messes were keeping the firewood inside their tents as the Senussi regularly tried to steal it during the night.

The sergeant told Lieutenant Tanner that he had received orders from Salem Effendi to immediately send Sub Lieutenant Dudgeon and Basil the interpreter, with two armed guides and a camel, to the wells at El Zebla to help in obtaining food, clothing and boots for the prisoners. Tanner wondered if the Senussi wanted somebody to speak English over the telephone to either the British in Sollum or the Italians in Tobruk to ask for these stores. Dudgeon however thought that the Senussi were to obtain stores from a vessel in an Italian port but the authorities required an officer and interpreter to certify that the stores were really for the survivors — another lie as it turned out.

At about 10.00 hours Dudgeon and Basil left the camp on camels, Captain Gwatkin-Williams and Lieutenant Tanner walking alongside to carry their water skins a little way into the desert. Their guides soon caught up and the captain and Tanner wishing them both 'God speed', handed over the water skins and waved them off. Tanner went on to say that he wished it had been him who had been chosen to go, but he had given his parole to Selim Effendi that the captain would not try to escape again. The prisoners' future looked bleak and their chances of survival very low. Before they parted Tanner and Dudgeon had exchanged messages to give to each others wives and families should any one of them fail to survive.

Several of the men were now down with dysentery, some were very ill, especially Quartermasters Abbit and Pritchard. All the others were very weak due to their meagre rations and the meat diet of the last few days. However, the weather was gradually improving so the men had been able to regularly boil their clothes in the cooking pans to try and eradicate the lice.

Having no food most of the survivors turned in at 15.30 hours

*Thursday, 16th March.* Things at the camp were now grim for everyone. Three more sheep were killed and the heads, intestines, liver and lights of two were retained kept by the guards for themselves, their wives and children. Lieutenant Tanner thought that the guards had some ground barley which they were also keeping for themselves.

Lieutenant Tanner insisted that all, except for the cooks, went out to look for firewood, only those who were seriously ill being excused. The simple tasks of pulling firewood and drawing water exhausted the men and they could not survive much longer. Mullah Osman decided that he had had enough, took down his tents and with his family set off westwards into the desert. Sub Lieutenant Marsh remarked that he was taking with him some bags of rice for which he couldn't blame him.

After a meagre supper, all the prisoners retreated to their respective messes and tried to sleep.

In Sollum the men of the rescue column were also trying to sleep but, perhaps due to the excitement or perhaps the cold, found it almost impossible and it did not seem long before the sentries were rousing everyone. There was no time for breakfast and by candle and torch light the cars were started up and blankets stowed. At 03.00 hours the column set off travelling by moonlight as they were under strict instructions not to use their headlights. The Duke of Westminster's Rolls-Royce (in which were travelling the duke himself, Lieutenant-Colonel Laycock, RHA, Captain Royle and two Arab guides) was at the front, followed by seven armoured cars and a long line of transport vehicles (carrying petrol, water, clothes and food) and the ambulances, with two armoured cars bringing up the rear.

They sped past Bir W'ar, surprising some Bedouin families who were scavenging amongst the detritus of battle, and on to the new camp at Bir Aziz where they stopped for a breakfast of bully beef and biscuits washed down by hot tea. As soon as they had finished they moved on, following the Tobrouk road, and whenever the going became firm, increasing their speed.

At 10.00 hours they came upon five horsemen and the Duke detached one car with orders to take them captive.[1] Two of the riders managed to reach stony ground where the car could not follow, and thereby escaped. The other three were caught and released after questioning. As the column sped onwards a caravan was seen in the distance which one of the guides pointed out could be carrying supplies for the Senussi. Once again, the column halted and some armoured cars were sent to carry out a stop and search. As he approached the caravan the commander of the leading car fired a burst of machine-gun fire over the heads of the camels which stopped immediately and their drivers threw up their hands. The camel's loads were searched but nothing incriminating was found, apart from a Turkish field service book, which the leader of the caravan said had been found lying on the ground. One of the guides insisted that it was a Senussi caravan as sometime previously he had been engaged in the same occupation and consequently the camels were shot and their loads confiscated and placed on the armoured cars along with the camel-drivers. The cars then returned to the main column where the prisoners and the camels' loads were distributed amongst the tenders and ambulances. It was now about midday and, time being of the essence, the column again set off westwards. A while later they came across a derelict Talbot car with a buckled wheel which was thought to have

1. After rescue, Captain Gwatkin-Williams, after hearing a description of these riders, was convinced that one of them was Dr Becki Faud.

been the Royal Navy wireless car that had been abandoned by the British but which had been repaired and used by the Senussi. Its pneumatic tyres had long gone and new tyres had been fashioned out of rubber sheets which had been cut into strips and lashed onto the wheels with wire. Apparently tons of rubber sheets littered the beaches around Sollum, part of a cargo originally destined for America, which had been washed ashore from a torpedoed ship.

After travelling eighty-five miles the column turned off the road into the open desert which Driver Rolls[2] later described as 'one of the most desolate pieces of country I have ever seen and what the guides steered by I have no conception.' First the cars headed south west, then south-south west, the guides urging them on over countless ridges. Eventually, the two Arab guides started arguing amongst themselves and suddenly they pointed into the distance. After a few words with Captain Royle the column was ordered to halt, having by now driven approximately 130 miles across unmapped territory. Everyone in the column followed the guides' pointing fingers, but even with field glasses were unable to see anything. Westminster ordered his tourer forward and, with the other cars following, slowly crept forwards some 200 yards. In the distance they could make out two mounds with what looked like a number of figures silhouetted against the sky line and who suddenly started waving their arms and shouting, whilst some removed their shirts which they started to wave.

*Friday, 17th March.* Dawn broke at Bir Hakkim and, although it was St Patrick's Day and nineteen weeks to the day since they had landed, nobody felt much like celebrating. During the morning another three sheep were killed and butchered. The flock was now down to thirteen which was reckoned would last them about another four days, and everyone was hoping that Sub Lieutenant Dudgeon and Basil would soon return with fresh supplies.

During the morning, the Mullah's wife returned to the camp to pick up some odds and ends she had left behind, which suggested that the family could not have moved very far away.

At 14.45 hours, whilst Lieutenant Tanner was on his daily rounds of the sick, visiting Quartermaster Abbit in the petty officers' mess, Leading Seaman Millward rushed in saying there was great excitement amongst the guards,

2. Pte Samuel C Rolls, ASC (No. M2/120791), driver of *Blast*, one of the armoured cars and author of *Steel Chariots of the Desert*.

possibly because a caravan was approaching. The two men dashed out and after staring to the north west for a few minutes, saw a car coming out of the desert towards the camp, then another, and another! Signaller Allen in another tent heard someone shouting, 'There's something the matter! The guards are all running out with rifles and baggage,' then someone else shouted, 'Good God, a motor car's coming boys.' We all sprang up and staggered across the camp, and lo and behold, not one motor car but a whole swarm of cars was approaching!'

In the officers' mess, Sub Lieutenant Marsh was acting as cook and had water on the boil and was busy stripping the meat from a goat's leg to put into the soup. Just as he was preparing to crack the bones to extract the marrow, someone at the tent's entrance shouted for those inside to come out as the Arabs were very excited and some of them had run to their tents to collect their rifles and were making for the mounds whilst others were rushing out westwards into the desert.

Some of the officers did go out, but most just lay where they were, too tired and too weak to move. Suddenly, a shout went up from those outside saying that they could see a car coming towards the camp. At this, everyone rushed and stumbled out of the tents and there, heading towards them were three khaki-coloured armoured cars. Behind them were more vehicles, armoured cars, ambulances, vans and opened-topped tourers. Some of the survivors started to climb up the mounds for a better view.

# 23. Rescue

As the survivors looked on the column halted, three armoured cars broke away and slowly made their way towards the camp. When the rescue column spotted the men on and around the mounds, three armoured cars broke away and slowly approached the camp, wary as to who they were. The prisoners started to wave and shout, some took off their shirts and waved them. The cars then halted and two men climbed onto the back of one and waved their rifles before getting back into the car. Then, with their motors roaring the three cars fanned out and raced in line abreast over the undulating ground towards the camp believing that speed was of the essence as the Senussi could well massacre the prisoners. A smattering of shots hit the cars, but the machine gunners held their fire as they could not distinguish the guards from the prisoners. As the cars entered the camp and came to a skidding halt they were immediately surrounded by the prisoners who were clad in old scraps of blue uniform, burnouses and flour sacks. The ambulances and tenders now surged forward into the camp and were also surrounded by the prisoners who cheered, shook hands with their drivers and slapped their backs. Eagerly they took the tins of chicken, mutton, corned beef, condensed milk, cigarettes, bread proffered by the well meaning crews of the tenders. From the ambulances, Royal Army Medical Corps orderlies alighted and went straight into the tents with medicines and stretchers, searching for the sick and infirm. Amidst all this confusion the crews of the armoured cars asked about the whereabouts of

*The Duke of Westminster with his tourer car [BRB (Residuary) Ltd]*

the guards and the prisoners, many now eating and nearly all crying tears of joy, pointed westwards into the open desert. The armoured cars then slowly moved off through the throng and before anybody could stop them flew off into the desert. A few seconds later, the prisoners heard the chattering of machine guns and drew the obvious conclusion. Some felt that the Senussi had got their just desserts, but others, those perhaps in the know, felt terribly sorry and ran after the cars in an effort try stop the killing, knowing that both the Arabs and prisoners had lived on basically the same rations and many had invited the prisoners into their own tents to meet their wives and families. The killing of the guards and their families was the only dark cloud of the rescue mission.

Gwatkin-Williams later recounted that he was gorging himself with tinned chicken and condensed milk when the Duke of Westminster dismounted from his tourer, came over and made himself known. Both men shook hands and the Duke asked about the whereabouts of the guards. The captain, because his mouth was full, waved his hand in the direction of the bushy plain to the west. Just then they heard the chattering of the machine guns and both ran after the cars trying to stop the killing but it was too late. As they walked into the desert they could make out the still forms of fifteen bodies — nine Senussi soldiers and their wives and some of the children. Seeing that there was nothing they could do they returned to camp. Lieutenant Tanner then came over and informed the Duke that Sub Lieutenant Dudgeon and Basil were at the Zebla Wells and not expected back on either Saturday or Sunday. The Duke expressed his regrets but insisted that, in accordance with his orders, they must leave immediately. He did mention, however, that he might return the following day. He also explained that they should not be too worried about their comrades as the British authorities held a number of very important Senussi prisoners. Whilst these assurances made sense, the former prisoners still felt very bad about leaving their comrades.

Having killed the guards, the crews of the three armoured cars returned to the camp bringing with them two wounded women, one shot in the abdomen the other in the thigh, and three children, one of whom had been shot in the leg. The cars were immediately surrounded by the prisoners who were still looking for food, forcing some of the medical orderlies to fight their way through to get at the women and children so as to attended to their wounds.

Private Sam Rolls later wrote that when *Blast* had been driven into the camp '[the prisoners] swarmed into my car and hugged and even kissed me. I have never before or since seen men in such a state. "Food!" they cried "Food!" I tore

*Three of the survivors in the camp at Bir Hakkim after the arrival of the rescue column*

open my locker and tipped out my emergency rations of bully beef, and in their ravenous haste to get at the contents they ripped the tins open with their teeth. We knew well enough that many of them must be suffering with dysentery and other diseases, but it was impossible to refuse them. Biscuits and beef they ate in great choking mouthfuls, and they drank condensed milk straight out of the tins.' Surprisingly, one of the 'prisoners' was remarkably well fed; Paddy, the little black and white mongrel, was running around yapping and barking, and was being fed corned beef, chicken and biscuits by both the prisoners and drivers. Many a time the prisoners had eyed him up for the pot, but resisted the temptation. Instead, they had gone without their full rations so that Paddy could have a feed.

Meanwhile Hospital Blues[1] — jackets, trousers, overcoats, socks and blankets – but no boots — were handed out to the prisoners who, due to the cold, quickly donned them over their verminous rags. Whilst all this was going on the Duke went around the camp taking photographs of the men as they ate, drank and smoked. His men were also moving about the camp, wondering at the great mounds of white snail shells outside each mess.

1. Hospital Blues – the uniform worn by British servicemen whilst in hospital, consisting of a blue peaked cap, blue suit (with white lapels), a white shirt, red tie and black boots.

More survivors preparing to leave the camp at Bir Hakkim

At 15.45 hours the Duke[2], after some small talk, shook hands with the senior officers of the *Tara*, climbed into his open-topped tourer and set off to report the success of the mission to the military authorities at Sollum. Whilst the doctors and orderlies carried the sixteen stretcher cases into the ambulances, other medical staff and the *Tara*'s officers urged the prisoners, who were still trying to gorge themselves, to collect their belongings and mementos and get onto or into the cars. Finally, at 16.30 hours, with the sun setting on the western plain, the column set off.

Lieutenant Tanner, W/T Neill, Clerk Manning and Paymaster Dutton got into the large, open-topped car which belonged to General Peyton. Sub Lieutenants Marsh and Griffiths and Asstistant Engineer Hughes were in one of the supply cars and Captain Gwatkin-Williams, with one of the Armoured Car Brigade's lieutenants, rode in the armoured car *Blast* where, according to it's driver, he never stopped talking all the way back to Sollum. Throughout the journey all the prisoners constantly nibbled at biscuits, corned beef, jam and drank condensed milk. Cigarette after cigarette was also smoked, the prisoners seemingly trying to make up for lost time. The driver of Tanner's car lent him his own pipe and tobacco for which the lieutenant was eternally grateful.

The column bumped its way across the desert until it found the Khedival road to Sollum which, although little better than a cart track, meant that all vehicles were able to pick up speed and their suspensions were tested to the limit as they bounced and bounded over the track. At 01.00 hours on 18th, after travelling some eighty-five miles, the column halted at a camp (Garrison Camp or Bir Anyiza?) which housed troopers of the Australian Camel Corps and a wireless-telegraphy station. Most of the drivers and their crews simply fell asleep in their vehicles, most having been on their feet since early the previous morning. For the prisoners it was a different story. All were given more clothing and blankets then Gwatkin-Williams and Tanner found an empty ambulance and laid down on stretchers but were too excited to sleep and talked all night. Some ate again before they went to sleep whilst others were given hot milk and brandy. Chief Officer Coalstead later recounted that the Australians, as soon as they learned that there were fellow countrymen amongst the survivors, produced whisky and beer and pressed these onto the survivors.

2. For the rescue of the *Tara* survivors and the action of 15th March, the Duke would be awarded the Distinguished Service Order, which was presented to him by the king at a special ceremony for the presentation of awards to the men of north Wales and the north-west of England at Chester Castle on 14th May 1917.

Three of the cars did not bother stopping, but simply sped past the camp. Sub Lieutenant Marsh, travelling in the last car with Sub Lieutenant Griffiths and Assistant Engineer Hughes, later recounted that they had to stop quite regularly to repair punctures which both he and Assistant Engineer Hughes assisted the driver to repair. The three drivers had misunderstood their orders and should have stopped at Garrison Camp, some twenty-three miles from Sollum. Instead they headed for a camp some four miles from Sollum. On reaching the position of the supposed camp, they discovered that there was no sign of it. The three cars separated to search for it and after an hour of going backwards and forwards and around in circles, repairing puncture after puncture, Marsh's car eventually lost sight of the other two. By now their driver was totally lost and a halt was called. Marsh suggested that they should steer south by means of the Pole star until they hit the main road. All agreed so off they went. Using this direct route meant that they had to go up and down sand dunes, which they did until 05.00 hours when they had yet another puncture. By now, dawn was breaking and the exhausted driver suggested that they should unship the waterproof canvas car cover and get underneath it for a sleep. The consensus of opinion, however, was that they should get the car fixed first. A brew was made and, whilst the water was boiling, the driver managed to lose the small leather patch from the tyre's valve and Hughes had to make another by cutting a piece of leather from Marsh's boot. By the time the puncture was repaired and the tyre pumped up, the sun was well up so it was decided to forego the sleep, stop searching for the road and point the car to the north-eastwards and head for the coast. After a time they passed a couple of dead Arabs, then saw two more in the distance who were very much alive and were relieved to see they were not armed. About ten minutes later, just the as the driver was telling Marsh that they ought to turn in the opposite direction, the Union Flag flying above Sollum fort came into view. The driver immediately turned around and offered his hand to Marsh and then drove, stopping just short of the fort where they all dismounted at 07.15 hours. They were quickly surrounded by officers and men from the fort's garrison and, after much handshaking and chatting, were ushered into a tent for something to eat. There they discovered that the other two cars had arrived in the early hours of the morning, but as yet there was no sign of the remainder of the column.

After a meal of biscuits, bread, fried bacon and marmalade they were asked to explain what had happened to them. To spare the driver's blushes and to save his reputation they said they had stopped for a sleep at the roadside. At 10.00

*Some of the survivors riding camels down to the beach at Sollum*

hours the main column arrived and was warmly greeted by the garrison and their comrades. Whilst they walked to the fort they were surrounded by members of the garrison, some of whom gazed at them curiously whilst others took photographs.[3] The senior army officer explained that the survivors would be taken down to the beach, the stretcher cases by motor ambulance and the walking wounded by camels, where they would be medically examined and any wound attended to. They would then be rowed out to a hospital ship, which was riding at anchor amongst the naval vessels out in the bay, and taken to Alexandria.

The stretcher cases were duly placed into ambulances and taken via a circuitous route down to the beach some 600ft below, whilst those that could walk were led to the waiting camels, each fitted with a seat to carry two men. The camels knelt, the men mounted, and each animal was then led down a precipitous zigzag path by an Arab attendant, the survivors clinging to their seats for dear life. On arrival on the beach they dismounted amidst more officers and soldiers, doctors and orderlies of No. 16 Stationary Hospital who busied themselves with the survivors and the wounded Senussi women and children.[4] Army officers handed out rice cakes and brandies and soda to the *Tara*'s officers, whilst the soldiers handed out mugs of Oxo to her crew. All the ministrations were very much appreciated by the survivors.[5]

*Tara*'s officers had a brief chat with the senior army officers who explained that after all the men had been seen to they would be rowed out to the hospital

3. Amongst the onlookers was twenty-year-old Trooper Thomas Oswald Forcer Williams (215023) of the Buckinghamshire Yeomanry. He resided with his parents at 10 Cybi Street in Holyhead and had enlisted in November 1914 but was unaware that the *Hibernia* had been requisitioned, renamed and sent to the Mediterranean. He did not know that he was looking at his own townspeople.
4. One woman had been shot in the abdomen and, although successfully operated on, died later that night. The second woman had her leg amputated and the boy's wound was cleaned and dressed.
5. On the beach Seaman Peter McMillan of Campbeltown, met a fellow townsman Ralph Dillon who was serving as a private with the 3rd County of London Yeomanry and who gave McMillan a pipe and tobacco.

Sub Lieutenant T H Coughtry, RNR

ship, the *Reschid* which was waiting to take them to Alexandria.

The survivors stood around on the beach in small groups, drinking, eating and chatting until told to embark at noon. They climbed into the lifeboats, turned around to face the shore and gave the garrison three hearty cheers as the boats pulled away to the *Reschid* where they climbed aboard. Once aboard the men were stripped of their verminous clothes bathed, shaved and given clean clothes and new boots – some of the men dumped their old clothes over the side, while others had theirs burned in the ship's boilers.[6, 7]

That evening, aboard the *Reschid,* Marsh received a visit from Sub Lieutenant Thomas Coughtry, RNR with whom had been at the Hibernian Sea School in Dublin and who was now serving on HMS *Lily,* a sloop which was anchored out in Sollum Bay. They chatted for a time and Marsh learned that the *Lily* had called

*The grave of the dog Paddy*

*The hospital ship* Reschid *at Alexandria having dischared the sick and wounded [T. Ashmore]*

6. Not all clothing was burnt or dumped as Chief Steward Morris kept one of his boots as a momento. On his return home this was given pride of place in a glass cabinet in the parlour, and kept by the family after his death in 1917 until well into the 1950s.
7. It was decided, however, that the dog, Paddy, could not be taken aboard the ship and he was presented to the Light Armoured Car Battery, joining their other mascot, a parrot, which had been found in a ruined house in Ypres whilst they were serving in France. Paddy's stay with the Light Armoured Car Battery lasted some four months. On 30th July, whilst the battery was at Matruh, he was killed by a sentry who had been ordered to shoot any stray dogs on sight to reduce the risk of rabbies. Unfortunately, being a new man, the sentry had not recognised Paddy. The dog died instantly and was accorded a military funeral, his grave overlooking Matruh was covered with a cairn of rocks and surmounted with a cross bearing the legend, 'In Memory of Paddy. Rescued by the D of W's Light Armoured Cars. Died 30.7.16.' On the arms of the cross was written 'Survived two wrecks. Found with *Tara* survivors.'

at Port Suleiman shortly after the survivors had left and a landing party had found the boats which they had burned before leaving. Coughtry and Marsh made arrangements to meet later at Alexandria and before leaving the former pressed £3 on Marsh which, after many protestations, he thankfully accepted.

# 24. Alexandria

After tea, supper and a night in a comfortable, warm bed with clean sheets, the men were awoken to a light breakfast after which, at 09.00 hours, the *Reschid* up anchored and made her way, never out of sight of land, to Alexandria. Although the sun was shining, it was a rough passage and the ship rolled heavily. The men spending their time either sleeping, reading, chatting, smoking, basking in the sunshine or eating, although their consumption of food was now being carefully monitored by the medical staff, as now some were beginning to suffer from their over indulgence during the previous forty-eight hours.

The following morning the *Reschid* berthed at Alexandria and among the first to come aboard were stretcher parties of the RAMC who carried ashore those survivors who were unable to walk. After some time they all made their way ashore where they were met on the quayside by Lady Carnarvon who presented each with a small Red Cross packet containing writing paper, envelopes, pencil, soap and a tooth brush. They were then ushered to a fleet of waiting ambulances which took them to N°. 21 General Hospital, Alexandria. The Indians were taken to the N°. 5 Indian Hospital where, sadly, Ali Mir, one of the *Moorina's* firemen,[1] died on the 26th April.

In the hospital the survivors were seen by Colonel D Sullivan, RAMC, and the petty officers and ratings were then detailed to various wards within the hospital. The officers were taken by ambulances to the Ras el Tin Military Hospital. Sub Lieutenant Marsh noting before he left that Quartermaster Abbit,

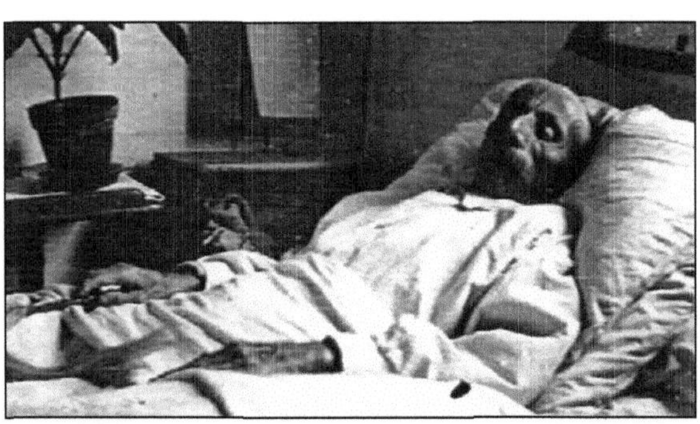

*Quartermaster Robert Abbit in hospital in Alexandria [T. Ashmore]*

1. Possibly one of the two Indian 'troops' who arrived at Bir Hakkim on 17th Janaury.

*Survivors at the Ras el Tin Hospital. Back row (L–R): W/T CW Birkby, Clerk WG Manning and 2 Eng TR Richardson. Seated (L–R): Ch/Off CS Coalsted, Lieut EB Tanner, Sister Stella Beavan (of Sydney, Australia), Capt RS Gwatkin-Williams and Surg Prob JD Arthur [BRB (Residuary) Ltd]*

although looking very ill, was very cheerful, as was Seaman Pritchard.

At the Ras el Tin hospital the survivor's story had obviously preceded them as they were warmly welcomed by both nurses and patients. Some took the opportunity to photograph them, whilst the matron handed each man packets of cigarettes (or a pipe and some tobacco) and a bag of clothing which contained clean hospital blues, before directing them to their respective wards. Marsh, Assistant Engineers Howarth, Hughes and David J Davies, Wireless Telegraphist Neill and Assistant Paymaster Dutton were all detailed to share Ward 7 with some army officers who had been wounded during the battles of January.

They wanted to let their families at home know that they were at last safe and sound and they jumped at the offer of Sister Margaret Blythe of the Territorial Force Nursing Service to send their telegrams at the cheap weekend rate. Their time was then their own and most took the opportunity to have another bath. Marsh weighed himself and found that he had lost a stone and a half.

Hospital routine provided lunch at noon, followed by an afternoon nap, and then tea at 3.30 pm. The men asked their new companions to excuse their table manners as they ate ravenously, their hunger still being unsated. Most of them found mail waiting for them; Marsh learned of the death of his brother-in-law, Richard D Roberts, chief steward aboard the *Anglia* and William Barton learned of the death of his nineteen-year-old nephew Albert Frederick Ashton, a cabin boy on the same ship.[2]

On 21st March, Lieutenant Tanner spent most of the day lying down, feeling 'out of it' suspecting that the cumulative effects of the previous few days, and perhaps overeating, was the cause. During the day he received a letter from home and, although it contained nothing but good news, he broke down uncontrollably. One of the nurses, Sister Josephine Costello, did her best to comfort him. The following morning he felt much better and, along with some other officers, went to purchase new clothes aboard HMT *Hannibal,* a pre-dreadnought battleship then being used as an Auxiliary Patrol Base Ship at Alexandria. He later recorded that he felt very weak and had to rely on handrails in order to negotiate the gangway and accommodation ladders. He put it down to muscle wastage during captivity.

Now that their families knew they were safe the survivors began to receive a steady flow of letters. In some the senders mentioned that they had also sent parcels but, perplexingly, none had arrived. Lieutenant Tanner took the matter up

*The survivors (wearing hospital blues) receiving Red Cross parcels at Alexandria, March 1916 [W Davies]*

2. No doubt others had lost good friends on the *Anglia.* Cook John Pritchard learned at this time of the death of his mother, with whom he lived. Seaman John Jones, having already having lost his father during the *Tara's* sinking, would shortly learn of the death in France of his brother Lance Corporal Owen Richard, killed in action on this very day.

with the Postmaster General of Egypt at Alexandria, Brigadier-General Neville Travers Borton, and explaining that there were about 300 parcels missing. Tanner later wrote that he had been told that the parcels, with the exception of those that had already been returned to sender, would most probably be delivered when they arrived back at Holyhead.

On 27th March they received news that Sub Lieutenant Dudgeon and Basil had been released and were with the Italians in Tobruk. Lieutenant Tanner immediately arranged an interview with the Italian consulate to request that the two men be sent to Alexandria as soon as practicable. It also seems that by this date the two *Moorina* officers, Coalsted and Richardson, had been transferred to the N° 19 General Hospital in Alexandria.

On 1st April, Dudgeon and Basil arrived at the Ras el Tin Hospital none the worse for their adventure, having reached Alexandria the same morning aboard the Italian transport *Minos*. Both Captain Gwatkin-Williams and Lieutenant Tanner wanted to know of Dudgeon's experiences and the following is the account he wrote.

*Wednesday, 15th March.* We left the camp in the company of two soldiers and a guide, heading north riding on a camel until we reached an Arab camp at about 16.30 hrs. That night we slept in Holy Joe's tent.

*Thursday, 16th March.* Up early and left at 07.00 riding on a camel, again heading north all day until we reached Salem Effendi's tent at 15.30 hrs. Very sore and hungry as had nothing to eat all day, slept in Salem Effendis tent, plenty to eat.

*Friday, 17th March.* After a late start, we set off at 10.30 hrs, accompanied by Salem Effendi and marched all day, riding on camel, now heading eastwards and arrived at a village of tents at 18.30, very tired.

*Saturday, 18th March.* Commenced march at 07.00 hrs but at 10.00 hrs we were ordered to rest in a ravine whilst Salem Effendi went ahead. He returned at 17.00 hrs accompanied by three Muhafizia, a Sergeant and two soldiers and explained that they would take us on to the Turkish Headquarters whilst he, the two soldiers and guide would be returning to Bir Hakkim with food. However, before leaving he demanded that Basil hand over the watch and chain he was wearing (the property of Mr Morris, the Chief Steward). The Muhafizia then marched us until we reached the Turkish headquarters at 18.30 hrs, here we met several Turkish officers including Tarik Bay, the former commandant of Sollum and learnt that we were not very far from the coast, and only some 12 miles from Tobruk. We were well fed and slept at the Turkish HQ.

*Sunday, 19th March.* This morning one of the Turkish officers Abdi Bey took us to his tent, some two miles to the east of the Turkish HQ and gave us socks and boots. We had an excellent lunch and met several other Turkish officers — Cassim Effendi, Selal Effendi, Sucri Effendi and some others whose names I cannot now recall.

At 14.30 hrs with Abdi Bey we rode on horseback some 2 miles to another tent, which apparently was an outpost of the Turkish lines. We were fed and then slept for the night — and where the fleas were both very large and very numerous!

*Monday, 20th March.* Up early this morning and again on horseback we rode for some six miles until we were about two miles from the Italian outposts. Here we were ordered to stay until a messenger informed us that a safe passage through the lines to the town of Toro had been arranged for us, however as there was no sign of him by 16.00 hrs we returned to Abdi Bey's tent for supper and the night.

*Tuesday, 21st March.* Spent all day in Abdi Bey's camp, and who during the whole time with him made us very welcome and treated us with utmost kindness.

*Wednesday, 22nd March.* Up early and with Abdi Bey left camp at 05.00 hrs, we marched to the fort outside of the town of Toro. Here we met and were handed over to Italian officers who escorted us to Tobruk, again we were treated with kindness and also given clothing, food and advance of money.

*Thursday, 23rd March.* Today we heard, thanks to an intercepted wireless message, of the rescue of the survivors from Bir Hakkim and of their arrival at Sollum.

*Sub Lieut Dudgeon (fourth from left) and Basil (sixth from left) with Italian soldiers at Tobruk after their release by the Senussi [W Davies]*

*Friday, 24th March.* I asked the Italians if they could contact Mersa Matruh to inquire about the whereabouts of the *Tara* survivors. Mersa Matruh replied that they had already gone on to Alexandria.

*Thursday, 30th March.* Embarked Tobruk on the Italian transport Minas and, escorted by the Italian destroyer Ostro we sailed for Alexandria.

*Friday, 1st April.* Arrived Alexandria at 09.00 hrs and were later invited to lunch aboard HMS *Hannibal,* but declined as had already eaten on the Ostro so, proceeded instead to the Ras el Tin Military Hospital to join fellow officers.

Meanwhile, at N° 21 Hospital the crew of the *Tara* had become minor celebrities. On Thursday, 30th March some fifty of them were invited to tea and an evening of song at Yr Hafod, the Alexandria home of a local Llanarmon-yn-Iâl-born businessman, Dr Joseph Davies Bryan. Davies Bryan had spotted convalescing officers wearing blue armbands and private soldiers in their hospital blues wandering aimlessly up and down the streets of Alexandria and had decided to open up his house to those Welsh members of the armed forces who were convalescing in the many hospitals in the city. No doubt well meaning, it was probably a bit stuffy and quaint for the younger patients, but was no doubt still much appreciated as evidenced by the letters of a Lieutenant Moore Haines, a dentist serving with the RAMC, who wrote that on Tuesday, 21st March he went to the Davies Bryan's 'Welsh Garden party' and noted that '... the old Welsh Fogies were there too', and by the looks on their faces it appeared that life in Egypt did not seem suit them at all! However, there were about 100 people in attendance and all had a good tea with home-made tarts and cakes and for Moore Haines it was the first time that he had tasted apple tart since he had left home. On 4th April he returned for another tea and noted that these parties had now become weekly affairs.[3]

A few days later Joseph Davies Bryan wrote to his friend the Rev John Williams, minister of Hyfrydle Chapel in Holyhead explaining that the

> ... medical authorities would not allow a few [of the *Tara*'s survivors] to come from hospital as they were still suffering from the effects of their terrible late experiences. Those that came looked very well although suffering much weakness of body. You can't imagine what progress they have made in a fortnight due to the great care, comfort and good food. The officers of the ship owing to their being housed in another hospital were not present but I have interviewed them also on several occasions and among them is a member of

*Yr Hafod, the Alexandria home of the Davies Bryan family [W Alister Williams]*

3. Dr Joseph Davies Bryan, vice president of the Alexandria YMCA, was one of three brothers from north Wales, who had created a business empire, Davies Bryan & Co, in Egypt during the late nineteenth and early twentieth centuries. In 1888, he had left college to join his brother John running a small outfitter's shop in Cairo. John died shortly afterwards and Joseph was joined by Edward and together they expanded the business until they had large department stores in Cairo, Alexandria, Port Said and Khartoum. They had a reputation for scrupulous honesty and were held in high regard by both the British and Egyptian population. The stores closed in 1934, Edward died in 1929 and Joseph in 1935. A fourth brother, Robert, was a noted poet and musician.

*The* Tara *survivors at Yr Hafod. Mr and Mrs Joseph Davies Bryan are standing at the back and their five daughters are standing wearing white dresses [W Davies]*

> your church, Mr W Griffith [sub lieutenant, RNR] ... They are, with one exception, gaining strength daily ... Hugh O Hughes and Richard Lewis both were operated on last Friday and are improving splendidly. All the crew hold a commendable reputation, and particularly Hugh O Hughes, 'The Leader'. If ever a man deserved the title of leader this man does. He held meetings of prayer; he heartened the despondent; he comforted the dying. All the boys are universal in their praises of his many good and kind deeds. I don't know of anything more to be desired than a 'good name' from your colleagues under exceptionally trying circumstances!

The survivors were later invited to a reception held by Lieutenant-Colonel Thomas Henley, a member of the New South Wales Legislative Assembly and assistant commissioner for the Citizens' War Chest Fund, who, having heard of their ordeal and rescue, arranged to give each man a present from the fund. In consequence, each man received a well filled billy-can containing a souvenir tin of cigars, cigarettes and tobacco and a souvenir tin of chocolates and sweets. Henley made a short speech which began — 'Four months of two ounces of goat and snails must have put a nasty taste in your mouths' — he felt sure that 'the people of Australia would approve of the small gifts to the survivors, and hoped that they would all soon recover and give further assistance to punish the Germans for their evil ways.' Lieutenant Tanner thanked him and the people of Australia on behalf of the officers and men. Those who were unable to attend were presented with their gifts in the hospital.

On 3rd April the British community in Alexandria threw a garden party and concert in the grounds of a house of the wealthy Greek merchant Anthony Autoniades, for the officers and men of the *Tara*.

Two days later, Thomas Pritchard died. Tanner recorded that he was just worn out, looked thin and drawn, pale, almost white, but gave the impression of being in good spirits. He was interred that afternoon in the Chatby Cemetery, and those of the crew who could, attended the burial, the stronger of his shipmates carrying his coffin from the ambulance to the grave followed by a military firing party. No volleys were fired over the grave, but a bugler played the *Last Post*. Lieutenant Tanner remarked that this was seventh funeral they had attended since 5th November.

*A group of he* Tara *survivors at the Soldiers & Sailors Institute, Alexandria [Courtesy Raymond Houston]*

# 25. Homeward Bound

Shortly after the death of Thomas Pritchard the medical authorities decided that most of the survivors had responded well to medical treatment and good food and were fit enough to travel and could return home . However, after a final examination, it was decided that Captain Gwatkin-Williams and Fireman Harold Jones were still too ill to travel had to remain behind. Twenty three of the survivors were to be moved on to hospital in England by hospital ship whilst the rest were fit enough to travel on an ordinary transport.

On 7th April, HM Hospital Transport *Dunluce Castle* set sail from Alexandria with twenty-six of the *Tara* survivors aboard (seven of whom were stretcher cases). After an uneventful voyage the *Dunluce Castle* arrived at Southampton on 18th April and the survivors were transferred to the Royal Naval Hospital Haslar at Gosport. They were not allowed to continue their journey home until at least the 3rd or 4th May.

*HMHT* Dunluce Castle *[Author]*

QM Robert Abbit
Smn Owen Hughes
Smn William Black
Smn Griffith T Jones
Smn John Jones
Smn Alfred Hughes
Smn John H Swaine
Deck Boy William Jones
Electrician Wallace CV Cooke
Fireman Hugh O Hughes
Fireman Owen Davies
Fireman Thomas Higgins
Fireman George A Wright
Fireman J McKinven
Fireman John Jones
Fireman Richard Lewis
Fireman John Williams
2nd Steward William Barton
Steward Hugh Jones
Eng's Boy Thomas A Thomas
Sig Boy Raymond Fulcher, RN (J30366)
Stoker John McNee, RNR (7971S)
Smn A. William Gunn, RNR (4369A)

*The Tara survivors who returned home aboard the HMHT* Dunluce Castle.

On 8th April the following officers and men embarked at Alexandria aboard HM Transport *T.46* (the former SS *Trafford Hall*) for passage to Devonport:

Lieut Edward B Tanner, RNR
Sub Lieut Leslie T Dudgeon, RNR
Sub Lieut William T Griffith, RNR
Sub Lieut Albert Marsh, RNR
3rd Mate John G Thomas, MFA
Asst Eng Howarth Hughes, RNR
Asst Eng David J Davies, RNR
Asst Paymaster Alfred Dutton, RNR
Surg Prob John D Arthur, RNVR
W/Tel Robert Neill, RNR
W/Tel Cyril W Birkby, RNR
Clerk William G Manning
Bosun Thomas Owen
Bosun's Mate John Owen
Smn William Rowlands
Smn William J Rowlands
Smn William T Jones
Smn William H Hughes
Smn William H Parry
Smn Albert J Learmouth
Smn Richard Williams
Smn John L Jones
Smn Griffith Griffith
Smn Peter McMillan
Greaser William G Cooper
Greaser Hugh O Hughes
Fireman Rhys Jones
Fireman T Jones
Fireman T Doughty
Fireman John O Bagnall
Fireman Richard Jones
Fireman Roland Williams
Fireman Hugh Hughes
Fireman Hugh E Wright
Fireman William Griffith
Fireman Hugh Jones
Fireman O Pritchard
Fireman William J Andrews

Fireman Richard Jones
Fireman Thomas Moorhead
Fireman Owen Gray
Trimmer Hugh Williams
Trimmer Thomas Wright
Trimmer Thomas Owen
Trimmer Richard J Williams
Chief Steward Andrew Morris
2nd Cook John Pritchard
Asst Steward Joseph Fenlen
Asst Steward William H Williams
Asst Steward Evan Evans
Asst Steward Thomas G Brosnan
Asst Steward John W Brosnan
Asst Steward William J James
Galley Boy William Parry
L/Smn William P Milward, RFR (SS1730)
Ship's Cpl Charles Mintram, RN (146622)
Yeo/Sglr Henry GJT Allen, RN (182570)
O/Tel George A Tanner, RN (J30698)
L/Smn James Marwick, RNR (3354C)
Smn Alexander Ross, RNR (3662A)
Smn Charles McNaughton, RNR (6218A)

As the men embarked they were seen off by Basil, who was by now a very good friend of Sub Lieutenant Dudgeon, so much so that the two of them would correspond regularly for a number of years. Basil, after his discharge from hospital, resumed his employment with the military being attached as an interpreter to the Australian Imperial Forces.

Once aboard the survivors found that the ship carried 430 passengers, most of whom were time-expired men from a variety of regiments and services returning

*HMT T.46 (formerly the SS* Trafford Hall *[Author]*

home for demobilization. There were also three or four women aboard accompanied by their children. Due to the threat of U-boats lifeboat drill was carried out every day whilst the ship was at sea.

Lieutenant Tanner was given a comfortable cabin on the main deck which he shared with Sub Lieutenant Dudgeon and Manning the clerk. He noted that the *Trafford Hall* was a well-found ship with a good library which would later be run by Manning on Tanner's suggestion.

At 07.15 hours on 9th April the ship set sail into a stiff, fresh breeze. There was a weak sun which made it rather chilly on deck. Two days later they were sailing along the northern coast of Crete and the weather had greatly improved, but, during the afternoon, a report was received of submarine activity some fifteen miles to their north which caused some excitement and anxiety amongst the passengers who spent the rest of the day wandering around the ship wearing or carrying their life jackets. Tanner later remarked that most people seem to be relaxed and got on well with each other and they were all certainly well looked after. Each morning they were woken up at 06.30 hours by a steward with a cup of tea, breakfast was at 09.00, lunch at 13.00, tea at 16.00 and dinner at 18.00. He also remarked that the catering was very good, so good in fact that by the time the ship dropped anchor at Gibraltar in the early hours of the 16th, most of the survivors had put on weight – Marsh had put on a stone in weight since the rescue.

At 15.00 hours the *Trafford Hall* left the Gibraltar anchorage heading for Devonport in a calm sea. Once they had passed Cape Trafalgar and were heading out into the Atlantic, the wind picked up, whipping up a heavy sea. Soon she was rolling, sometimes very uncomfortably, and although the weather was bright and clear, it continued to blow for the five days it took to reach Plymouth Sound where, in the early hours of Good Friday, she dropped anchor. The survivors were taken ashore after breakfast by tenders and Lieutenant Tanner was immediately interviewed by a rear admiral of the Royal Navy before proceeding to the Royal Hotel where he joined the other officers (the crew had been taken to the Naval Barracks in Devonport). The following morning, the 22nd, nine officers and forty-eight crewmen boarded a specially reserved saloon carriage on the 08.00 train bound for Holyhead.[1] Ordinary Signaller Tanner, Bosun Thomas

1. Among this number were William James Andrews (Larne) and Thomas Moorhead (Belfast) who, after the welcome at Holyhead, had caught one of the cross-channel packets over to Kingstown. Owing to the Easter uprising and the fighting that was then raging in Dublin they were unable to proceed any further and had to take shelter in Corrig Castle in Kingstown which was then a Red Cross Hospital.

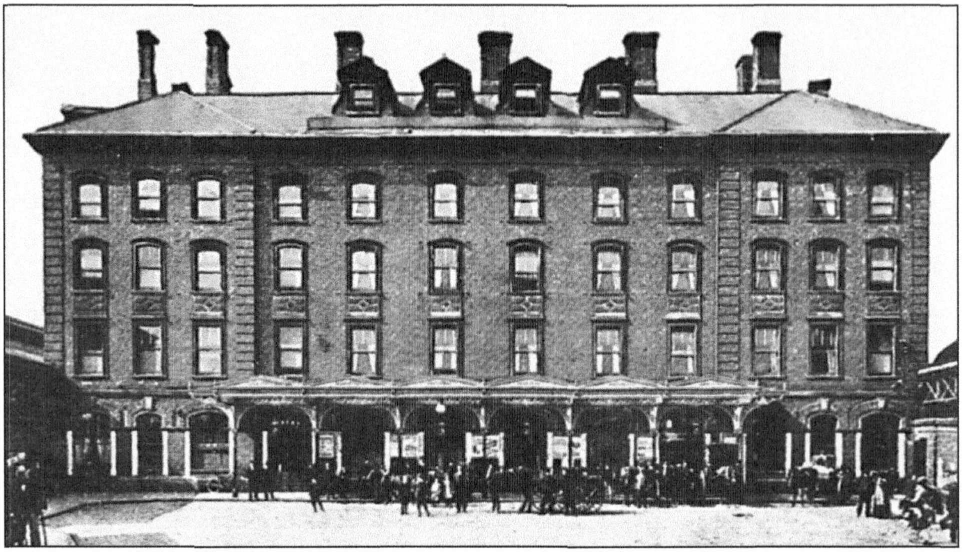

*Station Hotel, Holyhead [Author]*

Owen and Steward Evan Evans were confined in the local naval hospital suffering from enteric and therefore considered too unfit to travel.[1]

The train took the survivors (via Exeter, Bristol, Hereford and Chester) to Holyhead, arriving there at 22.45 hours. For some time, forewarned of its arrival, people had started to gather — families, relatives, friends, local dignitaries and sightseers. By the time the train pulled in, both the station platforms and the station approach were packed with people, who started to cheer. As the train came to a stop at platform Nº 1, an armed guard of honour stood to attention as the survivors, dressed in khaki, alighted from the carriage, seemingly dazed at the size of the crowd and the volume of noise. They were immediately surrounded by their families who were at the front of the crowd. Also to greet them, representing the L&NWR was F Bodvan Griffiths, the assistant marine superintendant of the port, who, despite the late hour, made a short speech of welcome and pointed out that there was a fleet of motor cars waiting to take the survivors to their homes.

Lieutenant Tanner thanked Mr Williams and the crowds for their overwhelming welcome and the survivors then made their way through the cheering crowds out to the station approach and the waiting motor cars, which they boarded and which then slowly carried them through the densely-packed, cheering, jostling crowds to their respective homes. Possibly unheard by the survivors as they made their way towards the cars, was a choir on the platform which began singing popular songs and Welsh hymns which the crowds took up and joined in with. All of the men were then given a period of sick leave, for which no doubt they were very grateful.

Of the Campbeltown men, James McKinven was deemed too ill to travel from Haslar, but Peter McMillan and Charles McNaughton were considered fit enough to travel to Glasgow by train where, on Tuesday, 25th April they made their way down to the quayside to catch the noon ferry, the SS *Davaar*. Much to their surprise they found she had been dressed overall in their honour. A further surprise awaited them as the ferry entered Campbeltown Loch when two shots rang out from her deck gun and, as they looked towards the town, they could see that there was a large crowd waiting for them on the pier. There were flags flying from the tallest buildings and the main street was decorated with flags and bunting. The *Davaar* came alongside and the two men stepped ashore amidst much cheering, McMillan dressed in khaki, and McNaughton in Royal Navy blues. As the crowd recognised them the cheering grew even louder and, as their families and friends surged forward to greet them, it was with some difficulty they were escorted through the throng to waiting cars which carried them to their homes. Like the Holyhead men, they had appeared dazed at their reception and no doubt were glad to slip out of the bustle and into the privacy of their own homes.

Two weeks later, on Tuesday, 9th May, Judge Samuel Moss, took his seat in the Holyhead County Court, to preside on the distribution of monies under the Workmen's Compensation Act to the widows and dependants of the thirteen petty officers and ratings of the L&NWR who had lost their lives during, or as a result of, the sinking of the *Tara*. On the requisition of the express steamers the

*SS* Davaar *[Author]*

company had insured each of their employees and the sum of £3,900 was to be paid out, approximately £300 for each rating lost. What the company's arrangements were for the families of the engineers killed is not known.[2] The judge heard evidence from the dependants, widows, children and / or their representatives, and then decided how much to award to each on a weekly or monthly basis, and how much to invest on their behalf. The outcome of his deliberations was reported in the local newspaper:

> Mrs Catherine Ellen Chorlton, the daughter of boilermaker George Mathew Cox, who was a widower, stated that on her father leaving with HMS *Tara* she and her husband, Francis Charlton, had been appointed guardians of her younger siblings. She was awarded £10 immediately with monthly payments of £2 10s 0d (£2.50).
>
> Mrs Mary Phillips, the widow of Leading Stoker Robert Phillips, stated that she had two children of her own and an adopted son dependant on her so asked for £1 5s 0d per week, but Judge Moss awarded her £3 10s 0d [£3.50] per month, with £250 to be invested in a 4½% War Loan.
>
> Mrs Margaret Williams, the widow of Carpenter Owen Williams, stated that she had no dependant children but applied for payment at £3 0s 0d per month [£3]. This was granted.
>
> Mrs Elizabeth Hodgson, the mother of Seaman John Hodgson, stated that she had been dependant upon her son since her husband died some thirteen years ago. She asked for £1 0s 0d per week [£1]. This was granted.
>
> Mr William Henry Thomas, the son of Quartermaster William Thomas. Acting on his behalf, as he was deaf was his aunt Mrs Margaret Lansbury who applied for £3 0s 0d per month [£3], this was granted.

2. The T.124 Agreement stated that widows of those engineers who were killed in action but had first-class certificates of competency, would receive a pension of £65 p.a. with £14–£8 p.a. for each dependant child, whilst those drowned or killed by acts of the enemy would get £50 p.a. with £12–£6 p.a. for each dependant child. In addition, the widow would receive a gratuity of one year's pay of her husband's corresponding rank in the Royal Navy and each unmarried child under the age of twenty-one would receive one third of the gratuity paid to the widow. The widows of those engineers who did not hold a first-class certificate would receive a pension of £60 or £50, with no pension for the children. The widows of petty officers and ratings would receive a gratuity of one year's pay of the corresponding non-continuous service ratings in the Royal Navy.

Fireman Owen Hughes Roberts. Acting on behalf of Owen's widowed mother, Mrs Jane Roberts, was a Mr Honeybill of Llaingoch who, when questioned by Mr R Gordon Roberts (solicitor), stated that she was his only dependant and could not attend the court as she was paralysed. In her absence Judge Moss awarded her £4 0s 0d [£4] per month.

Mrs Catherine Jones, the widow of Fireman John E Jones, stated that she had two children, aged five and four. Judge Moss awarded £3 10s 0d per month [£3.50p].

Miss Jane Pritchard, the daughter of Seaman Thomas Pritchard, stated that there were three children dependant upon her father's wage and, as she was the eldest, she had been acting as a housekeeper since her mother died eight years ago. The solicitor, Mr R Gordon Roberts, stated that there was an application for a sum of money to be paid out as the son, Robert, who had one month left of his apprenticeship to serve after which he was hoping to start a boot-making business in Cemaes. This was dismissed and Judge Moss awarded each child £1 10s 0d per month [£1.50].

Mrs Mary Ann Parry, the widow of Fireman John Parry, stated they had one daughter, Lillian Augusta, aged 22, who was in delicate health so was awarded £3 0s 0d [£3] per month.

Mrs Emma Jane Jackson, the widow of Cook Walter Jackson, stated that she had an invalid daughter, two sons and a second daughter who were dependant on her husband's wage and asked for £1 0s 0d [£1] per week. An order was made for £3 10s 0d per month [£3.50].

Mrs Elizabeth Catherine Jones, the widow of Acting Leading Stoker Thomas Robert Jones, stated that there were three children at home, one son Owen (aged 16) and two daughters, Lizzie (aged 25) and Annie (aged 23), both in poor health and 'could do nothing.' She asked for £1 5s 0d per week [£1.25]. Judge Moss made an order for £1 0s 0d per month [£1] and suggested that she got her daughters to do something as soon as possible!

Mrs Ann Marie Barber, the widow of Steward Frederick Barber, stated that she had a six-year-old daughter and a twelve-month-old boy and that the family had been dependant on her husband's wage. She was now applying for a large part of the money so as to enable her to start up a bottling business. After a few questions, Judge Moss disallowed the claim and ordered the money [£300 to be invested in the usual way and £3 0s 0d [£3] to be paid each month — although he did allow for this ruling to be challenged in future.

That same night, the monthly meeting of the Holyhead Urban District Council was held at the Town Hall, the last but one item on the agenda being headed 'The *Tara* Survivors.' The chairman, Mr John Clay, stated that there was a general feeling in the town that something should be done for the survivors, and that if a function was decided upon then the local member of Parliament, Mr Ellis Griffith, should be asked to attend. Councillor Bodvan Griffith suggested that a memorial to the *Tara* survivors be raised which was seconded, but Councillor Pratt asked what was to be done about the survivors of the *Anglia*? After further discussion it was decided to await the end of the war until they decided on what course of action to take.[3]

The L&NWR decided that they would give the *Tara* survivors a welcome home and would entertain them to a luncheon at Euston Station followed by a theatre show in London's West End. The invitation was extended to not only the Holyhead members of the crew but also to Mr Cooke (her electrician), the two Northern Irishmen, Andrews and Moorhead, two Liverpool seamen, Black and Hughes, and Fireman George A Wright, a Londoner, a total of sixty-six men. It is uncertain whether the men from Campbeltown attended but it was later confirmed that Captain Gwatkin-Williams, who had arrived back home on the 2nd May aboard the French Hospital Ship SS *Valdivia*, would attend. The date set was for Wednesday, 17th May and the men were duly notified. Unfortunately, six were unable to attend: Fireman Harold Jones was still in the N° 21 General Hospital and would not leave Alexandria until 24th May; Steward Evan Evans was in hospital in Devonport suffering from enteric fever (typhoid); Quartermaster Robert Abbit was still suffering from dysentery and was in Haslar Hospital; Firemen Richard Lewis and Hugh O Hughes had left Holyhead for Haslar Hospital on 16th for a check up, and the whereabouts of Fireman Thomas Higgins were unknown.

3. In the event, no further action was taken. The widows and dependants of those killed on the *Anglia*, the *Tara*, the *Leinster* and other ships lost during the war, were invited to a celebration at the Recreation Ground (Cae Mwd, then the site of Holyhead Town Football Club) on the afternoon of Saturday, 9th July 1919. Tents and stalls were erected and there was plenty of food and games for everyone, the whole being funded by the L&NWR's Hospital Fund.

*Survivors at Holyhead Station prior to departing for Euston [MM Hughes]*

At 06.00 hours on the appointed day the Holyhead survivors (accompanied by Andrews and Moorhead who had arrived the previous day) were conveyed by special train from Holyhead to London. A large crowd was at the station to see them off and the men were photographed before departure. Also aboard the train were A T Orr (the acting marine superintendent), F Bodvan Griffith, M G E Michael (outdoor superintendent at Euston) and G R O Shaw of the Marine Office.

At Euston Station they were welcomed by W M Turnbull, Assistant Superintendent of the L&NWR, photographed, and on entry into the large dining hall, met up with Captain Gwatkin-Williams. The place of honour was taken by the Chairman of the company, Sir Gilbert Claughton, who sat flanked by Captain Gwatkin-Williams and Lieutenant Tanner. Also in attendance were the General Manager, twelve directors and various other L&NWR officials.

After the luncheon Sir Gilbert rose and delivered a speech of welcome to the men and read telegrams from the Duke of Westminster and their old Marine Superintendent, Commander GE Holland. Captains Gwatkin-Williams and Tanner responded to the speech on behalf of all the crew. After lunch the survivors were conveyed to the Coliseum Theatre in a fleet of buses where, during the performance, much to their surprise, an announcement was shown on the screen informing the audience that amongst them were 'the Captain, Officers and men of HMS *Tara*', the message ended with the note that 'It is hoped that the audience will give them a cordial reception.' The audience did, clapping and cheering before breaking into the song *For He's a Jolly Good Fellow*. Whilst they sang a large portrait photograph of the Duke of Westminster was shown on the screen.

At 18.00 hours the survivors returned to Euston, where they boarded the 19.15 hours train which returned them to Holyhead at 00.38 hours.

Over the next few days those survivors who were L&NWR employees were given new appointments on the company's vessels in Holyhead and to the hospital carrier *Cambria* which was based in Dover. However, during the ensuing few months it became apparent that not all of them were fit to work. Some found the tasks too demanding and were discharged ashore, where they were either retired or were offered light-duty positions, such as gangway watchmen or boatmen, within the marine department or the Marine Yard Workshops. Some, like Firemen Richard Jones and Roland Williams, died within a relatively short time and others found that their time in captivity had taken its toll on their health and significantly contributed to their early deaths. One man, Fireman Richard Lewis, had a mental breakdown from which he never recovered.

Only forty-five of the survivors had been pre-war employees of the L&NWR's marine department, the others belonged to a variety of services, both naval and mercantile. Of the eleven naval survivor's most were posted to various vessels or shore bases whilst Ship's Corporal C Mintram was discharged from the Royal Navy on health grounds in late 1916. GA Tanner and R Fulcher, although only teenagers whilst serving on the *Tara,* had signed on for twelve years service in 1914. Both were discharged on health grounds soon after the war's end.

Of the mercantile survivors, the three Campbeltown men, the three remaining Federation men and two of the Larne men returned to their pre-war occupations, whilst W J Andrews (the third Larne man) enlisted in the RNR and was awarded a Distinguished Service Medal in 1918.

Of the twenty-two Holyhead and Anglesey men, who were for the most part deep sea seamen and firemen, some sought employment with the L&NWR whilst others returned to their pre-war employment. One of these, Seaman John Jones, was mentioned in despatches for an action against an enemy submarine in 1918. Others joined the RNR, one of whom Fireman H Hughes, lost his life later in the war. Seaman J H Swaine joined the Royal Engineers and served in Mesopotamia where he was promoted to sergeant and received a mention in despatches.

Those who had returned to or joined the L&NWR marine department, perhaps hoping for a quiet life, soon discovered that the war had not quite finished with them. Although the Irish Sea had been fairly quiet since November 1915 with only one ship attacked and three ships sunk, things changed in 1917 as the number of sinkings and attacks escalated. On 31st January, the German High Command announced that from 1st February their U-boats would commence unrestricted naval warfare and that all vessels, whether British, Allied or neutral, with a few exceptions, would be sunk without warning in certain sea areas including the waters around Britain.

In the Irish Sea the situation remained fairly inactive until the second week of February when in the area around Bardsey Island six ships were sunk within five days, all thought to be the work of *UC-65*. This set the pattern for the next twenty-two months when, in the area between Fishguard and the Isle of Man, approximately 110 vessels were sunk. Many others were attacked with gunfire and torpedoes and, whilst some managed to outfight their attackers, the damaged vessels would limp into Holyhead. Also in the port were those vessels that had been chased (or had simply sighted a surfaced U-boat) and their captains thought it prudent to take shelter until the danger had passed.

For the local populace there were the unsettling sights of vessels regularly putting into Holyhead's outer harbour and the rescued crews of torpedoed vessels being landed in the port. The dead and injured were taken to the Stanley Sailors' Hospital on Salt Island, whilst the uninjured were taken to the Sailor's Home on Newry Beach. There they recounted their stories to the staff and volunteers who worked there and they in turn would relate them to their families and friends.

These local submarine attacks and sightings clearly upset the timetables of both the L&NWR and the CofDSP cross-channel sailings, causing delay's and postponements. No doubt all of these factors must have had an effect on those men who worked on the local vessels and who had already been torpedoed — especially those employed in the engine or boiler rooms from which stations escape was at best difficult.

During the latter end of 1917 and the beginning of 1918, owing to the increasing submarine menace, the vessels of the L&NWR and CoDSPC were fitted with defensive armament, a single 4-inch gun mounted aft, and to man this two or three RNR gunners were attached to each vessel. This measure was in addition to the armed trawlers and drifters based at Holyhead and Kingstown who, with the airships based at the Anglesey Airship Station at Mona on Anglesey and the Malahide Airship Mooring Outstation near Dublin, regularly patrolled the area and escorted vessels across the Irish Sea. To further enhance the local anti-submarine measures, the Irish Sea Hunting flotilla was formed in 1918. It was based at Holyhead (commanded by Captain Gordon Campbell, VC, DSO, RN) and consisted of the cruiser HMS *Patrol* with the destroyers HMS *Mallard, Seal, Kestrel, Griffon, Stag, Sprightly, Earnest, Zephyr, Avon, Lively, Orwel*l with some sixteen trawlers and other small vessels. Also based at Holyhead were twelve American submarine chasers.

Further incidents involving Holyhead vessels which occurred during the following two years included:

During the night of 3rd November 1916, the SS *Connemara,* leaving Greenore in atrocious weather, collided with the collier SS *Retriever*. Of the ninety-four on board these vessels there was only one survivor. Of the thirty-two crew of the *Connemara,* twenty-five were from Holyhead, amongst whom was her chief engineer, Hugh Jones, *Tara*'s old second engineer.

On 15th February 1917, the SS *Slieve Bawn* rendered sterling service in taking passengers off the SS *Celtic* which had struck a mine off the Isle of Man laid by the *U-80* and landed them at Holyhead. The following night, the SS *Galtee More* sighted a U-boat but was not attacked. The *Connaught,* now one of His Majesty's transport ships, was torpedoed and sunk on 3rd March 1917 whilst on passage from Le Havre to Southampton, with three lives lost, none of them local to Holyhead.

On the morning of 13th October 1917, whilst on passage to Dublin, some fifteen miles WSW of South Stack, the SS *South Stack* came across an upturned lifeboat with three men clinging to it. On rescuing the men it was discovered that a fourth man was trapped underneath the boat and he was successfully extricated. The men were from the SS *Eskmere,* sunk the previous night, and were the only survivors out of a crew of twenty-four.

On 14th December, some 7–8 miles east of the Kish Light vessel, the SS *Slieve Bawn* came across a lifeboat containing five men, the only survivors of the sixteen-man crew of the SS *Hare* which had been sunk a few hours previously.

The SS *Cork* (City of Dublin Steam Packet Company), although not a Holyhead vessel, was of the company's Dublin–Liverpool service when she was torpedoed and sunk off Point Lynas, near Amlwch, Anglesey on 26th January 1918, with the loss of five crew and seven passengers. The survivors were landed at Holyhead.

On 30th January 1918, the SS *Slieve Bawn* was again attacked, the torpedo passing between her stern and log-line.

On 5th February 1918, five survivors of the SS *Mexico City* were picked up by the RMS *Leinster*.

On 25th February, the SS *Slieve Bawn* was shelled by a U-boat but suffered neither damage nor casualties.

On 13th March, the SS *Greenore*, under the command of Captain Nash, came across a raft with men aboard, surrounded by wreckage. A boat was lowered and the men brought aboard. They turned out to be the captain, chief engineer, second engineer and six crew members of the Spanish ship *Arno Mendi*. They were landed at Dublin. Some months later Captain Nash received the thanks of the Spanish consol at Dublin, and received a letter of thanks of behalf of the king of Spain and his government.

During the night of 14th March 1918, the SS *Rathmore* was rammed by HM Trawler *Mitres* but, although her engine room was flooded, there were no casualties.

On 22nd March a torpedo missed the RMS *Ulster* by ten yards whilst she was on day passage to Holyhead.

The SS *Slieve Bloom* was sunk after colliding with the American destroyer USS *Stockton* on the night of 30th March 1918. One passenger was killed.

On 6th April, RMS *Ulster*, escorted by two destroyers, was missed by torpedoes. The destroyers turned to attack and dropped three depth charges but without any results.

At 07.20 hours on the morning of 3rd May, when the SS *Rosstrevor* was some thirteen miles NNE of the Holyhead breakwater, a U-boat periscope was spotted. The *Rosstrevor* took avoiding action and the torpedo missed.

On 13th August, the SS *Greenore* sighted a submarine and opened fire with her 4-inch gun, forcing it to submerge.

On 15th August, the SS *Snowdon,* on passage to Dublin and escorted by an airship, was hit by a torpedo which failed to explode. She was dry docked and the dent in her hull plates was plainly visible.

The RMS *Leinster* was torpedoed twelve miles off Kingstown on 10th October 1918 with the loss of 501 passengers and crew, many of them were from Holyhead.

No doubt many of the *Tara* survivors were on board the L&NWR vessels at the time of the above incidents and they must have felt considerable relief when at 11.00 hours on 11th November 1918 the Armistice came into force.

# 26. Epilogue

With the war over both survivors of HMS *Tara* and their rescuers began to settle back into their peace-time occupations. There was however one piece of outstanding wartime business that needed to be addressed which stemmed from a question which had been raised on 17th May 1916. As the train carrying the survivors from their day out at Euston sped homeward to Holyhead, the reporter from the *Holyhead & Anglesey Chronicle*, R E Roberts, who had accompanied them, wrote that it had been muted amongst the officers and crew that a collection should be organised so as to present the Duke of Westminster with a souvenir of their rescue. Roberts went on to suggest that this be opened up to the general population of the town and that a meeting should be held to set up a committee to administer the fund.[1] Whether this was taken up or not is not known by the author but what is known is that a sum of £25 was found for a silver and ebony casket to be made which was surmounted by a silver model of an Rolls-Royce armoured car, with an inscription 'Presented to Major, his grace the Duke of Westminster, DSO, by the survivors of HMS *Tara* and PSS *Moorina* in grateful remembrance of the gallant deed by which they were rescued on St Patrick's Day 1916.' The casket was completed in January 1917 and put on display in the shop window of Victoria House (11–13 Stanley Street) in Holyhead, the business premises of D Jones & Sons, drapers, whilst notification was sent to the duke to arrange a presentation.

The Duke's secretary, H W Trott, replied on 14th March 1917 explaining that the duke was very grateful and very touched by the kind thoughts of the *Tara*'s crew, but begged the survivors to defer the presentation as he was going to London for further treatment to his knees and could not say when he would be allowed home. As he was still a serving officer, it would be contrary to military

1. The records of the Holyhead Urban District Council have been searched to ascertain how this fund was run and by whom, but there is no extant record of such a fund, nor of a silversmith being consulted; neither has any information been found in the local papers. Was the money donated by the L&NWR on behalf of the crew (£25 was a lot of money, most men would have had to contribute neary 10s (50p) which was approx 1–2 days pay for a steward)?

rule for him to accept such a presentation at that time and the casket remained on display until August 1919.

After the war, the Duke was again contacted to request an opportunity to present him with the casket. After some correspondence, a date was arranged and on 16th August 1919 sixty-five *Tara* survivors arrived at Chester Station (of whom about forty were from Holyhead, whilst the others were from London, Liverpool, Larne, Belfast and Portsmouth). They were ushered to charabancs and set off on a sight-seeing tour of the city and park before being taken to Saighton Grange where they were met by the duke, his mother, the Countess Grosvenor, his daughter Lady Mary Grosvenor and Major Ernest Bald (adjutant of N[os] 1, 2 and 3 LACB) amongst others. After lunch which was held in a large marquee on the lawn, the casket was presented to the Duke by Captain Tanner, who said that had his grace not arrived at Bir Hakkim when he did, they would all have died of starvation within five days. He added that the rescue was 'a wonderful feat of endurance, pluck and determination' and it had been a wonderful performance to get those cars from the sea and to drive them in the desert for the length of time they were driven. Captain Gwatkin-Williams then gave an outline of the whole story, after which the Duke rose and gave a short reply, expressing his thanks on behalf of both himself and the officers, non-commissioned officers and men who had served with him in Egypt. The ceremony concluded with the singing of the Welsh hymn, *O fryniau Caersalem ceir gweled*, which was led by Fireman HO Hughes and taken up by the rest of the Welshmen, it having been a particular favourite of the Welsh crew during their captivity.

The presentation concluded, the men shook hands with the Duke and boarded the charabancs which took them to the iron bridge from where they wandered

*HMS* Tara's *officers and engineers at Saighton Grange. L– R: J Thomas; Capt Gwatkin-Williams, RN; DJ Davies; Capt Tanner; H Hughes; R Neill; W Griffith; A Marsh; A Dutton; Lt LT Dudgeon [Mrs D Wise]*

*The Duke of Westminster was not the only recipient of an ornamental gift; this silver tray was presented to Bosun Thomas Owens by the Llanfairpwll Naval & Military Fund on 27th July 1916. It is engraved: 'The Great War, Llanfairpwll Naval & Military Fund. To Thomas Owen, Boatswain, HMS* Tara *with their congratulations on his escape after great sufferings when the crew were rescued from the Senussi in the Libyan Desert by the Duke of Westminster, March 1916.'*

around the grounds of Eaton Hall, and where sometime later they boarded motor launches which took them along the river Dee to Chester in time to catch the 17.07 hrs train to Holyhead.

# APPENDIX 1: Officers and ratings serving aboard HMS *Tara* at the time of her sinking

Ranks and addresses shown are those held at that time. All photographs courtesy of Southampton Libraries unless otherwise noted.

**Captain Rupert Stanley Gwatkin-Williams, RN (Retd)** [Author]

Born 3rd February 1875 as Rupert Stanley Williams, he joined the Royal Navy in June 1889 as a cadet. Later as lieutenant aboard HMS *Barfleur* he took part in the suppression of the Boxer Rebellion in 1900. After twenty years at sea and three with the Coastguard, he retired as a captain on 30th June 1912. The outbreak of war found him in Portugal where he was seeking employment with the railways and harbour board. On the call out of the Reservists he returned to Britain and was appointed to HMS *Tara*, taking command on 9th Aug 1914.

He survived the sinking and subsequent ordeal of the survivors, leaving Alexandria on 21st April 1916 and arriving in Portsmouth where he was admitted to Haslar Hospital on 2nd May. On 25th May 1916 he was appointed to HMS *Intrepid* and served at Murmansk, Russia. On 21st December 1917 he returned to England and on 21st April 1918 was appointed to the Naval Intelligence Division. On 25th April 1918 appointed captain of the armed merchant cruiser *Edinburgh Castle* which was employed on escorting convoys to and from the USA until the end of the war. For his services in the White Sea he was appointed a Companion of the Order of St Michael and St George in the summer of 1918. After the war, he returned to the Retired List and for a number of years toured the country giving talks on the story of the HMS *Tara* and her survivors.

In 1903 he married Miss Evelyn Gwatkin and assumed the additional name of Gwatkin after the marriage. There were two sons and one daughter of the marriage. The couple later divorced and in 1920 he married Miss Florence MC Scott, with whom he had son and one daughter. Sadly the only son, of his second marriage C/JX 406267 Ordinary Seaman Stanley Scott Gwatkin-Williams, RN died aged eighteen on 10th July 1944 whilst serving on HMS *Grey Goose.*

Captain Gwatkin-Williams died on 2nd August 1949 at his home 43 Lebanon Park, Twickenham and was cremated at Mortlake crematorium six days later. His second wife had predeceased him by twelve months. He was survived by the only daughter of his second marriage.

**Lieutenant Edward Butler Tanner, RNR** [W Davies]

Of Ormesby, Walthew Avenue, Holyhead. Born 10th July 1865 in Wexford, Ireland and had been in the employ of the L&NWR since 10th Feb 1891. On the 13th April 1914 Captain John

Evans of the *Hibernia* retired, Captain Tanner was appointed in his place, transferring from the SS *Cambria*. He volunteered to go on active service on the 15th August 1914 and survived the sinking. After rescue he returned to company service on 16th May 1916. His RNR commission was terminated on 23rd July 1916.

He later commanded the hospital transport *Cambria* and was awarded an OBE for his war service. After the war remained on the cross-channel services until retiring on 15th February 1927 and died on 10th June 1940, his body was interred at St Seiriol's Churchyard, Holyhead with his wife, Annie Esther Tanner, who had died 8th June 1931 aged sixty-six. They had three sons, two of whom served with the colours during the war: John Hollingsworth, the eldest, was commissioned into the RGA whilst William Butler, an officer in the Mercantile Marine, joined the RNR as a temporary midshipman. His youngest son, also called Edward Butler, had been born in 1903 and was therefore too young to enlist.

Captain Tanner had been favourably noted by the Admiralty for his conduct during the sinking of HMS *Tara*.

**Sub Lieutenant Leslie Thomas Dudgeon, RNR** [BRB (Residuary) Ltd]
Of 4 Plashyfryd Road, Holyhead. Born 2nd September 1870 in Killashee, Co Longford, Ireland, he first went to sea in 1887. In possession of a master's certificate of competency, he joined the L&NWR on 8th November 1899 and by the outbreak of war was chief officer on the SS *Galteemore*. On 24th August 1914 he was promoted to temporary captain on one of the company's cargo vessels. On 10th February 1915 he was granted a temporary commission in the RNR and joined HMS *Tara* on 10th March 1915.

He survived the sinking and after rescue, returned to company service on 16th May 1916 as chief officer on the SS *Rathmore* and his RNR commission was terminated on the 24th. He served on the Holyhead vessels for the rest of the war and in 1920 was promoted from chief officer of the new RMS *Anglia* to captain of the SS *Rosstrevor* and, in 1929, to captain on the passenger-service vessels. He retired at his own request on 31st March 1931 as captain of the RMS *Hibernia*. On 7th April he was invited aboard the *Hibernia* where a retirement gift of a silver salver from the officers and crew was presented to him by Albert Marsh (see later) who was her chief officer.

Captain Dudgeon and his wife Annie moved to Hatch End, Middlesex. She died in January 1937 and he died on 8th December 1950. Both were interred in the local cemetery. They were survived by their daughter, Milfred Kathleen (born in Dublin) and son, Charles William (born in Holyhead).

**Sub Lieutenant William Thomas Griffiths, RNR**
Of 31 Newry Street, Holyhead. Born in Holyhead on 24th May 1876 he joined the L&NWR on 1st January 1908. He held a master's certificate of competency and had since 24th August 1914 been acting as a temporary mate on one of the company's cargo vessels. He joined HMS *Tara* on 10th March 1915, having been granted a temporary RNR commission on 24th February. He survived the sinking and, after rescue, returned to company service on 16th May 1916. His

commission was terminated on 24th May 1916.

He retired in January 1938, aged sixty-two, due to ill health caused by an old injury sustained many years earlier after falling twenty-five feet into a hatch when his vessel was in San Francisco. His last command was the RMS *Scotia*, on which he had served from 1934. She was later sunk by enemy aircraft at Dunkirk on 1st June 1940. Captain Griffiths died aged eighty-one at the Valley Hospital on 2nd May 1958. He was then residing at 11 Alderley Terrace, Holyhead. He left his wife of forty-eight years, Margaret, two sons, William Owen and David Glynne, and one daughter, Elsie.

**Sub Lieutenant Albert Marsh, RNR**

Of 13 Roland Street, Holyhead, but had been born in St Anthony, Cornwall on 11th February 1887, one of seven children of William and Catherine Marsh. William Marsh was a chief boatman in the Royal Navy Coastguard Service and shortly after Albert's birth was posted to Holyhead. In the 1900's Albert went to sea where he gained his Masters Certificate of Competency and leaving Canadian Pacific's SS *Empress of Britain* joined the L&NWR on 24th May 1914 as a second mate. He volunteered to go on active service on 15th August 1915 as an additional second mate on HMS *Tara*, his temporary commission in the RNR was granted the same date. He survived the sinking and returned to company service on 16th May 1916 being appointed second mate of the SS *Slieve More*. His RNR commission was terminated on 24th May 1916. During the Second World War, he was master of the RMS *Cambria* when, in December 1941, she was attacked by a German Dornier which resulted in the death of one of her officers and the wounding of several passengers.

He retired as commodore captain of the port of Holyhead in May 1950 and died aged seventy-seven on 26th May 1964 at the Stanley Hospital, Salt Island and was interred in St Mihangel Churchyard, Valley. He was survived by his second wife, Elizabeth Margaret, and the children of his first marriage, a son, Jack, and daughters, Dorothy, Shelagh and Maureen. At the time of his death he was residing at The Wern, Valley.

NB His brother Alfred was serving as Chief Steward on the *Scotia* in the Red Sea at the time of the Tara's sinking, but died on 12th June 1916.

**Third Mate John Griffith Thomas, MFA** [Author]

Of Gwerin Alun, 26 Rhosygaer Avenue, Holyhead. Born in Bangor in 1862, he joined L&NWR on 30th April 1885 and was serving on the *Hibernia* when she was requisitioned. He volunteered to go on active service on 15th August but was not in possession of a certificate of competency so was granted a temporary commission in the Mercantile Fleet Auxiliary rather than the RNR. He survived the sinking and subsequent ordeal of the survivors and returned to company service on 16th May 1916.

He retired in 1927 or 1928 and died after a short illness on 8th January 1943, aged seventy-nine and was interred at Maeshyfryd

Cemetery, Holyhead. The funeral was attended by many of his old ship-mates, survivors of HMS *Tara,* and the coffin was draped with the Red Duster. He served over fifty years with the L&NWR and was survived by his second wife, Kate, and the children of his first marriage, Evan and Ellen. His first wife, Ellen, having died in 1899

**Engineer Robert John Seaborne Williams, RNR** [Author]

Of Glandwr, Bryngolau Avenue, Holyhead. He was the son of Captain Robert and Catherine Williams and had been born on 8th July 1863 aboard the sailing vessel *Bramley Moor* when some 150 miles NE of Pitcairn Island in the Pacific. He served an engineering apprenticeship and joined the L&NWR on 29th October 1884 and the marine department on 27th September 1887. Obtaining his second then first class engineers certificate of competency, he rose through the ranks and was appointed chief engineer on the passenger vessels on 1st February 1905. He was granted an RNR commission on 18th Sept 1915 and appointed to HMS *Tara* on 5th October 1915 after the disappearance of Chief Engineer Thomas Jones. Chief Engineer Williams died of sickness and malnutrition in captivity at Bir Hakkim on 28th January 1916. After the war, his body was exhumed and interred in Chatby Cemetery Alexandria, Egypt, grave 53.

He left a wife, Catherine, one son, Eric Seaborne, and one daughter, Margaret Olwen.

**Warrant Engineer James Hutton, RNR** [Media Wales Ltd]

Of 42 Wyndham Street, Barry, Glamorganshire. He was born in Manchester in 1867 and had served an engineer apprenticeship before going to sea as a marine engineer. In November 1892 he sat and passed his second class engineer's certificate of competency in Cardiff and gained his first class engineer's certificate on 28th February 1895. In1896, he married Eleanor Williams in Cardiff and the couple settled in Barry. Perhaps tiring of the sea, on 12th February 1900 he found employment as an engineer with the Barry Fire Brigade, a position that came with accommodation, a uniform and a wage of 35s per week (£1.75). The family, which then included a one-year-old son, Arthur Gilbert, moved from Aberystwyth Crescent to the Fire Station, Court Road, Barry.

On 23rd March 1896 James enlisted into the RNR at Barry Dock, being appointed assistant engineer. He was promoted to warrant engineer on 22nd June 1904 and a few years later left the Fire Brigade to be employed in one of the ship repair yards in the town, firstly as a fitter then as a charge-hand. By now the family had grown with the addition of another son, James Cyril, and a daughter, Phyllis Eluned.

On 2nd August 1914, on the mobilisation of the RNR he was appointed to the pre-Dreadnaught HMS *Majestic* and was on board when she was torpedoed and sunk on 27th May 1915 off Gallipoli by the *U-21*. After survivors' leave, he was appointed second engineer of HMS *Tara* and joined her at Devonport on 7th October. It was later recorded that he was last seen in the engine room by Fireman Roland Williams, one minute before the torpedo struck.

**Assistant Engineer Richard Lewis Phillips, RNR** [Capt G Pritchard]
Of Forcer View, Llasa Street, Holborn Road, Holyhead. Born on 7th July 1877 in Tyddun Llwyn Terrace, Minffordd, Meirionethshire, Robert served an engineering apprenticeship locally and on 27th September 1899 obtained employment as a fitter at the Marine Yard Workshops in Holyhead and lodged at 3 Cambria Street. On 9th February 1905, he transferred over to the L&NWR's Marine Yard Workshops to become an engineer on the local vessels. By the outbreak of war he was in the possession of a second-class engineer's certificate of competency and was serving on the company's dredgers at Garston. On 12th March 1915, he returned to the Holyhead vessels and volunteered for active service and was appointed an assistant engineer in the RNR with seniority dated to 22nd July, joining the *Tara* a few days later. When the *Tara* was in dry dock during September 1915, Richard Phillips was promoted to temporary second engineer, a position he held until 7th October 1915 when she called at Devonport and Warrant Engineer James Hutton, RNR, joined and took over the position, and Richard reverted to third engineer.

After the sinking, the second cook, John Pritchard, recalled that the last he had seen of Richard Phillips he was entering his cabin on the starboard side of the main deck shortly before the torpedo struck. He added that, as that cabin had been demolished, he had assumed that Phillips died immediately.

Robert Phillips had married Annie Pritchard of Cambria Terrace, Holyhead on 9th March 1904 and was the father of six children, Magwen, Gwylym Richard, Helena Crystal, Glynne, Robert Gerald and the youngest, Mary Glenys, who had been born on 28th July 1914 when the family resided at Glan-y-Don, Watkin Row, Boston Street. However, at the time of his death, the family were residing at Forcer View, Llasa Street, Holborn Road, Holyhead.

During the war, his brother, the Reverend J T Phillips, served with the 5th Bn The Cheshire Regiment.

**Assistant Engineer Griffith Hugh Roberts, RNR** [*Mrs B. Holmes*]
Of 56 Newry Street, Holyhead. Born on 26th January 1889 in Holyhead, he served an engineering apprenticeship in the Marine Yard before joining the marine department on 29th April 1912. By the outbreak of war he was in the possession of a second-class certificate of competency and was serving on the *Hibernia* as her third engineer when she was requisitioned. He volunteered to go on active service on 15th August 1914 and was on watch in the engine room when the torpedo struck. After the sinking it was ascertained that he had last been seen alive in the engine room by Fireman Roland Williams and it was assumed that he was killed instantly.

He had married Miss Ann Elizabeth Edwards of Refail Bach Farm, Penrhos Beach Road, Holyhead on 13th September 1912 at Bethel Capel, Edmund Street, Holyhead. on 16th September 1915 a daughter Isabella Eva was born.

Assistant Engineer Roberts is commemorated on his wife's grave in Maeshyfryd Cemetery, a white cross on whose base is inscribed 'In memory of my dear father G H Roberts, Eng Sub Lieut, RNR, HMS *Tara*.' Also inscribed is 'Dear mother Annie Roberts, died 30th January 1923, aged 37. Erected by his daughter.' He is also commemorated on the grave of his mother and father, Robert and Margaret Elizabeth Roberts, of Tan Rallt, Four Mile Bridge, who are buried in the Capel Wesla Cemetery, Rhoscolyn, Anglesey. Robert Roberts had been the *Hibernia*'s old chief engineer.

**Assistant Engineer Howarth Hughes, RNR**

Of 10 Mountain View, Holyhead. He was born in Liverpool on 3rd August 1890 and was the adopted son of Simeon (a ship's painter) and Elizabeth Hughes, and the nephew of Quartermaster William Rowlands (see later). After serving an engineering apprenticeship he joined the SS *Orcoma* as 7th Engineer on 14th November 1911, serving on her he rose to become 4th, and was discharged on 29th September 1913. He then sat and gained his Second Class Certificate of Competency and joined the L&NWR's marine department on 1st April 1914. Appointed to the *Hibernia* as an additional engineer on 12th August, he volunteered to go on active service on 15th August and was granted an RNR commission on the same date. He survived the sinking and returned to company service on 16th May 1916 and his commission was terminated on 24th May 1916.

On 18th June 1919 he was transferred to the company's dredgers at Garston where remained until 31st December 1919. Sometime later, he gained his first-class engineer's certificate and left the company. He then found employment with Evan Thomas, Radcliffe & Co of Cardiff and remained with the company rising to become chief engineer. During the Second World War he survived the sinking of the SS *Llancarvan* on the 30 May 1943 off the Portuguese coast, he later served on the newly-built SS *Fort Saleesh*, then the SS *High Park*. In June 1947 he was appointed to the SS *Llandaff*, from which ship, during the summer of 1951 he was taken to the Brisbane General Hospital, New South Wales, Australia suffering from broncho-pneumonia, and died there on 5th July. His remains were cremated at the Mount Thompson Crematorium and the ashes brought to Holyhead via London aboard the SS *Mooltan* and they were laid to rest in his parents' grave in Maeshyfryd Cemetery.

Howarth Hughes was a bachelor who still resided at 10 Mountain View and perhaps because of their shared experiences in the desert he and Assistant Engineer David J Davies (see below) became lifelong friends.

**Assistant Engineer David John Davies, RNR**

Of 17 Newry Fawr, Holyhead, but had been born at 9 Old Cross Street on 4th April 1887. He served an engineering apprenticeship and later went deep sea, where he gained his first-class engineer's certificate of competency. He left the SS *Consols* (R.J. Thomas & Co) to join the L&NWR's marine department on 30th November 1914 as a fourth engineer and volunteered to go on active service on 5th October 1915, receiving a temporary RNR commission on the same date. He survived the sinking and returned to company service on 16th May 1916; his commission being terminated eight days later. On 1st January 1919 he was appointed to the company's dredgers at Garston and returned to the Holyhead steamers on 30th May.

It is uncertain how long he remained on the railway vessels as by 1942 he was serving, as a chief engineer on the *PLM 13*, a French vessel which had been taken over by the Ministry of

War Transport and it is believed that he sailed on the Garston dredgers both before and after the war. However it is known that he retired as chief engineer from the local vessels in 1952.

He died suddenly on the 31st July 1967 and was survived by his brother Jack (who was also a marine engineer on the local vessels) and sister, Kate, both of whom were residing with him at Fenselar, Marine Square, Holyhead.

**Temporary Assistant Paymaster Alfred Dutton, RNR** [W. Davies]

Born 1890 in the Station Master's house in Pontrhythallt railway station, Llanrug, Caernarfonshire, where his father was the station master. His mother, Annie, had twelve children. By 1913, his father had retired and the family, without Alfred, were residing at Drury House, Westminster Road, Hoole in Chester. Alfred, an insurance clerk, had moved to Holyhead and found employment with the Holyhead Waterworks Company. A few months later he changed employer and became a clerk in the L&NWR's Marine Office while residing at 6 Roland Street. He was granted a temporary commission as an assistant paymaster RNR on 9th December 1914, on which date he joined HMS *Tara*, taking over from William T Davies. After the rescue, he resumed employment with the L&NWR, transferring to the catering office of the marine department. In 1939, he was appointed catering superintendent of the port, a position he held until his death on 26th November 1950, aged sixty. He was interred in St Seiriol's Churchyard, Holyhead; at the time of his death he was residing at 25, Porthyfelin. He was survived by his wife Ethel whom he had married shortly after returning home from Alexandria, and his daughter Mildred.

For twenty-eight years he had been the honorary secretary of the local yacht club and had served on their regatta committee. During the Second World War he took over the administrative duties of the local Sea Cadets and later became their commanding officer but had to relinquish the position due to pressure of other commitments.

Alfred Dutton had been favourably noted by the Admiralty for his conduct during the sinking of HMS Tara.

**Warrant Telegraphist Robert Neill, RNR**

Of Moonvane House, Portalington, County Loais, Ireland, but during the war he resided at 13 Holborn Road, Holyhead. He was born at 9, Broghill South, Charleville, Co Cork, Ireland on 12th December1895 and joined the L&NWR's Marine Department on 10th February 1914. He was serving on the *Hibernia* when she was requisitioned and volunteered to go active service on 15th August 1914. Initially he was given the rate of wireless telegraphy operator, a Mercantile Fleet Auxiliary rate, but on 30th November was appointed to the rank of warrant telegraphist, RNR. He survived the sinking and returned to company service on 16th May 1916 and his commission was terminated eight days later. He was paid off the railway vessels on 20th December 1917 and joined the Royal Naval Air Service as a second lieutenant, then transferred to the RAF on its formation in April 1918. He was demobbed on 18th March 1919 and returned to the local vessels, during which time he resided in Faughill, Bryngolau Avenue, Holyhead with his wife, Gertrude (née Morris), whom he had married on 16th May 1918 at St Cybi's Church, Holyhead.

He resigned from the L&NWR in 1920 and moved to Narberth in Pembrokeshire where he became a secretary for James Williams (Narberth) Ltd, wine and spirit merchants, and resided for a number of years at 48 St James Street in that town, although just before his death he moved to Bellmore Gardens.

He remained in regular contact with Sub Lieutenant Marsh and some of the other survivors until his death on 27th August 1979 at the Sunny Bank Nursing Home, Narberth. He had lost his wife in 1974 and in 1961 they had lost their only son, forty-two-year-old Major John Morris Neill, MC, Royal Welch Fusiliers, who died in a motor-car accident in Charlottenberg, Berlin, Germany on 4th September, leaving a wife and son.

Robert Neill had been favourably noted by the Admiralty for his conduct during the sinking of HMS *Tara*.

**Wireless Telegraph Operator Cecil William Birkby, MFA**

Of 228 Weast Lane, Weaste Drive, Salford, Manchester. He was born in Ballary, India on 28th August 1894. The date of his family's arrival in England is unknown, but prior to residing in Manchester it seems that they had resided for a time in Lichfield where Cecil was the principal boy in the cathedral choir. On 24th August 1910 he enlisted as a boy soldier in the 1st Bn, The Cheshire Regiment, aged fifteen years and eleven months, giving his trade as musician. On 21st October 1910, he suffered a chemical injury to his left eye which left him permanently scarred. He was promoted to private on his eighteenth birthday but was discharged on 6th January 1913 as his services were no longer required.

He joined the L&NWR's Marine Department on 27th July 1914 as a wireless operator and resided in Holborn Road. On 11th August 1914, he volunteered to go on active service, given the rate of wireless telegraphy operator, MFA, and appointed to the *Anglia* but was paid off on her de-commissioning on 24th April 1915. He then served on the passenger cargo/cargo vessels and passed his first-class Postmaster General's wireless operator certificate just prior to being appointed to HMS *Tara* on 2nd October 1915, taking over from Wireless Telegraphist Frederick J Chambers who had paid off on the 1st.

Birkby survived the sinking and returned to company service on 16th May 1916 being appointed to the SS *Greenore*. After the survivors returned to Holyhead, Lieutenant Tanner, knowing that Birkby held the same 'ticket as Robert Neill so should have held the same rank and the same higher rate of pay', wrote to the Admiralty in May 1916 pointing this out, but they replied in October, stating that there was nothing they could then do about it. By all accounts he was a very popular and well-liked man nicknamed 'Raj' or 'Rajah'.

He died of double pneumonia in his lodgings at 52 Newry Street, Holyhead on 28th October 1918. At the time of his death he was a wireless operator on the SS *Rathmore*, serving with his best friend, Wireless Operator John C Seed. His body was taken to Manchester where it was interred at Peel Green Cemetery, Salford. He was survived by his father, William James Birkby, and three sisters, Jessie, Winnie and Elsie. 1918 was a tragic year for the family as his mother had died in February, and his eldest brother Company Sergeant Major Hodgson Graves Birkby, aged thirty-five, of the 1/7th The Cheshire Regiment, had been killed in action in France on 14th October.

The Birkby's were a much-travelled family; the father, William, had been born in

Rawalpindi, India (a regular soldier for forty-four years, twenty-eight of which were spent as Bandmaster of the 1st Bn, The Cheshire Regiment. In 1915, still feeling that he had something to offer, he re-enlisted at the age of sixty-one); his wife, Mary, born in Preesall, Lancashire; their eldest son, Hodgson, born in St Helier and their daughters Dorothea Jessie in Gibraltar and Winifred Mary Stuart in Belgaum, India and Elsie Alice Wilhelmina in Rangoon, Burma.

**Writer William Gibson Manning, MFA**

Of Preswylfa, Valley, Anglesey. Born in Maes-yr-Haf, Longford Road, Holyhead in 1898, the son of Captain Lionel J Manning who, on the outbreak of war, commanded HMS *Anglia*.

William joined the L&NWR's Marine Department on 24th April 1915 as an assistant purser and was firstly appointed to the *Anglia*. On her decommissioning, he was discharged and appointed to HMS *Tara* as a writer, in effect a confidential secretary for both the captain's and the assistant paymaster. He survived the sinking and, after rescue, returned to company service on 19th May 1916. Promoted to purser, he was appointed to the HM Ambulance Transport *Cambria*, on which vessel he saw the war out. He left the company on 26th June 1919.

Some twelve months later he joined the White Star line's SS *Olympic* as a purser's clerk. Remaining with the company, he was promoted to extra assistant purser on the SS *Celtic* in 1923. Not long afterwards he changed companies and joined the Atlantic Transport Line's SS *Minnesawaka* as a purser. Unfortunately this company became a casualty of the depression of the 1930s and it seems that William came ashore to work. During the early 1920s he took up residence in New York and in 1930 he married Elizabeth, who was originally from Tullow, Ireland, and the couple took up residence in Brooklyn. On 12th November 1940 he became a US citizen and was employed as an assistant secretary for an instrument company, at the time the couple were residing at 80 Joralemon Street, Brooklyn. He died in New York in 1957 and is commemorated by name on the family's grave at St Seiriol's Churchyard, Holyhead.

**Temporary Surgeon Probationary John David Arthur, RNVR**

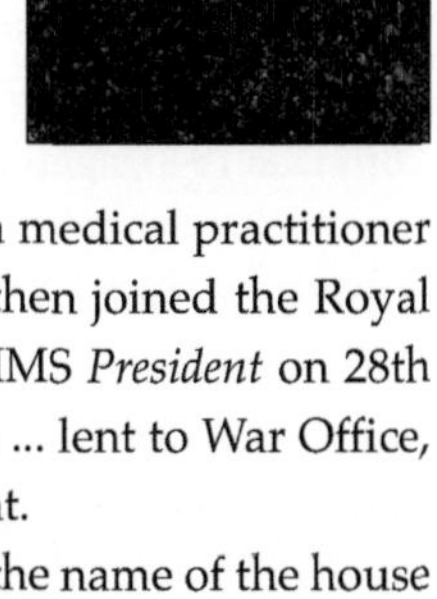

[BRB (Residuary) Ltd]

Born on 7th February 1894 in 16, Berkeley Terrace, Glasgow, he was the son of David (a dairyman) and Annie Thomson Arthur (née Sinclair). In 1915 John was studying medicine and residing at 3 Burnside Buildings, Eastfields, Cambuslang, Glasgow and volunteered for service as a temporary surgeon probationer RNVR on 15th September 1915 and was appointed to the *Tara* at the end of the month. He survived the sinking, but after rescue was 'demobilised' on 27th September 1916 so as to continue with his studies. Gaining his degree he registered as a medical practitioner in Scotland on 22nd July 1918 (MB, ChB University of Glasgow), but then joined the Royal Navy as a surgeon probationer on 8th August. He was appointed to HMS *President* on 28th September, from where he and a number of surgeon probationers were ... lent to War Office, John Arthur being posted to the 7th Battalion Royal West Kent Regiment.

In 1923 he took up a practice in Slamannan, Stirlingshire, changing the name of the house he had recently bought to 'Bir Hakim'. In July 1941, he was appointed physician to the Nervous

& Mental Disease Clinic of the Royal Infirmary, Glasgow. He died at Bir Hakim, Slamannan on 13th October 1969, aged seventy-five, having outlived his wife, Jane Bogue (née Stark), whom he had married in 1923. He left one son and a daughter.

**Basil/Vasili Lanbrimis** [Author]
Basil (real name Vasili Lanbrimis) was a Syrian-Greek by birth, fluent in English, Greek 'and many other languages'. On 7th May 1915 he was employed by the British Military as an interpreter and joined HMS *Tara* prior to her first patrol in October 1915. He survived the sinking and the subsequent ordeal of the survivors. After rescue, he remained working as an interpreter for the military, being attached firstly to the 1st Australian Light Horse then to the headquarters of the 234th Brigade in Egypt. He was released from military service on 11th February 1920.

Throughout his service on board the *Tara,* and during his time in captivity, he was known by all as 'Basil', and it seems that it was the name to which he clung to throughout his service with the military. It would also appear that after the war he was in regular correspondence with Sub Lieutenant Dudgeon and became the proprietor of the Bar Mishmish at 11 Bawaki Street, Cairo, Egypt.

*Petty Officers and Ratings of the Deck Department*

**Carpenter Owen Williams, MFA** [Holyhead Maritime Museum]
Of 14 Gilbert Street, Holyhead. Born in 1855, he was the son of John and Elizabeth Williams of Erw Wen, Newborough, Bodorgan, Anglesey. He had first gone to sea at the age of ten on sailing vessels and had lived for a time at Millom in Cumberland where he was believed to have been working in one of the shipyards. He joined the L&NWR's marine department on 20th April 1893 and was serving on the *Hibernia* when she was requisitioned. He volunteered to go on active service on 15th August 1914.

When the *Tara* was torpedoed Owen Williams had jumped over the side and was seen by Wireless Telegraphist Robert Neill struggling in the water, clinging to a life-raft, when a meat safe broke free of the wreck, fell on him striking him on the head, probably killing him instantly. He left a wife, Margaret, one son, John Oliver, and one daughter, Ellen. He is commemorated on the headstone of his wife's grave in Maeshyfryd Cemetery. She died on 15th May 1937, aged seventy-three. Also in the same grave is their son, who died on 28th Dec 1940, aged fifty-six.

**Boatswain Thomas Owens MFA** [Mrs G. Parillo]
Full name Thomas Henry Owens, he had been born 1869 in Pentraeth (Llaneugrad), Anglesey, but by the early 1900s had moved to Dryll-y-Bowl, Llanfairpwll (Llanfair PG), Anglesey. He joined the L&NWR's marine department on 17th March 1893, and was serving as boatswain on the *Hibernia* when she was requisitioned. He volunteered to go on active service on 15th August 1914 and survived the sinking. He returned to company service on 26th June 1916, but

left on 6th October 1917. He returned to the company's vessels on the 26 June 1916 but left on 6 October 1917. He later become the Foreman of the L&NWR's Marine Yard's Shore Gang – it is thought that the ordeal in the desert may have been too much for him so was given light duties ashore by the company.

On 27th July 1916, at a special concert at the Lecture Hall in Llanfairpwll, Owens was presented with a silver tray by the Llanfairpwll Naval & Military Fund upon which was engraved, 'The Great War, Llanfairpwll Naval & Military Fund. To Thomas Owen, Boatswain, HMS *Tara* with their congratulations on his escape after great sufferings when the crew were rescued from the Senussi in the Libyan Desert by the Duke of Westminster, March 1916.' At the presentation Fireman HO Hughes (see later) recounted the whole story to the audience.

Thomas retired in 1930 and died on 13th April 1941 and was interred in St Mary's churchyard, Llanfairpwll, in the same grave as his wife, Ellen, who had died in 1938, aged seventy-one. They had three children, Catherine Ellen, Erasmus and Elizabeth Olive.

**Quartermaster William Rowlands, MFA** [Mrs Ann Martin & Mrs Beryl Lloyd]
Of Penllechnest, Kingsland, Holyhead. Born in Holyhead in 1871 he joined the L&NWR's marine department on 20th February 1895, having previously worked for his father who was a butcher. He was serving on the *Hibernia* on the outbreak of war and volunteered to go on active service on 14th August. After rescue he returned to company service on 16th May 1916 and initially served on their Holyhead-based vessels but later transferred to, and saw the war out, on HMT *Scotia* which was employed as a transport sailing between Dover/Folkestone and Calais/Boulogne/Dunkirk. He remained with the company and rose to become boatswain.

He died aged seventy-six on 17th November 1947, at his home of Lybia, 2 Cyttir Road, Kingsland in Holyhead where he resided with his daughter and son-in-law, and was interred in Maeshyfryd Cemetery. He was the husband of Ann Ellen and father of John William and Elizabeth Mary. He was also an uncle to Assistant Engineer Howarth Hughes.

**Quartermaster William Thomas, MFA** [*Holyhead Chronicle*]
Of Hadley Villa, Rhosygaer Avenue, Holyhead. Born in Holyhead in 1852, he joined the L&NWR's marine department on 4th October 1882 from the vessels of the City of Dublin Steam Packet Company. He was serving on the *Hibernia* as a seaman when she was requisitioned and volunteered to go on active service on 15th August 1914 and is believed to have been promoted to quartermaster when Quartermaster John L Jones was unable to sail with the *Tara* on 18th August 1914.

Thomas broke and badly lacerated his right leg after being thrown out of the lifeboat when it capsized on launching, before its falls could be unhooked. He was picked up by Sub Lieutenant Marsh's boat and, although the break was correctly set, it became gangrenous. On 13th November Surgeon Probationer Arthur decided to amputate the leg at the knee by the under the supervision of the Turkish doctor, Bechi Faud. Having neither anaesthetic nor medical instruments they had to use a pair of scissors which had been sharpened on a stone by the crew. Sadly, Thomas died due to the shock of the operation and loss of blood. He was buried nearby next morning.

Thomas had recently been widowed as his second wife, Elizabeth, had died on 6th February, aged sixty-two. She had suffered a fractured skull after being knocked over by a horse and cart whilst crossing London Road from Wian Street to the Railway Barracks in Holyhead. The driver, and a police constable helped her to her feet and took her to Denbigh House (a nearby shop) from where a doctor was called. After an examination she was taken home and put to bed where she died. Her husband was contacted by wireless aboard HMS *Tara* which was then at anchor off Point of Ayr, north Wales and, even though on active service, was given compassionate leave to return to Holyhead where he could also make arrangements for their only child, William Henry, who, although aged thirty-one, had been born deaf. Elizabeth Thomas was interred in Maeshyfryd cemetery in Holyhead.

William Henry was the child of William's first marriage to Hannah Augusta Jones. They had married in St Cybi's Church on 8th January 1880, but she died nine years later and is buried in St Cybi's churchyard with their only daughter Hannah Augusta, who had died some nine month's previously, aged one year. Although William Henry had been born deaf he had served an apprenticeship as a tailor, and after the death of his step-mother he appears to have been sent to live with Thomas a marine engineer, and Margaret Sergeant of 53 Gloucester Road, Bootle, Liverpool (possibly his aunt). His adoptive family later moved to Holyhead and took up residence at Cartref, 20 Maeshyfryd Road, where William Henry died on 5th June 1967.

Elizabeth, his step-mother, had been interred in an unmarked grave in Maeshyfryd cemetery whilst, after the war, his father's grave could not be found and so he was commemorated by name on the Chatby Memorial in Alexandria, Egypt.

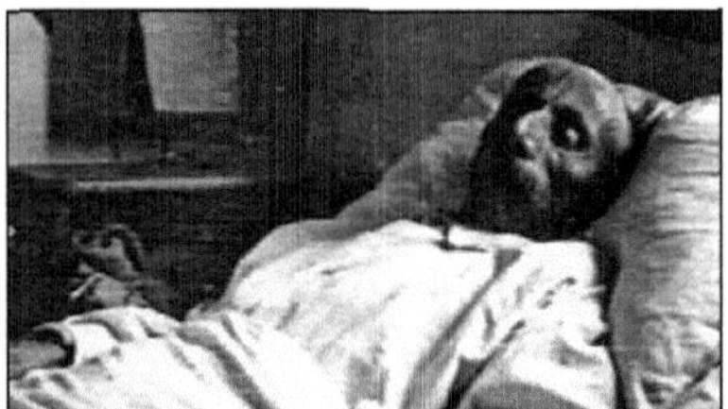

**Quartermaster Robert Abbit, MFA** [Mr T Ashmore] Of 37 London Road, Holyhead. He was born in Holyhead in 1853, the son of John, a carpenter, and Ann Abbit and had three brothers and one sister. At the time, the family were residing at 6 Mill Street. He joined the L&NWR's marine department on 2nd November 1878 and had volunteered to go on active service on 14th August 1914. During captivity he had suffered from dysentery for over four months and many of his shipmates thought that he would never pull through. However, after rescue, he recovered and returned to company service on 14th June 1916.

Abbit retired on 1st December 1917 and died on 25th May 1926, aged seventy-three. His wife, Elizabeth, died on 18th August of the same year, aged sixty-nine and was interred with him in Maeshyfryd cemetery. They had ten children, four daughters and six sons, two of whom became master mariners.

**Quartermaster Richard Williams, MFA** [Mrs Ann Denton & Mr D Reily]

Of Cadnant, 8 British Terrace, Holyhead. Born in Menai Bridge in 1868, he joined the L&NWR's marine department on 1st December 1893 and was serving on the *Hibernia* when she was requisitioned and volunteered to go on active service on 15th August 1914. He survived the sinking and, after rescue, returned to company service on 16th May 1916. On 30th November 1920 he was promoted boatswain from which position he retired in 1933.

He died on 27th January 1953, aged eighty-four, still residing in Cadnant and was interred in St Seiriol's Churchyard, Holyhead. He left four sons — Robert, Richard, Thomas and Owen, a daughter, Mary, and an adopted daughter, Olwen Jones. His wife Kate, died in 1946. During the war his son Thomas, an assistant at the Maypole Stores in Holyhead had enlisted in the Royal Welch Fusiliers and served in France where he was wounded in the left leg which had to be amputated.

**Bosun's Mate John Owen, MFA** [Mrs B Liepman]

Of 5 Lligwy Street, Holyhead, but born in Tai Coed Uchaf, Llangeinwen, Anglesey in 1862. He joined the L&NWR's marine department on 7th October 1891 and was serving as a seaman on the *Hibernia* when she was requisitioned. Volunteering to go on active service on 15th August 1914, he was promoted boatswain's mate after Richard Williams had been paid off due to illness. John survived the sinking and, after rescue, returned to company service on 19th May 1916.

John Owen was still residing at 5, Lligwy Street when he died, aged sixty-two, on 6th May 1925 and was interred in Maeshyfryd in the same grave as his wife, Mary Ellen, who had died, aged fifty-two, in 1923. They had one son, Robert Thomas, born in 1892, who served an engineering apprenticeship in the Marine Yard. He afterwards went to sea and, having gained his first-class engineer's certificate of competency, returned to the Marine Yard workshops where he rose to became Assistant Marine Engineering Superintendent.

**Seaman Griffith Griffiths, MFA** (Mrs Merfyn M Hughes)

Of 24 Gilbert Street, Holyhead. Born on 4th March 1866 in Llanbeblig, Caernarvon, he moved to Holyhead from 10 Uxbridge Street, Caernarvon in 1895. He joined the L&NWR's marine department on 13th December 1897 and was serving on the *Hibernia* when she was requisitioned. Electing to go on active service on 15th August 1914 he survived the sinking and, after rescue, returned to company service on 16th May 1916. He retired in 1931 having spent his career on the local railway vessels and died on 25th August 1940, aged seventy-four. He was interred in Maeshyfryd cemetery alongside his wife, Jane, who had died on 20th May 1938, aged sixty-eight. They left five sons: John Rees, Griffith Rees, Hugh Rees, Robert Griffith and Ellis Vaughan, and one daughter, Margaret Mary. During the war, their son, John Rees, a crane boy at the Goods Department of the L&NWR, served with the Royal Engineers.

**Seaman William Hugh Hughes, MFA**

Of 7 Rock Street, Holyhead. Born in Holyhead on 4th May 1885, he was not a pre war L&NWR seaman. His immediate pre-war employment in unknown (but thought to have been as a labourer in the Marine Yard), but his last deep-sea vessel had been the schooner *Dorothy* of Porthmadog which had been wrecked in Fago Bay, Newfoundland on 23rd October 1912. Two other men from Holyhead were on board, Joseph Lewis and David J Pritchard, and all three had made their way home, via New York, aboard the SS *Carthaginian*. He joined the vessels of the L&NWR's marine department on 11th August 1914 and was appointed to one of the Holyhead passenger/cargo vessels, from which he was discharged on 14th November 1914 to join HMS *Tara* at Larne. On the 9th June 1915 he was confined in the cells for an unknown offence. He survived the sinking and, after rescue, returned to the company's Holyhead-based vessels on 5th October 1916 , but was discharged on 17th February 1917. Joining the RNR he was given the service number 17261 and rated 'deck hand'. At this time he was residing at 23 Rock Street.

He was demobilised from HM Trawler *Daniel Harrington* and returned to the local vessels on 12th March 1920. He retired on the grounds of ill health in 1941 and died on 26th January 1945, aged fifty-nine, and was interred at Maeshyfryd Cemetery. At the time of his death he was residing at 4 Mill Bank. He was survived by his wife, Kate, and their three children.

**Seaman William John Rowlands, MFA** [Mrs Merfyn M Hughes]

Of 24 Cecil Street, Holyhead, he was born in Newborough, Anglesey on 16th June 1891. He was not a pre-war L&NWR seaman but is believed to have joined the company in 1915. After rescue, he joined the L&NWR's marine department on 30th July 1916.

On the outbreak of the Second World War Rowlands was serving on the RMS *Scotia* and volunteered to sail with her to evacuate members of the British Expeditionary Force from the beaches of Dunkirk. She was bombed and sunk on 1st May 1940 with the loss of thirty local crew members and 300 French troops. It was later estimated that at the time she was carrying over 2,000 troops. He survived the sinking and returned to the local vessels where he remained until he retired as boatswain in 1956.

On 24th January 1919 he had married Annie Jane Jones of 58 London Road at St Cybi's Church, Holyhead. They had one daughter, Edna. The family later resided at 147 London Road, Holyhead. Both his wife and daughter predeceased him and he moved to live in the Garreglwyd old people's home, where he died on 10th February 1981. During his service on the railway vessels he was known to all as Barney.

**Seaman John Hodgson, MFA**

Of 4 Wynne Street, Holyhead, he was born in 1870 at 2 North West Street in Holyhead, the son of Christopher Dodd, a servant, and Elizabeth Hodgson. The family later moved to 18 Summer Hill, Holyhead where two more children, Christopher and Isabella, were born.

He was not a pre-war L. & NWR man, but joined the Marine Department on 26th March and HMS *Anglia* on 9th April 1915 after leaving the SS *Olive Branch*. On the *Anglia's* decommissioning on 24th April it is believed that he was transferred to HMS *Tara*, when she was in dry dock in Holyhead.

He survived the sinking, but died of dysentery, malnutrition and lack of medication whilst in captivity on 10th January 1916 and was interred at Bir Hakkim. After the war, his body was exhumed and reinterred in the Hadara Military Cemetery, in Alexandria, Egypt (grave No 52).

**Seaman William Thomas Jones, MFA**

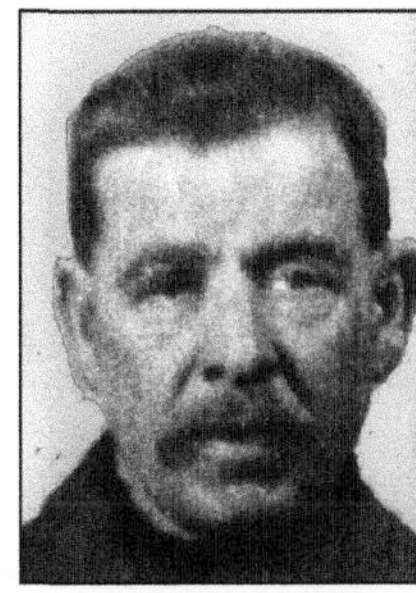

Of 5 Church Lane, Holyhead, he was born in Holyhead on 28th September 1874, one of three sons and two daughters of Thomas (a mariner) and Elizabeth Jones (an ex-stewardess on the steam packets). On leaving school, he had been employed in a bakery, but later went to sea. In January 1914 he joined the vessels of the City of Dublin Steam Packet Company, but was discharged on 10th April after which his movements are unknown. He is however believed to have joined HMS *Tara* in 1915.

He survived the sinking and after survivor's leave his movements are again unknown until 4th November 1916 when he married Miss Mary Jane Mullen at the Tabor Chapel in Valley, after which the couple resided at 22 Harp Street, Holyhead.

William joined the marine department of the L&NWR on 18th January 1918 and served aboard HM Transport *Scotia*. He left the company on 29th January 1920 and went/returned deep-sea. By December 1922 he was serving a bosun on SS *Hemisphere*. Sometime later he returned to the railway vessels where he remained until he retired aged sixty-five. He died on 29th May 1949 in Denbigh Hospital aged seventy-four and was interred in Maeshyfryd cemetery.

Although working full time on the railway vessels, he also served for a number of years with the steam lifeboat, firstly as a boatman, then for nine years as a bowman and eleven years as second coxswain. He was survived by his widow, his son, T W Jones, and his daughter and son-in-law.

**Seaman William Henry Parry, MFA**

Of 4 East Arthur Street, Holyhead. Born in Llaneilian, near Amlwch, Anglesey on 6th November 1881, he was the son of Henry, a copper miner, and Mary Parry, who at the time of William's birth were residing at Gadfa, Llaneilian with their daughter, Elizabeth. The family later moved to Glan-y-Don, Llaneilian by which time he had five more siblings: Hugh, Richard, Mary E (died in infancy), John and Owen. He joined the L&NWR on 10th May 1913 as a coal trimmer and was serving on the *Hibernia* when she was requisitioned and volunteered to go on active service on 15th August 1914 but, prior to 1 January 1915, he had transferred to the deck department and become a seaman.

Surviving the sinking of the *Tara*, he returned to company service on 19th May 1916 and remained on the railway vessels until retiring aged sixty-five. He died on 30th October 1955, aged seventy-four, and was interred in Maeshyfryd Cemetery. He left a widow, two sons and five daughters and resided at 4 East Arthur Street.

T.—124.

**This agreement is to be made out in duplicate. One copy is to be kept on board, and the other forwarded as soon as possible to the Director of Transports, Admiralty, London, S.W.**

**Particulars of Discharge, &c., of any Members of the Crew, and for the engagement of Substitutes, should be reported as soon as possible.**

# AGREEMENT AND ACCOUNT OF CREW.

## COMMISSIONED CHARTERED SHIP.

| NAME OF SHIP | Official No. | Port of Registry | Port No. and date of Register | Registered Tonnage | | Nominal Horse Power |
|---|---|---|---|---|---|---|
| | | | | Gross | Net | |
| | | | | | | |

| Registered Managing Owner | | |
|---|---|---|
| Name | Address | This ship is now chartered by the Lords Commissioners of the Admiralty under conditions which, during the continuances of the charter, constitute the ship one of His Majesty's ships. |
| | | |

The several persons whose names are hereunto subscribed, *being British subjects*, and whose descriptions are set forth against their signatures, hereby agree with ____________________ for and on behalf of the Lords Commissioners of the Admiralty to serve on board the said ship in the several capacities expressed against their respective names for any period not exceeding twelve months, or until seven days after the arrival of the ship in a port of Great Britain after the expiry of twelve months, but in no case to be bound to serve for more than 36 months.

(1.) The several persons whose names are hereunto subscribed agree that they shall be subject to the Naval Discipline Act:

(2.) Any offence committed by any such person shall be tried and punished as the like offence might be tried and punished if committed by any person in or belonging to His Majesty's Navy, and borne on the books of any of His Majesty's ships in commission:

(3.) Every such offender who is to be tried by Court-martial shall be placed under all necessary restraint until he can be tried by Court-martial:

(4.) On application made to the Lords of the Admiralty, or to the Commander-in-Chief, or senior officer of any of His Majesty's ships or vessels of war abroad authorised to assemble and hold Courts-martial, the Lords of the Admiralty, Commander-in-Chief, or senior officer (as the case may be) shall assemble and hold a Court-martial for the trial of the offender:

(5.) The officer commanding shall have the same power in respect of all other persons borne on the books or for the time being on board the same, as the officer commanding one of His Majesty's ships has for the time being in respect of the officers and crew thereof or other persons on board the same:

(6.) The Naval Commander-in-Chief and senior Naval Officer in His Majesty's Service shall have the same powers over the officers and crew as they have for the time being over the officers and crew of any of His Majesty's ships.

It is further agreed by the said ____________________ that provisions and clothing, and allowances in connection therewith, will be issued according to the Regulations for H.M. Naval Service, and that in the event of death or injury caused by acts of the enemy pensions or gratuities be granted in accordance with the Regulations printed on the last page hereof.

In witness whereof the same parties have subscribed their names on the other side hereof on the day specified against their respective signatures.

____________________ *Captain Royal Navy.*

This ________ day of ________________ 19

T. 1970/1908.

G & S 342 [2716] 500 4/08v P 342

**Seaman Albert James Learmouth, MFA**

Of 9 Leonard Street, Holyhead in 1922. He was the son of James (a boatman of the Royal Navy Coastguard Service) and Sarah Learmouth and had one sister and three brothers. During the 1870s the family moved to Holyhead and resided in Wynne Street. His father eventually left the coastguard and found employment with the steamers of the L&NWR.

Albert joined Trinity House, serving first as a seaman then as an electrical attendant on the Caernarfon Bay Light Vessel. On 18th June 1897, he was serving on the Bahama Bank light vessel off the Isle of Man and helped to affect the rescue of the crew of the SS *Roslin Glen* of Glasgow, a feat for which the crew of the light vessel — David Lewis, George Walford, Joseph Hughes, Richard Hughes and Albert Learmouth — were awarded the Lloyd's Bronze Medal for Saving Life.

On 26th December, in St Cybi's Church, he married twenty-four-year-old Mary Elizabeth Williams of the Cambrian Vaults, Holyhead. By the turn of the century the couple had a two-year-old daughter, May, and were residing at 12 Longford Terrace and Albert was serving on the SS *Triton,* a Trinity House vessel. He later came ashore and found employment as a cable jointer for the electrical department of the Holyhead Urban District Council.

On 11th August 1914 he joined the marine department of the L&NWR and volunteered to go on active service on the *Hibernia* on the 15th. He survived the sinking and, after rescued, returned to company service on 16th May 1916, but left on 17th April 1917 to go deep sea. At the end of the war he was serving as a lamplighter on the SS *Orotova* on the North Atlantic service. He died aged seventy-one on 13th August 1940 at West Orchard Lane, Fazakerley, Liverpool.

**Seaman John Jones, MFA**

Of 1 Erw Terrace, Holyhead. Born on 18th March 1885, he was the eldest son of William Jones of one of HMS *Tara*'s leading stokers (see below). He was a deep sea sailor who, on the outbreak of war, was serving aboard P&O's *Karmala,* which he joined on 12th June 1914, having been paid off the SS *Linmere.* He was paid of the *Karmala* on 8th March 1915 and is believed to have joined the *Tara* in May whilst she was in dry dock in Holyhead.

He survived the sinking but, after survivors leave, did not sign on the vessels of the L&NWR but returned deep sea. In early 1918, he was serving as bosun on the HMT *Carmania,* and later as quartermaster on the SS *Nellore.* He was mentioned in despatches (*London Gazette,* 7th August 1918) 'For good services and for his zeal

*Facing: Form T.124: Agreement and Account of Crew, Commissioned Chartered Ship. It is almost impossible to determine when some members of a ship's crew joined, as on her requisition the L&NWR's crew agreements could technically be done away with as the Royal Navy, having now in effect chartered the vessel, could employ their own crew, and only required their crew agreements to be signed. This was called Form T.124 in which the signatory signed that he was willing to serve under Navy terms and conditions on board a specific vessel for as long as she was under the White Ensign. Unfortunately these completed forms cannot now be found. However the L&NWR did continue to use their crew agreements to sign some of the company men on and off the four express steamers whilst they were under naval requisition.*

and devotion to duty for carrying on the trade of the country during the war.'

He remained deep sea and served on a wide variety of ships and companies as quartermaster, but mostly as boatswain, until he retired, aged seventy, in 1955.

**Seaman John Hughes Swaine, MFA**

Of 14 Robert Street, Holyhead. Born in Stanley Street, Holyhead on 19th June 1875. He first went to sea as an apprentice on the sailing vessel *Celtic Chief* (William Thomas & Co of Liverpool) then served on the vessels of the Royal Mail Steam Packet Company. Tiring of the mercantile marine he joined the Royal Navy on 1st March 1900, entering the shore-based HMS *Pembroke* at Chatham where he was rated as an ordinary seaman. Promoted to able-bodied seaman on 24th July 1900, he was appointed to HMS *Galatea* on 6th Sept 1900. On 5th September 1901 he deserted, but was caught, and on 31st December 1904 was dismissed the service as being 'not suitable to be claimed by the Royal Navy', during his service he had two spells in the cells.

He then found employment with Trinity House, serving on the SS *Triton* before joining the L&NWR as fireman on 18th January 1915. He was discharged on 6th August 1915, but re-joined the L&NWR and changed departments, from the Engine to the Deck Department and joined HMS *Tara* on the 14th as a seaman. After rescue, he returned to company service on 3rd July 1916 and joined the SS *Galteemore* but was paid off on 19th September. He then enlisted into the ranks of the Inland Waterways Transport Department of the Royal Engineers and served in Mesopotamia where he was employed on the River Tigris in shipping supplies for the advancing army up river from Basra. During his military service he was promoted to sergeant and, in 1918, was mentioned in despatches. He was demobilised in June 1919 and on 26th November rejoined the L&NWR where he remained until retirement.

In later life he resided in Kings Road but then lived with his daughter at 9 Windsor Avenue, Connah's Quay where he died, aged eighty. He was interred in St Seiriol's Churchyard, Holyhead on 17th November 1954.

He was survived by his daughter and two sons, Richard David and David Lewis, his wife Jane Ann having died in 1946.

**Seaman Griffith Tatem Jones, MFA**

Born 11 Britannia Terrace, Portdinorwic on 31st December 1895, he was the ninth child (six sons and three daughters) of Henry (a principle customs officer) and Grace Jones.

Griffith had signed off the schooner *David Morris of Caernarvon* in London on 7th February 1915 (having signed on at Hamburg on 22nd May 1914), then joined the City of Dublin Steam Packet Company's vessels at Holyhead on 20th May 1915. Leaving them he joined HMS *Tara* on 15th September. During this time he lodged at 16 Cybi Street, Holyhead. He survived the sinking but, after rescue, did not join the L&NWR cross-channel service.

Whether he returned to sea immediately after survivor's leave is unknown, but in December 1918 he joined the SS *Derbyshire* and thereafter it seems he remained deep sea. He later joined Ellerman Lines as a quartermaster and remained with the company until he died in August 1954, when his ship, the SS *City of Derby* was at Port Sudan

**Seaman John Lewis Jones, MFA** [Author]
Of 9 Water Street, Holyhead. Born 20th April 1870 in Tŷ Bach, Foel, Llangeinwen, one of six children of Lewis, a ship's carpenter, and Elizabeth Jones. John had been in the employ of the L&NWR since 12th July 1895 and, on the outbreak of war, was serving on the *Hibernia* as a quartermaster. He volunteered to go on active service on 15th August 1914 but it is believed through sickness or family matters he did not sail to the North Channel with *Tara* on 18th August, Seaman W. Thomas or R Abbit being promoted in his place. He did however join the *Tara* at Larne on 14th September as a seaman to replace seaman J Mitchell who had deserted (why he then did not claim his position back is unknown).

He survived the sinking and, after leave, returned to company service on 19th May 1916 in his old rank of quartermaster. He remained on the L&NWR's vessels until he died of a cerebral haemorrhage at his home on 14th August 1931, leaving a widow, Ann, and four children, Gladys, Thomas, David and Edith (Thomas emigrated to America in 1927 and David in 1937). Both his sons served in the American Mercantile Marine during the Second World War.

**Seaman Thomas Pritchard, MFA** [Author]
Of 1 Glascoed Road, Cemaes Bay, Anglesey. Born 1865 in Cemaes, the son of Owen, a mariner, he had been employed as a farm labourer before going to sea. In 1892, when he was an able bodied seaman on the sailing flat/lighter, *Reciprocity* (belonging to the lighterage company Thomas Thompson of Liverpool), he married Elizabeth Roberts, the daughter of Robert Roberts a farmer of Ty'n y Gors Farm near Llanfechell, in Bethesda Chapel, Amlwch. Shortly afterwards, on the death of his father-in-law, Thomas took up the running of the farm and over the next few years he and Elizabeth had four children Jane, twins Robert and John (John died shortly after birth) and Lizzie. Further tragedy struck the family on 26th March 1908 when Elizabeth died, aged forty-one, after which it seems Thomas gave up farming and returned to the sea.

For a time he was employed on the Liverpool & North Wales Steamship Company's paddler *St Elvies*, but she was withdrawn from service in 1914 to have new boilers fitted. He then found employment in Liverpool on the tugs belonging to Alexander Towing and served on the tug *Wapping* before joining the Marine Department of the L&NWR on 3rd December 1914. Initially serving on cargo vessels, he joined HMS *Tara* on 25th September 1915, relieving Seaman G J Jones whilst she was on refit at Holyhead. Prior to sailing for service in the Mediterranean it is thought Thomas may have lodged at Arthur Street, Kingsland whilst working in Holyhead.

Although Thomas survived the torpedoing and imprisonment, he succumbed to the effects of his ordeal in the N° 21 General Hospital, Alexandria on 4th April 1916 and was buried in Chatby Military Cemetery the following day.

**Seaman Owen Hughes, MFA**

Of 12, Ty'n Ffynnon, Cemaes, Anglesey. He had been born in either Liverpool or Birkenhead on 8th July 1894. Owen was not a pre-war L&NWR seaman and it is believed he joined HMS *Tara* in 1915. He survived the sinking and, after rescue and survivor's leave, enlisted into the Royal Navy Reserve on 29th May 1916 at HMS *Amethyst III*, the base ship in Holyhead(service number DA11294, rated deck hand) and was appointed firstly to the yacht HMS *Vanessa II*, then on 11th August 1918 to HM Trawler *Bengal II*, from which vessel he was discharged at Grimsby on 22nd March 1919.

On the 2nd August 1918 he married nineteen-year-old Annie Myfanwy Jones in St Cybi's Church and they resided with her parents at Porthyrafon, Baptist Street in Holyhead. After demobilisation he signed on the L&NWR's Holyhead steamers on 4th April 1919 but left the company on 4th October 1919, joining the SS *Nestor* of Alfred Holt & Co later the same month. He remained with the Blue Funnel Line for some time and served at sea throughout the Second World War. He was still at sea in December 1952, serving with Coast Lines, but after this date his movements are unknown.

**Seaman William Black, MFA**

Of 31 Cornwallis Street, Liverpool. Born Liverpool 2nd September 1882, he was amongst the first batch of men sent from Liverpool to Holyhead between 11th and 13th August 1914. On the 29th August 1914, when HMS *Tara* first called at Larne to replenish her bunkers, he was given extra duty and fined one day's pay for breaking leave. On 10th June 1915, he was placed in the cells, but his conduct and ability must have been satisfactory as he was allowed to remain on the ship. He survived the sinking and returned home on HMHS *Dunluce Castle* but was considered too ill to travel home to Liverpool so was hospitalised in the Haslar Naval Hospital. After his discharge and a spell of leave, he was to report to HMS *Victory* on 12th May 1916 'Prior to being re-employed on the Holyhead vessels.' Whether he reported as instructed is unknown but he did not report to Holyhead and it would appear that he left the sea.

William Black died in Liverpool in 1946 and was survived by his wife of forty years, Florence, and their four children.

**Seaman Henry Alfred Hughes, MFA**

Of 17 Sadler Street, Blowhill, Liverpool. He was born in Liverpool on 11th January 1887 and joined the Royal Navy on 1st Aril 1903 as a domestic third class, giving his civilian occupation as a waiter, and served in the shore base HMS *Vivid* at Portsmouth until 20th December of that year when he 'ran', (this was not considered to be desertion as he had not yet signed on to undertake a period of service with the Royal Navy). During his brief stay with the Navy his character was described as 'Fair' but had spent three days in the cells. Returning to Liverpool, he found employment as a dock labourer and later as a seaman. At the time of his serving on HMS *Tara,* he was single and residing with his parents, James and Margaret Hughes, at 17 Sadler Street, Liverpool.

Alfred Hughes had been amongst the first batch of seamen and firemen sent from Canning Place, Liverpool and during his time on HMS *Tara* he was given extra duty and fined one day's pay for breaking leave when she paid her first visit to Larne on 29th August 1914. His behaviour seems to have improved and he was retained and survived the sinking, eventually returning home on the *Dunluce Castle*. Like William Black, he was hospitalised at Haslar Naval Hospital and then ordered to report to HMS *Victory* on 12th May 1916, prior to being re-employed on the Holyhead vessels. Whether he reported to HMS *Victory* is unknown, but he did not report to Holyhead.

A few weeks after returning home he married Lily Ann Marshall of West Derby. It is not known whether he returned to sea but, in later life, he became a porter in a tobacco warehouse and died on 7th June 1950, aged sixty-three, at his home 25 Cupid Street, Liverpool.

**Seaman Peter McMillan, MFA** [Campbeltown Archives]

Of 14 Fisher Row, Campbeltown. Born 1879 in Campbeltown, the son of Peter and Mary McMillan, who had at least three sons and three daughters. He was a fisherman. On 21st June 1900, he married Jane McKerrel Howie. He joined HMS *Tara* when she was based at Campbeltown and survived her sinking and the ordeal of the crew. He arrived back in Campbeltown, with Charles McNaughton, on 25th April 1916, and, after survivor's leave, does not appear to have returned to sea-going employment.

He later worked at a local distillery and died on 14th October 1955, when he was residing at 131 Ralston Road in Campbeltown.

**Deck Boy William Jones, MFA**

Of 6 Baker Street, Holyhead. Born in Holyhead on 9th October 1899 he joined the L&NWR on 8th June 1914 and was serving on the *Hibernia* when she was requisitioned and he volunteered to go on active service on 15th August 1914. After rescue, he returned to company service on 16th May 1916 and was shortly afterwards promoted to ordinary seaman.

He retired as a seaman from the British Railways cargo vessels in 1964 when he was residing at 44 Queens Park in Holyhead. He died in the Stanley Hospital, Salt Island in Holyhead on 7th April 1968, aged sixty-eight, leaving a widow, Ann Ellen, one son, Cedric (who became a charge hand plumber at the Marine Yard workshops) and a daughter, Mildred. His body was interred in Maeshyfryd Cemetery.

William Jones's brother, John, served in France with the N° 2 (Holyhead) Siege Company Royal Anglesey Royal Engineers and survived the war.

*Petty Officers and Ratings of the Engine Room Department*

**Electrician Wallace Charles Vernon Cooke, MFA**

Of Belle Vue, St Helen's Street, Corbridge-on-Tyne, but had been born in Clerkenwell, London on 29th July 1877. He was one of the four children of Frederick William and Susanna L Cooke (née Yates). Shortly after his birth the family moved to Gravel Mount, Ordsall, Retford, where his father became a telegraph inspector for the Great Northern Railway. During the 1900s Wallace, by then a qualified electrical engineer, was the proprietor of a cycle repairer business in Retford.

On 24th April 1915 he joined HMS *Tara* at Holyhead to relieve Electrician Ernest Lawton. He survived the sinking, but, after rescue, his movements are mostly unknown although at the time he gave his home address as Corbridge-on-Tyne, but by 1918 he was residing in Islington, Liverpool.

He died suddenly on 30th March 1949, aged seventy-one, at the Llandough Hospital in Penarth, his home address at the time being 12 Greenfield Avenue in Dinas Powys. He left a widow, Mildred Jenny (née Harvey, of East Retford) whom he had married during the summer of 1921. It appears that Wallace Cooke was a quiet, reserved man who kept very much to himself, preferring to tend his garden. Prior to retiring had been employed as an electrician for British Railways.

**Boilermaker George Matthew Cox, MFA** [Holyhead Maritime Museum]

Of Arvon House, 3 Cybi Street, Holyhead. Born on 1st February 1858 in Waterside, Holyhead, he was the son of John, a seaman, and Mary Cox, and the only brother of Mary, Hannah, Elizabeth, Catherine and Susannah. In 1871, he joined the L&NWR as an apprentice boilermaker in their Marine Yard Workshops. On 10th May 1888 he married Mary Catherine Jones of Edmund Street. Initially the couple resided at 8 Park Street in Holyhead, during which time they lost a daughter, Annie Ada, who died aged two on 28th March 1894.

Sometime between the 11th and 15th August he volunteered for active service on the express steamers and was appointed to HMS *Tara*. He served on her throughout and survived the sinking. He was suffering a stricture of the urethra, for which he had to use a catheter to relieve himself, unfortunately, on abandoning ship, he had to leave this behind and in consequence suffered terribly until he died on 6th January 1916 of uric acid poisoning, compounded by dysentery and malnutrition. He was buried at Bir Hakkim. After the war his body was exhumed and reinterred in Chatby Military Cemetery, Alexandria (grave N° 51).

His wife Mary Catherine had died, age fifty, on 16th June 1913 and they had nine children, of whom eight survived — five sons, John Matthew, George Matthew, Richard, Edward Richard and William Meredith, and two daughters, Catherine Ellen and Beatrice. Two sons served with the colours during the war — George in N° 2 (Holyhead) Siege Company, Royal Anglesey Royal Engineers and Edward in the King's Liverpool Regiment.

**Leading Stoker Robert Phillips, MFA** [Mr R Phillips]

Of 14 Well Street, Holyhead. Born in Holyhead in 1859, he had been employed by the L&NWR since 6th February 1880. He was serving on the *Hibernia* when she was requisitioned and volunteered to go on active service on 15th August 1914. At the time the vessel was torpedoed he was off watch and in bed. The cabin was shattered by the explosion and it was assumed that he had been killed instantly.

Robert Phillips was the husband of Mary and they had six daughters, Mary Maria, Maggie, Hannah, Lizzie, Sarah and Lilly and two sons, Robert and James Merfyn. They also had an adopted son, Harry Evan Davies, aged only two when Robert Phillips died.

**Leading Stoker William Jones, MFA** (*Holyhead Chronicle*)
Born Llaindrain, Holyhead in 1859. In 1914 he was residing at Bryn Meilian, 1 Erw Terrace in Holyhead. He joined the L&NWR on 5th July 1880 and, on the outbreak of war, was serving on the *Hibernia* and volunteered to go on active service on 15th August 1914. He was off watch in his cabin asleep when the torpedo struck. The cabin was shattered and it is more than likely he was killed instantaneously. He left a widow, Martha Mary, and seven children; Elizabeth, Maggie Jane, John, Kate, Robert William, Owen Richard and Annie Grace.

In 1884, William Jones had come ashore to work as a railway goods porter but, by 1895, had returned to the ships where he remained until his death. His eldest son, John, an able seaman, was serving with him on HMS *Tara* and survived both the sinking and the subsequent ordeal of the survivors. Two other sons joined the colours, Robert William serving in France with the Nº 2 (Holyhead) Siege Company, Royal Anglesey Royal Engineers, who survived the war, and Owen Richard, a lance corporal in the 14th Royal Welsh Fusiliers, who was killed in action in France on 20th March 1916. William's wife, Martha Mary, died on 31st March 1935 at 1 Erw Terrace and was interred in Maeshyfryd cemetery. Both William and Owen Richard are commemorated on her headstone.

**Acting Leading Stoker Thomas Robert Jones, MFA** (*Holyhead Chronicle*)
Of 25 Cybi Place, Holyhead. Born in Holyhead in 1859 and had served with the City of Dublin Steam Packet Company for eighteen years before seeking employment with the L&NWR on 29th March 1900. On the outbreak of war, he was serving as a fireman on the *Hibernia* and volunteered to go on active service on 15th August 1914. When the torpedo struck he was in the engine room and it was thought he was most probably killed instantly by the explosion. He was last seen alive by Fireman William J Andrews.

Thomas Jones was the husband of Elizabeth Catherine and father of two daughters, Lizzie and Annie, and one son, Owen.

**Greaser Owen Davies, MFA** (W Davies)
Of 5 Trearddur Square, Holyhead. Born in Holyhead on 25th July 1868. Prior to joining the L&NWR on 1st October 1896 he had served with the White Star Line and had also seen twenty-years service with the RNR. He was serving aboard the *Hibernia* when she was requisitioned and volunteered to go on active service on 15th August 1914. He survived the sinking and, after rescue, returned to company service on 16th May 1916 but was discharged 31st December 1917. He does not appear to have returned to the steamers but retired as a donkeyman (possibly as a shore-donkeyman, tending the main, or donkey, boilers of the off duty or laid up vessels as they lay alongside), but retired in July 1933. The local paper stated in December 1950 that he '... still suffers from the injuries he received when he jumped into a lifeboat as HMS *Tara* was sinking.'

Owen Davies was married to Margaret and they had six children, three sons, Hugh John, Owen and William, and three daughters, Catherine Ellen, Ann Jane and Lizzie. He died on

31st December 1955, aged eighty-eight, still residing at 5 Trearddur Square, and was interred in St Seiriol's Churchyard.

**Greaser Hugh Owen Hughes, MFA**

Of 17 Queens Park, Holyhead. Born in 19 Llainfain, Holyhead on 2th December 1881, the son of Richard, a fireman, and Mary Hughes, and the brother of William, Richard, Margaret , Catherine and Mary. At the turn of the century he was residing with his brother Richard's family at Fron on Holyhead Mountain. He had been employed as an agricultural labourer until he joined the L&NWR on 14th August 1902 as a coal trimmer. He was serving on the *Hibernia* when she was requisitioned and volunteered to go on active service on 15th August 1914. Prior to the *Tara*'s sinking he suffered from a rupture on the left side despite which, during the period of captivity, he was noted as 'a tower of strength.' He returned to company service on 19th May 1916, his hernia having been operated on in Alexandria. In 1919 he was voted onto the Holyhead Urban District Council and on 9th November 1920 was promoted leading stoker on the railway vessels.

In August 1926, he was serving on the *Scotia* and whilst she was alongside at Dun Loaghaire, a passenger fell overboard at night, between the quay and ship. Immediately Engineer Officer Devonald and Leading Fireman Hughes dived overboard to his rescue, Further assistance was later given by Engineer Officer William Griffith. For their actions, the men received letters from Mr Glynne Roberts, the Assistant General Manager of the LMS Railway congratulating them on the part they had played in the rescue.

On the outbreak of the Second World War he was still serving on the *Scotia* and in May 1940 went with her to Dunkirk to help evacuate the British Expeditionary Force. He was wounded when she was sunk by enemy bombers on 1st June and spent some two months in a hospital 'somewhere in England.' After this he retired on health grounds. At this time he was residing at 9 Station Street.

Hugh Hughes died on 23rd June 1947 at his home, Bryn Maelog, 24 Station Street, aged sixty-five, a well-known and respected man. He had retired as a leading stoker having served some forty-two years at sea. His obituary recorded that 'By example and precept [he] made a valuable contribution towards sustaining the moral of his suffering fellow prisoners [and] upon returning to Holyhead ... took an active and leading part in the legitimate recognition of ex-Servicemen's rights.'

He had married Elizabeth Margaret Rae of 1 Hawthorn Terrace, Church Road, Dublin at the Welsh Chapel in Talbot Street, Dublin on 27th February 1908. He lost his wife on 4th December 1939 and was survived by his step daughter, Alicia.

**Greaser William George Cooper, MFA**

Of National School House, Holyhead but, prior to the war, he had resided at 12 Edgar Terrace, King's Road in Holyhead. Born in Portsmouth on 5th October 1880, he had joined the Royal Navy on 8th December 1895 and was posted to HMS *Ganges* as a band boy. He signed on for twelve-year's service as a bandsman on 5th October 1898 and served on various ships including *Hannibal, Majestic* and *St Vincent* until he was paid off at HMS *Victory* on 13th March 1907.

In 1903, George married Helena Thereza Tracey at St Mary's Catholic Church, Holyhead and it would seem that the couple made their home in the town. On 2nd April 1908 he joined the marine department of the L&NWR and by July 1914 was serving as a coal trimmer aboard the *Hibernia*. He volunteered to go on active service on 15th August 1915 serving as a greaser (a man who oiled and greased the machinery, which was mostly reciprocating within the engine room). After his rescue he returned to company service on 16th May 1916 and remained with the company, serving aboard both passenger and cargo vessels, until he retired in 1945.

George died in May 1961, aged eighty, and was survived by his son William Patrick and two daughters Lilian Ada and Mrs Helena Thereza May with whom he was residing at 65, Kilmore Road, Lewisham.

**Fireman Owen Hughes Roberts, MFA** [Holyhead Maritime Museum]
Of 23 Llainfain, Holyhead. Born in Holyhead in 1888, the son of Jane Roberts and the late Robert Roberts. He joined the L&NWR's Marine Department on 16th December 1913, prior to which he had been employed by the company as a pier trimmer (a member of the shore side coaling or bunkering gang). He joined HMS *Tara* on 13th March 1915 as a fireman and survived the sinking but died in captivity on 19th February 1916 of tuberculosis, dysentery and malnutrition and was buried later the same day. After the war his body was exhumed and reinterred at the Chatby War Cemetery, Alexandria. He was unmarried but had been courting Maggie, the daughter of Leading Stoker Robert Phillips.

**Fireman John Parry, MFA** (*Holyhead Chronicle*)
Of 7 George Street, Holyhead. Born in 1859 in Llanddeusant, Anglesey. On 9th September 1884 he joined the L&NWR's Marine Department (it is believed that he had worked in another department as he had been with the railway since he was seventeen-years-old). He was serving on the *Hibernia* when she was requisitioned and volunteered to go on active service on 15th August 1914. Although his rating was that of fireman he served as the ship's electric-light man — he looked after the electrical generating sets, putting the dynamos on and off on the main switchboard so as to supply electricity throughout the ship. At the time of the explosion he was in his bed and vacated his cabin immediately, but decided to return to obtain some clothing and his money. He was last seen going down to his room by Fireman Owen Pritchard who had tried to deter him. It was assumed that he was drowned when the ship went down.

John Parry left a widow, Mary Ann, and a daughter, Lilian Augusta. At the time of his death his parents, Robert and Margaret Parry, were residing at 8 Trearddur Square in Holyhead. John had been a deacon at the Mount Pleasant Congregational Church.

**Fireman John Ellis Jones, MFA** (*Holyhead Chronicle*)
Of 10 Lligwy Street, Holyhead. Born in 4 Back Jew Street in Holyhead in 1878, he had joined

the L&NWR as a brakeman in the shunting yards in 1895. On 23rd December 1907 he transferred to the marine department and was appointed a coal trimmer. By the outbreak of war he was serving as a fireman and volunteered to go on active service on 14th August. When HMS *Tara* was torpedoed, he was on watch and was last seen in the engine room some five minutes before the explosion by Fireman Owen Roberts. It was assumed that he was most probably killed at once. John was the husband of Catherine and the father of two children, Richard Ellis and Jane, who were aged four and five at the time of his death.

Further tragedy hit the family shortly after *Tara's* sinking, as his brother-in-law Robert Williams of Tandderwen, Garden Place, London Road, Holyhead a Cabin Boy was killed on 15th November 1915 in the sinking of HMHS *Anglia,* then on 24th June 1917. John's father-in-law, a fireman on the *Cambria,* and also of Tandderwen, died at home. .

**Fireman Thomas Doughty, MFA**

In 1916 he resided at Minffordd, Llanfihangel-yn-Nhowyn, Caergeiliog, Anglesey. He born at 26 Llaingoch, Holyhead on 21st October 1893. On leaving school he became a farm labourer then joined the L&NWR on 22nd December 1913 and was serving on the *Hibernia* when he volunteered to go on active service on 15th August 1914. He survived the sinking and, after rescue, returned to company service on 16th May 1916 joining the SS *Slieve Bloom,* and was on board when she was rammed and sunk by the USS *Eriksson* on the night of 30th March 1918. In 1940, he was on board the SS *Slieve Donard* when, about twenty-two miles from Greenore, she was attacked by a German torpedo bomber, but escaped unscathed.

Thomas Doughty retired as a leading stoker on the SS *Slieve League* on 24th October 1958. He died on 6th January 1971, aged seventy-seven, at Valley Hospital and was interred in Maeshyfryd with his wife, Ellen (née Parry), whom he had married on 21st December 1914 and who had died ten years previously.

**Fireman John Owen Bagnall, MFA**

Of 59 Foundry Street, Holyhead. Born in Holyhead on 12th August 1881, he had joined the L&NWR on 15th October 1912 from the City of Dublin Steam Packet Company. He joined HMS *Tara* on 18th September 1914 at Larne, to replace Fireman Richard Evans who was paid off due to illness. After rescue, he returned to company service on 16th May 1916. In 1918 he was serving aboard HM Ambulance Transport *Cambria.*

Sometime prior to the Second World War he suffered a breakdown and would not leave the house, only emerging on the death of his wife Jane Ann in March 1942. He later recovered and found employment in the officers' mess at RAF Valley where he met and in 1943 married Marcella Thompson, a widow from Scotland, who was a cook in the same mess.

John died in Denbigh on 9th October 1949, aged sixty-eight, and was interred in Maeshyfryd Cemetery. At the time of his death he was residing at 12 Bryn Môr, Turkey Shore Road. He was survived by his second wife and sons George, John Owen, Robert, Albert, Glyn and daughters, Annie and Joyce.

**Fireman Richard Jones, MFA**

Of 3 Mill Bank Terrace, Holyhead. Born in Holyhead in 1885, the son of Hugh and Annie Jane Jones and the elder brother of Annie, Jane, Lizzie and Owen. He transferred from the carriage cleaning department of the L&NWR to the marine department on 13th March 1913 where he was employed as a coal trimmer. On 1st July 1914 he was promoted to fireman and was serving on the *Hibernia* when she was requisitioned. On 15th August 1914 he volunteered to go on active service. He survived the sinking and, after rescue, returned to company service on 16th May 1916.

Richard Jones died on Tuesday 16th March 1920, aged thirty-five, and was interred in Maeshyfryd Cemetery. According to the local paper the privations he suffered during captivity had contributed in no small way to his death. He was a bachelor.

**Fireman Richard Jones, MFA**

Born on 19th July 1893, the son of John, a carter, and Margaret Jones, of 28 Mount Street, Bangor. He had two sisters, Kate and Sarah, and four brothers, John, Owen, Noah and William.

He is believed to have joined HMS *Tara* in 1915. After survivor's leave he enlisted into the RNR on 3rd July 1916 at the Holyhead Base Ship *Amethyst III*.and three days later joined HM Trawler *Daisy Bank*. He was demobilised from the paddle minesweeper HMS *Sandown* and joined the L&NWR on 27th November 1919. By this time he had married Ann Elizabeth Thomas and the couple had four sons Ernest, Idris, William and Idwal, and three daughters Sarah, Margaret and Eurwen. Initially, the family resided at 8 Kingsland, Holyhead, and later moved to 13 Kingsland.

He retired in September 1958 after forty-four years of service on the railway vessels and died in August 1973 aged eighty, at the home of his eldest daughter in Ashbourne, Derbyshire where he had been living for some twelve months. The funeral was held at Derby and his remains were cremated then brought back to Holyhead and interred in Maeshyfryd cemetery in the same grave as his wife, who had died on 1st June 1933. Also commemorated on the headstone is their son Ernest, a merchant seaman, who died aged nineteen, on the SS *Flying Kite* at Clydeside on 14th November 1939, and Idris, an ordinary seaman RN, also aged nineteen, who was killed when Landing Craft Infantry (Large) 162 was torpedoed by the *U-596* whilst en route to Algiers from Oran on 7th February 1943 (eighteen killed, seven survivors).

**Fireman Owen Pritchard, MFA** [Author]

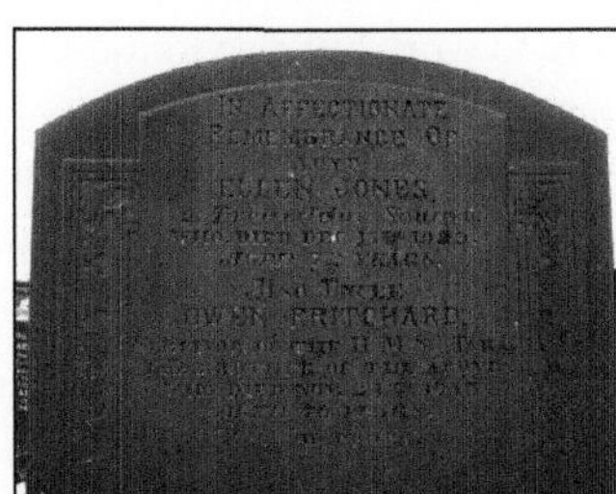


Of 2 Trearddur Square, Holyhead where he resided with his sister Ellen. Owen Pritchard was born in Holyhead in 1863 and joined the L&NWR on 29th October 1883. On 1st July 1914 he was serving as a coal trimmer on the *Hibernia* and volunteered to go on active service on 15th August 1914 and was promoted to fireman. He survived the sinking and, after rescue, returned to company service as a coal trimmer on 19th May 1916.

He died on 24th November 1933, aged seventy, at 2 Trearddur Square (where he was residing with his niece Elizabeth Williams and her husband Richard Robert Williams after the death of his sister in 1929).

On 1st November 1914, his sister Ellen's thirty-five-year-old adopted son, Able Seaman William Jones, RN (194073) was killed in action at the battle of Coronel when HMS *Monmouth* was lost with all hands.

**Fireman Hugh Hughes, MFA** [Brian Jones]
Of 1 Pump Street, Holyhead. Born in Holyhead on 25th August 1893. His pre-war employment is unknown but it is believed that he joined HMS *Tara* in 1915. He survived the sinking of the *Tara* and, on 27th June 1916, joined the RNR at the Holyhead Base ship HMS *Amethyst III* and was appointed to HM Trawler *Merse* as a coal trimmer. On 1st July 1917 he joined HMT *Sapper* and was assumed to have drowned with the rest of the crew when she struck a mine off the Owers Light Vessel in the English Channel on 29th December 1917.

Hugh was the son of the late Hugh (a fireman on the local vessels) and Mary Hughes and the brother of John, Anne, Grace, Mary Ellen and Maggie Elizabeth. Further tragedy hit the family in September 1918 when Mary Ellen's husband, Corporal Arthur Pidgeon (47482), 15th Battalion, The Welsh Regiment, was killed in action in France.

**Fireman Roland Williams, MFA** (*Holyhead Chronicle*)
Of 3 Old Station, Holyhead. Born in Llanynghenedl in 1887, he was the son of Richard (a foreman in the railway cattle yards) and Jane Williams and the brother of Ellen, Richard Morris, William Owen and Maggie. By all accounts Roland was a natural and a gifted football player, known locally as the 'The Doctor'. On 11th August 1914 he joined the L&NWR's marine department as a coal trimmer on the company's cargo vessels, transferring from the locomotive department where he had been employed as a footplate fireman. During September 1915 he transferred over to HMS *Tara* having been promoted to fireman.

He survived the sinking and, after rescue, returned to company service as a coal trimmer, however, owing to the privations he had suffered in the desert, he became seriously ill and was off work for sometime. Such was the concern for his health throughout the town that, on Saturday, 18th September 1920, when Messers McCormack & Davies donated the proceeds of the last house at the Empire Theatre to his family. He did eventually recover and returned not only to work but also to football as was a member of the Holyhead Railway Institute FC team that won the North Wales League (Division 1) in 1920–1.

On the night of 9th June 1924, whilst on his way to join his ship, the SS *Curraghmore*, he collapsed in the Holyhead Station approach and was taken to the Station Hotel where he died. Although he resided at 14 Millbank, Holyhead, his body was interred at Rhoscolyn. He left a widow, Mary whom he had married on 4th June 1918, and a daughter, Perry Kathleen.

At a meeting of the Holyhead Football Club on 27th June 1924, the chairman, when referring to Roland's death mentioned that he had rendered yeoman service for twenty years as a playing member of the local team.

**Fireman John Jones, MFA** (*Holyhead Chronicle*)

Of 3 College Lane, Holyhead. He was born in Holyhead in 1865, the son of Hugh and Jane Jones and the family resided at 5 Boston Street. His mother died in April 1892 and his father, a coal porter at the port, married Mrs Ellen Roberts, a widow of 3 College Lane, in January 1893. John Jones joined the L&NWR in their carriage and wagon department. On 26th May 1900 he transferred over to the Marine Department as a coal trimmer. By 1914 he was a fireman, serving on the passenger cargo/cargo vessels, but came ashore to work in the Marine Yard fitting shop as a labourer. It is thought that he joined HMS *Tara* sometime in 1915.

John survived the sinking but, by the time of his rescue, his weight had dropped down to six stone. He recovered and on 16th May 1916 returned to the L&NWR vessels but was discharged on 3rd August 1917. It seems he then worked ashore for the railway until he retired in 1930 aged sixty-five.

On the death of his father and step mother John remained at their home where he resided with his step brother and his wife. John died a bachelor on 19th March 1938, aged seventy-three, and is buried in Maeshyfryd cemetery.

**Fireman Rhys Jones, MFA**

Of 17 Harp Street, Holyhead, but born in Llanddeusant, Anglesey on 29th March 1877. Prior to serving aboard HMS *Tara* he was a general labourer in the L&NWR's goods yard. The date of his joining HMS *Tara* is unknown but is believed to be in 1915. He survived the sinking and, after rescue, joined the L&NWR's marine department as a coal trimmer on 27th July 1917. He left the railway vessels on 24th January 1920, possibly due to ill health, and died on 29th April 1933, aged fifty-six, the death certificate describing him as a 'Ships Stoker, Merchant Service (Retired)'. At this time, he was residing at 2 Queens Terrace with his wife, Mary, and two sons, Owen and Hugh. He is buried in Maeshyfryd cemetery

**Fireman Richard Lewis, MFA** (*Holyhead Chronicle*)

Of 22 Llainfain, Holyhead. Born in Holyhead on 23rd July 1875. Prior to the war he worked as a general labourer, probably for the L&NWR. He joined HMS *Tara*, his first ship, on 19th July 1915. When she was torpedoed, Richard had jumped into the sea, but, in doing so had collided with the gangway injuring his stomach. This problem was possibly aggravated by the conditions of his captivity so that, after rescue, he had to undergo a hernia operation at the N° 21 Hospital in Alexandria.

Richard Lewis returned to company service on 19th May 1916 but, due to his injuries, was discharged on 7th July. It seems he suffered a breakdown from which he never recovered and as a consequence, spent a number of years as an in-patient at Gors Hospital in Holyhead. Although he did undergo a series of treatments and operations, they all proved ineffective. He died, aged sixty-two, on 7th March 1938 at his home in Llainfain. He left a widow, Margaret Ellen, two sons, William and Richard, and one daughter, Sally. A second daughter, Elizabeth Ann, had died aged fourteen on 30th August 1922. He is buried in Maeshyfryd cemetery.

**Fireman William Griffith, MFA**

Of Fron, Holyhead Mountain. Born in Holyhead on 9th March 1892, he joined HMS *Tara* on 25th August 1915, from the vessels of the City of Dublin Steam Packet Company, although a deep-sea man, having previously served on the Cunard liner RMS *Mauretania*. He survived the sinking and, after rescue, joined the L&NWR's marine department on 19th May 1916. In July, he was appointed to the HMHS *Cambria* and on 11th December 1917 transferred to HMT *Scotia* from which he was discharged on 5th Feb 1918 and returned to deep sea, joining the Dominion Line's SS *Turcoman*. He saw the war out on the White Star Line's SS *Cretic*, having joined her on 3rd October 1918. He remained at sea, but eventually came ashore to work and retired from the carriage and wagon department of British Railways, Holyhead in 1957, aged sixty-five.

William Griffith died on 13th January 1971 at his home 7 Maes-y-Mynydd, aged seventy-eight, and was interred in Maeshyfryd Cemetery, leaving his wife of fifty years, Margaret, three sons, Hywel Morris, Hefin Vaughan, William John, and five daughters, Mary, Glenys, Megan, Elizabeth Mary and Eleanor.

**Fireman Hugh Jones, MFA**

Of Siloh Baptist Chapel House, Holyhead Mountain where he resided with his widowed mother (who ran a farm or small holding) and his four brothers, John, Owen, Richard and Harold (see below), and three sisters, Elizabeth, Hannah and Susannah. He was born in Holyhead on 13 April 1890 and had been a deep sea man prior to joining the *Tara* in 1915. He survived the sinking and, after rescue, married Elizabeth Jane Jones on 31st May 1916, then joined the L&NWR's Marine Department on 3rd October. He was discharged on 4th March 1919 and returned to deep sea, serving on a variety of ships as a fireman and a donkeyman until 1934 when he returned to the Holyhead railway vessels where he remained until he retired as a donkeyman on 21st April 1955.

Hugh died on 8th August 1975 at the Trevalyn Hospital, Rossett, near Wrexham, after a long illness. It may have been due to this illness that he had moved from his home at 26 Ucheldre Ave, Holyhead to live with his daughter, Annie (Mrs WE Roberts), in Dolgellau. After his death, his remains were brought back to Holyhead and interred in the same grave as his wife, Elizabeth Jane, in Maeshyfryd cemetery.

**Fireman Harold Jones, MFA**

Of the Siloh Baptist Chapel House, Holyhead. Born in Holyhead on 5th October 1893, he was a younger brother of Hugh (see above). He joined the City of Dublin Steam Packet Company on 6th June 1914 as a coal trimmer or fireman but left six days later. It is believed that he joined HMS *Tara* in 1915. He survived her sinking, but, due to the privations he had suffered in the desert, had to remain in N° 21 Hospital in Alexandria when all others had been allowed to travel home. He was eventually found to be fit enough to travel and returned home in late May or early June 1916.

He joined the Marine Department of the L&NWR as a trimmer on 27th November 1917, but was discharged at his own request on 8th May 1919. His employment details after this date are unknown, but in later life he took over the running of the small-holding at Siloh Chapel House, Llaingoch.

Harold died on 3rd July 1952, aged fifty-seven, and was survived by his only daughter from his first marriage Kathleen Stanley and his second wife. His body was interred in Maeshyfryd in the grave of his first wife.

**Fireman Hugh Ellis Wright, MFA**

Hugh Wright was born on 27th September 1891, in 4 Back Bath Street, Holyhead, the son of Henry (an L&NWR boatman) and Jane Wright. He had four brothers, Robert, George, John Henry and Thomas Richard (see below), and one sister, Catherine. Prior to sea service he was employed as a boilermaker's helper at the L&NWR Marine Yard Workshops, and joined the marine department on 16th December 1913. On the outbreak of war he was serving as a coal trimmer on the company's Holyhead-based vessels and was later promoted to fireman and transferred to HMS *Tara* during September 1915. After rescue, he returned to the company on 18th June 1916 to serve on their Holyhead-based vessels.

On 17th May 1917 he married Martha E Owen of 6 Wynne Street at the CM Chapel in Valley and they both moved to live at 10 Wynne Street. At the time, he was serving on the SS *South Stack*, but was discharged from the company on 29th August 1917. By early 1918, he was serving as a mercantile rating on *Hecla II*, the trawler base at Buncrana, Northern Ireland. His wife died on 6th September 1919. Hugh remained in Holyhead until the 1930s when he moved to the north-east coast of England where, during the Second World War, he served in the vessels of the east coast coal trade. He retired on 20th May 1952.

His sister, Catherine, became the first wife of William Williams, the highest-decorated naval rating of all time (he received the Victoria Cross, the Distinguished Service Medal and Bar, and the French *Médaille Militaire*. The Victoria Cross was awarded for an action during which the Q-ship *Pargust* sank the *UC-29* on 7th June 1917).

**Fireman Owen Gray, MFA**

Of 2 West Terrace, Llaingoch, Holyhead. He was born at 22 Llaingoch, Holyhead on 7th March 1897, the son of Roland and Mary Gray and the brother of Hugh. He joined the L&NWR on 29th October 1914, from the SS *Comic* (Belfast Steam Company) and served on the company's passenger/cargo and cargo vessels. Volunteering to go on active service, he transferred from the SS *Galteemore* to HMS *Tara* on 16th April 1915. He survived the sinking but, after the rescue, did not rejoin the vessels of the L&NWR and was paid off on 24th May 1916. On the same date he enlisted as a coal trimmer into the RNR and was promoted to engineman on 31st January 1918. After serving on a variety of trawlers of the Auxiliary Patrol he was discharged to shore in 1919 and on 3rd March took up employment on the L&NWR steamers. By now he was residing at 4 Pentre Canol, Llaingoch.

Owen Gray left the company on 27th August 1920 and worked for a number of employers including Trinity House, the silica quarry on Holyhead Mountain and the LMS railway's permanent way department. In later life, he resided at Ael-y-Bryn on Holyhead Mountain and died on 18th December 1973, aged seventy-six, at 37 St Seiriol's Close, Morawelon, Holyhead, the home of his daughter and son-in-law, Mr and Mrs Robert Owen. He is buried in Maeshyfryd cemetery.

**Fireman Thomas Henry Owens, MFA**

Of 4 Port Street, Holyhead. He was born on 19th October 1892 when his family was residing at 2 George's Place, Holyhead. His parents were John (a stoker on the L&NWR vessels) and Grace Owens, and he had two brothers, John and Robert, and six sisters, Elizabeth, Maggie, Grace, Hannah, Amie and Mary. Prior to the war, Thomas had been employed as a fisherman. He is believed to have joined HMS *Tara* in 1915.

He survived the sinking and, after capture, managed to escape and remained free for some four weeks before being caught. After the rescue and survivor's leave he enlisted into the RNR on 31st July 1916 as a deck hand (11751DA) on the local trawlers of the Auxiliary Patrol. He was discharged to shore on 16th October 1917 suffering from sciatica and was awarded a Silver War Badge, giving his address as 31 Thomas Street, Holyhead

Thomas Owens died, aged fifty-nine, in the Stanley Hospital, Holyhead on 25th June 1950 and was interred in Maeshyfryd cemetery. At the time he was residing at 14 Maes Hedd. His obituary stated that he had been employed for many years on the cross-channel services, and was an ex member of the Holyhead Lifeboat. He was survived by his wife, Ellinor (Nelli), two sons, Leonard and Robert, and three daughters Nellie, Violet and Lucy.

**Fireman John Abbington Williams, MFA** [Author]

Of 6 Baptist Street, Holyhead. Born in Holyhead in 1869 he had spent some time at sea, his last vessel being the SS *Norseman* of Liverpool on which he had served in 1896. It seems he came ashore and was employed for a time as a general labourer, possibly for the L&NWR. On the 29th October 1914 he joined the L&NWR's vessels as a coal trimmer, initially serving on their cargo vessels before being transferred to HMS *Tara,* probably during her dry docking in April/May 1915. He survived the sinking and, after rescue, returned to company service on 19th May 1916.

John Williams died of a cerebral haemorrhage on 14th January 1930, aged sixty-two, at his home 11 British Terrace. He is buried in Maeshyfryd cemetery. He was survived by his wife Martha Ellen, his sons John Pugh, William Hugh, Hamilton Malta and daughter Margaret Ellen.

**Coal Trimmer William James Andrews, DSM, MFA** [Author]

Of 72 Mill Brae, Larne. Born on 16th February 1871 in Keady, Armagh, he was the son of John and Martha (née McGaffen) Andrews. In 1893, he married Cassie (Catherine) Montgomery in Belfast, and they initially resided at Mayo Street and Imperial Street in Belfast. William first found employment in a linen factory and later a corn mill. Cassie died on 29th January 1911,

by which time they had four children, Wilhelmina, Edward, Martha and Ann. It is unknown when, or why, William moved to Larne, but he may have done so that his sister could look after his children whilst he tried to find employment locally.

After the outbreak of war, William was serving as a fireman on the SS *Princess Victoria*, a steam packet of the Larne–Stranraer service which had been commissioned on 11th October 1914–2nd May 1915 as a Fleet Messenger and which presumably had been manned as per HMS *Tara* on her commissioning.

He joined HMS *Tara* in 1915, but the exact date is unknown, however, he survived the sinking and, after rescue, travelled home on the SS *Trafford Hall*, landing at Plymouth on 21st April before going on to Larne via Holyhead. On 15th June 1916, he enlisted in the RNR and was rated as a trimmer. He served on the Larne-based trawlers and drifters of the Auxiliary Patrol and, whilst serving on HM Trawler *Hungarian*, was awarded the Distinguished Service Medal, 'In recognition of services in vessels of the Auxiliary Patrol between 1 January 1917 and 31 December 1917.' He was discharged to shore on 5th April 1919.

In later life, William resided with his sister at 3 Meetinghouse Street in Larne where he died, aged seventy-six, on 11th May 1947. He is buried in the Carnmoney Main Cemetery, North Belfast, in the same grave as his wife and their daughters, Lillie and Annie. Commemorated on the headstone is their third daughter, Martha, who died in Grimsby on 24th November 1918.

**Fireman Thomas Higgins, MFA**

Of 12 Waterloo Road, Larne. Born 1861 in Larne, it is unknown if he was a pre-war seaman or if he was amongst the second batch of (Belfast) Federation men who had either joined at Larne or had been engaged locally.

He survived the sinking of HMS *Tara* and was one of the hospital cases who embarked on the hospital ship HMHS *Dunluce Castle* at Alexandria bound for Haslar Naval Hospital and from where he was not discharged until the beginning of May 1916. He returned to sea-going employment but died, it is believed sometime before 1926, leaving Emily, his wife, whom he had married in 1883. Together they had twelve children. Five of his sons served during the war, one of whom, Lance Corporal William Higgins, RE, died in India on 23rd November 1918.

**73. Fireman James Alexander McKinven, MFA**

Of 12 Saddell Street, Campbeltown, Argyllshire. Born in Campbeltown on 14th January 1853, he was a herring fisherman by occupation. His wife Mary (née Russell) had been born in Ireland, as had the two eldest of their six children – Mary Ann, James (see later), Anna, Donald, William and Elizabeth (adopted). James Alexander was one of the locals who had been employed whilst HMS *Tara* was based at Campbeltown, but the date of his joining is unknown. He survived the sinking and it seems that, after the rescue, he returned to herring fishing.

James died on 13th June 1930 at his home 12 Saddell Street and his wife died on 10th January 1937, aged eighty-one.

**Fireman George Alfred Wright, MFA**

Of 52 Hooper Road, London, E1. A married man who joined HMS *Tara* at Holyhead on 3rd May 1915, having been transferred from the paddle minesweeper HMS *Lynn* (formerly the GWR ship *Lynx*).

**Fireman Thomas Moorhead, MFA**

Of 19 Greenmount Street, Belfast. Born on 9th April 1885 in Belfast. In 1908 he married Miss Elizabeth Spence of 20 Greenmount Street, Belfast and by 1911 they had one child, Mary Ann.

Thomas was probably a pre-war mercantile marine fireman and was amongst the second batch of (Belfast) Federation men who joined the *Tara* in November 1914 at Larne. He survived the sinking and after survivor's leave returned to the sea, and was still at sea in 1936 on middle and coastal trade vessels.

**Coal Trimmer Thomas Jones, MFA**

Of 30 Llaingoch, Holyhead. Born in Pentra Fferam Gorniog, Holyhead Mountain on 15th February 1889, the son of Humphrey (a seaman) and Margaret Jones and was one of their fourteen children. Prior to the war had been employed as a freight clerk for a shipping company in Liverpool whilst lodging in Bootle. He joined the L&NWR's marine department on 4th August 1914 and was one of the new men employed by the company on the outbreak of war to replace the reservists who had been called to the colours. The date of his joining HMS *Tara* is unknown. He survived the sinking and, after rescue, returned to company service on 19th May 1916.

He was still serving as a coal trimmer in 1920, but sometime later came ashore to work, either as a porter in the goods department or as a boatman in Holyhead harbour. He died whilst residing at Llyslew on Holyhead Mountain on 7th March 1962, leaving his wife, Annie.

**Coal Trimmer Thomas Richard Wright, MFA**

Of 21 Cross Street, Holyhead. He was born at 4 Northwest Street, Holyhead 6th December 1894 and was the brother of Fireman Hugh Ellis Wright (see above). After leaving school, he became employed as a ship's scaler by the City of Dublin Steam Packet Company until, tiring of this, he went to sea on the SS *Lime Branch* as an ordinary seaman on 18th April 1914 for a voyage to South America. On his return, he signed off at Liverpool on 2nd December 1914 and joined HMS *Tara* in 1915.

After the rescue, Thomas Wright enlisted in the Royal Navy Reserve as a trimmer on 3rd July 1916 (5731TS) and served on the Auxiliary Patrol vessels based at Holyhead, HM Drifter's *Merse, Berrie Braes* and *Fragrance*. He was discharged due to fibrosis of the lungs on 23rd January 1918 (officially 13th February 1918) which, according to the family, he contracted during captivity in the desert. He returned to company service, as a coal trimmer on 2nd March 1918. Later that year Thomas married Margaret McLeod (née Hambley) at West Derby, Liverpool in 1918. She was the widow of Thomas McLeod of 21 Cross Street, Holyhead, who was a troop-deck steward on board the SS *Royal*

*Edward* and had been killed when the ship was torpedoed by the *UB-14* in the Mediterranean on 13th August 1915.

In 1924, due to ill health Thomas came ashore to work, initially as a boatman, then a diver's attendant and finally a carpenter's mate in the LMS engineering department.

Thomas died in June 1945 of pulmonary tuberculosis and was interred in Maeshyfryd Cemetery, the local papers speculating that his death may have been accelerated by his experiences in the desert. He was still residing at 21 Cross Street and was survived by his widow, Margaret, his son, William, and daughter, Margaret Jane, and two step sons, Alexander and Thomas McLeod.

**Coal Trimmer Hugh Williams, MFA**

Of 9 Wian Street, Holyhead. Born in 1882 in Holyhead. The dates when he joined the L&NWR's marine department or HMS *Tara* are unrecorded, but he was one of the survivors of the sinking and he returned to the L&NWR vessels on 7th June 1918. He was discharged on 27th May 1919 and came ashore to find employment as a railway labourer, possibly with the LMS Marine Yard's Shore Gang but was retired on a pension in April/May 1920.

He died of tuberculosis on 21st December 1929, aged forty-seven, at his home, 9 Wian Street, where he lived with his sister Elizabeth and her husband John, a cook on LMS vessels. Also residing there was his younger brother, William John Williams, a fireman on the same vessels.

**Coal Trimmer Richard J Williams, MFA** (W Davies)

Of 41 Gilbert Street, Holyhead. Born on 3rd March 1894 in Holyhead, he joined the L&NWR on 12th July 1913 as a cabin boy then, on 12th February 1915, joined HMS *Tara* as a coal trimmer. He survived the sinking and, after rescue, returned to company service on 16th May 1916. On the 5th Sept 1918 he married Catherine Ellen Jones of 5 Trearddur Square (her father was unable to attend so she was given away by her uncle, Owen Davies, who had been a greaser on HMS *Tara*). The couple resided at 9 Gilbert Street.

Richard Williams was killed when the *Scotia* was sunk off Dunkirk on 1st June 1940, aged forty-six. He is commemorated in Maeshyfryd cemetery, on the headstone of his wife's grave. She lived at 3 Hedsor Street, Holyhead and died on 15th May 1973, aged seventy-six.

*Petty Officers and ratings of the Catering Department*

**Chief Steward Andrew Morris, MFA** (G Burnall)

Of Glanygarth 34 Holborn Road, Holyhead. Born in Holyhead in 1859 he joined the L&NWR as a railway porter before transferring to the marine department as an assistant steward on 30th November 1888. He was serving on the *Hibernia* when she was requisitioned and volunteered to go on active service on 15th August 1914. He survived the sinking and subsequent ordeal of the survivors, and returned to company service on 16th May 1916. He died, aged fifty-seven, on 14th December 1917 whilst still in their employ, leaving a widow, Catherine Ann, his wife of nineteen years. He is buried in Cormac Hill (RC) Cemetery, Cleveland Avenue, Holyhead. His funeral was a naval affair; a contingent from the naval base escorted the coffin to the grave. The chief mourners were his four brothers, George, William, Alfred and Louis (a sergeant in the Cheshire Regiment, who was killed in action on 30th May 1918). The family had suffered an earlier tragedy when, on the 25th November 1914, Andrew's brother, Joseph Augustine Morris, a private in the Royal Marine Light Infantry, drowned in Dover harbour whilst serving on the battleship HMS *Revenge*.

**Second Steward William Barton, MFA** (Mrs Glenys S Barton)
Of 4 Robert Street, Holyhead. He was born in Chelsea, London in 1867 and had initially joined the L&NWR as a porter at Holyhead Station. On 19th October 1881, he transferred to the marine department as a cabin boy and by the outbreak of war he was a second steward serving on the *Hibernia*. He volunteered to go on active service on 15th August 1914 and survived the sinking. After rescue and a period of leave, he returned to company service on 16th May 1916, joining the SS *Greenore*.

He retired, aged sixty-five, in 1932 and died on 27th July 1942 whilst still residing at 4 Robert Street. He was interred in St Seiriol's churchyard, in the same gave as his third wife, Ann Elizabeth who had died in 1940 aged seventy-two, he was survived by his two daughters, Frances Rebecca and Annie Emily, and son, William Frederick Stephen.

**Cook Walter Jackson, MFA** (*Holyhead Chronicle*)
Of 1 Hedsor Street, Holyhead, but had been born in Hamilton, Ontario, Canada on 29th April 1863, where his father was serving in the Royal Navy. The family later returned to England and settled in Portsmouth and in 1881 Walter found employment as an officer's servant at the Royal Naval College, Greenwich. On 2nd January 1882 he joined HMS *Defence* as a domestic (2nd class) and was discharged at Holyhead, where she was serving as a guard ship, on 2nd January 1884. Two days later he joined the L&NWR where he remained and was serving on the *Hibernia* when she was requisitioned and he volunteered to go on active service on 15th August 1914.

When the torpedo struck, Walter Jackson was wounded in the shoulder and was found wandering, dazed about the deck by the ship's electrician, Wallace Cook, who helped him into his life jacket shortly before the ship sank. He was last been seen alive on the boat deck by Fireman Richard Lewis. Jackson's body was picked up from the sea by Sub Lieutenant Marsh's boat and revival was attempted by Quartermasters Rowlands and Williams, and by Surgeon Probationer Arthur, but without success. His body was brought ashore and buried at Port Bardia. Surgeon Probationer Arthur stated afterwards that Jackson's wounds would in all probability have proved fatal, but the cause of his death had been drowning. After the war, his grave could not be found and he is commemorated on the Chatby Memorial in Alexandria and on the family grave in Maeshyfryd Cemetery.

Walter Jackson left a widow, his wife of 30 years, Emma Jane, and nine children, Emma

Mary, Maggie, Florence May, Annie, Alice Louisa, Walter James, William Edward, Rose and Albert Howard.

**Second Cook John Pritchard, MFA**

Of Craig Hyfryd, Cambria Street, Holyhead. Born in Holyhead on 11th April 1886, the son of Robert and Ellen Pritchard, and the brother of William, Richard, Alice, Ellen, Mary and Jane. He joined the L&NWR on 7th April 1902 and served on the *Hibernia* as her second cook sometime prior to the war. When hostilities began he was serving on the Holyhead-based passenger cargo/cargo vessels until, on 10th November 1914, he was sent to join HMS *Tara* at Larne. He survived the sinking and, after rescue, he learnt that his mother with, whom he was living, had died on 18th January 1916. He returned to company service on 16th May 1916.

John Pritchard died on 11th September 1933, aged forty-seven, at Bryn Seiont Hospital, Caernarfon, and is buried in Maeshyfryd Cemetery. Although his home address was given as 13 London Road, Holyhead, it would appear that he resided for a time with his sister, Alice, and her husband, Owen Thomas, at 19 Market Street, Holyhead.

**Assistant Steward William Hugh Williams, MFA** (Mrs G Jones)

Of 5 Old Post Road, Holyhead. He was born in Holyhead in 1884 and joined the L&NWR on 5th January 1899. He was the *Hibernia*'s pre-war steerage steward prior to her requisition and volunteered to go on active service on 15th August 1914. Surviving the sinking, he returned to company service on 19th May 1916, initially serving on their Holyhead-based vessels but on 11th December 1917 transferred to HMT *Scotia*. In July 1919, he returned to the Holyhead service where he remained until his retirement.

William Williams died on 27th March 1966, aged eighty-two, at his home 7 Old Post Road and was interred in Maeshyfryd cemetery. He left a widow, Margaret Elizabeth, two sons, William Hugh, Lewis Owen, and one daughter, Cissey.

**Assistant Steward Evan Evans, MFA**

Of 46 Cambria Street, Holyhead. He was born in Bangor, Caernarfonshire, on 21st April 1888, the son of Thomas (a labourer) and Jane Evans, and the younger brother of Robert Henry and Margaret Winifred. He was orphaned at an early age and, at the turn of the century, was living and working at Tan-y-Marian Farm, Llangoed. Evan joined the L&NWR on 12th November 1906 and, by the time the *Hibernia* was requisitioned, was her bar steward. He volunteered to go on active service on 15th August 1914. He survived the sinking and, after rescue, returned to company service on 16th June 1916, joining the SS *Greenore*.

In 1926, he went deep sea, firstly on passenger liners (mostly on the North Atlantic service), but in 1943, and was part of a crew which was sent to San Francisco to collect the SS *Empire Javelin*, a Landing Ship Infantry (LSI), which could carry 1,200 men and twenty landing craft. He was aboard her when she landed troops on Omaha beach on D-Day, after which Evan returned to the liners. On 20th November 1950, whilst the SS *Ceramic* was in Melbourne Australia, he was discharged to hospital where he died on 3rd January 1951. His body was interred in a Melbourne cemetery. He was survived by his children Anna, Gwendoline, Sylvia, Thomas, Henry, Dorothy, Leslie, Joyce and George.

Hannah, his wife had died in 1937 and is buried in St Seiriol's Churchyard; Evan is commemorated on his her headstone.

**Assistant Steward Fredrick Barber, MFA** (*Holyhead Chronicle*)

Of 6 Edmund Street, Holyhead. He was born in Roby, near Hyton, Liverpool, in 1877, the son of Frederick (a corn merchant) and Clara Barber, and was the eldest of two sons and three daughters. Over the years the family also resided in Liscard, Cornwall and Cilcain near Holywell. Frederick was employed by his father before joining the L&NWR's marine department as a steward on 12th March 1906. When the *Hibernia* was requisitioned he was her saloon steward and volunteered to go on active service on 15th August 1915.

At the time of the torpedoing, he was confined in the ship's hospital, suffering from an abscess of the left groin, but was last seen by George Tanner on the boat deck a few minutes before the ship foundered. He had advised Barber to follow him and get a lifebelt. For some reason Barber did not do so and it is assumed that he drowned.

Frederick left a wife, Anna Marie (née Graham), whom he had married in Dublin in 1908, and two children.

**Assistant Steward John William Brosnan, MFA**

Of the Victoria Inn, Porthyfelin, Holyhead. Jack Brosnan was born in Spa (near Tralee), Co Kerry in Ireland on 14th Feb 1892, the eldest son of John Vincent (a station master) and Margaret Brosnan, and the brother of Mable and Thomas (see Thomas Gregory Brosnan below). At the turn of the century the family resided at the Railway Station, Cullenagh, Ballina, Nenagh, Co Tipperary, but during the 1900s moved to Holyhead, where a second daughter, Margaret, was born. They took up residence at 3 West Terrace, Llaingoch. His father died in October 1910 at the Denbigh Hospital and his mother became a grocer. She remarried in 1915 to Farnham G Padfield, licensee of the Victoria Inn which became the family home. On the 28th December 1916 she gave birth to her third daughter, Beryl.

John Brosnan joined the L&NWR on 10th August 1909 and, on the outbreak of war, was serving on the *Hibernia* when she was requisitioned. He volunteered to go on active service on 15th August 1915 and survived the sinking. After the rescue, he returned to company service on 16th May 1916, but left to go deep sea, joining the SS *Grampian* on 4th April 1919. He later returned to the Holyhead vessels where he remained until he retired.

On 26th August 1919 he married twenty-three-year-old Jane Owen of 4 Rock Street, and resided at 3 West Terrace. They later moved to 19 Robert Street. He died in the Stanley Sailors Hospital on 6th June 1965, aged seventy-three, and was buried in St Seiriol's churchyard, Holyhead. His wife had died on 16th August 1962.

**Assistant Steward William John James, MFA**

Of the Sidney Inn, Rhosygaer Terrace, Holyhead. He was born in Holyhead on 4th June 1894, the son of William and Ruth James and the brother of William Hugh, Robert (Bob) and Mary. His mother died on 26th February 1917 and his father on 10th October 1920. William joined the L&NWR on 10th August 1910 and on the outbreak of war, was serving on the company's cargo vessels. He relieved Steward C H Gooding and joined the *Tara* on 12th February 1915. He survived the sinking and, after rescue, returned to company service on 16th May 1916. On 11th December 1917 he joined HM Transport *Scotia* and saw the war out on her.

On 18th May 1920 William James left the railway vessels to join the Canadian Pacific's SS *Metagama* on 26th June. He resided at the Sydney Inn until at least 1922 and it is unknown how long he remained at sea.

In 1930, he married Mrs Jean Liles (née Tranter) in Cardiff where he appears to have taken up shore employment. When he died on 25th June 1977 at the Lansdowne Hospital, Cardiff, his home address was 59 St David's Crescent, Penarth, and he was described as a widower and a retired conveyor attendant. He left behind one stepson, Kenneth, and a stepdaughter, Beryl. On the 12th April 1931, his brother, Robert, an engineer on the SS *Seaville,* fell into a dock at Antwerp and drowned. His body was interred in the Schooneelh Cemetery.

**Assistant Steward Hugh Jones, MFA**

Of 36 Gilbert Street, Holyhead. Born in 33 Cecil Street, Holyhead on 23rd May 1893 the son of Hugh (an engine driver) and Hannah Jones, and the brother of Robert, William John, Elizabeth Ellen, Annie Grace and Hannah Jane. Prior to going to sea had been employed for a time in the L&NWR's locomotive department. He joined the marine department on 11th September 1911 and was serving on the *Hibernia* as an acting assistant steward when she was requisitioned. He volunteered to go on active service on 15th August 1914 and survived the sinking of HMS *Tara*. During his captivity, on 1st January 1916, the company promoted him to assistant steward. He returned to company service on 16th May 1916 and on 11th December 1917 joined HMT *Scotia* and remained with her until after the Armistice.

Hugh Jones later left the company and moved to Manchester. On retiring from what was described as the security police, he returned to Anglesey, taking up residence at Kebius, Gorad Road in Valley. He died in Stanley Hospital, Holyhead on 4th April 1971, aged seventy-nine.

**Assistant Steward Joseph Fenlen, MFA**

Of 24 Cybi Place, Holyhead. He was born in Williamstown, Co Dublin, on 13th January 1882. He was a second steward with the City of Dublin Steam Packet Company before joining the L&NWR on 6th May 1912. On the outbreak of war, he was serving on the fleet messenger *Anglia,* but was discharged when she was decommissioned on 24th May 1915. On 14th August 1915 he joined HMS *Tara* to relieve William Henry Jones who had been discharged two days previously. He survived the sinking and, after rescue, returned to company service on 18th May 1916, joining the SS *Greenore*.

Joseph Felen died on 2nd February 1944, aged 62, at the C & A Hospital in Bangor, and was interred in Cormac Hill (RC) Cemetery, Holyhead, with his wife, Jane, who had died four years previously. At the time of his death he was residing at Berwyn, Porthdafarch Road.

**Cabin Boy Thomas Gregory Brosnan, MFA**

Of 3 West Terrace, Llaingoch, Holyhead. Born during the autumn of 1898, in Ballina, Co Tipperary, Ireland (although the *Mercantile Marine* records his date of birth as being 21st April 1894). He was the brother of John W Brosnan (see above) and had joined the L&NWR on 9th August 1913 and was serving on the *Hibernia* when she was requisitioned. He volunteered to go on active service on 15th August 1914 and survived the sinking of HMS *Tara*. After the rescue he returned to company service on 19th May 1916 as a cabin boy. In January 1918 he was promoted to assistant steward and was discharged on 23rd September 1918. On 6th January 1919 he joined Allan Line's SS *Grampian* as a steward and returned to her for a second trip to Canada, after which he joined the SS *Bayano* then the SS *Ebani*, on which vessel he died of bronchial pneumonia on 4th February 1920. He is buried in Accra, Ghana.

**Galley Boy William Parry, MFA**

Of 2 Gilbert Street, Holyhead. He was born in Holyhead on 7th October 1897. He joined the L&NWR on 8th July 1913 and was already serving on the *Hibernia* when she was requisitioned, volunteering to go on active service on 15th August 1914 and survived the sinking. After the rescue, he returned to company service on 16th May 1916. On the 11th December 1917 he was promoted to acting cook and appointed to HMT *Scotia*. On 7th March 1923 he married Hannah Sarah Parry of 37 Rock Street, Holyhead at the Bryn Du, Chapel, Llanfaelog.

During the Second World War, William Parry became a steward on the passenger vessels and died aboard the MV *Cambria* at Dun Loaghaire on 5th September 1957. His body was brought back to Holyhead and interred in Maeshyfryd cemetery. He left his wife, Hannah, three sons, Malcolm, William and Evan (twins) and a daughter, Mrs Mary Smith. Another daughter, Mrs Megan Bradshaw had died in 1946, aged twenty one. At the time of his death the family resided in 117 London Road, Holyhead.

**Engineer's Boy Thomas Arthur Thomas, MFA**

Of 2 George's Place, Holyhead. Born in Liverpool on 26th August 1896, the son of Thomas and Catherine Thomas, who had seven children, four boys and three girls. During the early 1900s the family had moved to Toxteth when the father was employed as a seaman but, on 7th October 1907, he took up employment with the marine department of the L&NWR and the family returned to Holyhead, initially residing at 2 George's Place.

Thomas Thomas joined the L&NWR on 6th February 1913 as an engineer's boy. On the outbreak of war he was serving on the company's cargo vessels, but joined HMS *Tara* on 23rd December 1914 as a cabin boy, although he is shown throughout the narrative as being her engineer's boy. After the sinking and subsequent rescue he returned to company service on 16th May 1916, having been promoted in his absence to ordinary seaman on 1st January 1916. He was discharged on 29th May 1916 at his own request and two days later joined the RNR (763TC) as a trimmer\ cook. Initially joining HMS *Amethyst III* (the base ship at Holyhead) he gave his address as 14 Stanley Crescent, Holyhead. In June 1917 he was promoted to deck hand, a rate which he retained until he was demobilised on 16th January 1919, which was about this time that he married nineteen-year-old Lilian Pellowe of 8 Webber Street, Falmouth. It would seem the couple initially lived in Holyhead but in June 1920 moved to her family home in Falmouth.

Thomas Thomas remained in Falmouth, living at 53 Pendarves Road, and working as a fitter's helper for Silley, Cox & Co Ltd at Falmouth docks for over forty-years, until his death on 2nd January 1966. He is buried in Falmouth Cemetery. Thomas and Lily had one son, Jeffrey, and a daughter, Gladys.

His father had joined the ranks of the Anglesey National Reserves before the First World War and served with them from August 1914 to 1917. Another member of the family, Thomas's brother, John Owen, a L&NWR coal trimmer in peacetime, served in France as a sapper in N° 2 (Holyhead) Siege Company, Royal Anglesey Royal Engineers.

*Royal Navy Personnel*

**Signal Boy Raymond Fulcher, RN (J30366)**

Born on 24th January 1899, he was the son of Walter (a fireman) and Bertha Fulcher, the brother of Walter, Bertha and Norman. The family resided at 4, Sophia Place, Park Road, Portsmouth. Raymond was employed as a hairdresser before enlisting in the Royal Navy as a boy rating on 25th April 1914 and was appointed to HMS *Tara* on 23rd February 1915, aged sixteen, becoming the youngest member of the crew. He survived the sinking and, after survivor's leave, was appointed to the battleship HMS *Renown* on 24th January 1917. He had volunteered to serve for twelve years but, on 12th February 1920, after serving both ashore and afloat, he was invalided out of the service. He remained at sea joining the Royal Fleet Auxiliary's SS *Serbol* on the 11th October, sometime late he came ashore and found employment with the Portsmouth Corporation as a bus conductor.

Raymond died in the Eye and Ear Hospital, Portsmouth on 9th December 1938, leaving behind his wife of sixteen years, Elsie, and two daughters, Iris and Olive, who resided at 32, Stamshaw Road, Portsmouth.

**Boy Telegraphist George Alfred Tanner, RN (J30698)**

Of Priory Street, Corsham in Wiltshire. George Tanner was born in Corsham on 12th September 1897 and employed as a rubber worker prior to enlisting into the Royal Navy as a boy rating on 29th April 1914. He was rated a boy telegraphist when he joined HMS *Tara* on 23rd February 1915. He survived the sinking and, after rescue, on 16th April 1916, was advanced to ordinary telegraphist in recognition of his services after the *Tara* was sunk. He was discharged from the service on 22nd August 1920.

Bob Tannner, a retired civilian radio operator of 45 Rosebery Avenue, Scarborough, died in

St Mary's Hospital, Scarborough on 13th December 1972 leaving his wife Dorothy and children Shelia and Dennis.

He had been favourably noted by the Admiralty for his services during the sinking of the Tara.

**Ship's Corporal 1st Class (Pensioner) Charles Mintram, RN (146622)**
Of Nocturnum, 51 Funting Street, North End, Portsmouth. Born in Southampton on 20th August 1870, Charles Mintram had enlisted 4th October 1888 as stoker second class. On the 21st August 1900 he changed departments and became a ship's corporal. He served on a variety vessels and shore bases until, on 10th December 1908, when he was discharged as time expired. When working as a commissioning agent for an insurance company he was recalled to HMS *Victory* on 2nd August 1914 and posted to HMS *Tara* at Larne on 15th September. After rescue and a spell in hospital, he was discharged from the Royal Navy as being unfit on 21st December 1916. He returned to the insurance industry and died at his home Holmlea, in Bartley, near Southampton, on 18th December 1934, and was survived by his second wife, Margaret, and the daughter of his first marriage, Christine. His first wife, Rosina, having died in 1930. In 1921, they had lost a son Charles Alfred Edward aged 26.

**Yeoman Signaller Henry George James Thomas Allen, RFR (182570 RFR B1650)**
Of 9 Salisbury Road, Greys, Essex. Born on 12th October 1879 at Woolwich in Kent, Henry Allen enlisted on 12th October 1897 and, after service both ashore and afloat, was invalided out of the service on 8th February 1906 due to defective hearing, and on the 1st May 1911 joined the Royal Fleet Reserves. Following his discharge from the Royal Navy he was employed as a dock's lock-man for the Port of London Authority, and resided at 121–2 The Dwellings in Tilbury with his wife, Mabel Lucy, his daughter, Winifred Grace, and son, William Henry Charles.

He was mobilized on 2nd August 1914 and posted to HMS *Tara* three days later. As a result of the explosion, or possibly his immersion in the Mediterranean, he became deaf in his right ear for which he was granted a hurt certificate. After rescue and survivor's leave, he served out the rest of the war mostly in shore bases until he was discharged on medical grounds on 14th February 1919.

On 4th December 1932 he collapsed whilst walking on Fore Street in Budleigh Salterton and was taken to hospital where he was pronounced dead on arrival. He was employed as an insurance agent residing at 15 Otter View Terrace, Budleigh Salterton, with his second wife, Ruth Mary (neé Murrin), a spinster , whom he had married on 7th April, his first wife, Mabel having died in 1930.

**Leading Seaman William Prince Millward, RFR (SS.1730, RFR CHB 8301)**
Of 13 Tiber Street, Lodge Lane, Liverpool. He had been born in Tideswell, Buxton, Derbyshire on 3rd December 1887 and was employed as a brass finisher prior to enlisting in the Royal Navy on 29th December 1906. He served on various ships and shore bases until, on 29th December 1911, he was invalided from the shore base HMS *Pembroke* at Chatham due to problems with his hearing. He joined the Royal Fleet

Reserve the following day. On 14th December 1912 he married Rosa Hall at All Saints Church, Prince's Park in Liverpool.

Mobilised on 2nd August 1914, he joined HMS *Tara* as an able seaman on 10th August 1914 and was promoted to leading seaman on 8th August 1915. He survived the torpedoing of the vessel and the subsequent ordeal of the survivors and was commended for his services. After release and survivor's leave he joined the new battleship HMS *Repulse* on 2nd August 1916, serving on her for thirty months before being demobilised on 8th February 1919. It would seem that he returned to the RFR as he was issued a Long Service & Good Conduct Medal on 15th February 1923.

On 17th June 1931, whilst returning to Liverpool from Derbyshire on his motorcycle combination, he was involved in an accident with another motorcycle. He was taken to the Stockport Infirmary where he died a few hours later. He left a widow Rosa with whom he resided at 30 Cam Street, Liverpool, and two daughters. At the time of his death he was employed as a captain on the Mersey ferries.

He had been favourably noted by the Admiralty for his services when the *Tara* sank.

**Leading Seaman James Brews Marwick, RNR (3354C)**

Of 125 Leith Walk, Leith. He was born in Kirkwell on the Orkneys on 22nd September 1882, the son of Hugh, a farmer/crofter, and took up a seagoing career serving mainly on home or Mediterranean trade vessels as an able seaman or mate. He enlisted into the RNR in 1909 and was mobilised on 2nd August 1914, serving first on the SS *Glenturret*. On 14th September 1914 he joined HMS *Tara* at Larne. He survived the sinking and eventually returned to naval service and was awarded the RNR Long Service & Good Conduct Medal on 27th November 1919 at Leith. For a time he went back to sea, joining the coaster SS *Clansman* (August, 1919), SS *Amelia* (March, 1920), SS *Somersby* (June, 1921) and later the SS *Baberton*. He came ashore in January 1922 and was employed by the Leith Dock Board as a labourer and was discharged from the RNR on 31st December 1923 as he was ineligible for re-enlistment due to his age.

James Marwick died at the Royal Infirmary in Edinburgh of chronic bronchitis, pneumonia and cardiac failure on 2nd May 1950. The death certificates gives his occupation as a retired coal trimmer. He was married to Margaret McKenzie Miller, of 22 Lorne Street, Leith.

**Seaman William Gunn, RNR (4369A)** (Donald R Gunn)

Born in Lamigo, Skerray, Sutherland on 13th January 1889, the son of James Murdo (an inshore fisherman) and Margaret Gunn, he was the brother of John, Ena and Margaret. William enrolled into the RNR on 29th July 1912, giving his occupation as being that of an inshore fisherman. On mobilisation, he was initially posted to the Drake Battalion of the Royal Naval Division with which he served at Antwerp in Belgium. On return to Britain he was posted to the armed boarding steamer HMS *Calyx* then, sometime during the summer of 1915, joined HMS *Tara*. He survived the sinking and, after survivor's leave, was posted to HMS *Gunner*, the Auxiliary Patrol Base at Granton on 22nd August 1916 for minesweeping duties. He remained on these duties until the 24th August 1919.

After the war, he lived for a time in Glasgow with his sister Ena and found employment with Singers Ltd and then became a conductor on the Glasgow Corporation trams. On the 10th September 1920, he married Andrewina Ross, a domestic servant from Edinburgh. During this time he remained with the RNR and was promoted to petty officer on 19th September 1922. In 1923, he went deep sea and served on a variety of vessels, including a whale factory/oil ship, doing a number of trips to South Georgia. In 1937, he was discharged from the RNR as time expired. On 12th October 1939 he was paid off the Duke of Sutherland's yacht the *Sans Peur* in Vancouver after she had been requisitioned by the Royal canadian Navy (she was under repair after hitting a reef off western Canada). The crew travelled across Canada and embarked at Montreal on the SS *Duke of Richmond* and landed in Liverpool on 29th October. He then found employment on the auxiliaries at Scapa Flow, supplying the British fleet with food and stores and later, with Balfour Beatty which company was charged with preparing and sinking blockships in the channels leading into Scapa Flow to prevent the entry of enemy submarines.

William Gunn left the sea on 27th June 1946 and returned to Lamigo and crofting. He retired in 1967 and died in Raigmore Hospital, Inverness on 13th February 1969.

**Seaman Charles McNaughton, RNR (6218A)** (Campbeltown Archives)
Born on 24th June 1888, one of the five children of David (a fisherman) and Maria McNaughton. Charles was also a fisherman prior to enrolling in the RNR on 29th September 1914 when he resided at 10 Burnbank Place, Campbeltown in Argyll. After survivor's leave he was posted back out to the Middle East where he served on HMS *Hannibal* and HMS *Egmont 2*. He was demobilised on 16th September 1919, but re-enlisted into the RNR on 26th Feb 1920. He died in 1973, aged eighty-four, still residing at Campbeltown.

**Seaman Alexander Ross, RNR (3772A)**
Of 104 Duke Street, Leith. Born at 52 Kirkgate, Leith on 27th December 1889, he was a mercantile marine able bodied seaman when he enlisted in the RNR on 2nd November 1911, and was posted to HMS *Tara,* at Larne, on 18th September 1914. He survived the sinking and on 6th September 1916, after survivor's leave, was posted to HMS *Excellent* then, two days later, to HMS *President III* for service on defensively armed mercantile ships. He survived the sinking of the SS *Australier* when she was torpedoed on 29th April 1918 by the *UB-57* in the English Channel, some six miles S by SW of the Dungeness Lighthouse, with the loss of five lives whilst on a voyage form Bilbao to Middlesbrough carrying iron ore. On 17th February 1919, he was demobilised and returned to the mercantile marine but in September of that year he came ashore and took up employment as a crane-man at Leith docks. He was discharged from the RNR on 21st December 1921 and later went deep sea.

**Seaman James McKinven, RNR (5031B)** (Campbeltown Archives)
Of 23 Argyll Street, Campbeltown. Born in Ireland on 14th January 1878, James McKinven, the son of Fireman James McKinven (see above), was a herring fisherman by trade when he

enlisted into the RNR on 1st April 1908. He joined HMS *Tara,* at Larne on 18th September 1914. On 3rd October 1914 he was rated leading seaman, RNR, but was reduced to seaman on 7th July 1915 for being drunk on duty.

After the torpedo struck the *Tara* he was last seen by George Tanner (see above) who stated that he had seen him in N° 5 Lifeboat which, owing to the speed and the list, had capsized before the crew could unhook her from the falls. All eight occupants were thrown into the sea, seven were rescued, but there was no sign of James McKinven and, knowing that he could not swim, it was assumed that he had drowned.

James was married to Jeanie (née Fullerton) and they had eight children whose ages, at the time of his death, ranged from two weeks to 13½ years. After his death, his wife became a domestic servant and died on 13th September 1921, aged forty-three. Their eldest son, James, later went to sea.

**Stoker John McNee, RNR( 7917S)**

Born on 25th May 1895, the eldest child of Donald (an engine fitter) and Mary McNee, and two brothers and four sisters, the family residing at 13 Menai Street, off Atholl Street, in Liverpool. After leaving school he became an apprentice pawnbroker but later went to sea as a coal trimmer, serving on the trans-Atlantic liners before enlisting in the RNR on 19th June 1915 and joined HMS *Tara* on 7th October. He survived the sinking and after leave was posted to the battleship, HMS *Lion* (Vice-Admiral Beatty's flagship at the battles of Dogger Bank and Jutland), serving on her from 4th June 1916 until 26th May 1919 when he was discharged to the Reserves.

During the sinking of the *Tara* he had been in the N° 5 Lifeboat and, on its capsizing, had broken his left arm and received a deep gash to the left hand. However, whilst in the water he saw Mr Manning, the clerk, a non swimmer, in great difficulties and swam over and supported him until they were both rescued by the N° 2 Lifeboat. For this gallant act, he was awarded the Bronze Medal of the Royal Humane Society in 1917.

After demobilization John McNee returned to the sea joining the *Mauretania* as a fireman then, in August 1920, the *Serbino,* but it is not known for how long he remained at sea.

He died in St Helens, Lancashire, during the late spring or early summer of 1962, aged sixty-seven.

*Local crew members who were paid off HMS* Tara *between 15 August 1914 and 7 October 1915 and died during the war.*

**Seaman Evan Davies, MFA** (Holyhead Chronicle)

Of 7 Ucheldre Avenue, Holyhead. Born at 50 Thomas Street, Holyhead in 1881, shortly before the death of his father, he was brought up by his mother, Jane, who also had to look after his older brother, William, and grandmother, Mary Hughes. Evan joined the L&NWR's marine department on 4th December 1901 and was serving on the *Hibernia* on the outbreak of war. He volunteered to go on active service on 15th August 1914, but was invalided home during the early summer of 1915. He died on 22nd January 1916, aged thirty-five and is buried in Maeshyfryd Cemetery. He was accorded a naval funeral. He left a widow, Margaret Ann (née Brown) to whom he had been married for 12 years.

**Bosun's Mate, Able Seaman Richard Williams, MFA**

Of 38 Gilbert Street, Holyhead. He was born in 1857 in Penrhoslligwy, near Amlwch and had been in the employ of the L&NWR since 7th July 1890. He was serving aboard the *Hibernia* when she was requisitioned and volunteered to remain with her during her naval service. On the 24th August 1914, whilst HMS *Tara* was on patrol, a boat was lowered and he was taken over to HMS *Juno* to be attended to by her surgeon. He resumed his duties on the 26th. He was again taken ill whilst she was on patrol and as a consequence was discharged and sent home, where he died on 25th June 1915. He is buried in Maeshyfryd Cemetery. He left a widow, Ellen, and a daughter, Jeannie.

At the time of his death, the *Scotia* was in dry dock and his coffin was borne to the grave by members of her crew. He left a wife, Ellen, and a daughter, Jennie.

**Engineer Henry Owen Roberts, RNR**

Of 37 Thomas Street. He was born in Valley on 23rd October 1856 and had served an engineering apprenticeship in the Valley Foundry before moving firstly to Liverpool in 1874 and then to Crewe where he was employed as an improver in the L&NWR locomotive works. He then joined the Guion Line of Liverpool as an engineer and rose through the ranks, gaining his first-class engineer's certificate of competency and was promoted to that rank at an early age within the company. Owing to ill health, he was forced to retire from foreign-going voyages and consequently joined the L&NWR's marine department as a second engineer on 15th August 1887. He married Eleanor Jones of Llanfair Mathafarn Eithaf, Anglesey, in West Derby, Liverpool in 1885 and they had four children, Margaret, Catherine Ellen, Olwen and Henry. Tragically, Olwen and Henry died in infancy and their mother died on 16th March 1894 at 54 Newry Street, Holyhead. In August 1895, Henry Roberts married Mary Elizabeth Jones. In 1899, he was promoted to chief engineer and in 1912 stood by the building of the SS *Greenore*, the company's first turbine steamer, where he remained as chief engineer until February 1914 when he joined the *Hibernia* on the death of her chief engineer, Robert Paton, who had died on 8th February. On the *Hibernia* being requisitioned, he volunteered to remain and was granted a temporary commission as an engineer lieutenant, RNR, on 15th August 1914. Owing to ill-health, he was paid off on 22nd December 1914 and discharged to pension from the company on 2nd August 1915. In late 1916 he was taken seriously ill and never fully recovered. He died on 29th May 1917, aged sixty. He was interred in Maeshyfryd Cemetery. He left behind the two daughters of his first marriage, Margaret and Catherine Ellen, and his second wife, Mary Elizabeth (née Jones), whom he had married on 14th August 1895. He had served for a number of years as a Sunday school teacher and was a deacon of Armenia Chapel, Holyhead.

**Engineer Thomas Jones, RNR** (Miss Jane Hughes)

Born on 18th March 1857, he was the son of William (a lead miner) and Mary Jones of High Street, Rhuddlan in Flintshire. He served an engineering apprenticeship with John Williams & Sons, the Phoenix Iron Works in Rhuddlan from May 1873 to March 1879. Leaving Rhuddlan

he found employment as an improver with De Winton's Foundry in Caernarfon. On 2nd June 1883, whilst residing at Pool Hill, Caernarfon, he married Annie Ellen Williams of New Street, Caernarfon. By this time he was an engine fitter and the couple resided at 4, Northgate Street, Caernarfon. He joined the L&NWR on 7th April 1887 and moved to Holyhead where he and his family resided at 3 Longford Terrace. He gained his second-class marine engineer's certificate of competency, and later his first-class certificate and the family moved to 6 Maeshyfryd Road, then Sunrise Terrace. He was promoted to chief engineer on the cargo service on 1st June 1907 and finally chief engineer on the passenger or express service on 1st March 1914, by which time the family were living at Riversdale, Four Mile Bridge. He relieved Chief Engineer HO Roberts during HMS *Tara*'s dry docking in Birkenhead in December 1914.

Thomas Jones disappeared on the night of the 10th / 11th September 1915 when *Tara* was on patrol duties off Northern Ireland. It seems that he had visited the engine room shortly before midnight and it was assumed by the watch–keepers that, after leaving, he had gone to his cabin. He did not appear for breakfast the next morning and a search of his cabin revealed that his bed had not been slept in. The bridge was informed and *Tara* reversed course but to no avail. After a thorough search of the vessel, it was concluded that he had fallen overboard. Fifth Engineer Howarth Hughes later remarked that he was the 'best liked man in the service' and that he was an abstainer. How the accident had happened was a mystery. His body was found at Sheephaven, Co Donegal, on 2nd October. After an inquest, it was brought to Holyhead and he was buried in Maeshyfryd Cemetery.

Thomas Jones left his wife, Annie, one son , Gwilym Goronwy, and three daughters, Ellen Mary, Gladys Laura and Joyce Dilys. He had served the company faithfully for thirty-two years.

**Assistant Engineer Hugh Jones, RNR**

Of 13, Moreton Road, Holyhead. Born in 12, Lower Park Street, Holyhead on the 9th May 1875, he was the son of Henry, a ship's carpenter, and Jane Jones, and had two brothers and five sisters. He served an engineering apprenticeship before joining the vessels of the L&NWR on 31st March 1898. On the outbreak of war was serving on the *Hibernia* as her second engineer and volunteered to go on active service on 15th August. Whilst HMS *Tara* was in Holyhead prior to her departure for the Mediterranean Hugh was sent on leave but whilst on leave was taken ill so could not rejoin. On 6th November 1915 he was promoted to chief engineer on one of the companies cargo vessels.

He died on the 3rd November 1916 as Chief Engineer of the SS *Connemara* when, in atrocious weather, she collided with the collier *Retriever* in Carlingford Lough, ninety-one people died in the disaster – twenty-eight from Holyhead, the only survivor being a fireman from the *Retriever*.

Hugh left a widow of some three years, Esther, and one daughter, Eunice, born on 7th August 1916.

**Fireman Richard Evans, MFA** (*Holyhead Chronicle*).
Of 6, New Street, Menai Bridge, he had been born in 35, Porthyfelin, Holyhead in 1866 and had joined the L&NWR on 13th July 1892. He was serving on the *Hibernia* when she was requisitioned and had volunteered to go on active service on 11th August 1914. He was taken ill on 2nd September when *Tara* was on patrol and was excused duties. On arrival at Larne six days later, Dr Thomas Killen was called who recommended that Evans be sent to hospital. He died in the Moyne Hospital, Larne, on 12th December 1914 and his body was brought back over to Holyhead and buried in St Seiriol's churchyard on the 18th, it is believed in the same grave as his parents, unfortunately the grave cannot now be found.

He left a widow, Sophia, and five children, Mary, William, Ebenezer, Albert and Sophie.

# Appendix 2: *Moorina's* crew and passengers held captive with the *Tara's* crew

**Chief Officer Charles Severin Coalsted** (Courtesy of Trove)
Born in Porsgrund, Norway on 9th August 1866, he first went to sea as a boy on sailing vessels. After being wrecked in the Gulf of Mexico, he made his way into the United States and entered the US Revenue Service. Tiring of shore life, he returned to the sea and made his way to Australia where he arrived in 1888. In 1893, after a number of voyages, he joined the private yacht *Sadie* belonging to Charles Gibson Millar, a wealthy railway engineer. Whilst aboard the yacht, Coalsted was awarded the Royal Humane Society's Bronze medal for rescuing a fellow crew member, a Japanese seaman who had fallen overboard. In 1900 he was master of the coastal vessel *Cambria* when she was wrecked whilst on a voyage from Fremantle to Bunbury and as a result his certificate of competency was suspended for six months. In 1903, he married Mary Ada Smith, a New Zealander, in Fremantle and they took up residence in Bunbury, and in 1904 he became an Australian citizen. For a time he worked as a pilot on the south coast after which he commanded the tug *Vigilant* in the port of Bunbury. On 21st October 1914, he was appointed mate of the *Thuringa* and remained with her until her sinking on 7th November 1915.

After the rescue, Coalsted and Richardson were admitted to the Ras el Tin Hospital with the *Tara* survivors, but were then transferred to the N° 19 General Hospital in Alexandria. On being passed fit enough to travel, they embarked on P&O ship *Medina* for the voyage home to Australia. Travelling via Bombay and Colombo, they arrived in Fremantle on 4th June 1916 where Coalsted disembarked to travel home to Wittenoom Street, Bunbury with his wife and sister-in-law.

In 1918 Coalstead took up employment with the Commonwealth Lighthouse Service and was given command of the lighthouse tender *The Governor Musgrave* and later the *Kyogle* and remained with the service until he retired in 1931. He later took up employment with the

Cossack Lightering Company. Whilst in command of the schooner *Uribes* and suffering chest pains, he was taken to hospital in Onslow, Ashburton, Western Australia where he suddenly died of a heart attack just after midnight on 12th November 1934. He left one son and two daughters, one of whom, Nora, became a classical concert pianist. At the time of his death his home address was 22 Hamilton St, East Fremantle.

**2nd Engineer Thomas Reid Richardson**

Born in Milnathort, Orwell, Kinross, Scotland on 8th July 1879, he was the son of John (a spinning mill manager) and Elizabeth Richardson. After serving an engineering apprenticeship he went to sea as a marine engineer and in 1907, whilst serving as fourth engineer on Blue Funnel's SS *Hyson* he first sailed to Australia. In 1910, he returned as third engineer of the SS *Levuka* on her delivery voyage from Britain, arriving in Sydney on 26th December 1910. Thereafter he remained with the company which had regular sailings on both the Australian coastal trade and to Fiji, carrying both passengers and cargo. On 12th May 1914, he married Ellen Murray Anderson in Queensland and they settled in Fifth Avenue, Neutral Bay, Sydney.

On the outbreak of war Richardson was serving as second engineer on the SS *Kyarra* and remained with her during her two-month conversion to a hospital ship. Leaving her in April/May 1915, he was appointed to the *Moorina* about a month later. He survived the ship's sinking and was, like Coalsted, admitted to the Ras el Tin Military Hospital. He also embarked on the SS *Median* at Alexandria and disembarked in Sydney on 12th June 1916.

Returning to the sea, further excitement came his way in 1919 whilst second engineer of the SS *South Bulli* . He was one of her lifeboat crew who successfully affected a rescue in atrocious weather of the survivors of the SS *Myola* during the early morning of 2nd April off Long Reef, some 1–2 miles off Sydney Heads.

In later life, he resided with his wife, Nell, son, John, and daughter, Betty, in the Mosman district of Sydney and died in hospital on 26th October 1950. His body was interred in the Northern Suburbs Cemetery.

**2nd Lieutenant Thomas Seth Apcar, IARO (Cavalry Branch)**

Of Armenian descent, Thomas Apcar was born in Calcutta, India in 1875 to a well-to-do family whose interests included coal mining and ship-owning. After school and college, he entered the family business and on 21st June 1898 married Elizabeth Dishkone Gregory at Calcutta. A daughter, Mathilda Elizabeth, was born on 13th June 1904. The family later moved to London where, on 7th November 1912, Thomas joined the Royal Aero Club. On the outbreak of war he joined the N° 2 Motor Ambulance Unit of the British Red Cross Society as a driver and landed in France with the unit on 12th November 1914. A few months later, he broke his arm whilst attempting to start a car which backfired causing the starting handle to break his arm. After recovering he returned to India and on 4th June 1915 joined the Indian Army Reserve of Officers (IARO). On 2nd August he was appointed a 2nd Lieutenant in the IARO (Cavalry Branch) and joined the *Moorina* in Bombay as the senior office (second lieutenant) of a detachment of reinforcements for the 32nd Lancers.

He survived the ordeal of the survivors and, after recovery in July 1916, was posted to the 34th (Prince Albert Victor's Own) Poona Horse in France. He was promoted to lieutenant in 1917 (antedated to May 1916) and in February the Poona Horse was posted to Palestine. On 26th August 1918 he retired on the grounds of ill health due to field service, and was granted the honorary rank of lieutenant. He then returned to the family business where he remained until retiring as an exchange banker of T S Apcar & Co. He died on 18th October 1947 on his house boat, *Victory*, at Srinagar, India. He also had another home at 15 Queens Park, Ballygunge, Calcutta.

## Appendix 3: Mercantile Marine officers and men appointed to HMS *Tara* who did proceed to the Mediterranean

(those without the suffix MFA may only have served aboard for a few days)

Sub-Lieutenant. Charles Proteous Copland, of Witchingham, Walthew Ave, Holyhead.
Sub-Lieutenant. William Hughes. RNR, of Trewerin, Cyttir Road, Kingsland, Holyhead.
Assistant Engineer Robert Edward Jones, RNR, of Llwyn Idris, Plashyfryd Rd, Holyhead.
Surgeon Probationer. George William Marshall Findlay, RNVR, of Brailes, Warwickshire.
Assistant Paymaster William Thomas Davies, RNR, of Caemawr, Turkey Shore Rd, Holyhead.
Assistant Paymaster Walter Frank Street, RNR, of 104 Risby Gate St, Bury St Edmunds.
Warrant Telegraphist Fredrick John Chambers, RNR, of St Helier, Jersey.
Electrician Ernest Lawton, MFA, of Crewe.
Able Seaman David Clements MFA, of 15 Pound St, Larne.
Able Seaman William Close of Larne.
Able Seaman William Gough of 49 Silvio Street, Belfast.
Able Seaman David Hayes, MFA, of 11 Victoria Street, Carrickfergus, jumped ship Larne, 13 January 1915, arrested Belfast and returned to vessel.
Able Seaman William Low, MFA
Able Seaman John McAllister, MFA
Able Seaman Albert Edward Milner, MFA, of Wakefield, Yorks, ex RN
Able Seaman J Mitchell, of 4 Rowland Street, Liverpool, jumped ship in Larne, 8 September 1914
Able Seaman G Simpson, MFA.
Seaman Ernest Banks, MFA, of 88 Anthony Street, Liverpool.
Seaman James Anderson
Seaman R Davies
Seaman Gerald Byrne, MFA, of Arklow.
Seaman Griffith John Evans, MFA, of 19 Lligwy Street, Holyhead.
Seaman James Gannon, MFA, lodging/residing London Rd, Holyhead

Seaman Edward Derbyshire, of 175 Chatsworth Street, Liverpool.
Seaman William Larner of 20 Horatio Street, Liverpool.
Seaman R Pritchard
Seaman Michael Joseph Ryder, of Liverpool, left *Tara* and enlisted in the King's Liverpool Regiment, 1 February 1915, but was discharged 6 May 1916 and returned to sea-going employment
Seaman Thomas Williams, of 54, Porthyfelin, Holyhead
Fireman James Blackwood, of 20 Roseleigh Street, Belfast.
Fireman William J. Bunting, MFA, of 45 Mill Street, Larne; later served RNR.
Fireman John Casey.
Fireman John Currie, MFA, of Londonderry.
Fireman Thomas Dillon, MFA, of Larne.
Fireman W Fisher.
Fireman Michael Hennigan, MFA, of Ballina, Ireland.
Fireman Edward Jones, MFA, of 11 Queens St, Holyhead. He jumped ship Larne 23 November 1914.
Fireman John Jones, of 50 Thomas St, Holyhead.
Fireman William Jones, MFA, of 11 Wynne St, Holyhead.
Fireman Alexander Larmour of 83 Cosgrove St, Belfast.
Fireman J. Morrison, MFA, deserted.
Fireman William Pritchard.
Fireman John Sanders of 19 Rosecommon Street, Liverpool.
Fireman W H Smith, MFA.
Fireman Thomas Stafford.
Fireman Frank Walter, MFA, of Easton on the Hill, Northamptonshire.
Fireman Robert Wilson, MFA.
Fireman Madden, first name unknown.
Cook John Williams, MFA, of 11 Henry St, Holyhead.
Steward Charles Henry Gooding, MFA, of 33 Holborn Rd, Holyhead.
Steward William Henry Jones, MFA, of 10 Moreton Rd, Holyhead.
Engineer's Boy William James Williams, of 3 Well St, Holyhead.

*Royal Navy crew who did not proceed to the Mediterranean.*
Able Seaman Charles Lacey (159482, RFR Ch B 339), served 10 August 1914–11 January 1915
Stoker 1 Harold Cain (SS115288) served 3 March 1915–30 September 1915
Carpenter's Crew Frederick Young (M8961 ), served 23 February 1915–30 September 1915
Ordinary Seaman Henry James Avery (J20353), served 5 March–30 September 1915

*Royal Navy Reserve crew who did not proceed to the Mediterranean. All men joining HMS* Tara *on 2nd or 3rd March 1915 and discharged on 30th September in Holyhead unless otherwise noted.*
Skipper Frank Lilley (337 WSA)
Skipper Harry Dale (WSA 336)
Seaman John Edward Brodigan (350B)
Seaman David Coleman (2704C)
Seaman John Cooke (5117B)
Seaman John Hare (2860B)
Seaman William Ralph (2848A), served 18 September 1914–12 June 1915 when he deserted to enlist in the Suffolk Regiment but in 1918 was serving in France with the 1/7 Bn, Royal Scots Fusiliers when he was discovered by the authorities but, as he had enlisted, the charge

of desertion against him was dropped and was allowed to remain in the army.

Henry William Cole, ERA, (400 EB)
Robert Francis Jones, ERA, (1148EA)
Arthur Percival Miles, ERA, (946E)
Leading Stoker William King (1028U)
Stoker Michael Coughlan (2402T)
Stoker William Dickson (3619S)
Stoker John Donovan (7661S)
Stoker Arthur Raybold (3139T)
Stoker Thomas Riley (1080U)
Stoker John Roberts (1826S)

# Sources

**Published works**

*Prisoners of the Red Desert: the adventures of the crew of the* Tara *during the First World War,* Captain RS Gwatkin-Williams, London, 1919.
*A Black Hole in the Desert – being the diary of a Yeoman Signaller, one of the survivors of HMS* Tara, (edited by H R S), London, 1916.
*In the Hands of the Senussi,* RS Gwatkin-Williams, London, 1916.
*The Sea and the Sand,* W Davies, Caernarfon, 1988.
*Holyhead and the Great War,* RE Roberts, Holyhead, 1920.
*The Sanusi's Little War* by Russell McQuirk, 2007.
*Naval Operations,* Sir JS Corbett & Sir JH Newbolt. London, 1920.
*Military Operations Egypt & Palestine from the outbreak of war with Germany to June 1917,* GF MacMunn & Falls, London, 1928.
*The Merchant Navy,* Sir A Hurd, London, 1924.
*Danger Zone, the story of the Queenstown Command,* E Keble Chatterton, London, 1934.
*The Auxiliary Patrol,* E Keble Chatterton, London, 1923.
*The Big Blockade,* E Keble Chatterton, London, 1932.
*Navy List* (September, November, December 1914 & May, September and October 1915).
*Lloyd's Register of Shipping.*
*Jane's Fighting Ships 1914 and 1919.*
*Merchant Fleets – Britain's Railway Steamers,* Duncan Hawes, 1994.
*British Vessels Lost at Sea 1914-18,* London, 1919.
*British Warships 1914–19,* FJ Dittmar & JJ Colledge, London, 1972.
*The Cheshire (Earl of Chester's) Yeomanry,* Lieut-Col Sir R Verdin, Liverpool, 1971.
*My dearest Mamma & Papa The War Letters written by Octavius C Moore Haines,* Barbara Beck.
*O Gamddwr i Gairo, hanes y brodyr Davies Bryan (1851–1935),* Siân Wyn Jones, Wrecsam, 2004.

**Diaries**

Lieutenant EB Tanner, RNR
Sub Lieutenant A Marsh, RNR
Sub Lieutenant WT Griffiths, RNR
Assistant Engineer DJ Davies, RNR
Assistant Paymaster A Dutton, RNR
Quartermaster Thomas Williams, MFA
Fireman Owen Gray, MFA
CV Sankey, RNAS

**Newspapers – various issues**

*Holyhead & Anglesey Chronicle*
*Holyhead Mail &Anglesey Herald*
*Carnarvon & Denbigh Herald*

*The Times*
*Campbeltown Courier*
*Belfast Newsletter*
*The Straits Times* (Singapore)

Articles and photographs courtesy of Trove – the website of the National Library of Australia, from which the following newspaperswere consulted:

*The Cairns Post* (Cairns, Queensland)
*The West Australian* (Perth, West Australia)
*The Register* (Adelaide, South Australia)

**Archives & Museums**
National Museum Royal Navy Library, Portsmouth
National Archives, Kew, London (Files: TNA FO383/238; TNA MT23/303; TNA MT23/387; ADM53/47454; BT165/995; Admiralty Weekly proceeding's Egypt 51115 – 61215; Log Books of HMS *Tara,* HMS *Latona,* HMS *Scotia,* HMS *Jonquil,* HMS *Proserpine,* HMS *Minerva,* HMS *Diana).*
Anglesey Archives, Llangefni, Anglesey
Larne Library, Co Antrim, Ireland
Campbeltown Archives, Campbeltown, Argyllshire
Plymouth & West Devon Record Office, Plymouth, Cornwall
The Duke of Westminster's Archives
National Maritime Museum, Greenwich, London
Imperial War Museum, Lambeth, London
L&NWR Society
National Railway Museum, York
Anglesey Registry Office
Caernarfon Registry Office
West Ham Registry Office

**Photographs**
William Davies
Mrs Ann Martin and Mrs Beryl Lloyd
Mrs G Barton
Brian Jones
Mr & Mrs Merfyn Môn Hughes
Mrs G Owen
Thomas Ashmore
Raymond Houston
Donald R Gunn
Dorothy Wise
Southampton Libraries
Mrs Gail Parillo
Mrs Betty Liepman
Raymond Houston
Mrs Ann Denton & Dewi Riley
William Wright

Mrs Betty Holmes
Capt Glynne Pritchard
Mrs Dorothy Wise (daughter of Capt A Marsh)
Mrs Hillary Tipping
Robert Phillips
National Library of Ireland
Holyhead Maritime Museum
Rolls-Royce plc
BRB (Residuary) Ltd

# Index

Italicised *f* indicates footnote
Italicised page number indicates illustration


Abu Gerab 142, 160
Agagia 212, 213, 214
Baggush 160, 175
Baq Baq 109, 126
Belfast 34f, 48, 51, 52f, 53, 55, 56, 58, 59, 60, 65, 70, 81f, 251f, 264, 297, 298, 299, 300, 316, 317
Benghazi 76
Bir Aziz 217, 219, 220, 226
Bir Hakkim/Bir Hakkimm Abbyat (Wells of the White Doctor) 137, 145, 157, 164, 167, 188, 189, 218–9, 227, 231, 232, 238f, 241, 242, 264, 270, 275–6, 281, 288
Bir Shola 176–7
Bir Waer 216
Bir Zebla 134–6
British India Steam Navigation Co 82, 116
Campbeltown 7, 46, 62, 63, 64, 67–70, 173f, 235f, 253, 256, 258, 287, 299, 310
City of Dublin Steam Packet Co (CoDSPC) 11, 23, 24, 27, 34, 260, 277, 281, 284, 289, 292, 296, 300, 305
Coliseum Theatre 257
Dardanelles 82, 142f
Denny & Bros, Dumbarton (shipbuilders) 12, 15, 20, 21
Dublin 11, 12, 13, 21, 23, 23f, *30*, 39f, 48, 55, 236, 251f, 259, 260, 261, 262, 269, 290, 304, 305
Dumbarton 12, 20, 21
El Aziat 118
El Dabaa 109, 201, 330, 331
El Zebla 224
Fayoum 143
Fishguard 55f, 259
Folkestone 117, 277
Gallipoli 75, 79, 80, 83, 90f, 112f, 113, 176f, 212, 220
Gebel Howimil 175
Gebel Medwa 160, 161
Gulf of Xeros 90
Halazin 176
Halazin, Battle of 178
Halfaya Pass 216
Hospital Blues 231, 231f
Holyhead 5, 6, 7, 11, 12, 13, 20, 20f21, 22, 23, *24*, 25, 25f, 28, 33, 34, 34f, 35, 38, 39f, 40, *42*, 43, 44, 47f, 48, 51, 52, 53 54f, 55, 58, 64, 67, 67f, 68, 70, 70f, 71, 73,73f, 73, 80f, 81f, 83, 84 116–8, 150, 167, 172f, 173f, 235f, 241, 244, *251*, 252, *252*, 253, 256–307, 252f, 256f, 263f, 311–7,
Holyhead Dry Dock/Marine Yard Dry Dock 5, 40f, 51–2, 66, 71, 73, *73*, 80f, 271, 280, 283, 312, 313
Italian–Turkish War 1911–12 77
Jaghbub 76
Jerawla 143
Kingstown 6, 11, 23, 25, 55, 67, 251f, 259, 262
Larne 7, 44, 45f, 47f, 46–7, 48, 49, 50, 51, 52, 52f, 53, 54f, 58, 59, 62, 63, 64, 64f, 66, 67, 69, 252f, 258, 264, 280, 285, 286, 292, 299, 300, 303, 308, 309, 310, 311, 314, 316, 317
Liverpool 21, 36, 37, 39, 48, 49, 50, 53, 55, *56*, 59, 63, 102f, 256, 260, 264, 272, 278, 283, 24, 285
London & North-Western Railway Co (L&NWR) 11–21, 13f, 20f, 22, 23, 24, 24f, 27, 28, 33, 34, 34f, 37, 38, 39, 39f, 40,40f, 43, 52, 54, 68, 68f, 72,73f, 116, 128, 150, 172f, 173f, 252, 253, 256–9, 256f, 261, 263f, 267–98,283f, 300–6, 313–4
London & South Western Railway Co (L&SWR) 28
Luce Bay Airship Station 63f, 72f
Marine Yard Workshops, Holyhead 5, 21, 35, 36, 39, 39f, 40,43f, 58, 66, 71, 72, 80f, 258, 271, 277, 279, 280, 287, 288, 295, 297, 301
Malahide Airship Station 259
Marressa 130
Mersa Matruh 82, 108, 110, 113, 114, 115, 119, 141, 142, 142f, 143, 144, 156, 159, 160, 161, 168, 175, 176, 177, 179, *179*, 212, 214, 215f, 243
Midland Railway Co 28, 34f
Milford Haven 44, 49
Military formations and organisations
- 1st Australian Division 142, 160, 175
- 1st Australian Divisional Train 160, 175
- 2nd Composite Yeomanry Brigade 141, 159, 160, 176f, 212
- 2nd Mounted Division 141, 212
- 5th Indian Hospital, Alexandria 238

19th General Hospital, Alexandria 238, 314
19th General Hospital, Alexandria 241
21st General Hospital Alexandria 219, 238, 256, 285
137th Field Ambulance 175, 177, 212
New Zealand Stationary Hospital 90
Australian Camel Corps 212, 220, 233
Australian Light Horse 141, 159, 160, 175, 176, 276
Berkshire Battery (TF) Royal Horse Artillery 143
Berkshire Yeomanry 176, 220
Cheshire Regiment 34, 271, 274, 275, 303
Cheshire Yeomanry (Earl of Chester's Own) 178, 179
City of London Yeomanry 160
Derbyshire Yeomanry 160
Duke of Lancaster's Own Yeomanry 160, 176, 176*f*
Egyptian Army Artillery 142
Egyptian Army Military Works Dept 142
Egyptian Coastguard Camel Corps 115
Hertfordshire Yeomanry 160, 176, 176*f*
Hong Kong & Singapore Mountain Artillery Battery 212, 214
Honourable Artillery Company (A Battery) 175
Machine Gun Corps (Motors) 179
1, 2 and 3 Light Armoured Car Batteries 178, *179*, 236*f*
Middlesex Regiment 23*f*, 141, 142, 160, 161, 175, 176
New Zealand Rifle Brigade, 1st Bn 142, 160, 175, 176, 212
North Midland Mounted Brigade 143
Nottinghamshire Battery (TF) Royal Horse Artillery 141, 159, 160, 176, 176*f*
Notts & Derby Field Ambulance 160
Queen's Own Dorset Yeomanry 176
Ras el Tin Military Hospital, Alexandria 238, 239, *239*, 241, 243, 314, 315
Royal Buckinghamshire Hussars Yeomanry 160, 176, 212*f*, 214, 235*f*
Royal Naval Air Service Emergency Squadron 5
Royal Naval Armoured Car Division 110*f*, 112*f*, 114, 159, 178
Emergency Squadron, 108, 112, 112*f*, 113
Royal Scots Fusiliers 61, 67*f*, 141, 159, 176, 177, 212*f*, 318
Sikh Regiment 142, 159, 160–1, 176, 177, 212
South Africa Infantry 176, 177, 212, 213, 214, 216
South Midland Field Ambulance 159, 175, 212
Yeomanry Field Ambulance 160
Yeomanry Machine Gun Section 160
Milo, Crete 111, 143*f*
Moghara oasis 142
Moville, Loch Swilly 53
Muafizia 161, 211
Mull of Kintyre 44, 48, 49, 53, 62, 67*f*
Neuve Chapelle, battle of 178
North Channel 5, 35, 44, 48, 49, 52–9, 56*f*, *57*, 63, 63*f*, 68–72, 74, 134*f*, 285
Orak Island 90
Orkney Islands 83, 309
Point Lynas, Anglesey 261
Poperinghe road 178
Port Bardia 85*f*, 90, 90*f*, 91, 98, 98–9*f*, 99, 119, 125, 129*fg*, 150*f*, 175, 224, 302
Port Charlotte, Islay 49, 53
Port Suliman 90
Ras Lik 85*f*
Ras Manas 159
Rathlin Island / Sound 44, 48, 56, 57, *57*, 59, 66, 72*f*
Red Bay, Northern Ireland 64, 66
Senussi 5, 75–84, 78*f*, 85–°6, 85*f*, 90, 92, 92*f*, 98, 100, 107*f*, 110–5, 115*f*, 116*f*, 119, 120–4, 127, 130, 131, 133, 135, 139, 130*f*, 141, 143, 144–57, 159–62, 166, 167–9, 171, 174, 175–9, 181–8, 190–207, 209–11, 212–19, *217*, 219*f*, 221–3, 226–7, 229–31, *243*, *265*, *277*
Sheephaven Bay, Donegal 58, 70*f*, 313
Sidi Barani 87, 112, 113, 114, 115
Ships (Mercantile Marine)
*Adam Smith* 69
*Anglia* *13*, *21*, *28*, *34*, *36*, *41*, *43*, *51*, *64*, *67*, *117*, 118, 240, 240*f*, 256, 256*f*, 268, 274, 275, 280, 292, 305
*Arabia* *109*
*Arno Mendi* 261
*Atlantic City* 59
*Balmarino* 59–62, 61
*Banshee* 11, *12*
*Cambria* 11, 13, *14*, 20*f*, 21, 28, 34, 35, *35*, 41, 43, 51, 64, 258, 268, 269, 275, 292, 296, 306, 314
*Caria* 101
*Castlereagh* 62
*Celtic* 260, 275
*Clan MacAlister* 101
*Clan Macbrae* 59
*Clyde Valley* *46*
*Connaught* 11, 48, 260
*Connemara* 12, 260, 313

*Cork* 260
*Davara* 54
*Dorothea* (trawler) 44
*Duchess of Argyll* 28
*Duchess of Cumberland* 28
*Duchess of Devonshire* 28
*Eskmere* 260
*Florazan* 59
*Galtee More* 260
*Greenore* 25, 28, 48, 72, 261, 274, 302, 303, 305, 312
*Hare* 260
*Hartdale* 59
*Helen* 59
*Hibernia* *26, 30, 35*
  specification and building 13–21
  service 1897–1914 21–35
  conversion to Fleet Messenger / Armed Boarding Steamer 35–41
*Highgate* 44
*Hillary* 37
*Japanese Prince* 91, 91*f*
*King's Lynn* 66
*Laupar of Tonsberg* 53
*Leinster* 11, 55*f*, 256*f*, 261, 262
*Lily* 11, 13
*Lusitania* 82
*Manchester Commerce* 48
*Marquette* 90
*Medway* 22–3
*Mexico City* 261
*Moorina* 101, 102, 103*f*, *103*, 125*f*, 126, 131, 149, 161, 169, 169*f*, 183, 218, 238, 241, 263, 313–6
  capture as *Thuringen* 102
  as *Moorina* service 102–4
  sinking 104–5
  survivors join *Tara* survivors 130
*Normania* 28
*Princess Victoria* 59, 299
*Rathmore* 28, 72, 261, 268, 274
*Redbreast* 58
*Retriever* 260, 313
*Rosalie* 88
*Rosstrevor* 12, 33, 261, 268
*Scotia* 13, *17*, 21, 24, 26*f*, 28, 34, 35, 41, 42, *42*, 43, 43*f*, 49, 51, 73, *79*, 80, 81–4, 81*f*, 87, 269, 277, 280, 281, 290, 296, 301, 303, 05, 306, 312
*Shamrock* 11, 13
*Slieve Bloom* 261, 292
*Slievemore* 48
*Snowdon* 262
*South Stack* 260, 297
*Svend Foyn 1* 47
*Titanic* 23, 176
*Ulster* 11, 261
*Umina* 103
*Violet* 11
*Vulture* 58
*Woolwich* 91, 111, 126


**Warships, requisitioned merchant vessels and shore stations (Royal Navy unless otherwise specified)**


*Dunluce Castle* (hospital ship) 248, *248*, 249, 286, 287, 299
*Abergeldie* (armed trawler) 142
*Aboukir* (armoured cruiser) 43
*Abronia* (armed trawler) 142*f*
*Amphion* (crusier) 42
*Angerton* (armed trawler) 51, 54, 69, 70
*Alsatian Minor* (trawler) 54
*Aquarius* (depot ship) 80
*Audacious* (battleship) 48, 49
*Avon* (destroyer) 260
*B6* (submarine) 85*f*
*B11* (submarine) 85*f*
*Bayano* (armed boarding steamer) 59, 60, *60*, 62–3, *62*, 306
*Berkshire* (armed trawler) 54
*Berlin* (*Kaiserliche Marine* minelayer) 48–9, 82
*Bittern II* (armed trawler) 54
*Borulas* (transport) 179
*Boy Scout* (armed drifter) 49
*Calgarian* (armed merchant cruiser) 44
*Caronia* (armed merchant cruiser) 35
*Cerealia* (armed trawler) 49
*Ceresia* (armed trawler) 39
*Challenger* (2nd class cruiser) 35
*Clementina* (armed yacht) 56, 67, 69, 70
*Clematis* (sloop) 142*f*, 160, 161, 162
*Clonsit* (armed trawler) 54, 59
*Comrade* (armed trawler) 142
*Cornwall* (armoured cruiser) 78
*Cressy* (armoured cruiser) 43
*Davara* (armed trawler) 54
*Dee* (destroyer) 63
*Diana* (2nd class cruiser) *79, 80, 80*f, 81
*Dick Whittington* (requisitioned drifter) 49
*Diver* (armed trawler) 54
*Dove* (destroyer) 63
*Dragoon* (armed trawler) 69
*Dufferin* (Royal Indian Marine troopship) 79–0, 81
*Earnest* (destroyer) 260
*Eclipse* (2nd class cruiser) 35
*Falmouth III* (armed trawler) *142*
*Faulknor* (destroyer) 59
*Fishtoft* (armed trawler) 54

*Forward* (cruiser) 32
*Garry* (destroyer) 63, 63*f*, 65, 67, 70
*Glenroy* (armed trawler) 54
*Goshawk* (armed trawler) 54
*Griffon* (destroyer) 260
*Hannibal* (battleship) 31, 240, 243, 290
*Hermione* (2nd class cruiser) 73
*Hogue* (armoured cruiser) 43
*Howe* (battleship) 43
*Hungarian* (armed trawler) 54, 299
*Isis* (2nd class cruiser) 35
*Jannissaire* (*Marine Nationale* destroyer) 112
*Jeanette* (armed yacht) 55
*Jonquil* (sloop) 111, 12, 112f, 125*f*, 129*f*, 150*f*
*Juno* (2nd class cruiser) 35, 44, 45, *45*, 46, 312
*Kestrel* (destroyer) 260
*King Orry* (armed boarding steamer) 53
*Königin Luise* (*Kaiserliche Marine* minelayer) 42
*Latona* (2nd class cruiser/minelayer) 176
*Liberia* (armed trawler) 49, 53
*Lily* (sloop) 131*f*, 161, 236
*Lively* (destroyer) 260
*Lunka* (armed boarding steamer) 82, 87–9, *87*, *89*, 110–1
*Lynn* (minesweeper) 67, 300
*Magnificent* (battleship) 31, 280, 310
*Magnolia* (sloop) 161, 162
*Majestic* (battleship) 79, 83, 270, 290
*Mallard* (destroyer) 260
*Mallow* (sloop) 161, 162
*Margaret Duncan* (armed trawler) 54
*Marynthea* (armed yacht) 55
*Mars* (battleship) 31
*Medusa* (destroyer) 55
*Mimosa* (sloop) 161
*Minerva* (2nd class cruiser) 35, 81, 111, 113–4
*Minos* (*Regia Marina* transport) 241
*Misurata* (*Regia Marina* armed yacht) 79, 87
*Mitres* (armed trawler) 261
*Narcissus* (sloop) 55
*Nellie Braddock* (armed trawler) 51, 53–4, 70
*Ocean Harvest* (armed drifter) 49
*Ocean Princess* (armed trawler) 142*f*
*Ocean Retriever* (armed drifter) 49
*Oriana* (armed yacht) 49, 50, 51, 53
*Orwell* (destroyer) 260
*Patrol* (cruiser) 260
*Pelorus* (3rd class cruiser) 35, 43*f*
*Pembroke III* (RN shore base, Chatham) 178
*Philomel* (2nd class cruiser) 79
*President* (RN shore base, Crystal Palace) 178
*Proserpine* (3rd class cruiser) 88, 111, *111*
*Remagio* (trawler) 142
*Revello* (armed trawler) 49, 51, 53
*Riano* (armed trawler) 49, 53
*Rodosto* (armed trawler) 142
*Rononia* (armed trawler) 142
*Rose II* (armed trawler) 54
*Roxana* (armed trawler) 54
*St Clair* (trawler) 142*f*
*Sapphire II* (armed yacht) 55
*Scooper* (armed trawler) 142*f*
*Scuter II* (armed trawler) *142f*
*Seal* (destroyer) 260
*Slasher* (armed trawler) 142*f*
*Stag* (destroyer) 260
*Stockton* (USN destroyer) 261
*Sprightly* (destroyer) 260
*Tara* (armed boarding steamer)
  requisitioning of SS *Hibernis* 36–40
  renaming of *Hibernia* 41–2
  service at Larne 43–54, 55–62
  service at Campbeltown 62–74
  service in Mediterranean 82–4, 85–9, 90–2
  sinking 92–101
*Thorn* (destroyer) *63*, *63*f, *65*, *67*, *70*
*Trafford Hall* (transport) 249, *250*, 251, 299
*Triumph* (battleship) 78
*U-20* (*Kaiserliche Marine* submarine) 59, 82
*U-21* (*Kaiserliche Marine* submarine) 55*f*, 78, 82, 270
*U-27* (*Kaiserliche Marine* submarine) 59, 62, 63
*U-34* (*Kaiserliche Marine* submarine) 82–3, 162
*U-35* (*Kaiserliche Marine* submarine) 5, 82–3, 90–101, 91*f*, 104, 105*f*, 110, 111, 112*f*, 113, 120, 124, 130
*UC-12* (*Kaiserliche Marine* submarine) 77, 77*f*, 161, 162
*Valdivia* (*Marine Nationale* hospital ship) 256
*Valiant II* (armed yacht) 55
*Venus* (2nd class cruiser) 35
*Veronica* (sloop) 161
*Victorious* (battleship) 31
*Walthem* (armed trawler) 54
*Zephyr* (destroyer) 260
Sheerness 178
Siwa oasis 154, 212
Sollum 78–82, 77*f*, 85–9, *86*, 92–3, 92*f*, 98–9, 98*f*, 101, 106, 107*f*, 108, 109, 110–5, 116, 116*f*, 118, 122, 124, 125, 16, 127, 129*f*, 136, 141, 144, 150, 151, 152, 154, 156, 156*f*, 161–2, 167, 168, 169, 171, 174, 175, 178, 181
Suez Canal 75, 77, 82, 104, 141

Torr Head Coastguard Station 44, 51, 53
Unjeila 212
Queenstown *34f*, 35, 44, 67, *81f*
Wadi Majid *107f*, 161
Wadi Maktil 212
Wadi Natrun 143
Wadi Senaab 159, 161
Wadi Shaifa 189
Wormwood Scrubs 178
Well of the Red Doctor 147, 151, 153
Western Approaches *32f*, 35, 67, 75, 82
Yorkshire & Lanacshire Railway Co 128

**People**

Bailey, Cdr HGF, RN
Barlow, Adm CJ, DSO, RN 55, 56, 59, 64, *72f*
Bayly, Adm Sir L, RN 67, 68
Bey, Gen Nuri 77,100, 120, 123, 127, 143, 149, 151, 154, 169, 182, 195, 208, 212
Binnie, Capt WH 20
Boyle, Rear Adm HF, RN 64, 66, 67, 69
Briscoe, Brig-Gen JT
Bryan, Dr J Davies, of Alexandria 243–4, *244f*, *244*, *245*
Cannon, WT/Op JD 24
Chadwick, T, galley boy 25
Chambers, WT/Op FJ 40, 51, 274, 316
Clay, Capt TG 21
Coalsted, Ch Off CS 104, 105–6, 130, 139, 145, 152, 186, *239*, 241, 314, *314*
Coke, Vice Adm Sir CH, RN 44, 67
Copland, Sub Lt CP *37f*, 45, 47, 64, 316
Coughtry, Sub Lt Thomas H, RNR 236–7, *236*
Creer, 2/Off AJ *106f*, 108, 109
Dare, Rear Adm CH, RN 55
Davies, Asst Paym'r WT, RNR 38, 47, 52, 273, 316
Dawson, Cmdr ABF, RN 84, 88
de Robeck, Rear Adm JM, RN 80, 81
Enver Pasha 77, 100
Evans, Capt J 25, 267–8
Faud, Dr B 122, 123, 124, 125, 126, 127, 128, 197, *226f*, 278
Fevsi, Lt 120
Findlay, Surg Prob GWM, RNVR 69, 72, 316
Foster, Capt J 60, 61
Gooding, Asst Stwd CH 58, 305, 317
Gradwell, 3/Eng F 108, 109, *125f*
Grand Senussi *77*, *77f*, *85f*, *92f*, 111, *115f*, 124, 143, 195, 208
Grosvenor, Maj HRA, second duke of Westminster 5, 7, 178–9, 213, 216, 218, 219, *219*, 220, 226, *229*, 230, 231, 233, 257, 258, 263–5
Hayes, AB D *52f*, 316
Henley, Lt-Col T 246
Hersing, *KaLt* O *55f*, 78
Hickey, Capt B 103, 108
Holbrook, Lt ND, VC, RN 85
Holland, Cmdr GE 23, *23f–4f*, 24, 33, *34f*, 35, 36, 37, 38, 39, 40, 150, 153, 257
Hughes, Mrs Elizabeth (Holyhead) 172
Hughes, Sub Lt W, RNR 37, 64, 316
Hunsi, Lt, 120
Jaafar Pasha al-Askari, Gen *76*, 77, 122, 123, 212, 213, 214
James, Ch Eng C 91
Jenkins, Capt AH 91
Jones, E, boatman 24
Jones, Fmn E 51, 52, 317
Jones, Asst Eng H, RNR 37, 70, 73, *73f*, 313, *313*
Jones, Asst Eng RE, RNR 37, 68, 316
Jones, Ch Eng T, 52, 70, *70f*, 312–3, *313*
Kophamel, *KorvKap* W 83, 90–3, *92*, 98–101, *98–9f*, 105
Lacey, AB C, RN 40, 44, 53, 317
Laycock, Lt-Col 226
Lawton, Elec E 40,67, 288, 316
Lettow-Vorbeck, Col P von *75*
Lewis, Lt-Col RR, 219
Lister, Lt Cmdr C, RNVR 112
Lucan, Brig-Gen, earl of 141, 161
Lukin, Brig-Gen, 212, 213, 215, 216
Le Marchant, Rear Adm ER, RN 55
McGarrick, Capt 62
Mannesmann, O *85f*, 91, *91–2f*, 92, 100, 126, 127, 128
Manning, Lieut LJ, RNR 62, 64, 275
Maxwell, Lt-Gen Sir J 141, 178
Mitchell, Smn J 47, *27f*, 285, 316
Mohamed al Mahdi *76*
Mohamed bin Ali al Senussi *76*
Moss, Judge S 253, 254, 255–6
Murphy, Mate R 60, 61
Mustapha, Lt 154
Nash, Lt WJ, RNR 64, 261
Osman, Mullah ('Holy Joe') 137, 138, *138*, 139, 144–9, 156, 164, 171, 184, 186, 188, 206, 208, 211, 223, 225
Owen, J, (farmer) 22
Owen, Std L *24*
Paton, Ch Eng R 25, 312
Petterson, AB J 21
Peyton, Maj-Genl WE, CB, CVO, DSO 212, 214, 215, 216, 218, 219, 220, 233
Pinchin, Capt LJ 22, *25f*
Roberts, Ch Eng HO 25, *39f*, 52, 131, 312, 313
Raby, Capt RA, RN 68

Ralph, AB W, RNR *47f*, *67f*, 317
Richardson, 2/Eng TR 104, 105, 107, 130, 156, 241, *239*, 314, 315, *315*
Rockey, WT/Op D *24f*
Rolls, Pte SV, ASC 227, *227f*, 230
Royle, Capt LVA *77f*, 85, *92f*, *117f*, 126, 176, 218, 226, 227
Rücker, *KaLt* C 82
Schwiger, *KaLt* W 82
'Snail King' 186
Salim Effendi 169, 170, 171, 174, 181 182–3, 186, 187, 208, 211, 221,
Sola, messroom boy (aka Portugese Joe, real name A E Rodrgues) 130, 183
Souter, Col 213–4
Snow, Lt-Col CL 77, *77f*, 85, 86, 87–8, 89
Starkey, CPO CV, RNAS
Street, Asst Paymr WF, RNR 58, 63, 316
Sullivan, Col D, RAMC 238
Tarrick Bey 181, 189
Varian, Capt TJ 13
Walker, Fmn 52
Wallace, Maj- Gen- A 141, 142, 143, 159, 160, 161, 175, 176, *176f*, 178
Webster, 4/Eng J 108, 109
Wegener, *KaLt* B 62
White, Capt RB 85
White, Lt RW, RNR 87, 88, 110, 111, 114
Williams, Lab J 53
Williams, 2/Cook J 50
Williams, PC RH 25
Williams, Tpr TOF *235f*
Wood, CPO RA, RN 61
Wright, Fmn GA 67, 256, 249, 300
Zoue, Mohamed (Mohamed Effendi) 130, 134, 138, 152–3, 154, 155, 156, 167, 168, 169, 181, 184, 185, 186

***Tara* Crew**

Abbit, QM R, MFA *47f*, 152, 164, 165, 167, 169, 170, 173, 182, 186, 222, 225, 227, 238, *238*, 256, 249, 278, *278*, 285
Andrews, Coal Trim W J, DSM, MFA 96, 249, *251f*, 256, 257, 258, 289, 298–9, *299*
Arthur, Temp Sur Prob JD, RNVR 72, 98, 119, 120, 125, 127, 135, 151, 165, 170, 171, 172, 182, 187, 208, *239*, 249, 275, *275*, 277, 302
Bagnall, Fmn JO, MFA 47, 249, 292–3, *292*
Basil, interpreter, see Lambriadis, V
Black, Smn W, MFA 47, 249, 256, 286
Barber, Asst Stwd F, MFA 126, 255, 304, *304*
Barton, 2/Stwd W, MFA 168, 240, 249, 302, *302*
Birkby, Warrant Tele Op CW, MFA 96, 99, 120, *239*, 249, 274, *274*
Cooke, Elect WCV, MFA 67, 98, 135, 256, 249, 287
Cox, Artif GM, MFA 40, 134, *134f*, 136, 148, 163–7, 254, 288, *288*
Davies, Asst Eng DJ, RNR 72, 95–6, 130, 135, 164, 170, 172, 173, 209, 221, 241, 249, *264*, 274, *274*
Doughty, Fmn T, MFA 52, 249, 293, *293*
Dudgeon, Sub Lt LT, RNR 64, 145, 173, 210, 224–5, 227, 230, 241, *243*, 249, 250, 251, *264*, 268, *268*, 276
Dutton, Asst Paym A, RNR 52, 63, 96, 134, 149, 152, 153, 154, 182, 208, 210, 221, 223, 233, 239, 249, *264*, 273, *273*
Evans, Asst Stwd E, MFA 250, 252, 256, 303, *303*
Fenlen, Asst Stwd J, MFA 250, 305, *305*
Gray, Fmn O, MFA 134, *134f*, 250
Griffiths, Sub Lt WT 64, 95, 99, 131, *132f*, 134, 151, 155, 164, 165–6, 173, 183, *183f*, 209, 210, 221, 222, 233, 234, 268–9, *269*
Gwatkin-Williams, Capt RSG, RN 37, 38, 44, 45–6, 47, 50, 53, 58, 61, 63, 66, 69–71, 74, 84, 87, 88–9, 93, 96–7, 98, 100, 101, 114, 118 –24, *124f*, 127–8, 130, 133, 135, 138, 139–40, 144, 147–9, 151–7, 162, 166, 167, 169, 171-2, 174, 181–2, 184–5, *184f*, 186–8, 190–207, 218, 221, 225, *227f*, 230, 233, *235f*, 241, *239*, 248, 257, 264, *264*, 267, *267*
Higgins, Fmn T, MFA 249, 256, 299, *299*
Hodgson, Smn J, MFA 67, 154, 164, 166–7, 254, 280–1
Hughes, Smn A, MFA 47
Hughes, Asst Eng H, RNR *37f*, 40, 139, 172, 173, 209, 233, 234, 239, 249, 272, *272*, 277, 313
Hughes, Greaser HO, MFA 101, 119, 167, 171, *172f*, 173, 187, 246, 249, 256, 264, *264*, 277, 290, *290*
Hutton, Warrant Eng J, RNR 83, 94, 270, *270*, 271
Jackson, Cook W, MFA 25, 98, 99, 100, 120, 121, 255, 302–3, *302*
Jones, Fmn Harold, MFA 73, 181, 248, 256, 296, *296*
Jones, Fmn Hugh, MFA 97, 249, 296, *296*
Jones, Fmn J, MFA 96, 249, 258, 282, 283, *283*
Jones, Smn JL, MFA 47, *240f*, 249, 285, *285*
Jones, Fmn JE, MFA 291–2, *252*
Jones, Act Ldg Sto T, MFA 94, 255, 289, *289*
Jones, Ldg Sto W, MFA 95, 289, *289*
Jones, Deck Boy W, MFA 96, 249, 287, *287*
Lambraidis, V (interpreter, aka Basil) 96, 97, 119, 120, 123, 137, 144, 154, 155, 164, 169, 170, 171, 174, 181, 188, 189, 208, 224, 225, 227, 230, 241, *243*, 250, 276, *276*

Lewis, Fmn R, MFA 101, 246, 149, 256, 258, 295, *295*, 302
Manning, Writer WG, MFA 98, 233, *239*,, 249, 251, 275, *275*, 311
Marsh, Sub Lt A *37f*, 53, 56, 93, 95, 98, 99, 100–1, 120, 123, 131, 132, 139, 148, 150, 157, 164, 166, 168, 171, 173, 174, 181, 182, 186, 209, 211, 221, 225, 228, 233, 238, 239, 240, 249, 251, 268, 269, *269*, 274, 277, 302
Moorhead, Fmn T, MFA 250, 251*f*, *256*, 257, 300, *300*,
Morris, Ch Stwd A 188, 209, 236*f*, 242, 250, 301–2, *301*
Neill, Warrant Teleg R, RNR 5, 96, 121, 233, 239, 249, *264*, 273–4, *273*, 275, 2761
Owens, Bos T, MFA *265*, 276–7, *277*
Owens, Fmn TH, MFA 73, 133–4, *133*f, 139, 152, 298, *298*
Parry, Fmn J, MFA 96, 97, 255, 291, *291*
Parry, Smn WH, MFA 93, 249, 281, *281*
Phillips, Ldg Sto R, MFA 95, 254, 288, *288*, 291
Phillips, Asst Eng RL, RNR 68, 73, 83, 271, *271*
Pritchard, Cook J 50, 241*f*, 271, 303, *303*
Pritchard, Smn T, MFA 54*f*, 73, 222, 225, 239, 246, 248, 250, 255, 285, *285*
Roberts, Asst Eng GH, RNR 37*f*, 94, 131, 271–2, *271*
Roberts, Fireman OH, MFA 255, 291, *291*
Rowlands, QM W, MFA 7, 96, 98, 127*f*, 147, 157, 183, 186, 272, 277, *277*, 302
Tanner, Lt EB, RNR *37f*, 38, 44, 70, 94, 96, 98, 118–20, 123, 127–9, 130, 133, 135, 13, 146–8, 150, 151, 155, 164–7, 173, 182, 183–4, 185, 186–7, 196, 207, 208–11, 221–5, 227, 230, 233, 240–1, 246, *239*, 249, 251, 252, 257, 264, *264*, 267–8, *268*, 274
Thomas, QM W, MFA 58, 98, 100, 101, 119, 122, 123, 126–7, 254, 277–8, *277*
Williams, Carp O, MFA 254, 276, *276*
Williams, Eng RJS, RNR 131
Williams, QM R, MFA 53, 94, 98, 125, 167, 172, 173
Wright, Fmn GA, MFA 67, 249, 256, 300


**Royal Navy Personnel**


Allen, Yeo Sig HGJ, RFR 38, 38*f*, 99, 101, 124, 157, 228, 250, 308
Fulcher, Signal Boy R, RN 58, 93, 149, 258, 307, *307*
Gunn, Smn W, RNR 93, 249, 309–10, *309*
McKinven, Smn J, RNR 47*f*, 98, 173*f*, 249, 253, 310–1, *311*
McNee, Sto J, RNR 83, 249, 311
Marwick, Ldg Smn JB, RNR 47*f*, 144, 250, 309, *309*
Millward, Lgd Smn WP, RFR 38, 44, 94, 227, 308–9, *308*
Mintram, Sh Cpl C, RN 47, 250, 258, 308
Tanner, Boy Tel GA, RN 58, 93, 96, 98, 250, 251, 258, 304, 307–8, 311

An environmentally friendly book printed and bound in England by www.printondemand-worldwide.com

PEFC
PEFC/16-33-415

PEFC Certified

This product is from sustainably managed forests and controlled sources

www.pefc.org

This book is made of chain-of-custody materials; FSC materials for the cover and PEFC materials for the text pages.